Seeds of Empire

The David J. Weber Series in the New Borderlands History

Andrew R. Graybill and Benjamin H. Johnson, EDITORS

EDITORIAL BOARD

Sarah Carter

Kelly Lytle Hernandez

Paul Mapp

Cynthia Radding

Samuel Truett

The study of borderlands—places where different peoples meet and no one polity reigns supreme—is undergoing a renaissance. The David J. Weber Series in the New Borderlands History publishes works from both established and emerging scholars that examine borderlands from the precontact era to the present. The series explores contested boundaries and the intercultural dynamics surrounding them and includes projects covering a wide range of time and space within North America and beyond, including both Atlantic and Pacific worlds.

Published with support provided by the William P. Clements Center for Southwest Studies at Southern Methodist University in Dallas, Texas.

Andrew J. Torget

Seeds of Empire

Cotton, Slavery, and the Transformation
of the Texas Borderlands, 1800–1850

THE UNIVERSITY OF NORTH CAROLINA PRESS   CHAPEL HILL

This book was published with the assistance of the Anniversary Endowment Fund of the University of North Carolina Press.

Short sections of chapters 2 and 3 appeared previously in "Stephen F. Austin's Views on Slavery in Early Texas," in *This Corner of Canaan: Essays on Texas in Honor of Randolph B. Campbell*, edited by Richard McCaslin, Donald Chipman, and Andrew J. Torget (Denton: University of North Texas Press, 2013).

Set in Calluna
Manufactured in the United States of America

The paper in this book meets the guidelines for permanence and durability of the Committee on Production Guidelines for Book Longevity of the Council on Library Resources.

The University of North Carolina Press has been a member of the Green Press Initiative since 2003.
Jacket illustration: unknown American artist, *Cotton Plantation near Columbus, Texas* (ca. 1860), watercolor on paper. Collection of William J. Hill; courtesy of the Museum of Fine Arts, Houston.

Complete cataloging information can be obtained online at the Library of Congress catalog website.

ISBN 978-1-4696-2424-2 (cloth: alk. paper)
ISBN 978-1-4696-4556-8 (pbk.: alk. paper)
ISBN 978-1-4696-2425-9 (ebook)

For Alexandra,
My forever

So where the greatest blessings may be found,
The greatest miseries also curse the ground,
And where the grain the careful farmer sows,
Waiting with patience till his harvest grows,
Satan comes also with his sack of seeds,
And scatters o'er the field his noxious weeds.
— "Texas," by M. Twichelle, *Telegraph and
Texas Register*, October 13, 1838

CONTENTS

A Note on Names *xi*

Introduction. Cotton, Slavery, and Empire *1*

Part I. In the Shadow of Cotton

1 The Texas Borderlands on the Eve of
   Mexican Independence *19*

Part II. Bringing Mississippi to Mexico

2 American Migration to Mexico, 1821–1825 *57*

3 The Politics of Slavery in Northeastern Mexico, 1826–1829 *97*

4 Cotton, Slavery, and the Secession of Texas, 1829–1836 *137*

Part III. Cotton Nation and Slaveholders' Republic

5 Creating a Cotton Nation, 1836–1841 *179*

6 The Failure of the Slaveholders' Republic, 1842–1845 *219*

   Epilogue. Migrations and Transformations *255*

   Appendix 1. The Texas Slavery Project *267*

   Appendix 2. Cotton Prices and Trade *272*

   Acknowledgments *275*

   Notes *281*

   Bibliography *325*

   Index *343*

MAPS, FIGURES, TABLES, AND GRAPHS

Maps

Texas Borderlands, 1820 *18*

Texas Borderlands, 1835 *56*

Texas Borderlands, 1845 *178*

Figures

Mexican Huts 21

Military Plaza, San Antonio, Texas 33

Comanche Feats of Horsemanship 38

Portrait of Stephen F. Austin *60*

Camara de los Diputados 74

*Stick Stock, or Surveying in Texas before Annexation
    to the U.S. 83*

Gin House and Cotton Screw or Press 89

Main plaza of Saltillo, Coahuila *112*

Section of map of Anglo settlements in
    Stephen F. Austin's colony *123*

Photograph of José Antonio Navarro *132*

Texan Farm in Montgomery County 139

Portrait of Agustín de la Viesca y Montes *143*

Advertisement for runaway slaves Will and Adam *148*

McKinney's Warehouse, or Quitana, 1835 159

View on the Guadalupe, Seguin, Texas 172

Detail of *View of Galveston Harbor* *198*

Young Texas in Repose *207*

Portrait of Juan Seguín in 1838 *223*

Republic of Texas and McKinney-Williams currency *225*

Photograph of Juan Seguín after the U.S.-Mexican War *265*

Tables

1. Aggregate Slave and Slaveholder Populations, Republic of Texas, 1837–1845 *270*

2. Average Annual Price of Cotton, 1815–1845 *273*

Graphs

1. Value of Texas Commerce by Department in 1834 *161*

2. Slave and Slaveholder Population Increases, Republic of Texas, 1837–1845 *271*

3. Imports of Raw Cotton by Great Britain, 1815–1845 *274*

A NOTE ON NAMES

Because the Texas borderlands served as the epicenter for so much migration and transformation in North America during the first half of the nineteenth century, writing about the region presents a challenge in finding accurate and consistent terms for identifying the numerous groups and people who lived in the territory during those tumultuous years. As such, I have followed a few conventions in the interest of clarity. Everyone who lives in the Americas, for example, has equal claim to the term "American," even if that word has tended to be monopolized by citizens of the United States. In the pages that follow, however, I have generally referred to people who lived within modern-day Mexico as "Mexicans" and people from the United States as "Americans." I do this for the simple fact that there is no elegant alternative for referring to people from the United States.

Whenever possible, however, I have been far more specific. Ethnic Mexicans in Texas often referred to themselves as "Tejanos," tending to emphasize their connections to the territory where they made their homes, and I have followed their lead. Similarly, I usually refer to other Mexicans by their regional locations, such as using "Coahuilans" for Mexicans living in Coahuila (even when the region was part of the state of Coahuila-Texas). For citizens of the United States who came into Texas during the 1810s, 1820s, and early 1830s, I use "Anglo-Americans" and "Anglos" interchangeably. I often use "Anglo-Texans," however, for the period during the 1830s and 1840s when these men and women began developing a national identity distinct from both Mexico and the United States. Native Americans are nearly always referred to by their group or tribal names. For enslaved people brought into Texas by Anglo-Americans, I have generally used "African Americans," although some of them were natives of Africa rather than the Americas.

For locations, I have tended to use names that survive today, even if they were not always the most common forms used during the early nineteenth century. For most of the period between the 1730s and 1830s, for example, people knew San Antonio as "San Antonio de Béxar" and most referred to the village simply as "Béxar." That practice, however, shifted during the late 1830s and early 1840s, as immigrants from the

United States flooded into the region, and by the mid-nineteenth century most people referred to the town as "San Antonio." For the sake of clarity, I have used "San Antonio" throughout this book, and have done the same with other villages and towns—such as Saltillo in Coahuila, which was also known as Leona Vicario from 1827 to 1831—solely as a means of avoiding confusion.

Perhaps most important, I describe Texas as a "borderlands" territory. Throughout the first half of the nineteenth century, the regions known as "Texas" were never controlled or dominated by any single people or nation. Texas was, instead, a territory defined by the crashing together of numerous forces and peoples coming from multiple directions, each colliding in this particular corner of North America. What made Texas a "borderlands" during the half century that led to the U.S.-Mexican War, in other words, was how the territory became a central crossroads for overlap, collusion, and conflict between various powers—not only Mexico and the United States, but also Indian nations and European countries. It was, indeed, the combination of those forces and peoples, rather than the domination of any single power or group, that remade Texas during those tumultuous decades. Understanding how those overlapping influences shaped and reshaped this borderlands territory in ways that would transform both the United States and Mexico is the heart of the book that follows.

Seeds of Empire

Cotton, Slavery, and Empire

Riding two stolen horses and a mule, three runaway slaves—Marian, Richard, and Tivi—waded across the Sabine River during the depths of winter in late 1819. Reasoning that the laws that made them slaves in the United States could not follow them into New Spain, the fugitives had escaped their master in western Louisiana, a cotton planter named James Kirkham, in hopes of making their way into the Spanish province of Texas. Carrying what little food they could, the runaways moved quickly to avoid pursuit, following a scattered trail that ran through western Louisiana on its way into northern New Spain. Once across the river that marked the international border, the band pushed through dense forests of pines, oaks, and cedars as they continued west in search of freedom and new lives.[1]

Not far beyond the Sabine, the runaways came upon a detachment of Spanish soldiers camped along the roadside. Probably in hopes of asylum, and perhaps because none of them knew the geography of the region, Marian, Richard, and Tivi marched into the camp and surrendered themselves. The troops took them into custody and escorted them 350 miles southwest to San Antonio, the Spanish capital of Texas, where they were presented to Governor Antonio Martínez. Lacking the resources to hold or feed them, Martínez soon decided to send the fugitives another 300 miles south to Monterrey, Nuevo León, where they could be housed and interrogated.[2]

The runaways soon had a chance to tell their story. Speaking through an interpreter, with a clerk nearby to transcribe the exchanges, Spanish officers asked Marian, Richard, and Tivi why they had run from the United States. One by one, the runaways recounted their escape from James Kirkham's plantation, defending their actions by describing the cruelty of their master. Richard testified that Kirkham's brutality pushed him to cross into Spanish territory "because he wished for freedom." Marian said much the same, recounting the "very bad treatment" that forced him to seek "protection in the domains of Spain." Tivi reported that Kirkham's wife was as vicious as her husband, prompting her to escape in hopes that "the Spaniards would treat her better." They were, they explained, refugees of the expanding U.S. cotton frontier. And particular questions during the interrogations brought to the surface, if only momentarily, flashes of the anger and pain each felt about their enslavement. When Spanish officials asked Marian if he understood the financial damage he had caused his master by running away, Marian shot back that "he was wronged too when he was taken away from his relatives" in South Carolina and sold to Kirkham's Louisiana plantation. Following their testimony, soldiers escorted the runaways to a nearby prison to await a decision on their fate by Monterrey authorities. And as they waited, the man who claimed to own them made his way into northern New Spain.

James Kirkham, having guessed where his slaves had gone, set out to reclaim them in November 1820 on the same road that guided Marian, Richard, and Tivi. As he approached the Sabine River, Kirkham met another traveler, Moses Austin, also making his way into Texas. The two men decided to make the month-long ride to San Antonio together, setting out on a journey that would become famous when Austin asked for—and received—permission from Spanish authorities to begin settling American families in Texas.[3] Opening the territory to immigration from the United States would turn out to have momentous consequences, and Austin's ride to San Antonio has since become widely known as one of the pivotal moments in the history of the U.S.-Mexican borderlands. Indeed, Austin's proposal to offer Americans cheap land in northern New Spain has provided historians ever since an elegant shorthand for explaining the beginning of American movements into what would become Mexican territory, a story so easily compressed into the fateful journey of a particular man.

Yet Austin did not ride alone, and the specter of James Kirkham accompanying him in pursuit of Marian, Richard, and Tivi points toward a larger, more complicated story surrounding that moment and its aftermath that has somehow been lost. More than Austin, Kirkham and the runaways represented broad and powerful changes remaking the entire Gulf Coast of North America during the first half of the nineteenth century. Austin came to Texas, for example, because hundreds of thousands of men like Kirkham had already made their way to the southwestern edge of the United States throughout the late 1810s as part of a massive expansion in American cotton farming. Austin's plans to colonize Texas, indeed, depended on extending that cotton frontier beyond U.S. borders by convincing people like Kirkham to move their plantations into northern New Spain. Yet to make that happen, Austin needed the Spanish government to approve more than just American immigration—he needed it to endorse the enslavement of men and women like Marian, Richard, and Tivi, since American farmers would not abandon the United States if they also had to abandon the labor system that made their cotton fields so profitable. That meant that opening the territory to American settlement would ultimately depend as much on the perspectives of Spaniards like Antonio Martínez—and their ideas about what cotton, slavery, and migration would mean for the region—as the designs of Austin, Kirkham, or the runaways. What was so remarkable about Austin's famous journey in 1820, it turns out, was not the plan or actions of any single person. It was, rather, how that moment represented the convergence of forces, actors, and agendas from both sides of the Sabine River that would collectively remake the shared edge of the United States and Mexico.

This is a book about the larger world that converged in that fateful ride to San Antonio, and all the consequences that followed in its wake. It is the story of how powerful economic and political forces swirling throughout the northern Atlantic world crashed into one another during the first half of the nineteenth century, swept across North America, and transformed Mexico's northeastern frontier into the western edge of the southern United States. That process would, in time, redistribute power on the continent as it remade the border between the United States and Mexico, leaving both countries with enduring tensions that reverberate to this day.

THE SEEDS OF THAT TRANSFORMATION—and the journeys of Austin, Kirkham, and the runaways to San Antonio—had been sown in a quiet revolution in textiles that began when British industrialists started feeding their machines cotton instead of wool. More comfortable, stylish, and affordable than its competitors, cotton cloth became a sensation by the early 1800s within Britain's rapidly expanding commercial empire. English mill owners, as a result, began buying as much of the fiber as they could (British imports soared from 56 million pounds in 1800 to more than 660 million by 1850) as the plant became one of the most valuable commodities in the entire Atlantic world. The economic opportunities presented by this revolution in British textiles, in turn, prompted a flood of American farmers like Kirkham to pour into the territories that would become Mississippi, Alabama, and Louisiana, where they established expansive new plantation districts in order to grow cotton for these ravenous new markets. The result was an unprecedented expansion of the southern United States during the early decades of the nineteenth century, as the region rapidly transformed into the epicenter of international cotton production.[4]

At that same moment, a small—but growing—contingent of antislavery activists rose to political prominence in the north Atlantic and presented a terrifying challenge to American cotton farmers. This movement also traced its origins to the British Empire, where Quakers and Anglican evangelicals established antislavery societies during the late eighteenth century in an effort to pressure London to extricate Great Britain from the horrors of slavery. Politically active antislavery groups soon emerged on both sides of the ocean, and by the early 1800s Great Britain and the United States each outlawed the international slave trade. By the early 1830s, aggressive antislavery forces had pushed a massive emancipation bill through the British Parliament at the same moment that U.S. abolitionists launched bold new attacks on American slaveholders in the U.S. Congress. Alarmed, farmers in the American South struck back. Slave labor served as the engine of their expansive new cotton economy (enslaved people, indeed, made up more than 50 percent of the population of Mississippi by 1850), and so proslavery forces in the U.S. South mounted their own militant defenses of the institution and its pivotal role in the expansion and prosperity of the United States.[5]

The result was one of the most consequential alignments of the nineteenth century: at precisely the same moment the cotton revolution made slave labor more profitable than ever, the rising power of global antislavery forces put that labor system under sustained political attack for the first time in human history. That remarkable confluence, in turn, produced a series of escalating battles between pro- and antislavery forces that polarized politics within the United States and drove an ever-widening divide between the northern and southern halves of the country. Those struggles culminated with the secession of the South from the United States in 1860–61 and the establishment of the Confederacy as a republic dedicated to defending slave-based agriculture in a world increasingly hostile to slave labor. Historians working on the effects of the cotton revolution in North America, as a result, have focused most of their attention on the internal development of the United States, and the central roles that slavery and cotton played in creating political battles within the United States that led to the cataclysmic events of the American Civil War.[6]

Yet the global forces that created the Confederacy washed over far more of North America than just the United States, and the profound changes that followed were never confined solely to the American experience.[7] This book examines the Texas borderlands as the far-western front of the cotton revolution in North America, arguing that the same economic and political forces that created Mississippi and Alabama reached beyond U.S. borders and remade northeastern Mexico into the western edge of the American South. The wrenching changes that overtook this corner of the U.S.-Mexican borderlands, in turn, brought far-reaching consequences to both Mexico and the United States, as struggles over cotton and slavery helped reshape the wider continent.

THAT PROCESS UNFOLDED over the course of a tumultuous half century. Although Spaniards had long claimed the territory they called "Texas," by the early 1800s the Spanish crown had failed for more than a century to wrest the region away from the Indian nations that controlled it. By the late 1810s, indeed, this borderlands territory served primarily as a profitable raiding ground for the vast Comanche empire that stretched across both Texas and New Mexico. When Mexico gained its independence from Spain in 1821, Mexican leaders opened the region to foreign colonization in a desperate bid to bring stability to their northeastern frontier by populating it. During the fifteen years that followed, as tens of thousands of American expatriates poured into northern Mexico, the Texas borderlands shifted rapidly from entrenched Comanche territory to a thriving Anglo-Mexican state. Then, in 1836, a rebellion sheared Texas away from Mexico, and Anglo-Americans rebuilt the territory once again as a newly independent nation. The sudden emergence of the Republic of Texas isolated the region's Indians and ethnic Mexicans and set off pitched international conflicts between the United States, Mexico, and Great Britain over the future of North America. By 1845, those struggles—combined with the failure of the Texas nation—resulted in the annexation of Texas to the United States and set the stage for the U.S.-Mexican War.

Although there were innumerable factors and people at play, the roiling turmoil of those decades could be traced to the powerful influence of three forces that combined to determine the ultimate fate of the region: the rise of the global cotton economy, the international battles over slavery that followed, and the struggles of competing governments to control the territory. These were the three driving forces—cotton, slavery, and empire—that brought Austin, Kirkham, and the runaways to San Antonio in 1820 and then shaped the unlikely evolution of this borderlands territory from Comanche hinterland to American state.

The first of these defining forces was the influence of empire: that is, the ever-shifting political states (such as the successive governments of New Spain, Mexico, and the Republic of Texas) that attempted to control the region. The official policies of those governments, as well as their frequent inability to enforce those policies, deeply influenced the movement, actions, and decisions of people throughout the region. It mattered enormously, for example, that New Spain's leadership failed to secure or populate Texas, just as it mattered that Mexico's leaders then chose to endorse the migration of Americans into the region in order to solve problems they inherited from the Spanish. The collective decisions and competing agendas of native Indian nations, the neighboring United States, and distant European powers also played defining roles, and it was the ambitious failure of the Republic of Texas that set the region on its final path toward U.S. statehood. As they noted time and again in public debates and private conversations, the people who lived in these borderlands took seriously the policies and decisions of these various governments, and much of what follows is a chronicle of their efforts to shape and reshape those policies to their own advantage.

These chapters, as a result, spend a significant amount of time eavesdropping on political discussions that took place within congresses, parliaments, community halls, and the homes of everyday people. What happened in peripheral places like Texas, as we shall see, often played pivotal roles in determining the policies of leaders in political centers like Mexico City, Washington, D.C., and London. Decisions made in these national capitals, in turn, shaped the actions of people living in the Texas borderlands, which again influenced the decisions of various governments and people outside the region. There was, in other words, a perpetual back-and-forth relationship between developments *within* these borderlands and developments *outside* the territory, as each continually reacted to and influenced the other. One of the central themes of this book, therefore, is that understanding the complex relationship of the Texas borderlands to the rest of the world is central to understanding the evolution of this portion of the U.S.-Mexican borderlands.

And nothing so profoundly shaped the worldview of those who came to live in Texas as the spectacular rise of cotton during the early 1800s, the second defining force in the territory. When cotton became a driving economic power in the Atlantic world during the first decades of the nineteenth century—sending hundreds of thousands of Americans into the Mississippi River Valley—the Texas borderlands stood along the western edge of those great changes. By the mid-1840s, nearly all the raw cotton that drove Great Britain's massive manufacturing and export economy came from the Gulf Coast of North America.[8] As a result, the forces unleashed by the cotton revolution began washing over Texas as early as the 1810s and would play a powerful role in reshaping the territory during the decades that followed.

The world that cotton made continually shifted the political and economic circumstances surrounding the Texas borderlands. As we shall see, the sudden emergence of the U.S. cotton frontier during the 1810s played a crucial role in bringing Spain's presence in Texas to its knees, and Mexico's plan during the 1820s to secure Texas through migration from the United States was built upon the realization that Americans wanted to take advantage of the region's potential for growing cotton. Indeed, the rapid movement of U.S. expatriates into northern Mexico was—more than anything—a continuation of the endless search by Americans during those years for the best cotton lands along North America's rich Gulf Coast. The relentless waves of immigrants pouring into their far-northeastern territories that followed, in turn, forced Mexican leaders to grapple with how such rapid population shifts would affect Mexican authority in the region. By the 1830s, battles over the consequences of that transnational migration drove a wedge between people in Texas and leaders in Mexico City, setting the stage for the region's secession from Mexico. When Texans rebuilt the territory during the late 1830s and early 1840s as the Republic of Texas, they constructed their new nation explicitly on the foundation of cotton, staking their future on the hope that their cotton fields could bring them power in the global marketplace and therefore on the world's political stage.

Because cotton production was so tightly interwoven with enslaved labor during the first half of the nineteenth century, international disputes over slavery emerged as the third defining force shaping the Texas borderlands. In an age marked by revolutions for liberty in both the Americas and Europe, antislavery activists made the institution a political, economic, and moral problem for Atlantic world nations dealing in cotton. The growing tide of American cotton farmers and slaveholders moving into northern Mexico during those decades, therefore, became deeply entangled in the battles that erupted between pro- and antislavery forces, as the region emerged as a key battleground in the fight to determine the future of slavery in North America.

Disputes over slavery came to define relationships between Mexicans and Americans in the Texas borderlands. Nearly every Anglo-American who came into northern Mexico during this era—such as Austin and Kirkham—considered slavery to be the indispensable institution for building a successful cotton economy, and so they demanded that the institution remain legal in the region. Mexicans, by contrast, were anything but united on the question of slavery's future on the continent. Although most Mexicans proved themselves to be opponents of chattel slavery, a smaller group of Mexicans emerged as full-throated supporters of slave-based agriculture as practiced by the U.S. immigrants. There was, it turned out, no single position on slavery within Mexico, setting off a series of fierce debates among Mexicans and Americans over the institution's future in Texas. Struggles over slavery, indeed, became the defining point of contention between those in Texas and the Mexican government during the 1820s and early 1830s, disputes that eventually became enmeshed in larger battles over federalism that drove Mexico into civil war and Texas into rebellion.

Shifting attitudes toward slavery, in turn, affected how Americans and Europeans reacted to the expansion of the cotton frontier into Texas. Quarrels over slavery within Mexico regularly found their way onto the pages of U.S. newspapers, where they shaped the ebb and flow of migrants moving from the southern United States to northern Mexico. When Texas emerged during the late 1830s as an independent nation, the efforts of its leaders to wield cotton as a diplomatic weapon in their quest for international assistance meant that the Republic of Texas's commitment to slavery became a painful political liability. The attempts of Texas leaders to gain assistance from foreign powers crashed time and again against the politics of slavery, as did their struggles to annex the region to the United States. Slavery became a diplomatic burden that the Texas nation could not overcome, a circumstance the British attempted to exploit in their search for a free-labor supply of cotton for their textile mills. Throughout the 1830s and 1840s, questions of Texas invariably became entangled in international disputes over what cotton and slavery would mean for expansion and political power in North America. The result was a decade-long struggle between Mexico, the United States, Great Britain, and the Republic of Texas over the fate of this borderland region.

None of these three forces changed Texas by themselves. What each of them did, instead, was powerfully shape the challenges and opportunities facing both the people who lived in the territory and the various governments that attempted to control them. This is a history of how the rise of a particular form of capitalism—the cotton complex, which relied on enslaved labor and intricate systems of finance and international trade regulated by various governments—shaped the movement of people and ideas into the U.S.-Mexican borderlands during the first half of the nineteenth century.[9] It was a complex and confusing process, but one that followed a consistent pattern: it was cotton commerce that moved so many people into the region, it was slavery that so often put them into conflicts, and it was largely through their governments that they struggled so mightily to define the region's future. Each of these forces played upon and influenced one another, each wielding different roles at different moments as circumstances changed over time. The result was an evolution of the region that was volatile, unpredictable, and anything but foreordained.[10]

THIS IS NOT THE STORY that we usually tell about how Mexico's Far North became the American Southwest. Explanations for how the United States came to control Mexico's far-northern territories, for example, have long centered on notions of "manifest destiny" propelling Americans westward in an inexorable march toward the Pacific Ocean.[11] Yet the Americans who abandoned homes in the United States to come to Texas during this period rarely described themselves in such terms. Rather than seeing themselves as the forward guard of an inevitable United States takeover of the continent, these men and women said that they risked their lives and their families for what seemed to be better opportunities in northern Mexico or the Republic of Texas. This is not to say that white Americans of the era did not think of themselves as racially or culturally superior to Mexicans, Indians, or people of African descent. Most of them did. Nor is it to say that Americans did not believe that these territories would be better governed by the United States. Many certainly did, and at times said as much. But feelings of superiority did not, by themselves, collectively convince tens of thousands of Americans to abandon their native country and undertake the arduous trek westward. The movement of Americans into Texas was, instead, the result of global economic forces and specific government policies that together convinced tens of thousands of individuals to seize opportunities in the region on their own behalf rather than as the vanguard of the United States.

If pointing toward "manifest destiny" obscures the motivations that drove Americans into the region, invoking the concept also blinds us to the central role that Mexicans played in these transformations of the Texas borderlands. The rush of Americans into Texas during the 1820s, for example, simply could not have happened as it did without the consent—if not outright support—of the Mexican government and people. Mexicans were never passive observers of these momentous changes, as leaders on the local, state, and national levels sought to shape the movement of Americans into their northern territories toward their own particular ends. These were not always the same ends, however. Mexicans who lived in the Texas borderlands—usually called Tejanos—often held different perspectives and goals from Mexicans elsewhere in the country. Tejano leaders, for instance, forged an alliance with Anglos to preserve slavery in the region against the repeated efforts of Mexicans from other regions to outlaw it, a move that proved crucial to the continued influx of Americans during the late 1820s and early 1830s. Even after Texas broke away in 1836, competing groups within Mexico continued to shape the fortunes of the region in ways that would help ensure the ultimate failure of the Republic of Texas. Assigning nearly all responsibility for these transformations to American designs has, strangely, left historians little room to acknowledge the differences that Mexicans made.[12]

The same must be said for Indian nations in the region, who also played central—sometimes defining—roles in the drama that unfolded during those decades. Recent work on the U.S.-Mexican borderlands has revealed in stark detail the powerful influences that native peoples wielded in the tumultuous changes of that era. The military and economic power of Indian nations, the Comanches in particular, decimated the Spanish presence in the region, pushed Mexicans toward embracing American immigration, and fundamentally shaped Spanish, Mexican, and Anglo-American government policies by forcing non-Indians in the territory to address the demands and agendas of native groups. As both Mexicans and Americans in the region understood, local Indian nations often wielded immense power over the choices available to men and women attempting to build new lives and societies within the Texas borderlands.[13] Yet these Indians also found themselves often overwhelmed and overrun by the sheer crush of Americans coming into the region to claim cotton lands, forcing many tribes to abandon native homes and territories.

Perhaps most important, the rapid expansion of cotton and slavery across the Gulf Coast of North America—particularly as they related to global economic and political shifts remaking the larger Atlantic world—has never been central to our understanding of the evolution of the Texas borderlands and northern Mexico. Despite the pioneering work of a handful of historians who have delved into the expansion of American slavery into the Mexican frontier, that story has remained a sidelight within the literature that rarely connects the evolution of the U.S.-Mexican borderlands to the rapid development of the Mississippi River Valley.[14] The history of cotton in pre-annexation Texas has received even less attention, with mentions of the industry—and its connections to controversies over slavery—scattered among a handful of works.[15] In explaining the vast transformations that overtook the Texas borderlands during these years, scholars have tended to focus instead on other—usually related—factors. Some, for instance, point toward the availability of cheap Mexican land as the prime mover of Americans into the region. Others argue that it was the power of the expanding U.S. economy, primarily through trade with northern Mexico, that helped overwhelm Mexico City's weak hold on the territory.[16] Yet, unless issues like land and trade are placed squarely within the broader context of rising cotton markets in the Gulf of Mexico, such explanations can tell only part of the story. The value of these lands, for example, rose and fell in Americans eyes in direct proportion to their ability to support cotton and therefore always moved with the shifting attitudes of the Mexican government toward slavery. It is similarly difficult to understand the far-reaching influence of the U.S. economy on northeastern Mexico without cotton commerce serving as the center point.

This work, in other words, attempts to provide a new orientation within which to understand the transformations of the Texas borderlands. In all of this, I am attempting to combine ideas and insights spread across a wide variety of usually segregated fields—the early Mexican Republic, the American South, the expansion of the United States, New World slavery, and the recent outpouring of work on the U.S.-Mexican borderlands, among others—to expose broad overlaps of influence shaping both Texas and the continent. And as my notes attest, I owe a deep debt to the work of groundbreaking historians in all those fields. Yet the story presented here—based on archives in both Mexico and the United States—places the connections between cotton, slavery, and empire at the very center of the evolution of these disputed lands, emphasizing how powerful undercurrents swirling throughout the Atlantic world continually reshaped the shared edges of the United States and Mexico.

When cast into the shadow of those three dominating forces, much about these decades that once seemed so familiar takes on a different hue. Comanche and Apache raids that devastated Spanish settlements in Texas during the 1810s, for example, were not driven solely by the weakness of Spain's presence in the region; they were also driven by the rise of lucrative new markets for horses created by the expanding U.S. cotton industry. The decisions of Anglo-Americans to move into northeastern Mexico during the 1820s and 1830s, it turns out, were only partially tied to the availability of cheap Mexican land. The politics of slavery in Mexico, the rise and fall of global cotton prices, and the flow of information through newspaper networks played even more powerful roles. Because Americans in Mexico had to operate within Mexico's federal political system, it was the Mexicans of Texas—not the Anglo-Americans—who became the essential powerbrokers in forging political alliances that brought the global cotton market into northern Mexico. And when Texans finally tore the region from Mexico, the Republic of Texas that emerged during the late 1830s and early 1840s was never simply a collection of disgruntled Anglo-Texans in rebellion from Mexico. The Texas nation was, instead, a dress rehearsal for the creation of the Confederacy two decades later, offering a remarkable window into the worldview of nineteenth-century American slaveholders and their hopes for building a cotton empire along the Gulf Coast of North America.

There was, in other words, a strange unity to the rapid evolution of this territory during that fateful half century. The central premise of this work is that common threads ran throughout those decades that tied together disparate events—ranging from Comanche raids in New Spain during the 1810s to fights between the United States and Mexico over annexation during the 1840s—which have long appeared to have little in common. These were, indeed, the same threads that tied the territory and its people to the larger world around them.

STRIPPED TO ITS BASE, the transformation of Mexico's northeastern frontier into the western edge of the U.S. South is the story of how American migration to Mexico reordered power in the region. And that tide of Americans making their way across the Mexican frontier was never confined to just Texas. From the 1810s through the 1840s, Americans trekked across the entire expanse of northern Mexico, moving into places like New Mexico and California. Most Americans who ventured past Texas came to trade goods, either with Mexican villages like Santa Fe and Taos or with the powerful Indian nations who controlled the majority of the territory. Others came as trappers, hunting the region's beaver and other animals for pelts that brought high prices in American and European markets. Impoverished *nuevomexicanos* and *californios* generally welcomed the commerce that came with these Americans, although Mexico's profound weakness in the region meant there was little that Mexico City could have done to stop them. Connections forged between American merchants and Mexican buyers began reorienting the economy of northern Mexico away from Mexico City and toward the United States. The result was a weakening of ties between the Mexican frontier and the rest of the nation during the decades that preceded the U.S.-Mexican War, as the region came under the expanding influence of the American economy. What happened in Texas, in other words, was part of a larger process overtaking the whole of northern Mexico during those crucial decades.[17]

Yet what happened in Texas was also profoundly different, and that made all the difference. The trappers and traders who came to New Mexico and California never intended to stay. Despite colonization laws that allowed Americans to acquire land as settlers in nearly any territory of northern Mexico, there were never more than a few hundred Americans in the expansive regions west of Texas. An 1839 census found just 39 foreigners living in New Mexico, and as late as 1845 only 680 foreigners could be found in all of California.[18] The tide of Americans pouring into the Texas borderlands, by contrast, became an unceasing flood. More than 30,000 Americans abandoned the United States for Texas during the 1820s and 1830s, and by the mid-1840s the region's Anglo-American population exceeded 100,000 souls. The reasons for these differences went beyond the sheer proximity of Texas to the United States. Although much of New Mexico and California were arid, Texas offered fertile soils and lush river valleys that seemed perfectly suited for Gulf Coast agriculture. Texas therefore drew a particular *kind* of American, as farmers from the southern United States made up the overwhelming majority of migrants into the region, leading to rapid shifts in the region's economy and populations that made Texas increasingly unlike the rest of Mexico's northern frontier.

The transformation of Texas, as a result, proved far more volatile and destabilizing for Mexico than the evolution of New Mexico or California. Texas was, for example, the only portion of Mexico's frontier where expatriate Americans became the dominant population, the only region where plantation agriculture came to define the economy, and the only territory in Mexico that evolved into a slaveholding society. Becoming the epicenter of such rapid and profound changes along the U.S.-Mexican border meant that Mexicans and Anglo-Americans in Texas often found themselves in struggles with Mexican officials over questions of American migration, slavery's future in Mexico, and issues of regional autonomy. When those conflicts boiled over into war in 1835–36, Texas became the only portion of northern Mexico to secede from the nation. While Mexico's leaders certainly worried about American influence in New Mexico and California, neither territory came close to wielding the influence that Texas did in shaping Mexico City's policies toward its far-northern provinces.

Texas was also, therefore, never simply an extension of the American frontier. Although men and women from the southern United States did their utmost to transform the region into a Mexican version of Mississippi, they instead found themselves attempting to build a plantation society in circumstances unlike anything they encountered in the American South. The dogged efforts of some Mexicans to abolish slavery during the 1820s and 1830s meant that Anglo-Texans never succeeded in forcing Mexico to support slave-based agriculture in the image of the Mississippi River Valley. Anglo-Texans then failed once again when they attempted to create their own nation to serve that same end, this time because of the international constraints surrounding their political and economic vision for the territory. In the end, what was so remarkable about the Texas Republic was its swift downfall, and how its collapse marked the first failure of American farmers to construct a nation built atop cotton and slavery. The story of Texas lays bare not only the powerful role that cotton played in shaping a particular vision for the Gulf Coast among American slaveholders during the first half of the nineteenth century but also the profound limits of that vision.

What follows is a chronicle of how Mexicans, Indians, Anglo-Americans, Europeans, and African Americans competed for space and power in the Texas borderlands in a world dominated by the Atlantic cotton economy. When Marian, Richard, and Tivi made their desperate trek into northern New Spain, they hoped to escape the cruelty of James Kirkham and the power of the U.S. cotton frontier that had torn them from families and homes in North Carolina, South Carolina, and Kentucky. Yet Texas never became the refuge from cotton and slavery that these runaways imagined in 1820. The cotton frontier instead followed them into the territory when Anglo-Americans like Moses Austin and James Kirkham forged an alliance with leaders in San Antonio that would eventually transform the Texas borderlands into everything Marian, Richard, and Tivi had hoped to escape.

That story begins in San Antonio on the eve of Mexican independence from Spain, at a moment when struggles between Indians, Spaniards, and Americans for control of the region reached a flashpoint. During the decades that followed, numerous other peoples and nations joined the fray, each failing in their attempt to master the region, even as the demands of cotton and slavery slowly tightened their hold on the territory. What emerges is a detailed history that dwells on the contested nature of these lands, where the clashing of people and ideas about the future of North America brought enormous consequences for both the United States and Mexico.

PART I

In the Shadow of Cotton

*From now on, I am not responsible for defending
and controlling this province that has been placed
under my protection.*

—Governor Antonio Martínez, 1820

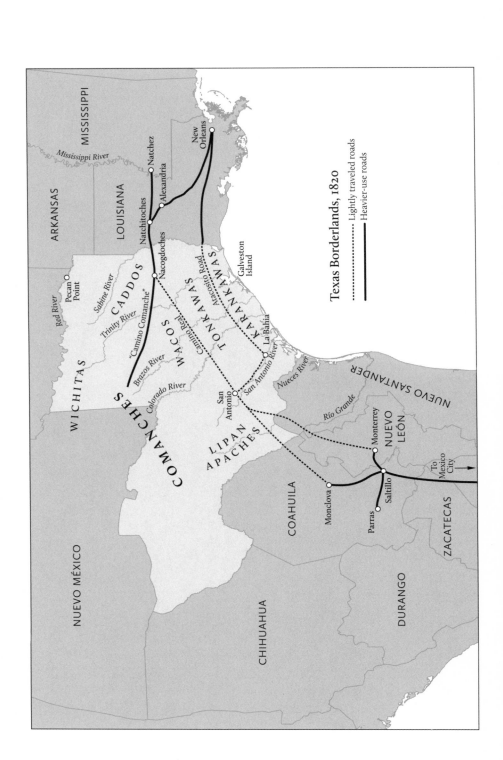

Texas Borderlands, 1820

········· Lightly traveled roads
─────── Heavier-use roads

MISSISSIPPI

Mississippi River

ARKANSAS

LOUISIANA

Natchez

New Orleans

Alexandria

Natchitoches

Nacogdoches

Atascosito Road

Galveston Island

Pecan Point

Red River

Sabine River

CADDOS

Trinity River

"Camino Comanche"

WICHITAS

WACOS

Brazos River

Colorado River

Camino Real

TONKAWAS

KARANKAWAS

La Bahía

San Antonio River

San Antonio

Nueces River

NUEVO SANTANDER

COMANCHES

LIPAN APACHES

Río Grande

Monterrey

NUEVO LEÓN

Saltillo

To Mexico City →

NUEVO MÉXICO

CHIHUAHUA

COAHUILA

Monclova

Parras

ZACATECAS

DURANGO

ONE

The Texas Borderlands on the Eve of Mexican Independence

During the night of July 4, 1819, a soft rain began falling north of San Antonio, beating the parched earth with an endless stream of desperately needed water. A severe drought had seared the region for the past several years, burning away vast swaths of native grasslands and decimating herds of bison and wild cattle. Fields withered by the sun that summer had been unable to support the corn crops needed to sustain the Spaniards huddled in San Antonio, leaving the village gravely short of food. Even the horses were starving, with the Spaniards' mounts so malnourished that some could barely stand. Yet the rain had finally come. Rolling across the burned ground, water began to fill the dried creek beds and *arroyos* that twisted their way southward. Eventually the storm made its way to San Antonio. For those who lived in that small, parched village, the din of rain on their rooftops surely sounded like mercy sent from the heavens.

San Antonio was a town in need of divine grace. Founded in 1718, a little more than a century earlier, the town sat on a stretch of land between the San Antonio River on the east and the San Pedro Creek on the west. Growing in spurts over the course of the eighteenth century, the village served as the makeshift capital of Texas, the most remote province along New Spain's far-northeastern frontier. Despite its political status, the village had always languished in isolation as Spanish authorities refused to put significant resources into the region, sending only as few troops and supplies as necessary to keep alive their military presence in Texas. When the governor of Texas filed a report on the region in 1803, his assessment of San Antonio was grim. The village had, he lamented, "absolutely no commerce or industry" to support its modest population of twenty-five hundred, and were it not for a handful of hunters providing the town with buffalo meat, "the greater portion of the families would perish in misery."[1]

If the village failed to prosper during the eighteenth century, it had been ravaged during the nineteenth. When the Mexican War for Independence broke out during the early nineteenth century, rebels captured the town in 1813 and executed the governor. Spanish authorities, in retaliation, launched a bloody military campaign to reclaim the region, killing hundreds of suspected rebels in San Antonio and sending hundreds more fleeing into the countryside. Those who survived the vicious reassertion of Spanish authority found themselves, in the years since, living under siege. Emboldened by the weakness of San Antonio, Comanches and Apaches launched an endless series of raids that bled the Spaniards of what few horses, cattle, and crops they still had. Wars, drought, and famine reduced the population of San Antonio to a mere sixteen hundred by 1819, almost a thousand fewer than lived there only two decades before.[2]

On that July evening in 1819, however, the rains had finally come. And they continued overnight, though too quickly for the drought-hardened ground. Shallow creek beds soon began funneling a torrential gush into the San Antonio River, which picked up speed and force as it moved south toward the village. By dawn, the river was straining at its banks. A wall of water broke into the north side of San Antonio just after daybreak, rushing through the streets with frightening momentum. The only bridge spanning the river cracked and shattered under the power of the rising tide. Water continued to force its way into the town, drowning every street and plaza, before finally joining the San Pedro Creek on the far-western side of San Antonio. Almost as soon as the flood began, there was no longer a town—only a wide, angry river that subsumed everything.[3]

The governor, Antonio Martínez, awoke to water pouring into his home. Wading out into the flooded streets, the aged patriarch could hardly comprehend the scene. Every avenue had been transformed into a furious river sweeping away screaming men and women who flailed about in desperate attempts to pull themselves to safety. Those lucky enough to snag tree limbs climbed high into the branches seeking refuge. Others tore off their clothes to keep from being pulled to their deaths beneath the water. The raging tide even unmoored homes from their foundations. Poorer families in San Antonio lived in rickety wooden huts, known as *jacals*, built of timber plastered together with mud and clay. Martínez watched, powerless, as the flood ripped apart *jacals*, often with families inside, and "houses began to disappear, leaving only fragments afloat to indicate the disaster that overtook them."[4]

The governor ordered his soldiers to pull anyone they could from the

Mexican Huts, by James Gilchrist Benton, 1852. Most Tejanos in San Antonio lived in rickety jacals, many of which were swept away and destroyed by the 1819 flood. (Amon Carter Museum of American Art Archives, Fort Worth, Texas)

water, sending the best swimmers to rescue people who had taken refuge in treetops. As the deluge continued, Martínez decided to abandon the town before the water rose any higher. Ordering all survivors to follow him, Martínez led a march toward the hills outside San Antonio, where they huddled beneath trees. Then, as quickly as they had come, the flood waters began to recede.

When they returned, the survivors surveyed the destruction. San Antonio in 1819 was divided into four neighborhoods that corresponded roughly to the directions on a compass.[5] The northern and southern neighborhoods—where the wealthiest and most influential families lived —had been completely inundated, with homes and buildings near the town's center sustaining the worst damage. The flood, however, had concentrated its fury on the poorer neighborhoods on the eastern and western sides of town. Raging waters had slammed hardest into the eastern neighborhood of Valero, where nearly every home had been a rickety *jacal*. Hardly a structure survived, as the flooding destroyed and killed indiscriminately. In the small western neighborhood of Laredo, the water rose so quickly that people, trapped within their homes, lashed together makeshift rafts in a desperate bid to avoid drowning. Many had not succeeded, and most of those who died in the flood came from either Valero or Laredo.

Governor Martínez returned to his residence on the east side of the military plaza, near the center of town. The receding waters swept away many of the governor's household effects, and extensive damage made the home uninhabitable. Most other government buildings met similar fates. The royal corrals had been ruined, and the livestock lost. Storehouses of corn had flooded, spoiling what little food reserves the town had. There would now be no harvest that year—the fields just outside the village had been leveled. Like the governor, most residents had either been made homeless or lost their few possessions to the raging waters. Many no longer had clothes, having shed them to keep afloat during the height of the flood. No one could even be sure how many had died, and for days survivors toiled at the grim task of recovering the dozens of bodies that washed up on the riverbanks downstream.[6]

Three days after the flood, Martínez wrote two reports of the disaster, one for the commandant general in Monterrey, Nuevo León, the other for the viceroy of New Spain in Mexico City. Martínez described, in frank and brutal terms, the desolate scene in San Antonio, begging both men to send whatever aid might be possible to salvage the town. Martínez also brooded on the dark irony of a flood ravaging the same village that had prayed for an end to the drought. God, it seemed to Martínez, was mocking the impoverished people of San Antonio. "Divine Providence," he wrote to the viceroy, "lets them exist in order to witness and participate in the misfortune which His Divine Majesty dispenses with impenetrable judgment."[7]

Though he railed at God, Martínez saved most of his anger for the leaders of New Spain. The flood, while devastating, had merely exposed the decay left by what the governor saw as a century of neglect and mismanagement by Spanish authorities. Texas, he recognized, had always been treated by the Spanish crown as a distant, unimportant hinterland, leaving outposts like San Antonio—even before the flood—in desperate straits. When the violence of a revolution shook New Spain during the 1810s, the result had been the rapid erosion of an already weak Spanish presence in Texas. In the years since, authorities in Monterrey and Mexico City had been either unable or unwilling to bolster Spain's position in the region, which struck Martínez as an almost willful abdication of their responsibilities. In nearly every letter he wrote as governor, Martínez complained that lack of support from his superiors had effectively abandoned Tejanos—as Spaniards in Texas called themselves—along New Spain's northeastern frontier to their enemies. His tirades about the "impenetrable judgment" of Providence, then, poorly masked Martínez's underlying conviction that the misery of Spaniards in Texas was tied directly to the poor judgment of authorities in New Spain.[8]

What Martínez did not know, however, was that powerful forces had been destabilizing the Texas borderlands in ways that Mexico City could not control. Far beyond the confines of New Spain, a revolution in cotton had begun in Europe during the early 1800s when the burgeoning British textile industry developed an insatiable hunger for cotton as a cheaper, more comfortable, more durable alternative to wool. The crop became, almost overnight, one of the most valuable commodities in the Atlantic world, unleashing an economic storm that soon swept across the Atlantic Ocean and began reshaping the North American continent. One of the largest migrations in United States history ensued, as hundreds of thousands of Americans poured into the Gulf Coast region that would become the Cotton South of the United States—places like Mississippi, Alabama, and Louisiana—where alluvial soils and a long growing season promised ideal conditions for cultivating this newly profitable crop. By 1819, as Martínez despaired for Texas, the revolution in cotton had remade the southwestern United States into one of the primary engines of a new global cotton economy. And because all of this took place along the northeastern edge of New Spain, powerful forces unleashed by cotton began making their way across the landscape of Spain's tenuous holdings in Texas.

Although Martínez could not know it, the desolate condition of Spanish settlements in Texas owed as much to the rise of this new global cotton economy as it did the failings of Mexico City. Alongside the Americans who flooded into places near the Spanish border had come an equally powerful new trading market geared toward supplying them. Indian nations in Texas, as a result, had vastly escalated the frequency and violence of their raids against Spanish villages in order to feed this voracious new market with horses and mules. American traders hoping to profit from those tribes, in turn, established illegal trading posts in eastern Texas, while smugglers used the Texas coast to funnel enslaved Africans into the flourishing new slave markets of the Mississippi River Valley. The result was a dramatic reorientation of economic and military power along the U.S.-Texas border that forced impoverished communities like San Antonio to expend their few resources on repelling invaders and began to collapse Spain's presence in the region. Indeed, by the late 1810s Indian raids and armed incursions by foreigners had become so unceasing that Martínez feared he might have to abandon the province entirely. While it brought prosperity to the southern United States, the revolution in cotton brought chaos and turmoil to northern New Spain.

Governor Martínez had seen firsthand how the neglect of Mexico City and the forces unleashed by cotton had combined to overwhelm Spain's presence in the Texas borderlands, even if he did not fully understand their origins. And in the aftermath of the 1819 flood, Martínez would turn to the very source of his troubles as an unlikely means of salvation, making the remarkable decision in 1820 to invite the cotton revolution into the Texas borderlands in order to save the region for New Spain.

Indian Country

As the people of San Antonio attempted to rebuild, Governor Martínez struggled to understand how Spain's presence in Texas had edged so close toward ruin. The Spanish, he knew, had claimed control of the region since the sixteenth century, although that had long been more an assertion than anything else. When conquistadors found neither gold nor silver in Texas during the 1540s, Spanish authorities chose to ignore the region throughout most of the sixteenth and seventeenth centuries. Only when French explorations of the Texas coast during the late 1600s threatened their claims did Spanish officials push to establish a permanent presence in the region. Numerous Spanish forts and missions were erected throughout the province during the years that followed, nearly all of which ended in failure. Reading through the reports of his predecessors in San Antonio's government archives, Martínez could easily understand why. Letters from officials in Texas during those years invariably complained of inadequate support from Mexico City: too few troops assigned to defend such a vast and unsettled frontier; heavy-handed trade restrictions enforced by the crown that retarded the region's economic growth; the lack of a shipping port, combined with undeveloped roads, that left the region dangerously isolated from the rest of New Spain. Few settlers, as a result, proved willing to abandon New Spain's interior for the insecurities of this far-flung frontier, leaving the Spanish population in Texas perpetually anemic.[9]

By the onset of the nineteenth century, the permanent Spanish presence in Texas had not grown beyond a handful of small villages. San Antonio, the capital, was the largest and most developed in the province, boasting around twenty-five hundred people divided between civilians and the royal troops who guarded the town and nearby decaying missions. A hundred miles downstream stood La Bahía del Espíritu Santo, a small settlement of about seven hundred scattered around a dilapidated presidio and two missions.[10] Originally located on the site of an abandoned French settlement, La Bahía had been moved in 1749 to its permanent location along the southern San Antonio River, near the Gulf of Mexico.[11] Villagers in both outposts depended on ranching for their survival—running horses, cattle, and goats on ranches fronting the river—although that provided only a meager existence.[12] Three hundred miles farther east, along the Louisiana border, stood the hamlet of Nacogdoches. Founded in the late 1770s, in the wake of the collapse of nearby missions, Nacogdoches had managed by the early 1800s to grow into a hardscrabble community of around eight hundred. Isolated by hundreds of miles from any other settlement, Spaniards in Nacogdoches survived on ranching and an illegal trade in contraband goods—including a small trade in slaves—that locals maintained with Louisiana.[13] Life along the farthest edge of New Spain was precarious, and Spaniards in Nacogdoches struggled. "There," the governor of Texas noted in 1803, "the inhabitants subsist with scarcely as many articles as are necessary to sustain life."[14]

Despite what maps in Madrid said, Spain never controlled Texas. Power in the region always resided with the province's numerous Indian tribes, whose frequent clashes with local Spaniards was another reason settlements in the region refused to grow. The tens of thousands of Indians who made their homes in the Texas borderlands during the early 1800s far outnumbered the approximately four thousand Spaniards who lived there.[15] The Caddos of eastern Texas dominated the territory along the Louisiana border, farming and trading with Wichitas, Kickapoos, and others in the region. Tribes such as the Tonkawas and Wacos hunted in the central parts of the province, while Karankawas lived in the swampy lowlands of the Texas Gulf Coast. Lipan Apaches roamed throughout central and western Texas on horseback, hunting buffalo and raiding weaker tribes. The Comanches, however, reigned as the acknowledged masters of the region. Operating out of the central and western plains, the Comanches established themselves during the eighteenth century as the dominant military and trading force across Texas and neighboring New Mexico. Whereas the Spanish controlled only a handful of small villages, "the remainder of this extensive, immense, and spacious region," observed one Tejano resident of San Antonio, "is occupied by the different tribes of barbarous Indians." It was, he lamented, the Comanches and the Lipan Apaches "who, at all times, have been masters of the possessions and lives" of Spaniards in the region.[16]

Every effort of the Spanish to establish dominion over Texas and its Indians had failed. Crown officials originally hoped to conquer both with the mission system, which called for Franciscan friars to establish mission complexes (a collection of buildings resembling a small village, centered around a chapel) near Indian tribes in order to minister to them. Indians, they hoped, would come to live in these missions, where the friars would instruct them in the Catholic faith and Spanish civilization, eventually converting powerful enemies into loyal, tax-paying subjects of the Spanish crown. While a remarkably cheap method of conquest—requiring only that Mexico City invest in a handful of soldiers at each mission to guard the Franciscans—it also proved remarkably ineffective. Throughout the entire eighteenth century, no Caddo, Wichita, or any other Indian nation in eastern Texas showed any interest in becoming either Catholic or Spanish. Tonkawas, Karankawas, Comanches, and Apaches all rejected numerous other Spanish missions established in central Texas and along the Gulf Coast. Only the missions around San Antonio attracted any Indians, mostly members of impoverished tribes who sought the missions largely as shelter from their enemies. Although they traded with the missions, or raided them when convenient, Indians in Texas simply had no interest in converting to Spanish ways. By the late 1700s, Mexico City acknowledged that the system was an unmitigated failure and began shuttering missions across the region.[17]

Rather than converting Indians, Spaniards found themselves perpetually locked in violent confrontations with particular tribes. When the Spanish founded San Antonio in 1718, they had unknowingly established themselves within the southern expanse of Lipan territory. Apache warriors soon began raiding San Antonio's horse herds and killing Spaniards who resisted. A vicious cycle of bloody confrontations ensued for decades, as Apaches and Spaniards killed, kidnapped, and raided one another's settlements. When Comanches moved into the region during the 1730s and 1740s, challenging the Lipan Apaches for control of the Texas Plains, a desperate struggle ensued. Comanche raiders devastated Apache villages, forcing the Apaches to compensate by raiding their own neighbors, including the Spanish. Following years of warfare, the Spanish made a pact with the Comanches in 1785 to maintain peace between them and to unite in an effort to exterminate their common enemy, the

Lipan Apaches.[18] By forging an alliance with the Comanches, the region's most powerful military force, Spaniards groped for any means of stemming the bloodshed that undermined every effort at developing their Texas settlements.[19]

By the time of the Comanche-Spanish 1785 truce, officials in New Spain had come to embrace trade with Indian nations—rather than the mission system—as the most promising means for advancing Spanish interests in Texas. Guided by regulations issued by the crown in 1786, Spanish authorities began licensing agents to establish commerce with the tribes of Texas at authorized trading posts. Regular shipments of goods were to be sent to San Antonio and Nacogdoches, where they could be distributed among tribes as a means of maintaining both military and political alliances. It proved a practical arrangement. The costs of the merchandise distributed were unlikely to exceed the value of what otherwise would be lost to Indian raids, and with peace came the possibility for growth of Spanish settlements. Most Indian tribes were directed to make annual treks to Nacogdoches, where a new trading warehouse distributed gifts and conducted trade. The powerful Comanches, however, would be received in the Spanish capital where they enjoyed preferential treatment. The governor ordered the construction of a massive new lodge to house his Indian visitors in comfort while in San Antonio, and the first shipment of gifts earmarked for Comanches arrived in August 1786. The results of this tactical shift were immediate, as Spaniards secured tentative peace agreements with almost all Indian nations and Indian visitors streamed into Spanish settlements for trade. From 1794 to 1803, more than forty-two hundred Comanches visited San Antonio.[20]

Yet from the outset this new emphasis on mercantile diplomacy suffered from an unstable supply chain. San Antonio, La Bahía, and Nacogdoches remained at an extreme edge of Spain's New World holdings, several hundred miles from authorized ports of commerce like Veracruz. Transporting matériel to such remote locales presented innumerable challenges, not least because the Spanish crown refused to authorize construction of a port along the Texas coast. Shipments had to be trekked overland hundreds of miles by mule trains along the royal highway out of Mexico City. When wars in Europe following the French Revolution badly disrupted Spain's transatlantic commerce, the flow of supplies bound for Texas slowed to a trickle. Terrified of not meeting his trade obligations to the Comanches, the governor began stockpiling dwindling supplies in San Antonio, leaving the trade house at Nacogdoches with chronic shortages. Tribes across eastern Texas soon grew frustrated with the inability of Spaniards to live up to their commitments and lodged frequent complaints with Spanish officials. Although promises of trade had allowed the Spanish to stabilize their settlements during the late 1700s, the inability of Mexico City to maintain a steady flow of supplies to its frontier outposts threatened to undermine the fragile peace in Texas.[21]

When the United States purchased the Louisiana territory in 1803, the failure of the Spanish to satisfy the trade needs of Indians in eastern Texas became an urgent liability. Because the line between Louisiana and New Spain had never been clearly defined, President Thomas Jefferson made the audacious claim that U.S. territory now stretched all the way to the Río Grande. Spain vehemently disagreed, and both Washington and Mexico City rushed troops toward the Louisiana border as the conflict escalated into a full-blown military crisis. Seeking to undermine Spain's military capabilities in Texas, the U.S. government dispatched John Sibley into western Louisiana in 1805 with orders to distribute gifts and foster trade connections with Indians in Texas. Sibley's charge was to sway the allegiance of Texas tribes toward the United States as a means of isolating the Spanish, and his overtures were well received by Caddos and Wichitas along the border. The United States even established a government-sponsored warehouse in Natchitoches, Louisiana, to ensure the steady flow of American goods into the region. Such efforts incensed Spanish authorities, yet there was little they could do to counter them without a more stable supply of their own trade goods. U.S.-Spanish tensions finally began to diffuse when both sides signed an armistice in November 1806, agreeing to observe a "neutral ground" that separated Louisiana and Texas until a final border agreement could be hammered out. The episode, however, exposed how deeply vulnerable Spanish-Indian trade alliances in Texas were to powerful new economic forces brewing along the border in the United States.[22]

By 1810, Spaniards walked a precarious line in Texas between stability and disaster. Paying tribute to the Comanches had staunched the worst of the violence against their settlements, and trade alliances with most other tribes had ushered in twenty-five years of relative peace. Although the United States now loomed as a meddlesome neighbor in Louisiana, the Americans no longer posed an immediate military threat. Yet Texas remained, indisputably, Indian country, leaving Spaniards in the region fearful of anything that might undermine their strategic alliances with powerful tribes. Spain continued to control, after all, only a handful of isolated outposts: San Antonio, its largest, was no more than a tiny island within the greater sea of Comanchería. And so the governor focused his few resources on what he deemed the greatest potential threat—commerce between American traders and Texas Indians—although it had little effect. Most Indian nations saw the advantages of engaging both Spanish and American markets, pitting Anglos and Spaniards against one another, and so they welcomed American merchants into their villages, while also making regular trade visits to Spanish towns (more than two thousand Indians visited San Antonio during 1807 alone).[23] The survival of the Spanish presence in Texas, therefore, depended entirely on Spain's ability to maintain alliances with powerful Indian nations like the Comanches while also guarding against the potentially disruptive influences of the Americans.

Rebellion

The fragile peace in Texas would be undone, in part, by a rebellion that began in central Mexico during the fall of 1810. In the centuries since the fall of the Aztecs, Spanish monarchs had attempted—with varying levels of success—to control the development of colonial Mexico. Mexico's primary purpose, according to Madrid, was to enrich Spain itself, and during the late eighteenth century the crown moved to tighten its control over the economic life of the colony. All commerce had to be routed through a single port, Veracruz, so that crown officials could monitor the shipments of silver that transferred wealth from Mexican mines to the Spanish treasury. The viceroy in Mexico City, in turn, attempted to reserve top administrative positions in New Spain solely for Spaniards born in Spain (known as *peninsulares*), shutting out Spaniards born in the Americas (*criollos*) from the upper echelons of Mexico's power structure. Such efforts to centralize power bred distrust and resentment among Spanish *criollos* in Mexico. Ranking far below both *peninsulares* and *criollos*, in both political power and social standing, stood everyone else deemed less "white" and less "Spanish" and therefore less worthy: *mestizos* (those born of Spanish-Indian unions), Indians, and anyone of African descent (such as "mulattoes" and "negroes"). Representing more than racial categories, these terms defined a social and economic hierarchy in Spanish New World society, where "white" blood represented the top and "black" blood the bottom. By the early nineteenth century, stark divides of power and wealth separated most Mexicans from the handful of *peninsulares* who held the majority of power in Spanish Mexico, fostering distrust and resentments between classes.[24]

Those frustrations boiled over in September 1810, when a *criollo* priest named Miguel Hidalgo delivered an impassioned address denouncing Spanish rule. Hidalgo's protest became a rallying cry for the disaffected within Mexico, sparking a massive uprising that launched the Mexican War for Independence. Within weeks, tens of thousands of *mestizos*, Indians, and mulattoes formed themselves into an unlikely army of liberation behind Hidalgo's leadership and began overrunning Spanish strongholds along the road toward Mexico City. When Hidalgo's forces sacked Guanajuato in the silver-rich region northwest of Mexico City, the rebels slaughtered hundreds of men, women, and children in an orgy of violence that terrified Spanish officials and stunned even Hidalgo. The rebel army then marched to the outskirts of Mexico City where, for reasons that remain unclear, Hidalgo chose not to attack. He instead turned his army northward, whereupon many insurgents began deserting. When the rebel army subsequently suffered a series of crushing military defeats, Hidalgo and other rebel leaders fled toward the northern borderlands of New Spain. They ended up in the province of Coahuila along the southern border of Texas, where Hidalgo was captured in March 1811. Following a speedy trial in Chihuahua City, a firing squad executed Hidalgo four months later. His severed head was sent to Guanajuato, where it hung in a cage for ten years as a warning to other would-be rebels.[25]

The rebellion, however, lived on and engulfed Spain's vulnerable outposts in Texas. When word of the Hidalgo revolt reached San Antonio, Governor Manuel Salcedo feared that local Tejanos might join its ranks. Hoping to slow the movement of revolutionaries and their ideas, the governor clamped down with prohibitions on Tejano travel and restrictions on the mail. Revolutionary talk nevertheless raced through the streets of San Antonio, as some Tejanos—likely tired of Spain's inability to provide for frontier settlements—began plotting the overthrow of Governor Salcedo. In January 1811, as Hidalgo retreated northward, a retired captain named Juan Bautista de las Casas led a small militia force into the governor's house, where they captured Salcedo in the name of the revolution. Most other outposts in Texas, like Nacogdoches, also surrendered to Las Casas. Numerous Tejanos, nevertheless, remained wary of the rebel leaders, and Las Casas's overbearing ways—jailing anyone he suspected of royalist sympathies, confiscating property at will—quickly eroded his base of support. A counterinsurgency formed, and a contingent of Tejanos overthrew Las Casas in March 1811, allowing Manuel Salcedo to return royal rule to Texas. Almost as soon as it began, Hidalgo's revolution had begun eroding New Spain's already weak hold on its most isolated frontier settlements.[26]

A far more destructive wave of the revolution soon washed over Texas. In December 1811, an agent of Hidalgo's, José Bernardo Gutiérrez de Lara, traveled to the United States seeking aid for the rebellion. In New Orleans, Gutiérrez joined forces with Augustus W. Magee, a former U.S. Army officer, and recruited Americans for an army to liberate Texas from Spain. In what became known as the Gutiérrez-Magee expedition, around 130 men made their way across the Sabine River in August 1812. As the self-styled "Republican Army of the North" began its march toward San Antonio, the paltry Spanish military presence in east Texas effectively vanished. Rather than fight, all but ten of the royal soldiers stationed in Nacogdoches deserted or joined the rebels, as did numerous local citizens, swelling the expedition's ranks to about three hundred. The Spanish commander at La Bahía abandoned his post as the insurgents approached, retreating toward the capital.[27] The culminating fight came in late March 1813, when rebels routed Spanish forces just outside San Antonio, forcing Governor Salcedo to surrender the capital. Salcedo and his officers were imprisoned and then brutally executed—a wayward contingent of the insurgents slit their throats and then stabbed them to death. The savagery of Governor Salcedo's murder prompted some in the rebel army to desert, including many Americans. More important, the rebellion and murder infuriated the viceroy of New Spain, who moved to reassert royal authority in Texas with vicious force.[28]

The viceroy sought a commander who could destroy the rebels, and so he appointed José Joaquín de Arredondo as the new commandant general of the Eastern Interior Provinces—an area that included Texas—with orders to crush the Gutiérrez-Magee rebellion. Arredondo quickly built an army of more than eighteen hundred royalist troops and marched toward Texas. Meanwhile, in San Antonio, hundreds of Tejanos joined the rebel forces, increasing their numbers to around fourteen hundred. While some of these new recruits surely volunteered for sheer adventure, many others plainly hoped for an opportunity to better their miserable position in Texas. A number of Tejanos, less convinced that rebellion could bring prosperity, sided with the royalists. When scouts brought word that Arredondo's forces were approaching San Antonio, the rebel army marched six miles southward to meet them along the Medina River.

On August 18, 1813, the two armies battered each other for four hours in blistering heat. The disorganized rebels proved no match for Arredondo's more experienced and disciplined soldiers, and the fight degenerated into a one-sided slaughter. All but one hundred of the rebels were killed, effectively destroying the Gutiérrez-Magee revolt. And as the tattered remnants of the rebel army fled back toward San Antonio, with Arredondo's troops in pursuit, the full-scale destruction of the rebellion in Texas began in earnest.[29]

News of the insurgents' defeat set off panic throughout San Antonio. Apache riders, fresh from the battlefield, brought the first reports of the rout as they galloped through the village. The families of those who had joined the rebellion began a desperate scramble to gather their possessions and flee the capital, knowing they would be held liable for the defections of their fathers, brothers, and sons. When the first survivors from the rebel army staggered into town, they joined the frenzied scene of men, women, and children clambering into wagons for a terrified exodus toward Louisiana. With whatever little they could carry, hundreds of Tejanos then abandoned San Antonio before Arredondo's forces could arrive. Several hundred other Tejanos—who, for one reason or another, could not flee—crowded into the Catholic chapel at the center of San Antonio, praying for mercy and hoping for sanctuary.[30]

When Arredondo finally rode into San Antonio, he began exacting royal vengeance upon the villagers. His troops rounded up hundreds of Tejanos, including everyone cowering in the church, and jammed them so tightly into makeshift jails that at least eight people suffocated. The next morning, Arredondo berated the terrified villagers and selected forty to be shot—at a pace of three per day, for almost two weeks—while another 160 were chained together in work gangs. Women and children deemed disloyal were imprisoned in "La Quinta," a makeshift building on the main square, where guards forced them to grind corn and make thousands of tortillas needed to feed Arredondo's troops.[31] Every firearm in the village was confiscated, as were the homes and property of all suspected insurgents. Anyone resisting was whipped on the public square.[32] Arredondo's methods were as ruthless as they were vindictive. Yet they served a strategic goal of Spanish authorities in Mexico City: to stamp out any vestige of rebellious sentiment within Texas that might challenge the authority of the Spanish crown.

Royal forces moved quickly to wrest the other Texas outposts from rebel hands, and Arredondo dispatched eighty soldiers to reclaim La

Military Plaza—San Antonio, Texas. This plaza served as the scene for most public events in San Antonio, including the mass executions ordered by Arredondo during his bloody reassertion of royal authority in Texas. (General Collection, Beinecke Rare Book and Manuscript Library, Yale University)

Bahía. Word of the ongoing purge of disloyal Tejanos, however, preceded the troops, prompting many families from La Bahía to join their San Antonio compatriots in fleeing toward Louisiana. Arredondo then sent several hundred cavalrymen, under the command of Ignacio Elizondo, to chase down the rebels and refugees escaping eastward. Elizondo rode out of the capital with five hundred soldiers, but moved with such ferocious speed that only half his men could keep up. At the Brazos River he ran down the slowest of the escaping families, executing the men upon capture.[33] Thundering on toward the Trinity River, Elizondo's men began overrunning scattered bands of refugees, capturing women and children and usually executing the men. In his after-action reports, Elizondo reported that his men shot 71 insurgents, although Tejanos who survived his wrath remembered a bloodier affair.[34] When Elizondo's men arrived at the Trinity, recalled two survivors of the purge, they slaughtered more than 100 of the 150 refugees they captured. One Tejana survivor would later remember with horror how Elizondo's troops lanced her cousin after shooting him. When the young man's mother protested that he needed to be allowed to confess before dying, Elizondo's troops declared that "he should confess himself to the Devils" in hell.[35]

Arredondo's scorched-earth policy burned down Spain's feeble presence in eastern Texas. By the time Elizondo reached the outskirts of Nacogdoches, all but three families had fled in terror to either Louisiana or the countryside. Elizondo emptied the town entirely by ordering those three families to join his march back to San Antonio, as his men drove hundreds of prisoners back to the Spanish capital. When they arrived, they were paraded through the streets before being presented to Arredondo, who ordered that every man be executed, the women sent to "La Quinta," and the children abandoned to the streets.[36] By the end of Arredondo's purge, approximately a thousand Spanish residents of Texas had been killed, and another thousand had fled to the United States, effectively halving the Spanish population of Texas.[37] Nacogdoches had been completely abandoned; La Bahía had been gutted. San Antonio endured as the only significant outpost left, although its people had been decimated.[38] Through brutal suppression of the rebellion, José Joaquín de Arredondo reduced the Spanish presence in eastern Texas to almost nothing, reordering power dynamics in the region in ways that would haunt San Antonio for the rest of the decade.

Cotton Farms and Horse Raids

Indian nations of Texas reassessed their priorities in the aftermath of the Spanish tearing themselves apart. With fewer settlements, Tejanos now had little contact with most tribes, and the violence of 1811–13 badly disrupted the already unstable supply of trade goods that Spain shipped into the region. The Spanish, moreover, had lost their entire military presence in eastern Texas, and Arredondo had disarmed the civilian population of San Antonio. Tejanos, as a result, had no ability to challenge tribes militarily and almost nothing to offer in trade, thereby losing all leverage in their dealings with nations like the Comanches. As such, the strategic alliances upon which Tejanos survived unraveled quickly in the aftermath of the Gutiérrez-Magee rebellion.

Perhaps more significant, the decimation of Spanish settlements in the region happened at precisely the same moment that the growing American presence along the Texas border offered alluring new trade opportunities to those same tribes. During the years following the U.S. acquisition of Louisiana in 1803, thousands of American migrants began pouring into the Gulf Coast territories. In the Natchez District of Mississippi (an area much closer to the Sabine River than San Antonio), the American population had more than tripled—exceeding thirty thousand—during the decade that preceded the Hidalgo revolt.[39] A similar phenomenon took place in Louisiana, where as early as 1810 the combined population of just two Louisiana parishes—Natchitoches and Rapides—exceeded the entire Spanish population of Texas.[40] Enough people had migrated by 1812 for Louisiana to attain statehood, and the end of the War of 1812 unleashed a torrential flood of new settlers into the region. So many migrants staked claims in Mississippi that it became a state in 1817, followed by Alabama in 1819. Such vast new populations building along the American side of the Texas border offered lucrative new trading opportunities to Indians willing to engage the rapidly expanding economy of the southwestern United States.

The creation of these new populations—and markets—alongside Texas was the result of a profound economic transformation in cotton taking place on both sides of the Atlantic Ocean. Starting in the 1770s, English textile manufacturers began experimenting with the possibilities of cotton, and although cotton cloth proved tremendously popular in both domestic and European markets, they could not find a reliable supplier of raw cotton, despite a willingness to pay handsomely for it. American planters remained largely uninterested in the crop, as did farmers in other parts of the world, for the simple reason that separating the seed from the fiber by hand was so labor-intensive as to make it unprofitable. Then, in the 1790s, the invention of various machines to remove seeds from cotton mechanically—to "gin" them—changed everything. This newfound ability to gin raw cotton into profitable bales produced, almost overnight, a rush of American farmers eager to supply textile mills in the U.S. northeast and England. New plantations sprang up across South Carolina, Georgia, and the Mississippi River Valley in rapid succession. From 1794 to 1800 virtually every tobacco planter in the territory around Natchez, Mississippi, converted his farm to cotton, and in only six years the Natchez District increased its cotton production from 36,000 pounds annually to more than 1.2 million.[41] During the decade leading to the Hidalgo revolt, the U.S. cotton industry surged: in 1806 the annual production of American farms surpassed 80 million pounds, and by 1810 more than half of Britain's cotton supply came from the southern United States.[42]

Yet nothing compared to the explosive transformations that cotton brought to the American Gulf Coast during the 1810s, at the same moment the Mexican War for Independence greatly weakened Spaniards in Texas. A series of favorable circumstances converged to set off the frenzied rush. With the defeat of the Creek Indians during the War of 1812, the U.S. federal government opened up 14 million new acres of prime Gulf Coast cotton lands (an area equal to half of modern-day Alabama) for public purchase at rock-bottom prices.[43] Because several new strands of hybrid cotton seeds—which produced bigger bolls that were easier to pick—had also recently become available, each of those acres promised farmers more profit than ever.[44] The tipping point came, however, when the market price for cotton doubled to thirty cents per pound in 1815, making the crop more valuable than almost any other commodity in the Atlantic World.[45] The result was one of the largest migrations in North American history, as hundreds of thousands of Americans raced to the Gulf Coast territories to establish cotton farms and plantations. By the late 1810s, the combined population of Louisiana, Mississippi, and Alabama surpassed 370,000, while the production of cotton in the region exploded.[46] The number of cotton bales exported by the United States increased tenfold during the 1810s, and by 1820 the southern United States surpassed India as the world's leading cotton producer.[47] The result was the complete transformation of the Gulf Coast of North America, making vibrant new markets available to Texas Indians to trade buffalo hides and deerskins for goods they could no longer obtain from the Spanish.

Yet it was horses, above all else, that U.S. cotton farmers wanted from Texas Indians. The southwestern United States remained in desperate need of horses and mules to plow fields for planting, power gins that cleaned crops, cart finished bales to market, and otherwise serve as the engines of nineteenth-century agriculture. Because the massive volume of Americans moving into the Gulf Coast persistently outstripped the local supply of such animals, finding some means for funneling new horses into Louisiana, Mississippi, and Alabama became indispensable to sustaining the continued growth of the U.S. cotton frontier. Texas, with its massive herds of wild mustangs, thus became a central focus of American merchants along the border. A trader named Philip Nolan made the first such forays into Texas during the 1790s, at the outset of the cotton revolution, where he captured horses that he later sold in Louisiana and Mississippi.[48] Rumors of Mexican horses soon spread across the U.S. South (even grabbing the attention of Thomas Jefferson), as accounts of the "innumerable herds" in Texas made their way into the U.S. press. The *Democratic Clarion* of Nashville published a breathless account in May

1812 of "The Wild Horses of Mexico," detailing how herds of "six to eight thousand" roamed the Texas plains and could be captured to feed the ravenous needs of the southern United States. American traders, the editors observed, promised Indians an eager market for any horses they could deliver to the Sabine River.[49]

The Comanches, in response, declared war on the Spanish, unleashing horrific waves of violence that washed over Texas during the years after 1813. Spanish-Comanche relations had begun to fall apart even before the Gutiérrez-Magee debacle, and in its aftermath Comanche warriors proved eager to reorient their economic and political priorities toward raiding Spanish settlements in order to supply horses for American markets. A drought that began around 1800 had decimated the region's buffalo herds—cutting their numbers by as much as half—and thus made the economic opportunities offered by U.S. trade all the more alluring.[50] Comanche warriors descended upon the ranches south of San Antonio with relentless fury during the winter of 1813 and spring of 1814.[51] Driving off horses, slaughtering cattle, and murdering anyone who challenged them, Comanches destroyed the livestock and livelihood of those Tejanos who had somehow managed to survive Arredondo's wrath.

Recognizing what was happening, the governor of Texas begged Arredondo to spare enough funds to reestablish trade with tribes like the Comanches so "that the Indian may not have the allurement of greater advantages with their sales among the Americans." "Preventing the trade of the Indian Nations with the Anglo-Americans," he pleaded, was the only way to prevent Indians from "committing hostilities upon our properties with the greatest forces, in order to increase the theft of herds of horses, and introducing these to the United States."[52] Arredondo, however, had no funds to spare and instead ordered that all Tejanos abandon their ranches and retreat into San Antonio in the face of the Comanche onslaught.[53] Wichita Indians joined their Comanche compatriots in the new horse trade, and by the summer of 1814 most Tejano ranches around San Antonio smoldered in ruins.[54]

An extensive trading network soon emerged to connect Comanche and Wichita raiders with buyers in the United States. American traders made regular purchasing trips into eastern Texas, visiting Wichita villages along the Red River and Comanche trading parties that moved herds toward Louisiana. Many of these traders gathered in Nacogdoches for such commerce, turning the abandoned Spanish village into a hub of the new economy of eastern Texas.[55] As U.S.-Texas traffic increased,

Comanche Feats of Horsemanship, by George Catlin, 1834–35.
(Smithsonian American Art Museum, Washington, D.C./Art Resource, N.Y.)

numerous men in eastern Louisiana came to be known as "old Comanche traders" whose deep forays into Indian territory established a "Camino Comanche" trail.[56] Tonkawas and Apaches began raiding and trading in earnest as well, while numerous other tribes in eastern Texas became horse brokers in order to profit from stolen herds flowing into American territory. Even several tribes that had recently moved into eastern Texas from the southern United States to seek shelter from the expanding cotton frontier, such as the Alabamas and Coushattas, built their own networks for fencing horses into Louisiana.[57]

Trade in stolen horses was nothing new for the Comanches, Wichitas, Tonkawas, or Apaches, and most had engaged in at least some trade with the Americans since the early 1800s. What had changed by the late 1810s, with the rise of the U.S. cotton frontier, was the scale and profitability of that trade. One American who lived among the Texas Comanches during the late 1810s reported that "the number of mules and horses that these Indians capture annually from the Spaniards is immense, probably not less than 10,000."[58] A Tejano testified in 1818 that he saw the Comanche trade bring more than three thousand horses and mules through Natchitoches, Louisiana, over the course of a single month.[59] American merchants squatting in Nacogdoches conducted an astounding $90,000 in trade during 1820, and the volume of money to be made along the border led to the establishment of "Pecan Point," a new settlement of Americans south of the Red River.[60]

What made commerce on this scale so appealing to Comanches and their allies was that it brought them steady access to firearms. With the Spanish trade gone, all Indian nations in the region sought a new supplier of the arms and munitions that gave them a military advantage over their enemies. U.S. traders happily complied, converting horses into weapons for Indian raiders in Texas.[61] The growing movement of American armaments into Texas, in turn, spurred escalating cycles of violence. Comanche warriors, now better armed than Spanish troops, continued to attack places like San Antonio in order to maintain the flow of their military supplies coming from the United States.

Within a few years, the terrifying violence in Texas spread into northern New Spain. Having destroyed nearly all Tejano herds, Indian raiders sustained the volume of the horse trade by extending their attacks southward to encompass Spanish settlements in territories beyond Texas. War parties began crossing the Río Grande as early as 1815, laying waste to Spanish ranches and haciendas in the provinces of Nuevo Santander, Nuevo León, and Coahuila.[62] To facilitate these extended forays, the Comanches forged an alliance in 1816 with their Apache rivals that allowed Comanches to move freely through Apache territory (often with Apache guides) on their way through the Río Grande Valley. The pact further amplified the scale of violence. The following year, a thousand warriors stole ten thousand horses and mules in Refugio during a single raid.[63] By the late 1810s, the destruction unleashed by the U.S.-Texas horse trade had engulfed four Spanish provinces, as Texas became a launching point for Indian assaults on all of northern New Spain.[64] Joaquín de Arredondo, now serving as the military commander of the region from his base in Monterrey, groped for any means to staunch the bleeding. In 1817 he published an open letter authorizing the Caddo Indians of eastern Texas "to kill and destroy" anyone trafficking in stolen Spanish horses and mules, which was then reprinted in newspapers across the U.S. South. When the editors of Mississippi's *Natchez Republican* protested that Arredondo's decree meant "the murder of our citizens is not only *authorized*, but strictly *enjoined*," they openly acknowledged that Mississippians were buying horses in northern New Spain.[65]

By the time Antonio Martínez arrived in May 1817 as the new governor in San Antonio, the destruction of Spain's outposts in Texas was nearly complete. As his convoy rode onto the dusty streets of San Antonio, Martínez saw firsthand how the ongoing war with the Comanches, Apaches, and Wichitas had gutted the Spanish capital. The few royal troops still stationed in the province were a bedraggled and pathetic lot: almost none had mounts; few had shoes or a full set of clothes. Many had no weapons, while others carted firearms that were useless for want of basic tools to repair them. Far more troubling, however, was that the soldiers, their families, and the civilians in San Antonio were all starving. Incessant Indian attacks had prevented the Tejanos from cultivating crops, leaving the villagers to survive on whatever could be grown in gardens next to their homes and the occasional shipment of corn that arrived from other parts of New Spain. Indian raids on Spanish supply wagons made those shipments increasingly rare, and by the late 1810s Spaniards in Texas had been reduced to living under siege. Almost every basic need in the village could not be met—there were no clothes, food, medicines, blankets, tools, weapons, or even paper available—as Tejanos endured life in San Antonio in abject poverty.[66]

Martínez scrambled to stabilize the Spanish position but soon realized that the situation was largely beyond his control. Attempting to break the cycle of unceasing violence, the new governor sent out detachments of troops to confront Indian raiders. Yet many of the soldiers were too terrified to challenge the better-armed, better-mounted, and more numerous Indians. "Being afraid," Martínez noted with disgust, soldiers sent to chase down raiders often "hide in some forest and after a sufficient number of days, they return and report whatever they wish to show that they have discharged their commission."[67] Other soldiers in San Antonio and La Bahía simply abandoned their posts altogether, preferring to risk being shot for desertion rather than remain on the perilous Texas frontier.[68] Martínez then attempted to address the crippling food shortage. The governor formed the remaining soldiers into armed escorts for Tejano farmers, providing them enough protection from Indian attacks—Martínez hoped—to ensure a sufficient corn crop for the coming season. Yet that plan, too, failed when Martínez's superior in Monterrey, Joaquín de Arredondo, rebuked him for using royal troops to assist civilian projects. Arredondo ordered Martínez to abandon the enterprise as an unacceptable breach of army protocol—the fields would remain barren.[69]

Martínez also discovered that Tejanos were themselves participating in the American horse trade that had so decimated Spanish settlements in Texas. All but forsaken by Monterrey and Mexico City, many Tejanos began turning toward the cotton-driven economy growing along the U.S.-Texas border as their only realistic economic outlet in an increasingly desperate situation. Although Tejanos had engaged in varying levels of contraband trade with Louisiana since the eighteenth century, the near-complete devastation of their settlements after 1813 forced Tejanos to begin herding stock toward the Americans as a means of survival. Numerous merchants and soldiers, from both San Antonio and La Bahía, drove some of the few remaining horses and mules into southern Louisiana, trading them for food and supplies unavailable in Texas. No less a figure than the commander at La Bahía, Juan Manuel Zambrano, ran his own extensive smuggling operation. Although Martínez attempted to stop such illicit trade, occasionally arresting some offenders, there was little he could do without more capable troops at his command.[70]

Perhaps most disturbing, some Tejanos had even joined the Comanches and other tribes in their horse raids on San Antonio and La Bahía. Many of these Tejano raiders were refugees from Arredondo's vicious 1813 purge, who now lived in exile in Louisiana or among various Indian nations in eastern Texas. One prominent Tejano refugee, Francisco Ruíz, moved back and forth between western Louisiana and eastern Texas as he built his own trading network among the Comanches to funnel Spanish horses to American merchants. A prominent Tejano community leader before the 1813 rebellion, Ruíz's participation in the Gutiérrez-Magee revolt meant he would likely be executed if he returned to San Antonio. So Ruiz built a new life by integrating himself so deeply into the U.S.-Comanche trade that Governor Martínez feared Ruíz might lead a Comanche assault on the capital.[71] Hundreds of other exiled Tejanos had also been forced into the shadows along the border, and reports continued to filter into San Antonio and La Bahía of other "traitorous Spaniards who were among this nation."[72] Residents of the villages could sometimes spot Tejanos riding among the Indian raiding parties that continually harassed their settlements.[73] The presence of these Tejano raiders, although few in number, exposed how badly the Spanish presence in Texas had crumbled by the late 1810s.

Martínez thus found himself attempting to govern chaos, an intractable situation that he blamed primarily on lack of support from Monterrey and Mexico City. And so he penned an endless stream of petitions to his commander at Monterrey, begging for resources. When those failed to come, the infuriated governor took his case directly to the viceroy in Mexico City. It was the abysmal weakness of Spain's military in Texas, Martínez argued, that invited such unrelenting attacks from the region's Indians. "The condition of these troops, who are unpaid, unclothed, and on foot," he insisted, "accounts for the daring with which these savages attack us so frequently."[74] If the viceroy would simply bolster the defenses of San Antonio and La Bahía, went Martínez's logic, tribes like the Comanches would retreat, and the violence would abate. Yet the participation of Tejanos in the same raid-and-trade economy as the Comanches, supplying horses and mules to U.S. cotton frontier, belied the governor's assertions that Spain's demise in Texas could be blamed solely on insufficient support from the crown. Powerful new markets in the southern United States were also reshaping northern New Spain, with devastating effect.

A Vast and Noiseless Desert

Spain's forced abandonment of eastern Texas and its coastline transformed the territory into a haven for revolutionaries, smugglers, and pirates hoping to profit from the simultaneous rise of the U.S. Southwest and demise of New Spain's northeastern frontier. Galveston Island's natural harbor and proximity to New Orleans made it a hub of these efforts. Louis Michel Aury, a French-born revolutionary and privateer, established a pirate operation on Galveston in 1816, using the island to capture ships participating in the gulf's growing merchant trade.[75] Mexican rebels operating out of New Orleans also began using the island as a base for their ongoing effort to achieve Mexican independence, and in 1817 an insurgent named Francisco Mina launched an invasion of Tamaulipas from Galveston. Although Mina's expedition failed, it nonetheless made Mexico City painfully aware of the growing risks that an undefended Texas coastline posed to the rest of New Spain.[76]

Like the horse trade, much of the smuggling that emerged along the Texas coast served the growing U.S. cotton frontier. The hundreds of thousands of Americans who had moved into the region represented a massive new market for Gulf Coast pirates, and Louisiana farmers proved eager to purchase the infinite variety of goods that smugglers made available at cut-rate prices, such as silks, linens, dry goods, gold, silver, flour, jewelry, wine, whiskey, and weapons. When American officials sent the U.S.S. *Boxer* to intercept this illicit sea traffic spewing out of Galveston, the smugglers adapted by sneaking in their goods overland on mules that followed the same routes as Spanish horses into southern Louisiana.[77]

Some of the greatest profits were to be had in smuggling slaves. When American farmers began pouring into the Mississippi River Valley during the 1810s, they brought with them tens of thousands of enslaved people to serve as the labor force of their new plantations. As demand for cotton boomed, so did the enslaved population of Alabama, Mississippi, and Louisiana. By 1820, the combined slave populations of those states approached 150,000—every third person in Alabama was enslaved, while nearly half of all Louisianans were.[78] Although cotton could be grown profitably without slaves (and often was on small family farms throughout the southern United States), most white Americans of the era believed that only slave labor could enable plantations to achieve the scale that would make a man wealthy. And so white men of all classes—whether they already owned slaves or not—hoped to buy enslaved people for their farms, creating voracious new markets for slaves along the Gulf Coast. Because the United States had outlawed the international slave trade in 1808, an extensive domestic trade soon emerged to transport hundreds of thousands of men and women from places like Virginia to slave markets in Mississippi and Louisiana.[79] Hoping to profit from this lucrative new market, smugglers of all stripes began exploiting the unregulated Texas coast in order to funnel enslaved Africans into the southern United States.

Galveston quickly became the epicenter of this illicit trade. Louis Aury's pirating operation preyed primarily on Spanish ships, which regularly transported hundreds of slaves in and out of the Havana markets in Cuba. Aury's men snuck captured Africans into New Orleans and within months smuggled so many into Louisiana that Washington, D.C., began receiving alarmed reports from U.S. officials stationed along the gulf. "The most shameful violations of the slave act, as well as our revenue laws," reported one American agent, "continue to be practised, with impunity, by a motley mixture of freebooters and smugglers, at Galvezton." Louisiana planters, for their part, rushed to snap up every available slave, and some farmers proved so eager that they trekked all the way to Galveston in search of new field hands at rock-bottom prices.[80]

The trade reached new heights when Pierre and Jean Laffite took over piracy operations in Galveston in 1817 and transformed the island into the hub of a massively profitable smuggling ring. While the Laffite brothers trafficked in every good imaginable, they developed a particularly clever system for transporting enslaved Africans into the United States. The brothers constructed a slave-trading barracks on the western side of the Sabine River and posted advertisements along Louisiana roads whenever they planned to sell a cache of captured slaves. Planters, farmers, and slave traders who arrived on the appointed days could buy new slaves—who were weighed on sale days—at a dollar a pound. By holding the sales on the Texas side of the border, the brothers operated beyond U.S. jurisdiction and transferred all the burdens and risks associated with transporting the slaves into the United States to their American buyers. And with prime field hands fetching $1,500 in the New Orleans markets, the opportunity to buy slaves for $150 seemed well worth the risk to many white Americans along the cotton frontier.[81] The commerce thrived as thousands of enslaved Africans were funneled through Texas on their way to plantations as far east as Mississippi.[82] At times, the Laffites could not keep up with demand. When Randall Jones arrived in Galveston in 1818 to purchase slaves for Louisiana planters, Jean Laffite informed him that "he was out of Negroes at that time but he expected some before long."[83] Other Americans, such as James Bowie, began shuttling between Louisiana and Texas as middlemen in the smuggling process—buying Africans from Galveston, transporting them into the United States, and then creating fraudulent paper trails to protect buyers from prosecution.[84] The result was a booming trade in eastern Texas in slaves, as well as numerous other smuggled goods, that served the same purpose as the horse trade: to support and profit from the rapid growth of the southern United States.

By the late 1810s, the Spanish had lost almost all control over eastern Texas as the region evolved into an ungoverned appendage of the southwestern United States. The sheer volume of people tramping through the territory began overwhelming local Indian nations, increasing conflicts between Americans and various tribes along the border.[85] What little reliable information the Spanish could get about the region often came from the steady stream of enslaved people who fled into Texas as refugees from the U.S. cotton frontier.[86] When a forty-eight-year-old enslaved man named Andrés rode into San Antonio in March 1817, three weeks after escaping his master's plantation in Natchitoches, Louisiana, Governor Martínez had him interrogated for whatever news Andrés could provide about developments in eastern Texas.[87] When three black men escaped Laffite's smuggling camp at Galveston, the Spanish learned in alarming detail what a threatening operation it had become. According to the three refugees—who had run away when they learned they were to be smuggled into the New Orleans slave markets—Laffite's crew was actively preparing for an invasion of New Spain.[88] Outraged officials in Monterrey and Mexico City demanded that Governor Martínez lead a military campaign to reclaim eastern Texas. Yet Martínez refused, pointing out that San Antonio's complete lack of men, horses, and supplies "makes it impossible for me to attempt even a minor expedition."[89]

The governor, indeed, was barely holding onto San Antonio and La Bahía. Indian attacks remained unceasing. Over the course of several days in April 1819, nightly raiding parties killed or wounded at least fifty Spaniards.[90] An ongoing drought had so parched the region that "there is hardly a blade of grass in the fields," and starvation became a serious threat for San Antonio and La Bahía.[91] Martínez reported that soldiers were now deserting because "they were dying of hunger," and the few horses left in Spanish corrals were often too weak to saddle.[92] Then, in July 1819, the great flood ripped San Antonio to pieces—shattering houses, destroying crops, and drowning dozens of Tejanos. In the flood's aftermath, Governor Martínez himself seemed shattered as he railed at both God and his superiors for what had become of the province. Later that summer, a newspaper in Natchez, Mississippi, joined Martínez in lamenting the fate of the region. "Texas is undoubtedly a rich and fertile tract of country," wrote the editors, "but from the desultory and savage warfare which has desolated the land, that vast extent presents almost literally a vast and noiseless desert."[93]

Opening Texas to Cotton

In February 1819, the United States and Spain finally agreed on an official boundary between Louisiana and Texas, something that had been in dispute since the Louisiana Purchase. In the Adams-Onís Treaty, Spain ceded control over Florida to the United States in exchange for the United States' relinquishing its dubious claims to Texas and establishing the Sabine River as the undisputed border. Although practical and advantageous for both Madrid and Washington, D.C., the deal roiled Americans along the cotton frontier. The potential agricultural value of Texas land had become a regular point of discussion in Alabama, Mississippi, and Louisiana newspapers, and numerous U.S. politicians and newspaper editors attacked the Monroe administration for giving away the chance for Texas.[94] A group of disgruntled Americans in Natchez, Mississippi, organized an armed expedition to nullify the treaty by invading and "liberating" Texas from Spanish rule. Under the leadership of James Long, a motley army of several hundred Americans made its way into east Texas during the summer of 1819, using the abandoned Spanish post of Nacogdoches as its base.

News of the invasion terrified Spanish authorities who feared that Long's forces might represent the forward guard of a larger U.S.-backed attack. As the military commander responsible for northern New Spain, Arredondo immediately ordered the governors of Coahuila and Nuevo Santander to send all available troops to San Antonio, where hundreds of royal soldiers and new supplies began arriving by early August. In the face of an American invasion, Martínez would finally have the military backing for which he had long begged. At the end of September, Martínez dispatched Lt. Col. Ignacio Pérez at the head of 550 men with orders to destroy Long's army and drive out any other Americans they could find hiding in eastern Texas.[95]

As Pérez marched toward the Sabine River, the disorganized Long expedition fell apart. Unable to supply themselves, Long's men ran short of food and failed to forge an alliance with Laffite's pirate operation at Galveston. When news arrived of the approaching Spanish army, most of the invaders—including Long himself—fled back toward Louisiana. By the time Pérez's forces arrived in Nacogdoches, the Long expedition had evaporated, and so Pérez set to his second task: rooting out American squatters, traders, and smugglers.

As bands of Spanish soldiers fanned out to comb the region, Pérez's troops discovered no fewer than thirty illegal American farms in the territory surrounding Nacogdoches, where squatters were growing cotton in "extensive fields which they have opened for cultivation." Pérez's soldiers burned every cabin they found—often chasing away the trespassers in the process—and appropriated any food they could find. Spanish troops also ran off dozens of American traders who had been purchasing "horses & mules," and warned nearby tribes against trading with the Americans. Local Indians, however, appeared unfazed, telling Pérez they had received reports that in La Bahía and San Antonio "there were nothing but a few half naked, half starved miserable old men." Despite their success in clearing out the territory around Nacogdoches, Spanish forces learned of several other American settlements growing along the Neches and Red Rivers. The largest of these was Pecan Point, where several hundred

Americans had gathered. Pérez hoped to lead his forces in an expedition against these squatter villages, but shortages of food and supplies forced him to begin the three-hundred-mile return march to San Antonio.[96]

In their sweeps of eastern Texas, Pérez's troops captured more than forty Americans and forced several hundred others to retreat into Louisiana. They also took into custody several runaway slaves who had approached the Spanish in hopes of asylum from their American owners. Marian, Richard, and Tivi had run from their master—a cotton planter in western Louisiana named James Kirkham—along with another fugitive slave named Samuel. At Nacogdoches, the four runaways surrendered themselves to Pérez's troops just in time to join dozens of American prisoners in a forced march to San Antonio. When they arrived at the capital, the prisoners and runaways were taken to a makeshift jail, where they met another runaway, John, who had escaped his plantation by walking from St. Landry Parish, Louisiana, to La Bahía. The decrepit conditions of San Antonio meant that Martínez had "no place to hold them in safety or even any means of sustaining them," so the governor ordered a detachment of soldiers to escort the captives to Monterrey, where they could be interrogated. Tied together with rope, fugitive slaves joined American prisoners on a forced march that would take them several hundred miles into the interior of New Spain.[97]

If he lacked the resources to sustain several dozen prisoners, Martínez soon discovered he was even less equipped to support the several hundred new troops now stationed in San Antonio. The soldiers quickly consumed what little food the village had, and Martínez was forced to confiscate corn from Tejanos to feed the troops when no new supply wagons from Monterrey arrived. The enlarged military force, surprisingly, did little to deter the constant barrage of Indian attacks, as Comanches and others continued to assault Spaniards at every opportunity. Under such horrific conditions, the newly arrived soldiers began to desert, leaving "daily in parties of six, eight, and more" in hopes of escaping back to their home provinces of Nuevo Santander, Nuevo León, and Coahuila.[98] Within two months, more than 160 had abandoned their posts. Not even reports of deserters being killed by Comanches (in April 1820 nine mutilated bodies were found a short distance from San Antonio) could stem the tide. By June, more than three hundred soldiers had chosen to risk death by walking back into the interior of New Spain rather than remain any longer in San Antonio.[99] The Spanish civilian population of Texas also edged closer to open rebellion. Martínez reported to the viceroy that Tejanos were "so distressed, dejected, and desperate" that he believed they might abandon Texas en masse. "And I am in a quandary," he wrote, "because I do not consider that I have a right to stop them."[100]

As the winter of 1820 approached, the Spanish position in Texas neared complete collapse. With his people starving, his troops abandoning their posts, Comanche and American invaders surrounding them, and no help coming from either Monterrey or Mexico City, Martínez effectively gave up on the region. "From now on," he warned the viceroy, "I am not responsible for defending and controlling this province that has been placed under my protection." Like the Tejanos, Martínez saw no future under such impossible circumstances. "Without resources and utterly helpless," he wrote, "I can only join them in their sorrow and grief and grow despondent and weak."[101] Two weeks later, the governor convened an emergency meeting with the Tejano town council—the *ayuntamiento*—to discuss the gravity of the situation. At that very moment, as Tejanos huddled in deep crisis, several Americans were riding toward San Antonio with a proposal to bring new settlers into the region that would offer an unlikely solution. Although the forces of cotton had brought nothing but devastation to Texas during the past decade, the crop's stunning transformation of the southwestern United States into an economic juggernaut during that same period would be offered by these Americans as a possible model for how Spain might salvage its dying presence in the region.

James Kirkham, James Forsythe, and Moses Austin had set out from western Louisiana in late November 1820, on their way to the Spanish capital of Texas. Kirkham, a thirty-seven-year-old cotton planter, was the master of Marian, Richard, and Tivi, and he intended to ask Martínez for their return.[102] Originally from Virginia, James Forsythe was a thirty-two-year-old farmer living in Natchitoches who planned to ask the governor for permission to settle his family on the Spanish side of the Sabine River. Moses Austin, a fifty-six-year-old lead mine owner from Missouri, had in mind a design similar to Forsythe's, although on a grander scale. Austin planned to petition the Spanish government for permission to establish a colony of three hundred American families in Texas, an enterprise that he hoped would enable him to escape crushing debts he had accumulated in Missouri. Encountering each other at a Louisiana tavern along the road to Texas, the men decided to make the long journey together, accompanied by Austin's enslaved servant, Richmond.[103]

Austin and Forsythe both hoped to find cheap land in New Spain, something that had suddenly become difficult to come by in the United States. After enjoying a remarkable run-up following the War of 1812, the U.S. economy suffered a widespread financial crisis during 1819 that destroyed the credit market. Soon thereafter, the U.S. Congress—in an effort to discourage the land speculators who were blamed for the panic—passed a bill that greatly toughened the terms on which government land could be purchased. While it had once been common to finance the majority of a land purchase, the U.S. government now required buyers to produce enough cash to cover the full price of at least eighty acres. At $1.25 per acre, a potential farmer had to scrape together $100 if he wanted to buy U.S. federal land along the Gulf Coast. Few people in the aftermath of the 1819 panic could come up with that much cash, and so U.S. government land sales plummeted by nearly 80 percent from 1819 to 1820.[104] For those who had lost everything in the panic—as Moses Austin had—the prospect of cheap land on the Spanish frontier suddenly had a powerful appeal.

After four weeks in the saddle, the small party finally rode into San Antonio two days before Christmas. Their reception by Spanish authorities was not what they had hoped. Deeply distrustful of any American, Martínez refused to discuss any of the reasons that brought them to Texas and ordered the travelers to return immediately to Louisiana. Dejected, Kirkham, Forsythe, and Austin had little choice but to begin making preparations for the long ride back to the United States. On his way to pack for the return trip, Austin happened to cross paths with a man who went by the name of Baron de Bastrop. The Baron was actually Felipe Bögel, a Dutchman who migrated to Spanish Louisiana in the 1790s and then made his way to San Antonio in 1806. Austin and Bastrop apparently knew each other from a chance encounter years before at a tavern in the United States, and after listening to Austin's story, the Baron offered to intercede on his behalf with the governor. Martínez, who thought highly of Bastrop, then reversed himself and allowed the Americans to stay temporarily in San Antonio.[105]

When the three Americans returned to the governor's office that afternoon, Martínez asked each of them to state his background and why he had come to Texas. Austin produced a Spanish passport and explained that he had once been a Spanish subject when he lived in Missouri, until the transfer of the Louisiana territory to France and then to the United States put him under U.S. jurisdiction. Since the Spanish king had declared that Spanish subjects in Louisiana could resettle in any part of New Spain, Austin requested that he be allotted land in Texas for himself and three hundred other families from the United States. These settlers, Austin told the governor, would become Spanish subjects and provide for themselves "by raising sugar and Cotton," indicating that these recruits would come from the southern section of the United States. Austin would, in other words, redirect hundreds of farmers from the U.S. cotton frontier into northern New Spain, where they would build a colony of Anglo-Spaniards that would help finally secure the region for Spain. James Forsythe also asked for permission to settle in the region, although just for his own family. Kirkham explained that he wanted only to reclaim the slaves who escaped his cotton plantation and presented Martínez with a letter from the governor of Louisiana requesting their return.[106]

Despite strong reservations about Americans, Antonio Martínez recognized that Austin's colonization proposal offered perhaps the last possible solution to Spain's intractable situation in Texas. After years of relentless violence, dissolution, and misery had battered Spain's presence in Texas into near abandonment, Martínez saw no other options before him. Various other colonization plans had been contemplated over the years, although the Spanish had never managed to convince their own people to move to the insecure northern frontier. Previous schemes had ranged from forcibly resettling Tlaxcaltecan Indians on territory in Texas to granting tracts of land to ten thousand farmers from Switzerland—all of which came to nothing.[107] The governor decided to take several days to consult with local Tejano leaders and carefully consider the ramifications of both accepting and rejecting Austin's offer. Then, on December 26, 1820, Martínez forwarded Austin's application to Joaquín de Arredondo for official approval, with his own strong endorsement. "The proposal which he is making is, in my opinion, the only one which is bound to provide for the increase and prosperity in his settlement and even others in this Province," the governor wrote to Arredondo. "Otherwise I look upon the appearance of such a favorable development as quite remote."[108]

Arredondo had, remarkably, come to the same conclusion. By 1820 the commandant general was spending three-quarters of his entire military budget for northern New Spain on problems related to Texas, and the U.S.-Comanche horse trade had so devastated the wider region that Arredondo predicted "the complete depopulation of these provinces will result."[109] Endless waves of raiding warriors had convinced Arredondo that military efforts alone would never bring security and prosperity to the region—only increasing the non-Indian population and building up the local economy could accomplish such things. Perhaps a colony of

Anglo-Spaniards, he reasoned, could help make that possible and usher into northern New Spain some of the prosperity that had come to the southern United States. "They will bring with them," he advised the viceroy, "the arts and industry, commerce and prosperity which is offered by that other vast and ferocious nation."[110] And so Arredondo approved Austin's colonization proposal. That the Spanish would strike such a deal makes sense only in the context of the devastation that their settlements suffered in the wake of the Mexican War for Independence and the rise of the U.S. cotton frontier.

That Austin believed he could convince hundreds of American families to abandon the United States for the uncertainties of northern New Spain makes sense only in the context of the rise of the international cotton economy. The spectacular rise of cotton prices and subsequent massive migration of Americans into Mississippi, Alabama, and Louisiana had remade the southern United States into a central player on the global economic stage. The money to be made in cotton, in turn, had transformed Gulf Coast acreage into highly valuable property, and by the late 1810s the best cotton lands sold at auction for fifty dollars an acre.[111] When the Panic of 1819 put that land out of the financial reach of small-time American farmers, Moses Austin recognized a remarkable opportunity. Because Texas shared the same long growing season, rich soils, and ready access to Gulf Coast shipping ports that made Mississippi acreage so appealing—a point made repeatedly by U.S. newspapers during the late 1810s—Austin was betting that American farmers who found themselves priced out of the U.S. land market would take a chance on Texas if they could obtain cheap cotton lands there. Austin had, in fact, said as much in his petition to Martínez. And because he would be granted his own large tracts of lands, which he could then resell to new migrants, Austin was betting that by redirecting the American cotton frontier into northern New Spain he could make himself a wealthy man.

Austin's colonization contract thereby became the legal wedge that opened Texas to sanctioned American settlement. As written, the agreement stated that prospective settlers had to practice the Catholic religion, bring letters attesting to their good character and background, and swear allegiance to the Spanish government.[112] Austin would take responsibility for recruiting, transporting, and settling the families. The contract said nothing about slavery, likely because the institution remained legal in both New Spain and the United States, and thus neither Austin nor Spanish officials felt the need to broach the matter. Slaveholders were, in fact, the very sorts of recruits that both Austin and the Spanish hoped to attract: wealthier people with a vested interest in their lands, farms, and plantations. Left unspoken, however, was the implication that Americans who came to New Spain would leave behind the legal traditions of the southern United States that protected the property rights of slaveholders. Such explicit assurances by state and federal governments in the United States had, quietly, made it possible for so many white Americans to invest with confidence in cotton farms in the Mississippi River Valley. Austin's colonists, in contrast, would be faced with an entirely different set of legal circumstances, although what that would mean in practice—if anything—was yet to be determined.

For the moment, Austin was simply elated that his proposal had been accepted. James Forsythe's application had also been forwarded for approval, although James Kirkham received less favorable news. Martínez informed the Louisiana planter that his slaves could not be returned because they had been transferred to Monterrey, although he promised to forward Kirkham's request to the proper authorities. Kirkham and Austin then began the long journey back to the United States. When they reached the San Marcos River, fifty miles east of San Antonio, Kirkham informed Austin that he had struck a deal with some Tejanos. Five men would meet them at the Colorado River, about thirty miles ahead, with a drove of mules stolen from the royal corral that Kirkham had promised to purchase. Fearing that such illicit dealings could jeopardize his colonization plans, Austin berated Kirkham for colluding to rob the Spanish government, and after some heated exchanges the men maintained an uneasy truce for several days. Then, one night, as they camped along the banks of the Trinity River, Kirkham disappeared into the darkness with Austin's horses and most of their supplies. Abandoned, Austin trekked on foot through harsh winter weather the rest of the way. He was nearly dead when he arrived in Louisiana, though he eventually managed to struggle his way back to Missouri. Moses Austin, however, never recovered his health and succumbed in June 1821 to a "Violent attack of Inflamation on the brest and lungs." Austin's death threatened to destroy Tejano hopes for using American colonization as a means for stabilizing New Spain's presence in the Texas borderlands.[113]

Events farther south also threatened to overthrow the enterprise. As Moses Austin lay dying in Missouri, the long-simmering revolution in Mexico came to fruition in the spring of 1821. Agustín de Iturbide, a royal military officer, defected to the side of the rebels and declared Mexico free of Spain in February 1821. Within months, Spanish power throughout the entire region crumbled. Mexico had suddenly become free, although what that meant for the territory and its people was far from certain. With independence, Mexicans now faced momentous challenges in building a new nation from the rubble of New Spain, and among the most daunting was what to do with the unstable northeastern borderlands that Spain had never managed to secure. Mexicans had inherited Spain's strange solution to that problem in the agreement that Spanish officials struck with Moses Austin. They would now have to decide whether they wanted Americans, cotton, and slavery bringing a new flood into their northern territories.

PART II

Bringing Mississippi to Mexico

The primary product that will elevate us from poverty is Cotton and we cannot do this without the help of slaves.
—Stephen F. Austin, 1824

If all knew like me the hard and cruel treatment with which the Anglo Americans treat the slaves, they would provide a means for saving them.
—José Francisco Madero, 1827

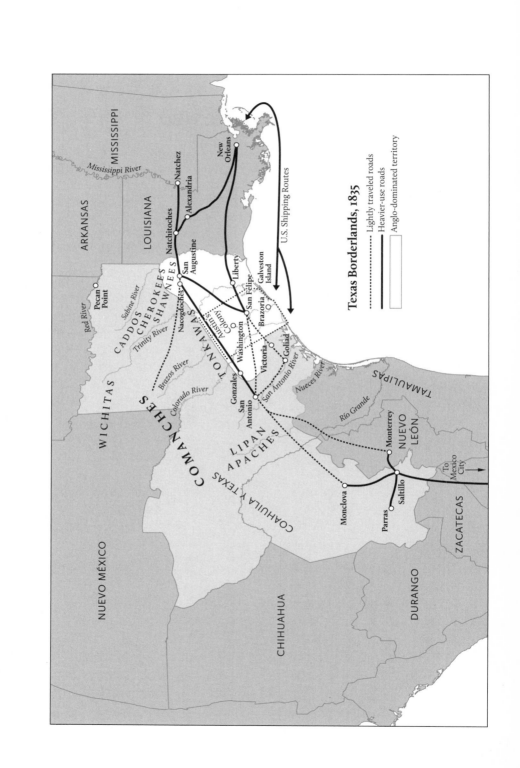

Texts Borderlands, 1835

.... Lightly traveled roads
– – – – Heavier-use roads
_____ Anglo-dominated territory

TWO

American Migration to Mexico, 1821–1825

In the early summer of 1821, fourteen Tejanos rode eastward out of San Antonio on their way toward the Louisiana town of Natchitoches. Erasmo Seguín rode at the front of the small force, although no one strayed too far behind as they followed the faint trail that wound through the wilderness. Once beyond the confines of their desolated village, the Tejanos found themselves deep within Indian country, and they moved cautiously—always armed—ready to defend themselves against any sudden Comanche onslaught. Most of Seguín's men were already familiar with the trail's perils, having made the trek numerous times on trading trips to American markets in Louisiana. One of his companions, Juan Martín de Veramendi, had built his family's fortunes and influence throughout the 1810s by shuttling goods from New Orleans into northern Mexico. This journey, however, was about matters far more grave than trade. Seguín carried with him official approval of Moses Austin's colonization proposal, as well as royal pardons for all Tejano families still hiding in Louisiana following the Gutierrez-Magee expedition of 1813–14. Seguín's band was riding to the United States in order to throw open the gates of Texas to American immigration and returning Tejano refugees, which they hoped would begin a process of repopulating and rebuilding their shattered corner of northeastern Mexico.[1]

The journey east took the Tejanos through a landscape still smoldering from the violent convulsions of the 1810s. San Antonio crumbled beneath the weight of incessant Indian raids and the 1819 flood, the small Tejano population surrounding La Bahía teetered near collapse, and Nacogdoches had been abandoned by all but a handful of families. In a letter to the governor, the town council of San Antonio bemoaned what years of Indian attacks, civil war, and royal neglect had wrought. There were, they observed, no improved roads, bridges, schools, hospitals, ports, agriculture, manufacturing, mining, commerce, or infrastructure of any kind within Texas. Indeed, the most well-worn road in the territory was the highway from Louisiana into Comanchería, the thriving thoroughfare for transporting stolen Mexican horses into the southern United States, serving as a painful metaphor for the fate that had overtaken the territory during the 1810s. Life in Texas had simply become intolerable for Tejanos. "Since 1813, when this Province was reconquered," concluded the San Antonio council, the province "had advanced at an amazing rate, towards ruin and destruction."[2]

Seguín's mission to Louisiana was the Tejanos' best last hope to save the territory. Only by increasing the non-Indian population of the region, they believed, could they shield their homes from "incessant Indian aggressions." Opening the territory to transplanted American farmers could accomplish that, while also bringing new commerce and economic development into the impoverished province. "The soil is well qualified for the production of every kind of grain, plantation and vegetable," observed the Tejanos. "Let hands be introduced to till this immense territory." Those new farmers, in turn, would "export the productions of the country to the most advantageous markets," opening potentially lucrative opportunities for places like San Antonio and La Bahía to profit from new "interior consumption and commerce."[3] Authorizing American colonization thus served two overlapping goals for the Tejanos: it would help secure their own settlements from Indian raids, while also vastly expanding their economic opportunities within the region. Tejanos had used that reasoning to secure approval for the enterprise from royal authorities at Monterrey, Nuevo León, who agreed that allowing Americans to settle in Texas offered the only practical means "to increase its population, and thus, to oppose a more effective resistance to the Indians, and give a greater development to Agriculture, commerce and mechanical arts."[4]

When Seguín and his men finally rode into Natchitoches, Louisiana, in early June 1821, they found that Moses Austin had not yet arrived. As they waited, the men spread the word that all Tejanos still living in exile in Louisiana could now return safely to Texas; news that brought "rejoicings" from several hundred refugee families eager to reclaim their abandoned homes. For Seguín, the journey to Louisiana had been a sobering reminder of the urgency of his mission. Near the ruins of Nacogdoches, his party had passed several American families squatting illegally on land in far-eastern Texas—"a scandalous proceeding," he grumbled, and the consequence of Spain losing almost all influence over the territory. Seguín hoped that Austin's colonial enterprise would allow San Antonio

to regain some measure of control over the border and American movements into Texas.[5] A few weeks later, Moses Austin's son, Stephen, arrived
in the village. Stephen F. Austin had agreed to join his father's Texas
venture and told Seguín that he would accompany them on the journey
back to San Antonio. Along with several other Americans, Stephen Austin followed the Tejanos to the Texas border. There, at daybreak, a rider
brought news of the death of Moses Austin, leaving his saddened son to
carry forward the colonization venture. On July 16, 1821, Stephen F. Austin and his American party followed Erasmo Seguín and his Tejanos as
they splashed up the western bank of the Sabine River, ready to begin the
American colonization of Texas.[6]

For Austin and his Anglo companions, the appeal of Texas was in the
land and—more important—what it could produce. During his ride from
the Sabine to San Antonio, Austin scribbled meticulous notes in a journal
on the quality of the soil, water, timber, and geology of the ground they
covered. The territory closest to the border reminded him of "the Barrens
of Kentucky," and he was heartened to see fields boasting "more luxuri-
ant growth than I have ever seen before in any country and is indica-
tive of a strong rich soil." Some areas Austin deemed second-rate, usually
places where the soil was sandy, but most of the territory impressed him
deeply, and he delighted to discover so much "soil very black and deep."
By the time the Anglo-Tejano party neared the outskirts of San Antonio,
Austin had become convinced of the wisdom of his father's enterprise. It
was land rich enough to support farming of nearly any sort—"the most
beautiful I ever saw," he wrote—and Austin believed that his new Texas
colony could offer American farmers everything that had made the Mississippi River Valley so appealing for cotton cultivation: rich soils, a long
growing season, ready access to Gulf Coast shipping.[7] The fact that the
recent Panic of 1819 had put similar acreage in the United States beyond
the financial reach of most Americans only made Austin's prospects for
success more enticing.

But, as it turned out, it would take more than promises of cheap cotton lands in northern Mexico to entice Americans to abandon the United
States for new lives in Texas.[8] Accounts of the devastation that ravaged
Texas during the 1810s had appeared regularly in U.S. newspapers, and the
apparent inability of the Spanish to govern the province had prompted
many American editors to portray Texas as a lawless haven for "bands of
outlaws in arms, tribes of Cannibal Indians, gangs of daring smugglers,
with hordes of miserable African slaves."[9] Such disparaging accounts

Portrait of Stephen F. Austin. (Prints and Photographs Collection, Dolph Briscoe Center for American History, University of Texas at Austin)

helped shape how Americans imagined the Texas borderlands during the early 1820s and were enough to give any would-be migrant pause. When Mexico became independent of Spain in 1821, the determined efforts of numerous Mexican legislators to outlaw slavery in their new nation only heightened the concerns that many farmers in the American South held about abandoning the securities of the United States for an uncertain life in northern Mexico. As Austin and his Tejano allies would discover, opening Texas to American migration proved far more difficult than simply advertising cheap land. They would somehow have to convince American farmers that both their property—particularly in slaves—and their futures would be secure in northern Mexico.

As they rode together toward San Antonio, Erasmo Seguín and Stephen Austin represented the beginning of a remarkable Anglo-Tejano alliance that would open the Texas borderlands to American settlement. Both groups wanted colonization for their own purposes—Tejanos to stabilize and enrich communities like San Antonio, Anglo-Americans to enrich themselves by developing an agricultural powerhouse along the Texas coast. And so both sides came together to support, defend, and expand the stream of Americans that began flowing into northeastern Mexico. During the early 1820s, such efforts put them at odds with legislators in

Mexico City who sought to abolish chattel slavery as part of their efforts to establish the new Mexican nation. Anglos and Tejanos responded in unison with an intense lobbying campaign, arguing that the preservation of slavery was indispensable to ensuring the continued migration of American cotton farmers into Texas and thus the security of northern Mexico. In so doing, both Anglos and Tejanos recognized the intricate connections between regional development in Texas and national policies being forged in Mexico City, and so they both focused intensely on convincing national leaders that maintaining the legality of slavery was the key to maintaining American migration into Mexico.

The movement of Americans into northern Mexico that began during the early 1820s was the result of a remarkable confluence of factors, driven in large measure by the overlapping visions that Americans like Austin and Tejanos like Seguín held for the development of the Texas borderlands. Yet, in the aftermath of Mexican independence in 1821, both Austin and Seguín also recognized that this movement of American expatriates would happen within the context of the rise of Mexico as an independent nation, and would therefore be deeply shaped by the debates, decisions, and policies being forged within the new Mexican capital. Whether American farmers would be allowed into northern Mexico, as both Anglos and Tejanos desired, would depend on whether men like Austin and Seguín could convince Mexico City to allow American slavery into the region.

Envisioning Northern Mexico

As Seguín and Austin approached the outskirts of San Antonio on August 12, 1821, word reached them of the success of the Mexican War for Independence. The news had arrived in the Texas capital three weeks before, when town leaders declared in favor of the revolution and swore to support the new Mexican nation. Seguín and the Tejanos greeted the news "with acclamations of 'viva Independencia' and every other demonstration of joy," although what Mexico's independence would mean for northeastern Mexico and Austin's colonization enterprise remained uncertain.[10] The new government of Mexico, whether a monarchy or democracy, might choose to uphold Spain's decision to encourage American migration into Texas as a means of controlling the frontier. Or the new government could change the terms of American colonization, perhaps even reversing the policy. Spain might even reconquer Mexico

before any change could take place, leaving the original colonization policy in force. With nothing certain, Governor Antonio Martínez welcomed
Austin to Mexico and assured him of the support of the local leadership
in San Antonio. Martínez also recognized Austin as the heir to his father's
grant—he would be an *empresario*, or land agent—and gave the American
permission to explore the territory around the Colorado River where his
proposed colony would be located.

With the enthusiastic support of the local Tejano leadership, Austin
set his colonization plans into motion. His first step was to draw up a
formal plan for distributing land to American settlers in Texas. Although
he would later adjust the specific number of acres granted, Austin's land
policy followed a basic rule: each settler would receive land in proportion
to the number of people—primarily family members and slaves—they
brought to Texas. His initial proposal to Governor Martínez suggested
that each family receive 320 acres of land for farming and 640 for raising
livestock (allotments which would later be adjusted to 177 acres for farming and 4,428 acres for ranching). A man would get an additional 200
acres for bringing his wife to the colony, and another 100 for every child.
Austin made no effort to hide the fact that he planned to attract slaveholders to Texas, proposing that families receive an additional 50 acres
for every enslaved person they brought to the region.[11] Indeed, the idea
was to encourage Americans to bring their entire families into Mexico
and to provide a premium to slaveholders willing to make the journey.
Austin then began extensive explorations of the countryside as he pondered which lands would best serve his purposes, surveying in detail the
region between the Colorado and Brazos Rivers.

As he scouted locations for his colony, Austin also began the work of
enticing Americans to abandon the United States for Mexican territory.
Before leaving for Texas, Austin had partnered with a family friend from
New Orleans named Joseph Hawkins, who agreed to provide financing
for the venture in exchange for a 50 percent stake in whatever profits the
colony produced. Once in Mexican territory, Austin began sending letters
to Hawkins describing the land in Texas and asking his partner to adver-
tise the colony to potential colonists. "The objects of this settlement are
entirely agricultural," Austin wrote to Hawkins as he toured the region.
"The richness of the soil, healthfulness of the climate, contiguity to the
sea, and other natural advantages" promised Americans who came to
Texas "a reward to our labors, which few spots on the globe could furnish
to an equal extent." The empresario asked his partner to publish their

colonization plans in the New Orleans newspapers. Once news of cheap cotton land in Mexico began appearing in the Louisiana papers, Austin anticipated that word would soon spread across the American South. "I hope the newspapers in Mississippi, Tennessee, Kentucky and Missouri, will republish," he wrote to Hawkins.[12]

In advertising for potential settlers, Austin counted on news of the venture filtering across the United States through informal networks of newspapers reprinting from one another. Americans during Austin's time had a voracious appetite for news, and even the smallest communities boasted their own newspapers. Some of what appeared in these papers came from local sources, such as editorials on political and social matters, advertisements from area businesses and merchants, and the occasional local event significant enough to merit a story. Most of the news that filled their columns, however, had been lifted and reprinted from other papers. When newspapers from one part of the country found their way to another—whether by ship, through the mail, or in the satchel of a traveler—editors pored over them in search of stories intriguing enough to merit inclusion in their own publications. A story chosen for reprinting could be as profound as the outcome of a battle or as trivial as an amusing anecdote, depending on what caught the editor's eye. This haphazard information network, as imperfect as it was, enabled people throughout the United States to know what was happening in places far from their homes.

Within weeks, Austin's descriptions of the wonderful lands and generous government in Mexico were reprinted in the *Arkansas Gazette*, *St. Louis Enquirer* in Missouri, *Frankfort Argus* in Kentucky, *Edwardsville Spectator* in Illinois, *Richmond Enquirer* in Virginia, and *Washington Gazette* in Washington, D.C., among others.[13] One widely reprinted account quoted Austin as promising "to each individual settler at least 1000 acres of land, for agricultural purposes, and an additional quantity to settlers in proportion to the size of their families, number of their slaves, and resources they possess for cultivating the soil." In another reprinted letter, Austin laid out a hypothetical scenario to illustrate the vast land grants he would be making to colonists. "A married man with two children and ten slaves would receive 1360 acres of land" for farming, he wrote, "and 2840 acres for a vachery [cattle pen], making together 4200 acres of land besides a town lot." Nearly every advertisement emphasized that colonists would receive additional land for every dependent—including slaves—they brought with them to Texas. Austin's letters seemed to promise migrants vast tracts of land for nearly nothing, and the empresario was anything but timid in his claims about northern Mexico. "The country is superior to any other part of the United States I have seen," he proclaimed.[14]

Austin was offering Americans far more land in Mexico than they could ever hope to own in the United States. During the 1820s, the U.S. government sold public land at $1.25 per acre—already too expensive for most farmers in the aftermath of the 1819 panic—and the cotton boom of the 1810s had driven up the costs of premium cotton lands alongside major rivers in Mississippi and Alabama to as much as $50 per acre, far beyond the reach of all but the most well-heeled Americans.[15] Those same farmers, however, could now acquire premium cotton lands in Mexico for nothing more than the costs of surveying, for which Austin planned to charge 12.5¢ per acre. Anyone could easily do the math: the very best lands in Texas could be claimed for a fraction of the price of the most meager tracts available along the Gulf Coast of the United States.

American newspapers would prove the most powerful medium for advertising the colony to potential settlers, and other accounts that appeared in U.S. papers helped Austin's efforts by extolling the great agricultural promise of northeastern Mexico. Noting the recent return of several local planters from a survey of Texas, one newspaper in Mississippi reported that "they all unite in representing this great body of country as superior to any of equal extent they ever passed over."[16] Another Mississippi paper printed a glowing account by "a Traveller in Texas" who described the region as remarkably well watered, unusually healthy, and particularly suited to cultivating the crops of the southern United States. "The lower range of lands bordering on the Gulf of Mexico are peculiarly adapted to the cultivation of sugar, cotton and corn," wrote the anonymous traveler, "the middle range to that of cotton, corn and tobacco."[17] Nearly all descriptions that appeared in U.S. newspapers—whether written by Austin or not—lavished praise on the quality of the lands in Texas, prompting many American editors to grumble loudly about the United States' decision in 1819 to relinquish its claims to the region.[18]

Such press allowed Austin to portray the Texas borderlands as a natural extension of the American cotton frontier. During the years that preceded his arrival in Mexico, newspapers across the United States had carried innumerable stories describing the rich soils, temperate climate, and extensive river system of the Gulf Coast as ideal for ambitious farmers serving the rapidly expanding cotton markets. Such advertisements had convinced tens of thousands of Americans to pour into the Mississippi River Valley, where U.S. cotton production increased by more than 400 percent between 1800 and 1820. Indeed, by 1821, massive migration had transformed Alabama and Mississippi into states where—combined with Louisiana—farmers produced more than 40 million pounds of cotton annually.[19] Austin's advertisements employed the same language and phrases that had brought so many people into Mississippi, as the empresario worked hard to describe the geographic virtues of northern Mexico in terms that would resonate with farmers in the southern United States.

Yet, for every description in the American press about the wondrous agricultural potential of Texas, numerous others portrayed northern Mexico as a lawless, unstable, and chaotic land. Anyone reading Austin's generous descriptions of Texas lands had to weigh them against the endless procession of stories about Indian raids, slave smugglers, and invading filibusters that dominated U.S. newspaper coverage of northern Mexico at the time Austin arrived. This was the legacy of the devastation of Spanish settlements in Texas during the 1810s, which continued to shape how Americans imagined Mexico. As Austin made his way into Texas during the summer of 1821, newspapers from Louisiana to Rhode Island reported that Tejanos cowered in San Antonio on the edge of starvation, "afraid to venture a mile on account of the Indians."[20] The most damaging stories portrayed the region as an unregulated refuge for fugitives and criminals. One widely reprinted article blamed "inefficient government in the Mexican provinces" for chaotic conditions in Texas, where—according to the story—Mexican bandits murdered innocent travelers with impunity, American criminals escaped the reach of U.S. law, smugglers operated unchallenged, and Louisiana slaves ran "from their masters and find an asylum." Land in northeastern Mexico may have been reputed to be among the most fertile in North America, but the apparent absence of any effective government in the territory cast doubt on the real value of such land.[21]

The challenge facing Austin and his Tejano patrons in early 1821 was not to convince Americans that land available in the new colony was well suited for cotton production. Newspaper reports on the region had been near unanimous in their praise of the agricultural promise of Texas. The challenge, rather, was to convince Americans that the government of Mexico would support them and protect their property. Repeated stories of armed revolutionaries and incompetent bureaucrats, violent bandits and brazen smugglers, vicious Indians and starving Spaniards prompted men and women in the United States to imagine northeastern Mexico as a chaotic place. If Austin and the Tejanos hoped to convince would-be colonists to abandon their native country for opportunities in a foreign territory, those settlers would need confidence that their new government would grant them the support and protection necessary to make the endeavor worthwhile.

This uncertainty about the Mexican government proved particularly salient for those hoping to bring slaves into the new Anglo colony. All Americans recognized that the stunning success of cotton in the Mississippi River Valley had been built upon the backs of enslaved laborers. By 1820, enslaved people composed more than 40 percent of the combined population of Alabama, Mississippi, and Louisiana, and Austin had purposefully structured his colony's land policy in order to attract slaveholders.[22] Yet, more than any other property holders, slaveholders depended on the government to endorse and protect their property rights, and the empresario soon found himself fielding numerous letters from potential colonists in the United States asking about the attitude of the Mexican government toward enslaved property. Austin advertised his colony as an agricultural paradise, but the truth was that he could deliver on that promise only if the new national government of Mexico endorsed the labor system that white Americans believed necessary for truly profitable cotton cultivation.

Framing a New Nation

Questions about colonization and slavery would need to be answered in Mexico City. When Texas governor Antonio Martínez forwarded details of Austin's colonization efforts to his superiors in Monterrey, he received word back that nothing about Austin's grant could be confirmed. With the upheavals following independence, it remained unclear what the new government in Mexico City would decide in regard to the far-northern frontier and colonization policy. Until the national government determined such matters, authorities in Monterrey informed the Texas governor, Austin had no power to distribute land and American colonists could be settled in northeastern Mexico only provisionally. Martínez urged Austin to take his case directly to the new government forming in Mexico City, and so the American set out with two companions in the spring of 1822 on a two-thousand-mile journey to the capital of the new Mexican nation.[23]

Colonization was only one of many challenges facing Mexico's provisional government in the wake of independence. Sweeping across thousands of miles, Mexican territory ranged from the lush rainforests of Chiapas and the snow-capped mountains surrounding Mexico City to the brutal deserts of Chihuahua and the barren plains of New Mexico. Some 6 million people lived within that overwhelming expanse, divided from one another by sharp lines of race, region, and economics. Three centuries of Spanish rule and a decade of intermittent rebellion had done little to foster any coherent sense of unity or nationalism among Mexico's inhabitants, most of whom—about 60 percent—were Indians who felt little affinity for an independent Mexican nation. The rest of the population divided into various minority groups—such as *mestizos* (those of Indian Spanish heritage), *creoles* (Spaniards native to Mexico), Europeans, and free and enslaved Africans—whose mutual mistrust and racial divides from one another were reinforced by stark economic inequalities. The long-standing isolation of most regions within Mexico, due to few roads and poor communication between provinces, meant that local affiliations mattered far more to most people than the abstract notion of a Mexican nation. The country itself, moreover, was mired deeply in debt that threatened to bankrupt the government before it could even begin. Such stark divisions among the Mexican people, along with mounting financial burdens facing the country, presented a daunting challenge to leaders in Mexico City hoping to somehow forge a unified nation.[24]

Among the most difficult challenges facing Mexico City was the problem Spain had never overcome: how to secure the sparsely populated northern hinterlands. The northern border of Mexico ranged across thousands of miles, from the Gulf of Mexico all the way to Oregon, with potential invaders looming on all sides. The Russians hovered just north of California, where they coveted the rich coastline and had established a fort north of San Francisco Bay in 1812. Only thirty-five hundred Mexicans lived in the California territories at the moment of independence— far too few to repel an invading force—and reports had already reached Mexico City of Russians taking possession of the region.[25] The new nation had a much larger presence in New Mexico, where around thirty thousand Mexicans lived in the territory surrounding Santa Fe. Although it was the most populated portion of Mexico's northern frontier, New Mexico also remained its most isolated. Sheer distance from Mexico's interior meant that trade along the Santa Fe trail had begun to connect the region's economy more closely to the United States than to Mexico.[26] Yet the most pressing challenge to securing Mexico's northern frontier remained the territory along the shared border with the United States. "The most important problem is the security of the Province of Texas," reported a Mexico City commission in December 1821. "It would be an irreparable loss to the Empire if this beautiful Province is lost. In order to save it there remains only one recourse—to populate it."[27]

It is not hard to see why the commission feared for Texas. The surge of Americans making their way into the Gulf Coast territories during the cotton revolution had created a wild imbalance of populations along the U.S.-Texas border that clearly disturbed Mexican authorities. In Arkansas and Louisiana alone more than 167,000 Americans crowded up against the border with Mexico by the early 1820s, with another 220,000 in nearby Mississippi and Alabama. In stark contrast, authorities in San Antonio reported that only about 2,500 Mexicans made their homes in Texas in 1822—most of them several hundred miles from the border—and Mexico's entire military presence in the region amounted to a mere 186 soldiers.[28] Leaders in Mexico City recognized the alarming vulnerability of the country along its northeastern border: there was simply nothing to stop the Americans from forcing their way into Texas and claiming the region for the United States.

The Indian problem in Texas, moreover, remained as painful and intractable for the Mexican government as it had been for the Spanish. In the immediate aftermath of independence, Mexico attempted to establish peace through a treaty signed in 1822 by a Comanche delegation to Mexico City. The measure, however, could not end the tremendous demand for horses and mules in the southern United States, and so Comanche raiding to feed that market continued to threaten all settlements throughout northeastern Mexico. Several Comanche raids swept through Texas during the early 1820s, terrorizing and killing Mexicans all the way into Coahuila, prompting renewed cries from officials in northern Mexico for measures that could stem the violence.[29] The nation's empty treasury meant, among other things, that Mexico simply could not afford to send enough troops to pacify hostile tribes threatening settlements in northern Mexico.

Leaders in Mexico City soon acknowledged what Tejanos had already concluded: colonizing Texas seemed to offer the only viable option for shoring up the nation's perennially weak presence in its northeastern territories. Persistent reports from leaders in San Antonio about the dire need for more loyal citizens in Texas helped convince them. "It is absolutely necessary that the nation make some effort to populate it," wrote an exasperated Antonio Martínez, who insisted that "admitting foreigners would be the easiest, least expensive, and fastest mode."[30] Although legislators in the Mexican capital remained leery about inviting foreigners of unknown loyalties to settle in Mexico, many were also willing to take a chance on foreign colonists if they could not convince their own people to move to an isolated and violent frontier. Vibrant colonies could solve the intractable Indian problem in Texas and enable Mexico to counter the growing American presence along the border, all without taxing the nation's treasury. The dangers of taking no action, moreover, appeared worse than the risks foreign colonization could bring. "If we do not take the present opportunity to people Texas," warned the Mexico City commission, "day by day the strength of the United States will grow until they will leave their center and annex Texas, Coahuila, Saltillo, and Nuevo Leon like the Goths, Visigoths, and other tribes assailed the Roman Empire."[31] Mexico's national congress thus formed a committee in March 1822 to begin drafting the framework for a national colonization law.

Foreigners of all stripes hoped to profit from that colonization law. By the time Stephen Austin arrived in the Mexican capital in late April 1822, the congress was besieged by people hoping for their own contracts to colonize northeastern Mexico. Upon arriving at his hotel, Austin ran into two Tennesseans, Robert Leftwich and Andrew Erwin, representing a collection of United States investors hoping to capitalize on American interest in Mexican land. Some of the would-be empresarios infesting the capital offered to transport settlers from Europe to northeastern Mexico. Diego Barry, Tadeo Ortiz, and Felipe O'Reilly hoped to secure permission to bring fifteen thousand Catholic colonists from Ireland and the Canary Islands off the coast of Africa. P. B. Leuba and Juan Rosset both asked for permission to create Swiss colonies in Texas. Most petitioners, however, hailed from the United States, including Benjamin Milam, Arthur Wavell, and Haden Edwards. Even James Wilkinson, a former U.S. Army general and ex-governor of the Louisiana Territory, arrived in Mexico City with hopes of securing permission to begin his own colony. The Mexican congress fielded nearly a dozen proposals during 1822 for schemes to colonize the Texas borderlands, nearly all of them from men like Austin hoping to open Texas to American farmers. "In my Opinion," wrote one American living in Mexico City at the time, "the Austin Grant will have as much to fear from the encroachment of new grantees as from any other cause."[32]

As Mexicans debated colonization, it was not the prospect of bringing Americans into the country that proved controversial. It was, instead, the insistence of those Americans that chattel slavery accompany them into Mexico that sparked heated debates. Three competing colonization bills emerged from the Mexican congress by late summer 1822, as legislators sought to establish a framework for turning Mexico's vacant lands into a source of strength for the nation. Although leaders in Mexico City squabbled over details, all three proposals agreed on several points of broad consensus. Each bill, for example, mandated that native Mexicans be given priority in claiming vacant lands along the nation's northern territories. Because everyone understood that few Mexicans showed interest in relocating to the nation's distant frontier, each of the proposed colonization bills focused on regulating how foreigners—Americans, in particular—would be incorporated into the nation. Each bill thus required all migrants to be professed Catholics, a reflection of the fact that religion would serve as part of Mexico's early national identity. Yet one point of consensus among Mexican legislators stemmed directly from the lobbying of numerous would-be empresarios milling around Mexico City, who had collectively made clear that Americans intended to bring slave-based agriculture with them into northern Mexico. All three colonization bills, in different ways, called for the eventual abolition of slavery as a central condition for allowing Americans into Mexico.[33]

The common approach of the bills toward slavery reflected a widespread desire among Mexicans during the early years following independence to abolish the institution from their new nation. For some, antislavery convictions grew out of the fervor of the revolution itself. Father Miguel Hidalgo, whose protest began the movement for independence from Spain, had decreed an end to enslavement at the outbreak of his rebellion in 1810.[34] In leading the final charge toward overthrowing Spanish rule, Agustín de Iturbide had declared everyone in Mexico to be social equals as one of the Three Guarantees of his Plan de Iguala. In neither case did slavery appear to comport with the ideals that had animated the War for Independence. And for those legislators taken with the ideas of the Enlightenment, enslavement clashed violently with liberal concepts of the natural rights of man. Thus, the opportunity to create a new nation in Mexico based on principles consistent with the revolution and liberalism seemed to present a unique opportunity to abolish the institution. "There is not a better moment than this to prohibit slavery in the Mexican Empire," Juan Francisco Azcárate observed from the floor of congress in October 1821.[35]

There were also practical reasons for Mexicans to oppose slavery.

Although chattel slavery had once been an important part of the Mexican economy, the institution had withered to near insignificance by 1821. Over the centuries Indian labor had proven far cheaper than enslaved labor, and by the nineteenth century debt peonage provided the majority of unfree labor in the country. In a nation of more than 6 million, there were perhaps only eight thousand enslaved Africans still toiling in Mexico by the early 1820s.[36] Because the Mexican economy no longer relied on slave labor in any meaningful way, abolishing the institution appeared to require no significant sacrifice on the part of the country's industry, agriculture, or trade. Similarly, there were few incentives for Mexico to involve itself in the international slave trade. Both Great Britain and the United States had recently abolished the practice, and the British navy had even begun intercepting ships that trafficked in slaves. As a new nation setting itself up on the world stage, Mexico would do well to avoid conflicts with England—which, at the time, was both the dominant global power and the biggest foreign investor in Mexico's economy—over an institution that had little value for the national economy. In the eyes of many politicians in the nation's capital, there appeared to be no meaningful advantage to keeping the institution of slavery legal in Mexico.[37]

The prime exception, however, were the Mexicans in Texas. For many Tejanos, the dire necessity of populating the region—and thus providing some measure of security for their settlements against ongoing Indian raids—overpowered any abstract notions about whether chattel slavery was consistent with the ideals of the new Mexican nation. And the sheer proximity of their villages to the United States also provided Tejanos with powerful economic incentives to support American immigration, incentives that no one else in Mexico had. Practically every prominent and politically influential Tejano family in San Antonio—including the Casianos, Seguíns, Navarros, Veramendis, Ruizes, and Musquizes—made their money in trade with the southern United States by importing American goods into northern Mexico where they brought high prices in Texas, Coahuila, Nuevo León, and Tamaulipas. Allowing American settlers into Texas would mean bringing those markets closer to Tejano villages, offering easier access to goods and an expanding new population of local buyers, while also providing greater security from the Indian raids that continued to threaten their families and livelihoods.[38]

Most Tejano leaders also had personal connections and exposure to the southern United States that helped shape their perceptions. José Casiano, Ramón Músquiz, Erasmo Seguín, and Juan Martín de Veramendi had each spent a great deal of time making trade trips to New Orleans, which by 1820 had become the central hub of the cotton revolution overtaking the entire Mississippi River Valley. Several hundred Tejanos, including such prominent men as José Antonio Navarro and Francisco Ruíz, had spent much of the late 1810s living as refugees in Louisiana in the violent aftermath of the Gutierrez-Magee expedition. They had, in other words, witnessed firsthand the rapid transformations in populations and wealth that slavery and cotton had brought to the southwestern United States, and they wanted to bring a similar transformation to northeastern Mexico. Endorsing American-style chattel slavery was primarily a practical consideration for most Tejano leaders: if defending the institution was necessary in order to bring American farmers into Texas, then they would defend slavery as a means to greater ends. As Francisco Ruíz later explained to Stephen F. Austin, "I cannot help seeing the advantages which, to my way of thinking, would result if we admitted honest, hardworking people, regardless of what country they come from . . . even hell itself."[39]

The Americans, for their part, made it clear to both Tejanos and legislators in Mexico City that without slavery there would be no mass exodus of Anglo farmers into northern Mexico. General James Wilkinson reported to a friend in Baltimore about his effort "to acquire a precious tract of Land in the province of Texas" and his work to curry favor with Mexican officials on the matter, arguing that building "extensive productions of Sugar & Cotton" required that his settlers "be permitted to introduce negroes." Stephen F. Austin lobbied with ferocity on behalf of his own colony, meeting personally with legislators to stress that opening northeastern Mexico to American colonization depended on ensuring that slavery remain legal in Texas.[40]

Debating the Americans

When the Mexican congress opened formal debates over colonization in August 1822, representatives squabbled over numerous details. Some demanded that prohibitions against non-Catholic settlers be strengthened, others wanted greater resources directed toward tackling the Indian problem, and still others wrangled over how to guard against unscrupulous settlers from the United States. Slavery, however, was woven throughout the entire debate. Francisco García, for example, argued that there could be no higher justice than outlawing "the fatal abuse" of enslavement and urged the congress to abolish the institution immediately in a national antislavery law. A representative from Guanajuato, Juan Ignacio Godoy, railed against the idea of permitting American colonists to bring their slaves into Mexico as a "property right," which Godoy felt was "repugnant to natural reason." Lorenzo de Zavala, a prominent congressman from Yucatán, was one of a handful of voices seeking a middle ground. De Zavala urged Godoy and others to permit Anglo colonists to import slaves in the short term (thus providing an immediate solution to the need to stabilize Texas) by adopting a gradual approach to abolition, which would ensure the populating of Texas while also providing for the eventual end of the institution in northern Mexico.[41]

Ongoing turbulence in Mexico City, however, meant that questions about colonization and slavery would remain unresolved until the following year. During the early summer of 1822, supporters of Agustín de Iturbide—the man who had led the final charge in overthrowing Spanish rule in Mexico—mobbed the streets and congressional building, demanding that Iturbide be crowned emperor of Mexico. The national congress gave in and Iturbide became Emperor Agustín I in July 1822. When some legislators then attempted to rein in the power of their new emperor, Iturbide jailed his political opponents and dissolved the elected congress, replacing it with a handpicked junta composed of his supporters. All matters related to colonization were set aside during this period, as the overthrow of congress and associated controversies took center stage in Mexico City.[42]

Petitioners from the United States, regardless, continued pressing for passage of a colonization law that would enable Americans to begin claiming land in Mexico. Austin petitioned the emperor himself and pressed his case personally with every legislator he could corner.[43] "I talked to each individual member of the junta of the necessity which existed in Texas, Santander, and all the other unpopulated provinces for the new colonists to bring their slaves," Austin reported to the governor of Texas.[44] Despite his efforts, Austin continued to encounter fierce resistance from legislators unwilling to permit slavery to continue in Mexico, even if such concessions would help populate and secure the nation's northern frontier. "The principal difficulty is slavery," Austin told a friend. "This they will not admit." More disheartening, the new Mexican congress was even contemplating a sweeping antislavery measure that proposed to free all enslaved people within ten years. "I am trying to have it amended so as to make them slaves for life and their children free at 21 years," Austin wrote,

Camara de los Diputados. The floor of the national Congress in Mexico City, where fierce debates raged over whether Anglo colonization and slavery would be allowed into the Texas borderlands. (*Album Pintoresco de la Republica Mexicana*, DeGolyer Library, Southern Methodist University)

"but I do not think I shall succeed."[45] Although Austin and others continued hammering at individual Mexican lawmakers, the national congress remained stubbornly resistant to granting American colonists any more liberty on the matter of slavery.

When Iturbide's handpicked congress took up the question of colonization in November 1822, debates again turned on slavery. The imperial junta decided to take up Lorenzo de Zavala's middle-ground approach, proposing to allow colonists to bring their slaves into Mexico while also outlawing the slave trade itself and mandating that the children of enslaved parents be freed at the age of fourteen. Such a gradual approach to abolition was not swift enough for legislators like José Mariano Aranda, who insisted that Mexico not even consider American colonization until a comprehensive law regarding slavery could be passed. Francisco Argandar went further, denouncing slavery as "inhumane and against all right" and imploring his fellow congressmen to "abolish it for all time." As for any Americans who wanted to bring slave-based agriculture into northeastern Mexico, the representative from Michoacán had little sympathy.

"If they wish to come, they will do it under the condition that they will not have slaves," thundered Argandar. "This will be the highest honor of the Mexican nation."[46]

Other legislators, however, remained deeply concerned about securing the nation's northeastern border and were willing to forgo immediate prohibitions on slavery if it would bring American colonists into the region. Salvador Porras, representative from Durango, noted that U.S. petitioners for colonization contracts had argued repeatedly that outlawing slavery would create "powerful and invincible obstacles" to bringing American settlers into the region. Porras himself had been "assured that on the contrary, they would not come, since the colonists would lack the might for their work" without enslaved laborers to plant and pick their cotton. Porras thus came out in favor of the gradual approach toward abolition as the only practical means for ensuring that Americans would colonize Texas, sentiments seconded by Ramon Estévan Martinez de los Rios and numerous others. Iturbide's congress finally approved the colonization bill, which promised to open Mexico to both American settlers and slavery, while also mandating a gradual end to the institution. Emperor Iturbide signed the measure into law on January 3, 1823.[47]

Stephen Austin believed that the law's passage—and the fact that it did not outlaw slavery outright—was due to his own persistent lobbying. Austin's greatest fears had been that no colonization law would be passed (preventing him from settling anyone) or that whatever bill became law would abolish slavery entirely. The colonization law of 1823 avoided both problems, and Austin reported that the fervent antislavery sentiments of legislators in Mexico City meant the settlers had been lucky to secure the right to bring any slaves at all. "No article of any kind permitting slavery in the Empire would ever have been passed by Congress for a time," Austin recalled, and he believed that without his own member-by-member lobbying campaign "the law would never have passed."[48] Although Austin gave himself all the credit, the truth was that numerous other would-be empresarios from the United States had also lobbied hard for preserving slavery in northeastern Mexico.

Tejanos, as it turned out, had also played a crucial role in getting the colonization law passed. Father Refugio de la Garza, the forty-six-year-old pastor of San Antonio, arrived in Mexico City during the spring of 1822 to represent Tejano concerns in the national congress. As the deputy from the province most deeply involved in American colonization, de la Garza's opinions on the matter carried great weight in Mexico City, and he soon found himself appointed to the committee that drafted the final colonization law. Had the Tejano congressman expressed reservations or come out against American immigration, the bill would never have passed. Yet de la Garza represented Tejano enthusiasm for the project (he even approached Austin about becoming the official pastor for the colony) and thereby helped ensure the bill's final passage.[49] In so doing, de la Garza made it possible for Austin to secure formal approval for his colonization venture, which finally came in the spring of 1823.

Yet, once again, political turmoil in Mexico City threatened to overturn all that had been settled in regard to colonization. A revolt against Iturbide's rule began in the province of Veracruz in December 1822, when Antonio López de Santa Anna issued a proclamation demanding the overthrow of the empire and the establishment of a republic. By March 1823, the emperor had been forced from his throne and sent into exile (he would attempt to return in July 1824, only to be captured and executed). All legislation passed under Iturbide, including the national colonization law, was promptly annulled by the new Mexican congress. Because it had already been approved, Austin's empresario contract remained valid. But his was the only application granted such approval, and the subsequent revocation of the colonization law meant that, until another was passed, Austin now had a monopoly on settling Americans in Mexican territory. With his approved documents in hand, Austin left Mexico City in April 1823 on his way back to Texas. All other would-be empresarios had to remain in the Mexican capital, awaiting passage of another national colonization law.

Constitution of 1824

The overthrow of Iturbide brought with it a seismic shift in Mexican politics that tipped the balance of power away from monarchists and conservatives and toward liberals, republicans, and federalists. In the immediate wake of Mexican independence, leaders in Mexico City could be divided into two general political camps. On one side stood conservatives, who hoped to keep power centralized in Mexico City (as the Spanish had) and who feared the discord and disruptions that widespread diffusion of political power across Mexican society could bring. On the other side stood those inclined toward liberalism and republicanism, whose ranks often included representatives from provinces (particularly those along the frontier) that had not fared well under Spain's policy of centralizing power in Mexico City. These republican-minded legislators, as a consequence, tended to embrace federalism—with its promise of granting more power to state governments than the national government—as a means for uniting the country under a unified system of government, while also empowering the provinces to legislate on matters of regional importance. Conservatives and centralists had enjoyed the upper hand in political matters during the first year of independence, when they had succeeded in establishing a monarchy. The overthrow of Emperor Iturbide, however, discredited centralism and swelled public sentiment in favor of federalism. The break was both abrupt and profound, with the exile of Iturbide emboldening formerly reticent republicans to come forward and assert their desire to make Mexico a federal republic.[50]

The rapid shift in sentiment toward federalism would have far-reaching consequences for the way that Mexico's national government dealt with the unresolved issues of slavery and American colonization. A glimpse into that transformation could be seen in the colonization law passed by the new national congress in August 1824. Unlike its previous incarnation, the new law delegated practically all authority on the matter to "the Congresses of the States," charging them with framing "laws or regulations for the colonization of those lands which appertain to them." The national government, of course, set certain parameters—such as a ban on settlements within a certain distance of foreign countries or the sea coast—but otherwise left the details to individual states. One practical result of this shift from a centralized to federal approach toward regulating colonization was that the new bill placed no restrictions on the institution of slavery. The new law, in fact, said nothing on the matter, pointing toward a profound turn in Mexican politics. Mexico City's embrace of federalism in the wake of Iturbide's downfall had begun a process of delegating numerous—and often contentious—policy questions to the state governments.[51]

None of this meant that antislavery sentiment in Mexico City had been swept aside with the fall of the emperor. Legislators from across the country continued to loathe the institution, and the national government still had numerous opportunities to set antislavery policies into place. In July 1824, for example, the national congress passed a law banning the slave trade. "Commerce and traffic in slaves," read the bill, "proceeding from any country and under any flag whatsoever, is forever prohibited in the territory of the United Mexican States." Enslaved people brought into Mexico contrary to the law would be deemed free by "the mere act of treading Mexican soil," and anyone caught smuggling such human merchandise would face a year's imprisonment. The bill's language made clear that its primary purpose was to halt Mexico's involvement in the international slave trade. What remained unclear, however, was whether this provision also outlawed the importation of slaves for personal use. The emphasis on prohibiting "commerce and traffic" in slaves left murky the question of whether the measure applied only to the slave markets or covered any movement of enslaved people into Mexico. Tejanos in San Antonio decided to interpret the law as applying only to the commercial slave trade and assured Austin that it would not be enforced against Americans transporting their own slaves into Texas. Yet, such assurances aside, it remained to be seen whether Mexico City would move to outlaw slavery throughout the country or would cede the matter to the states as part of the nation's recent embrace of federalism.[52]

The central venue for deciding such questions would be the new national constitution of Mexico. Erasmo Seguín, the man who had guided Austin into northern Mexico, represented Texas in the national legislature during the spring and summer of 1824 as debates raged in Mexico City over the writing of the constitution. Austin immediately began coordinating with Seguín, urging him to do all in his power to ensure that the new constitution did not outlaw slavery. "There are two obstacles that slow down emigration to this province and the entire nation," Austin reminded Seguín. "One is the doubt that exists if slavery is permitted and the other is Religion." The empresario knew they could expect no concessions on religion, but he begged Seguín to use "all your protection and influence" in the national legislature to ensure that Americans "could bring and keep their slaves" in northeastern Mexico. There was absolutely nothing, he insisted, that would play a greater role in determining whether Americans would abandon the United States for Mexico. "They cannot emigrate without bringing them," Austin declared.[53]

While most Mexican legislators in the national congress continued to openly oppose slavery, Seguín articulated the different perspective embraced by the Mexican leadership in San Antonio. Seguín considered himself a dedicated liberal and federalist, yet his driving concern—above all else—remained the rapid stabilization and development of Texas. As a result, Seguín threw himself into lobbying on behalf of the fledgling Anglo colonization project, emerging during the constitutional debates as a fierce advocate for preserving slavery in Mexico. When some representatives again tried to outlaw slavery throughout Mexico, Seguín pushed back, arguing that preserving slavery was indispensable to securing the nation's northern frontier through Anglo colonization. Austin, for his part, remained in constant—and perhaps exhausting—contact with his Tejano ally in the national capital. "Tell Austin that I am well aware that abolition of the Slaves will hinder emigration," Seguín told a friend in San Antonio. For his part, Seguín believed that the nation's embrace of federalism would mean that Anglos and Tejanos could secure protections for slavery and colonization at the state level, once the national constitution was completed.[54]

Although most legislators in Mexico City could unite in their opposition to American-style slavery, the practical need to populate Texas—combined with strident Tejano lobbying—left antislavery forces in the capital divided. The result was that when Mexico published its Constitution in 1824, the new document made no mention of slavery whatsoever, deferring the matter—like most divisive issues—to the individual states. Indeed, the 1824 Constitution represented a resounding victory for federalists. Although the national government reserved jurisdiction in several matters (such as the right to declare war, engage in foreign relations, levy taxes) the bulk of policy decisions were made the purview of the states. Such an embrace of divided government was, in part, a practical means of uniting Mexico's different provinces under a single government by not challenging the power of states to enact policies suited to their own circumstances. It also enabled the national legislature to defer difficult matters, such as finding a practical means for enacting emancipation, to regional authorities.[55]

The decision by Mexico City to delegate slavery policy to the states had sweeping implications. Because state legislators could write their own laws on the matter, the institution would now remain legal in Mexico for as long as any individual state chose to allow it. This approach had the potential to blanket Mexico with a patchwork of conflicting slavery statutes, although the fact that most regions held few enslaved people meant that the majority of states simply outlawed the institution. The national Constitution's approach to slavery also shifted the financial burdens associated with emancipation—such as the need to compensate slaveholders for freeing their property—onto state treasuries, which may account for why some states chose to enact gradual emancipation measures. The strongest reverberations of this approach, however, would surely be felt in northeastern Mexico. Unlike their counterparts in any other part of Mexico, Anglos and Tejanos in Texas hoped to foster a thriving new Anglo-Mexican society built atop slave-based agriculture. And since regional officials had been empowered to establish policies on both slavery and colonization according to local circumstances, the embrace of federalism by Mexico's national government appeared poised to grant Texans the freedom they needed to entice large numbers of American cotton farmers into northern Mexico.

Yet the small Mexican population in Texas, the most enduring legacy of Spain's failure in the region, ensured that Anglos and Tejanos would not be granted sole jurisdiction in determining the future of northeastern Mexico. Because Texas had too few people to become an independent state, the Mexican congress had to determine whether to make Texas a territory (which would put it under the jurisdiction of the national government) or to join the province with a more populated neighbor to create a combined state. Miguel Ramos Arizpe, the representative from Coahuila, pushed hard for Texas to be united with his own province, a move that would help Coahuilans avoid territorial status while also granting them control over valuable unsettled lands in Texas. Tejanos opposed the union, objecting that the merger would place all legislative decisions regarding Texas hundreds of miles away in the Coahuilan capital of Saltillo. Yet territorial status promised its own problems, because it would place those same decisions even farther away in Mexico City. Following vigorous protests, Erasmo Seguín eventually conceded to the union after gaining permission for Texas to seek independent statehood once its population justified it. The national congress thus grafted Texas onto Coahuila in May 1824, creating the new state of Coahuila-Texas. This ensured that even though decisions concerning colonization and slavery in northeastern Mexico would no longer be made in Mexico City, neither would they be made in Texas. They would instead come from the Coahuilan capital of Saltillo, where Texans would be outnumbered in the state legislature by ten to one.[56]

The prospect of legislative power moving from Mexico City to the Mexican frontier nonetheless sparked great hope among proslavery Anglos and Tejanos. Austin celebrated the news by issuing a proclamation praising "the prospects of Freedom, Happiness, and Prosperity" that Mexican federalism would bring to the region. Most Tejanos, too, shared Austin's optimism and hoped that the Saltillo congress would prove more responsive to their desires to foster conditions in the region that would appeal to potential American colonists. "The State government will be more aware of the issues for which they are responsible and have more authority when they meet than the Provincial congress," Seguín told Austin. "They will put an end to your problems."[57]

Americans in Mexico

While politicians in Mexico City wrangled over the structure of their national government, and Austin's descriptions of lush cotton lands in Mexico appeared in U.S. newspapers, Americans began migrating into northern Mexico with their slaves. No fewer than thirty-nine American families passed through Nacogdoches on their way to Austin's colony during the last three months of 1821, and the evident hunger among Anglo farmers for cheap cotton lands reaffirmed Austin's conviction that he could flood the region with Americans. "I am convinced," he wrote in a letter to the Texas governor, "that I could take on fifteen hundred families as easily as three hundred if permitted to do so." Hoping to begin his colony with the right men, Austin shipped fourteen handpicked colonists, along with a mountain of farming supplies, to the Colorado River. Although the schooner never reached the river (thrown off course, it eventually landed on the Brazos), Austin himself arrived at the Colorado to discover that a number of Americans, rather than wait for the empresario, had already begun scraping out farms along the river. A steady influx from the United States continued, and by the time Austin left for Mexico City in March 1822 there were a hundred Americans settling themselves along the Colorado River and another fifty along the Brazos.[58]

As soon as they arrived, Austin's colonists began changing the landscape. These were men and women who shaped their lives around the lifecycles of the plants they grew, and most hoped to arrive in northern Mexico during the winter so they could prepare their new lands for spring planting. The first task was to clear fields for corn and cotton. Settlers used axes to chop down small trees and hoes to scrape the ground free of wild vegetation and vines. To fell larger trees, colonists stripped off the bark around the trunk—a process known as "cinching" or "girdling"—that robbed the tree of the ability to nourish itself until it died and eventually collapsed in a rotten heap. Once cleared, the fields could be tilled. Using plows carted in from the United States, the settlers cut long, deep furrows across their new land, each spaced several feet apart. They needed draft animals for this work—mules or oxen were considered ideal, but strong horses could do the job. Corn went into the ground first in order to ensure food for the coming year, and would grow into ripe ears with relatively little tending.

Cotton, however, demanded unceasing attention, and the new Anglo settlements became hives of activity. Following a careful regimen honed in the southern United States, they began planting during early spring, usually between mid-February and mid-March, whenever farmers believed they were past the hard freezes of winter. Once cottonseed went into the furrows, farmers fought an endless battle to protect their budding plants from the encroachments of nature. When cotton seedlings emerged a few weeks after planting, they had to be protected from aggressive weeds and grasses that threatened to invade the cotton rows and choke them out. Farmers continually "scraped" their crop lines with hoes, clearing their fields of anything that might compete with new cotton shoots for water and sun. If all went well, farmers would thin out the growing seedlings around early April (leaving one stalk every two or three feet) in order to give the strongest plants sufficient room to grow. With enough rain, the cotton plants would become well established sometime in May, although the onset of warmer weather also signaled an acceleration of the endless battle with grasses and weeds for control of the fields. Those who managed to keep nature at bay would be rewarded with mature plants and the first budding cotton bolls by midsummer.[59]

Much of what went into these Anglo cotton fields had their origins in Mexico. Most of Austin's settlers likely hitched their plows to horses and mules stolen by the Comanches from Mexican settlements during the late 1810s and early 1820s, and many of the mounts that the Anglo colonists rode into Texas were probably returning to their native territory. More important, these Anglo farmers sowed their fields with a new variety of "Mexican" cottonseed. When a fungus began ravaging cotton fields across the Mississippi River Valley in 1811, local farmers had searched in desperation for a resistant variety of cotton that could save their fledgling industry from what became known as "the rot." After several failed experiments with seeds from Georgia, some planters near Natchez, Mississippi, tried a small batch imported from Veracruz, Mexico (where cotton had been grown in small quantities since before European contact). The new "Mexican cotton" proved immune to the fungus, and soon spread from the Natchez District to Alabama and Louisiana. Before long, these Mexican strands had been cross-pollinated with the Georgian variety, producing a hybrid Mexican-American seed that was resistant to fungus. The

Stick Stock, or Surveying in Texas before Annexation to the U.S., by Theodore Gentilz, shows a team of surveyors in the process of mapping and clearing the land for Anglo settlement. (Collection of Betty Lou and Larry Sheerin, San Antonio, Texas)

new seed also happened to produce bolls so large that field hands could pick far more "Mexicanized" cotton in a day—about three times more—than they could with the old Georgian variety, leading to even greater profits. The new strand soon became the standard within the U.S. cotton industry, and many of Austin's colonists carried these Mexican-American seeds in their saddlebags when they made their way into northern Mexico.[60]

The cabins of these new Anglo settlers had to be built by the end of summer, because the emergence of cotton bolls in full bloom during the early fall marked the beginning of a frenzied race to harvest as much cotton as possible before rains or frosts killed the plants. Picking cotton was brutal work; the plant's fibrous bolls had to be pulled from protective husks with knife-like edges that would lacerate any fingers not careful enough to avoid them. The work required concentration and a nimble touch, as each picker slowly filled a bag or basket towed down endless rows of stalks. The fruits of an entire year's labor now depended entirely on speed and volume, so every available set of hands toiled each day from sunup to sunset—often for weeks on end—throughout the fall. The most skilled pickers could collect upward of several hundred pounds in a single day, which would then be piled together into heaps for cleaning and processing.

No one mastered their fields like Jared Groce, the largest slaveholder and wealthiest colonist in Austin's colony. A Virginian by birth, Groce had meandered through South Carolina and Georgia, accumulating a large stock of enslaved men and women along the way, before ending up in Alabama in 1818. Like many Americans, Groce had been impressed with newspaper reports of Austin's glowing descriptions of the agricultural promise of the Texas borderlands. Determined to claim his share of northeastern Mexico's cotton lands, Groce began driving his ninety slaves westward in a convoy of fifty wagons toward Mexico. After a stopover in New Orleans to purchase farming supplies, the caravan rolled through Nacogdoches along the San Antonio Road before arriving at the Brazos River in January 1822. Christening the tract of land he claimed "Bernardo," Groce ordered his slaves to build cabins for their master and themselves and to begin planting the cottonseed they brought from Alabama.[61]

Because cultivating cotton required periods of such intense labor, the number of acres that a farmer like Groce could cultivate—and thus how much money he could make—depended entirely on the number of hands he could direct toward his fields. Austin's colonists had been granted more than 4,400 acres each, but their ability to capitalize on those grants was directly tied to the number of people available to work them. For most settlers, that limited them to cultivating only as many acres as they could manage with their wife and children. Those who owned slaves, however, had the ability to leverage their Mexican grants into far more acres of cotton than their nonslaveholding competition. Every additional worker in the field translated into an additional eight to ten acres in cultivation, which usually meant an additional bale of cotton for each of those acres.[62] Owning slaves, in other words, meant much larger profits for people like Jared Groce. Although most Anglo-Americans who came into Texas during these early years did not own slaves, all of them understood that harnessing enslaved labor would allow them to achieve a scale of production that could make a man wealthy. Thus even the poorest white man hoped one day to be able to purchase slaves for his own plantation.

Farming was not the only way Austin and his colonists hoped to profit from the expansion of the cotton frontier into Mexico. Austin, for example, grew no cotton himself, but his plans for becoming wealthy revolved entirely around speculating in cotton lands. For all his troubles as empresario, Austin received large allotments of premium land from the Mexican government, which he then intended to sell to future waves of American immigrants. If the colonies somehow managed to grow and prosper, Austin's lands would become increasingly valuable as the demand for them grew in direct proportion to the number of Americans moving into northeastern Mexico. The same equation was true for all of his early settlers, none of whom—not even Jared Groce—could come close to farming the nearly seven square miles of land granted to them by Mexican authorities. Each family, instead, farmed whatever portion of their land they could manage and held onto the rest as an investment that would grow in value with time. Every farmer who came to settle in Austin's colony was also, therefore, a land speculator.

No other colonist brought as many slaves or could cultivate as many acres as Groce, although most came from the same section of the United States that he did. From 1825 to 1831, Austin recorded the names of each U.S. state his colonists abandoned on their way to northeastern Mexico, providing a rough sense of where his advertisements resonated with the greatest force. Nearly 90 percent of Austin's colonists came from the slaveholding regions of the United States, with Louisiana, Alabama, and Arkansas accounting for more than half of the settlers. Proximity alone made those cotton states the most likely places for Austin to find settlers, something the empresario counted on. Although most of these people, like most white families in the southern United States, owned no slaves, almost all listed themselves as farmers and hoped to raise cotton. Yet a significant proportion of the colonists did bring enslaved property into Mexican territory. Those who imported slaves usually could afford only a few, such as William Rabb and Thomas Bell, who each brought one enslaved person into the colony. Others with more means had larger holdings, such as Alexander Jackson (who had four slaves), James Ross (six slaves), and Benjamin Beeson (seven slaves). By 1825, only three years after American settlers began legally migrating into northern Mexico, a census of Austin's colony revealed that a full quarter of the population was enslaved.[63]

More families in Austin's colony depended on enslaved labor than raw population numbers would suggest. Colonists with an abundance of slaves, such as Jared Groce, regularly leased slaves to settlers without the means to purchase their own. A settler named Churchill Fulshear, for example, approached Groce in 1824 in hopes of leasing one of his slaves.

Fulshear needed a slave to cut and split fence rails, most likely to fence in Fulshear's crop fields, and he offered Groce $20 to cover the "two or three months" he imagined the job would require.[64] Although Austin was fond of telling Mexican officials that he owned no slaves himself (in fact, he did from time to time), the empresario regularly relied on enslaved labor that he contracted from other slaveholders. In 1823, Austin leased from Groce the rights to Sally, Jack, and Kelly for $38 a month, and the following year he leased Lucy, Patsy, Elsy, and Henry for $180 a year from Thomas Westhall.[65] This practice of leasing vastly expanded the ranks of those with access to enslaved labor, as well as the investment of nonslaveholders in the institution's preservation.

Austin promulgated a legal code for his colony in January 1824 that demonstrated the extent to which slavery made up a significant portion of the settlement's business. Intending his code as a means for providing stability to the colony, Austin addressed issues he felt most likely to cause problems: murder, theft, robbery, assault, slander, drunkenness, immorality, gambling, horse racing, and counterfeiting. The legal issues concerning slavery merited special consideration—only Indian relations occupied as much of the code—and Austin sought to establish security in enslaved property by instituting harsh deterrents. Anyone who harbored a runaway slave could be fined $500 and sentenced to hard labor; anyone who stole slaves or helped them escape risked a $1,000 fine and hard labor. Slaves who stole would receive anywhere from ten to a hundred lashes of the whip. Any enslaved people found off their plantation without a pass were to be tied up, whipped, and returned to their master. And no one could trade with a slave without the permission of his or her master, lest such commerce encourage slaves to steal. The code itself was a clever mix of Spanish and English legal traditions, although its articles concerning slavery were thoroughly American. While the provisions for punishing slaves codified practices common in the southern United States, they violated Spanish precedents and Mexican laws dictating that slaves receive the same punishment as free men. Such contradictions apparently gave little pause to the Tejano leadership in San Antonio, as José Antonio Saucedo formally approved Austin's code when he visited the colony in May 1824.[66]

The legal code's support for slavery—like all issues relating to the institution—was a means to a greater end for Austin, his colonists, and the Tejanos: establishing the necessary conditions for fostering rapid development of a profitable agricultural industry in the region. "The primary product that will elevate us from poverty is Cotton," Austin explained to a Tejano friend, "and we cannot do this without the help of slaves."[67] And precisely because Austin recognized that the success of his settlements depended so heavily on this trade, he did everything he could to build the infrastructure his colonists needed in order to tap into the global cotton market. The empresario aggressively courted support from merchants in both New Orleans and New York, hoping to use the promise of boundless Texas cotton as collateral in order to obtain new cotton gins and equipment that could accelerate production in the colony.[68] He petitioned numerous Mexican officials for the authority to establish new seaports at Galveston and the Brazos River, arguing that they were indispensable for exporting Texas cotton on a grand scale.[69] Indeed, for Austin, gaining a seaport at Galveston would serve the same purpose as gaining legal protections for slavery from Mexico City: both were necessary conditions for developing a cotton empire in Texas. "Nothing but foreign commerce, particularly the exportation of cotton to Europe," Austin explained in a letter to the governor of the state, "can enrich the inhabitants of this section of the State."[70]

The Americans who came to Texas shared this vision, and cotton production took off during the earliest years of settlement. While it is impossible to know precisely how much cotton came out of Texas during this early period, Austin estimated that his fledgling colony annually shipped several hundred bales—probably around 200,000 pounds of cotton—by the mid- to late 1820s.[71] That meant that the Anglo colonies constituted only a tiny fraction of the cotton commerce coming out of the Gulf of Mexico. Mississippians, by comparison, produced 10 million pounds of cotton in 1826, while Louisiana and Alabama planters shipped 38 million and 45 million pounds respectively.[72] Yet Austin and his colonists saw their small shipments as the first fruits of a booming new industry in Texas, and they reveled in the success of plantations in the Mississippi River Valley as models of the rapid growth they hoped to replicate in Mexico. In letters to Mexican officials, Austin often cited the massive scale of cotton exported from places like Alabama and Mississippi, arguing that Texas—given the right support from the Mexican government—could one day exceed the southern United States in cotton production.[73]

The needs of this budding industry, in turn, shaped how capital was invested within Austin's colony. Cotton had to be cleaned and baled before it could be sold, and so a number of Austin's colonists financed the construction of local cotton gins during the early 1820s. Imported from manufacturers in the United States, these three-story structures relied on horses to turn large saws that slowly stripped cotton fibers from their seeds. Cleaned cotton fell through to the bottom floor, where it was taken to a "press" that compacted the collected fibers into dense rectangles that weighed anywhere from four hundred to six hundred pounds. Once bagged and tied, these massive bales were ready to be sent to market.[74] Although hauling gins into northern Mexico proved expensive, the machinery was indispensable for preparing cotton for shipment. The gins could also be highly profitable, allowing farmers to process the crops of their neighbors—for a fee—after cleaning their own. Within three years, Austin's colony already had four cotton gins in operation.[75] Eager to capitalize, Austin's brother and cousin set up a partnership in 1825 to erect another gin along the banks of the Brazos River.[76]

Getting those bales from the wild Texas interior to established markets, however, usually entailed an arduous trek. Every new colonist claimed waterfront land along either the Brazos or Colorado, hoping that Texas rivers would offer an efficient means for shipping crops to the Gulf of Mexico, much as the Mississippi River had for U.S. farmers in Mississippi, Alabama, and Louisiana. Yet Austin's colonists discovered that large sandbars at the mouths of both the Brazos and Colorado blocked most sizable ships from coming upstream, because any boat sitting more than five feet deep was likely to run aground while attempting to enter or exit the rivers. Roads were nearly nonexistent in the region, making it impossible to move bales by wagons or carts. During the earliest years of settlement, some Texas planters experimented with sending their cotton into the Mexican interior on mule trains.[77] Hauling overland to Mexican markets, however, proved impractical, and most colonists resorted to floating their bales downstream on rafts, keelboats, or small sloops. Once they arrived on the coast, bales were then piled up beachside to await the next commercial vessel from the United States.

Practically all those bales went to New Orleans, which had emerged during the early nineteenth century as the epicenter for buying and selling cotton in the Gulf of Mexico. Wealthy trade houses headquartered along the New Orleans waterfront coordinated the flow of millions of pounds of cotton coming down the Mississippi River Valley, connecting American farmers with mercantilists and buyers on both sides of the Atlantic Ocean.[78] Agents from Liverpool, England, and New York City (representing the two centers of global cotton manufacturing) competed

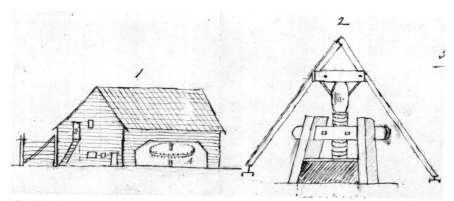

Sketch by British traveler William Bollaert of a *Gin House and Cotton Screw or Press* in Montgomery County, Texas, 1843. Austin's colonists invested in the construction of multistory cotton gins (*structure on the left*) that could separate seeds from cotton bolls on an industrial scale. Mounds of cleaned fibers were then loaded into a cotton press (*machine on right*), which compressed them into dense 450-pound blocks that could be shipped to market. (The Newberry Library, Chicago, Vault Oversize Ayers Art, Bollaert #45)

for the best bales, although buyers from across Europe and the Americas came to the Crescent City. The result was a thriving international cotton exchange that emerged during the cotton boom of the 1810s, and whose position alongside northern Mexico promised Austin and his settlers ready access to both U.S. and European markets. New Orleans also became the largest point of departure for people making their way into Austin's settlement. As the colony continued to grow, New Orleans shippers began making regular runs to the Texas coast, where—after discharging their cargoes of passengers and farming supplies—they gladly loaded up on cotton for the return trip.[79]

The growth of shipping lines between New Orleans markets and the Texas coast represented the very heart of what the Tejano leadership hoped that American colonization could do for the Texas borderlands. Every ship transporting new settlers meant a larger non-Indian population for the territory, which—they hoped—meant more security for places like San Antonio. Just as important, each ship that docked along the Texas coast to exchange its cargo of goods for Anglo cotton bales brought the New Orleans markets closer to Tejano villages, bringing everyone in the region closer to a thriving new Texan economy.

Perceptions and Realities

Yet a growing perception within the United States—that Mexico was both unstable and unfriendly toward slavery—continued to undermine the recruitment efforts of Austin and the Tejanos. Although Mexico had not outlawed slavery, reports about the debates in Mexico City over whether to abolish the institution found their way into the newspapers of the United States. These reports discouraged potential settlers from migrating to northeastern Mexico, and Austin received a steady stream of letters from the southern United States asking him about the state of slavery in Mexico. "Three months ago I received more than one hundred letters from individuals in that country, well-known men of character, asking for reports about whether the Government would allow the free entry of Emigrants, and especially if they can bring in their Slaves," he told Gaspar Flores in late 1824.[80] In one of those letters, an Alabama planter named Charles Douglas warned Austin that "our most valuable inhabitants here own negroes" and "our planters are not willing to remove without they can first be assured of their being secured to them by the laws of your Govt."[81] James Phelps sent a similar report to Austin from his home along the western edge of Mississippi. "Nothing appears at present, to prevent a portion of our wealthy planters from emigrating immediately to the province of Texas," Phelps wrote, "but for the uncertainty now prevailing with regard to the subject of slavery."[82] Even settlers already within the colony sent Austin similar pleas, telling the empresario that their compatriots in the United States would not join them without assurances that their slaveholdings would be secure. If Austin wished for his colony to fill up with Americans, advised Randall Jones, a settler already in the colony, "nothing would facilitate that more than the admission of Slavery in this state."[83]

Much of the uncertainty among Americans about Texas and Mexico stemmed from reports appearing in U.S. newspapers. During the early 1820s, dozens of stories circulated among American papers about troubles in Austin's colony. Some emanated from real events—such as a drought that hit the region in 1822, Austin's prolonged absence from the colony during his visit to Mexico City, and government prohibitions against Protestantism. Other stories had no basis in fact but were bandied about just as frequently—including reports of Americans being forcibly driven from Texas by Spaniards, widespread starvation and famine destroying the colony, news of Stephen Austin's death, and even a claim that "the whole country is infested with ticks . . . which are of an enormous size." At the same time, a wide assortment of stories praising the successes of Austin's colony and the potential of northeastern Mexico also continued to appear in the papers. Many of these stories reported the confirmation of Austin's grant, detailed the generous land grants available to emigrants, described the region as unusually healthy, and praised the colony's agricultural promise. In 1825 the *Kentucky Whig* declared Texas soil "to be inferior to none in the world," while the *Louisiana State Gazette* reported Austin's colony to be in a "flourishing and prosperous condition." The contradictory mix of positive and negative stories, swinging from one wild extreme to another, fostered confusion within the United States about conditions in northeastern Mexico.[84]

A steady stream of negative press flowed from newspaper editors in the western United States, some of whom openly campaigned to discourage emigration to Texas because they feared that American colonies in Mexico would compete with their own states and territories for population. One newspaper in Louisiana urged readers "to stay at home, and abandon the idea of trying new experiments of this kind."[85] Another Louisiana paper railed against Americans who would abandon "millions of uncultivated acres of land *in their own* country, to settle a foreign soil; a country not more fertile, a country no more healthy, and where the government is altogether inadequate to the protection of the citizen."[86] None, however, matched the vehemence of the *Arkansas Gazette*'s attacks against American colonization in Mexico. In a long-running series of articles about Texas, the paper printed exaggerated—and often outright false—reports depicting Austin's colonists as starving to death, stricken with disease, eating their horses, ruined by floods, losing their crops to drought, overrun by Indians, and abandoning Mexico as fast as they could.[87] "A large proportion of the population, is composed of the most abandoned of the human race," wrote the *Gazette*'s editor in a description of American expatriates living in Mexico. "Murderers, horse-thieves, counterfeiters, and fugitives from justice make this province their refuge."[88]

Slavery was a particular focus for the editor of the *Gazette*, who apparently believed that Mexican moves toward abolition could destroy American migration to Texas. In June 1822 the paper reported "a late measure adopted by the Mexican Congress, which prohibits the holding of slaves in the Mexican empire," which the newspaper's editor predicted "will operate as a material check to the emigration from the U. States and particularly from the Southern and Western States."[89] No such measure had been passed in Mexico, although that did not stop the *Gazette* from repeating the charge time and again in subsequent editions. In August 1822 the paper proclaimed that "slavery is expressly prohibited thro'out the Mexican Empire," and the following month it reported that all slaveholders in Austin's colony "were returning to the United States as fast as possible" in order to avoid having their slaves confiscated.[90] Newspapers ranging from South Carolina to Vermont reprinted the *Gazette*'s false claims of antislavery laws in Mexico, enabling the editor of one Arkansas newspaper to spread rumors of Mexican abolition across the entire United States. Following the *Gazette*'s lead, some newspapers like the *Baltimore Patriot* began to warn U.S. slaveholders against migrating to Texas since "in the Mexican Empire, the laws prohibit any person holding such property."[91]

Newspaper reports of antislavery efforts in Mexico continued to compete with stories praising the agricultural potential of Texas, producing widespread confusion—and therefore concern—within the United States about circumstances in the region. The result was a migration pattern from the United States that produced mixed results for Anglo-Tejano efforts to establish a cotton-based economy in Texas, the evidence of which Austin could see within his own colony. The fact that every fourth person within his settlement was enslaved placed Texas ahead of the rate of slaveholding in several southern U.S. states, such as Missouri, Tennessee, and Kentucky. Yet that rate also remained significantly lower than those found in the U.S. states that bordered Texas and the Gulf of Mexico, the regions of North America that dominated the cotton trade. A full third of the population in Alabama was enslaved, while slaves composed more than 40 percent of the population in Georgia, Mississippi, and Louisiana, suggesting that slave-based agriculture in the Texas colonies was not yet matching the successes of their American neighbors.[92] Every American who read Austin's advertisements of land in Mexico had to calculate the risks and rewards of moving to Texas, and several hundred American families had decided to seize the opportunities offered by northern Mexico. Yet the truth was that there were many thousands more Americans who chose not to come because of the uncertainties of life under the Mexican government.

BY 1825, STEPHEN F. AUSTIN managed to fulfill his original empresario contract, having settled the requisite three hundred families in his colony along the banks of the Colorado and Brazos Rivers. And that settlement was, by and large, what Austin had set out to establish. It was a collection of expatriates from the southern United States, dominated by farmers growing cotton for sale in the New Orleans markets that served the growing global textile markets. Fanning out alongside the rivers, the settlers had established a burgeoning network of new trails, roads, ferries, and bridges, which served as arteries of commerce and communication in eastern Texas. The most important roads led to San Felipe de Austin, a newly established village on the western bank of the Brazos that served as the headquarters for Austin's enterprise. Whenever American migrants arrived in Texas, they made their way to the empresario's rough-hewn cabin—which was both his home and the colony's land office—to claim their acreage and enter their names in Austin's register. From San Felipe, Austin coordinated the complex business of settling Americans in Mexico, surveying tracts, issuing land titles, managing legal disputes, advertising in U.S. newspapers, and representing the interests of his settlers to Mexican authorities.[93]

As Tejanos had expected, the movement of Americans into eastern Texas brought painful new pressures on the region's Indians. Southern portions of Austin's colony encompassed Karankawa lands, leading to violent encounters between the tribe's various nomadic bands and the new American arrivals. Austin began organizing militia raids on Karankawa camps in 1823 and then launched an all-out war of extermination—"to pursue and kill all those Indians wherever they are found"—that decimated the tribe and pushed the survivors west of the Colorado River by 1825.[94] With the more numerous Tonkawas, who lived along the northern edge of the new Anglo settlements, Austin pursued a peace strategy backed by the threat of violence. Having been deeply involved in the Texas-Louisiana horse trade since the 1810s, most Tonkawas saw the American emigrants as potential trading partners and hoped to profit from the growth of the colony. Some tribesmen, however, launched occasional raids of Anglo farms for horses and livestock. Austin encouraged the trade but threatened to wage war against the tribe if raiding continued. Following several shows of force by the empresario—Austin, in one case, forced a Tonkawa chief to whip several of his men for stealing Anglo horses—the Tonkawas signed a formal peace accord and then retreated northward, beyond the limits of the new Anglo settlements.[95]

The presence of the new colony, however, did little to shield Tejanos from the dominating power of the Comanches. Although officials in Mexico City signed a peace treaty with the tribe in 1822, Comanches persisted in their intermittent raids against Tejano ranches and villages.

Much of this raiding continued to serve the voracious horse markets in the southern United States, where the steady expansion of cotton in the Mississippi River Valley ensured high prices for whatever draft animals the Comanches could provide. Men and women in San Antonio and La Bahía tried to maintain peace by offering tribute gifts whenever they had goods to trade. But the lack of money from Mexico City for such gifts often left Tejanos at the tribe's mercy, and in June 1825 more than three hundred Comanches ransacked San Antonio over the course of six days. Although Austin's colony had nearly doubled the non-Indian population of Texas, bringing two thousand Americans into the territory in only three years, the new arrivals were not yet far west enough to offer much help to Tejanos suffering under the shadow of Comanche power.[96] This was, in part, a product of the developing split occupation of Texas, with Anglos establishing a zone of plantation agriculture in the east and Tejanos occupying the western territories along the edge of Comanchería.

The Tejano leadership in San Antonio nonetheless remained deeply committed to American colonization as the key to rapid development of northern Mexico. Austin's colony had already brought more improvements to the region's transportation infrastructure than had the previous century of Spanish rule. More important, the enterprise had vastly expanded commerce and trade between northern Mexico and the southern United States, as shippers in New Orleans established regular runs to the Brazos and Colorado Rivers. Although colonization had not yet solved the Comanche problem, American migration into the region had nonetheless begun remaking the territory in ways that gave Tejanos hope that there could be a prosperous future for the region, even without much support from Mexico City. When the new state legislature of Coahuila-Texas convened in early 1825, the Tejano leadership chose Baron de Bastrop—who was then serving as the land commissioner in Austin's colony—to represent Texas. One of the baron's first acts was to push through the passage of a state colonization law that ensured continued American settlement in northern Mexico, allowing Austin to apply for a second empresario contract.[97]

The Anglo-Tejano alliance had thus succeeded in opening northern Mexico to American colonization, in part because people like Erasmo Seguín and Stephen F. Austin—each for his own reason—saw great value in bringing the cotton frontier into Texas. Yet much of that success hinged on how Americans imagined Mexico, and Austin and the Tejanos spent enormous amounts of time attempting to persuade leaders in

Mexico City to establish policies and laws that would reassure would-be American migrants that life in northern Mexico would be as secure as life in the southern United States. Slavery therefore became the crucible of debate over American migration, as Anglos and Tejanos lobbied against those legislators in Mexico City determined to outlaw the institution in the new Mexican nation. In the end, questions of American migration into Mexico became swept up in a massive political shift that overtook Mexico City in 1823–24, which, in turn, opened the door for chattel slavery to remain legal in Mexico when national politicians embraced federalism and made the majority of policy issues—including immigration and slavery—matters for individual Mexican states to decide for themselves. By refusing to outlaw slavery, despite widespread antislavery sentiment within the congress, Mexico's national government made it possible for the cotton frontier to make its way into northeastern Mexico.

Yet Mexico had in no way embraced slavery. The institution had only been allowed to survive for the moment, enabling anti-Texas newspapers to spread rumors of Mexican abolition across the United States. Such tales of antislavery laws in Mexico were hard to counter because Austin had no definitive statement by Mexican officials endorsing the institution. As Austin lamented in a letter to a friend, he was unable to assuage the concerns of U.S. planters about the Mexican government's approach to slavery: "At the moment I cannot give them a definitive response."[98] The mere rumor of emancipation in Mexico, as Austin and Tejanos discovered, had the power to keep numerous American farmers from considering a new life in Texas.

The future of American migration into northern Mexico would be decided by the state legislature of Coahuila-Texas, which began writing its state constitution in 1825. Wasting no time, Austin and the Tejanos began work immediately on securing from the state government what they had never been able to wrest from the national legislature: a positive endorsement of slavery. "We cannot expect much emigration if not from the bordering states, which are Louisiana, Mississippi, Alabama and Arkansas, and there they permit slavery of the Blacks," Austin told his Tejano friend, Gaspar Flores. "If the colonists are permitted to bring slaves," he explained, "we will have workers to cultivate the land," but "without this, we will have nothing but poverty for a long time, perhaps the rest of our lives."[99]

Several hundred families, it seemed, might soon become several thousand, if the Coahuilan government could maintain the right policies to convince Americans to abandon the United States and seek their fortunes in Texas soil. Cotton from Texas plantations was already filling warehouses in New Orleans, and a newspaper from that city echoed Austin's observation that the congress of Coahuila-Texas now had the opportunity to pass legislation that could remake northeastern Mexico. "If their legislature would consent to the emigration of planters from the U. States, with their slaves," noted the *Louisiana State Gazette*, "it will only require a rise of the price of cotton in Europe, to give this state, a population and wealth, superior to many states in our confederacy."[100]

THREE

The Politics of Slavery in Northeastern Mexico, 1826–1829

Even though he had never met Stephen F. Austin, Peter Ellis Bean felt that he had no choice but to offer the empresario some advice. Bean, a resident of eastern Texas, had spent the last several months in Mexico City, visiting old acquaintances and conducting personal business. In July 1826 he received an urgent letter from a friend in Saltillo, the small town in the foothills of the Sierra Madres of northern Mexico that served as the state capital of Coahuila and Texas. Bean's friend had personal connections within the Coahuila-Texas state legislature, and he warned that the Congress was preparing to enact a constitution that would free all enslaved people throughout northeastern Mexico. Shocked, Bean quickly consulted the president of Mexico, Guadalupe Victoria, who was an old friend from their days fighting together during the Mexican War for Independence. Victoria had also heard the news and could offer no consolation—the Saltillo legislature, he confirmed, intended to outlaw chattel slavery, leaving the Anglo-Texan distraught. Bean harbored his own ambitions of becoming an empresario in Texas, and he feared that Mexican moves toward abolition would swiftly destroy the American colonization projects under way. So he decided to write to Austin to suggest a way around the problem of emancipation.

Bean's proposal revolved around a simple plan for changing the legal status of enslaved people in northern Mexico. He proposed that Austin's colonists take their enslaved laborers before the nearest Mexican official, declare how much they had paid for each slave, and then offer to allow those slaves to gain their freedom by repaying their own value through labor. Each slave would become, in effect, a contracted laborer, working for however long it took to repay their "debt" to their former master. Bean's proposal, however, was never meant to free anyone. Because masters would control the accounting, Bean pointed out, they would also make certain that a slave's debt could never be repaid, ensuring that enslaved men and women in Texas "will be the same to you as Before." If the outlawing of slavery in northeastern Mexico was inevitable—and Bean assured Austin that impending legislation meant that it was— then perhaps the American colonists could protect their investments in human property by legally reclassifying their slaves as indentured servants or indebted peons before the new constitution could take effect. All the colonists would need to do in order to preserve slavery in Texas, Bean explained to Austin, was simply call the institution something other than slavery.[1]

Bean's scheme exposed fundamental tensions over slavery that continued to divide Mexicans and shape the movement of American farmers into northern Mexico during the late 1820s. Although Mexico City had delegated questions of American colonization to individual states, that had done nothing to resolve disputes among Mexicans about the role slavery would play in the development of northern Mexico. The successes of Austin's settlement during the early 1820s demonstrated the potential of cotton to transform the territory, and Anglos and Tejanos remained fiercely committed to protecting the institution as the indispensable key to ensuring the rapid growth of plantation agriculture in Texas. The recent advances in population, infrastructure, and economic development brought by the movement of the cotton frontier into Texas, they argued, could not be abandoned at the very moment those forces had finally begun to remake the territory.

Yet, as both Anglos and Tejanos discovered, not everyone in northern Mexico shared their vision. When Coahuilans gathered in the state legislature to begin writing their state constitution, many of them proved just as eager to outlaw slavery as their counterparts in Mexico City had been during the early 1820s. Some Coahuilans emerged during this period as fiery opponents of slavery for ideological reasons, arguing that the institution was incompatible with a liberal democracy that recognized the inalienable rights of all men. Others opposed slavery as a practical means for undermining American migration into Mexico, realizing—just as the Anglo-Tejano alliance did—that the institution served as the foundation for the Anglo cotton economy. There was, however, a smaller contingent of Coahuilans who—having become convinced of the value of American immigration—joined forces with the Anglos and Tejanos. The debates that had once raged in Mexico City over slavery, colonization, and cotton thus reemerged with new intensity in Coahuila during the late 1820s, when Anglo-Americans, Tejanos, and Coahuilans fought with one another over the future of American migration into the territory.

These debates burned with such heat because they represented two incompatible, competing visions for the future of northeastern Mexico. Anglos and Tejanos, for their part, struggled to preserve slave-based agriculture as the means for recreating the successes of the southern United States in northern Mexico, which they believed represented the only practical way to ensure rapid development of the Texas borderlands. Antislavery Coahuilans, by contrast, rejected the American model, pushing instead for a northeastern Mexico free of enslavement and thus free of the contradictions that came with building a democratic society atop chattel slavery. The writing of the state constitution of Coahuila-Texas therefore became a brawl between these two visions, as Tejanos, Coahuilans, and Anglo-Americans confronted each other in heated exchanges about what they believed slavery and freedom would mean for the fate of the territory. Everyone understood that decisions forged during these debates would have profound and lasting consequences.

Yet the resulting battles produced a state that neither fully embraced nor fully rejected slavery, ensuring that neither vision for the future of Texas would be realized. The pro- and antislavery political coalitions that formed in the Saltillo Congress fought each other to a standstill during the late 1820s. The antislavery bloc in Saltillo eventually passed several pieces of emancipation legislation, yet those laws were tempered and blunted by relentless Anglo-Tejano lobbying and even ignored by authorities in Texas. Coahuilan legislators found they could outlaw slavery in theory, but they could not stop Anglo farmers and Tejano leaders from continuing the practice. Yet, at the same time, Texans also discovered that they could not force the state to openly embrace the institution of slavery, a problem that undermined the expansion of American migration into Mexico. Newspaper coverage of the slavery debates that raged in Saltillo reached tens of thousands of readers in the United States during the late 1820s, prompting many would-be American settlers to imagine Mexico as an unstable region overtly opposed to slaveholding.

Peter Bean understood those tensions and believed that his letter to Austin offered an elegant solution: allow the Coahuilans to outlaw the idea of slavery, while permitting the Americans to continue the practice under a different name. What he failed to grasp, however, was that outlawing slavery—even if only in name—would badly undermine Anglo and Tejano efforts to recruit new settlers from the southern United States, threatening the long-term stability of the colonization experiments. Although leaders of the Anglo-Tejano alliance might carve out a place for cotton and slavery to endure in Texas, they also came to realize that they could not build a thriving slave society while in conflict with their government.

Article 13

By the time Bean's letter completed its two-thousand-mile journey from Mexico City to the Texas colonies, Stephen F. Austin had already learned that abolition was part of the latest draft of the Coahuila-Texas state constitution. In June 1826 José Antonio Saucedo, the Tejano political chief of Texas, forwarded to Austin a letter written by Baron de Bastrop, Texas's sole representative in the state Congress. Bastrop had never intended for Austin to see the letter—he had, in fact, criticized Austin in the note. Yet Saucedo felt that the empresario needed to read the Baron's warnings that language in the new state constitution would free "all the slaves who set foot on our soil." Although Bastrop did not spell out the details of the constitution's anticipated antislavery article, he made dramatic predictions about its likely consequences: "If I cannot succeed in removing it, or at least modifying it," the colonies "will be completely ruined." Austin and the baron had previously discussed the possibility of Bastrop returning to Texas before the end of the legislative session, but Bastrop now believed the perils of the slavery issue demanded that he remain in Saltillo for the foreseeable future. Otherwise, he warned, "the enemies of foreign colonies would deal them a mortal blow without anybody being able to stop it."[2]

When another packet of mail from Saltillo arrived in San Antonio several weeks later, political chief Saucedo received a copy of the proposed state constitution and discovered what had so troubled the baron. As drafted by the legislature in Saltillo, Article 13 of the new constitution read: "The state prohibits absolutely and for all time slavery in all its territory, and slaves that already reside in the state will be free from the day of the publication of the constitution in this capital." Accompanying the article was a vague promise that "a law will regulate the mode of compensating those who held slaves at the time of said publication," although what that compensation would entail remained unclear.[3] If the article left compensation for slaveholders uncertain, it left no ambiguity about the future of slavery in Texas. All legal protections for the institution would end immediately upon the publication of the new state constitution, when slaveholders throughout Texas would lose all their enslaved property. The emancipated people would, presumably, be allowed to remain in Texas alongside their former masters, perhaps even as citizens of Mexico.

Article 13 had been drafted by Manuel Carrillo, one of three representatives from Saltillo in the state legislature and a leading voice for liberalism in Coahuilan politics during the late 1820s. Liberals in Coahuila tended toward a sympathetic view of the United States, generally favored the adoption of American-style federalism in their own government, and often supported inviting foreign colonists into the new Mexican nation. Slavery, however, was a practice that put men like Carrillo at odds with colonization efforts in Texas. While Mexican liberals frequently pointed toward the United States as a model for liberal democracy, chattel slavery stood out for many as a glaring contradiction in how Americans practiced their liberal creed. For some liberals in the state—such as Dionisio Elizondo, a representative from northern Coahuila—the development of the Texas colonies was far less important than ensuring that the state protected the "universal rights of men" that they recognized as the foundation of a liberal democracy.[4] Elizondo had, in fact, attempted unsuccessfully in 1825 to make abolition part of the state's colonization policy, although protests and pressure from San Antonio had thwarted his effort.[5]

Carrillo and Elizondo had nonetheless garnered enough support from like-minded legislators during the year since to write emancipation into the latest draft of the Coahuila-Texas constitution, in part by bringing conservatives into the antislavery coalition. Conservatives were fewer in number in the state (Coahuila was known as a bastion of liberalism and federalism during the early Mexican Republic), and they generally opposed American colonization. Some of this opposition was out of fear of economic competition from foreign merchants, although other conservatives were also concerned about the long-term consequences of a growing foreign population in the territory. Opposing slavery, for most conservatives, served largely as a practical means for opposing the potential dangers they saw in continued American colonization of Mexican territory rather than as an ideological end in itself. Eliminating slavery, moreover, would require little economic sacrifice on the part of individual Coahuilans. The enslaved population of Coahuila had never exceeded more than a hundred souls, and neither the region's economy nor its future development seemed to depend on the institution. Although all members of Manuel Carrillo's antislavery coalition wanted to establish a constitution that would promote the economic development of north-eastern Mexico—and Coahuila in particular—they saw no place for American-style slavery in the state's future.[6]

Mexicans in Texas saw the matter differently. Recognizing that the constitution's approach to slavery could destroy the new American colonies, Tejanos in San Antonio scrambled to contain the potential damage of Article 13. Without waiting to consult the Anglo colonists, San Antonio's town council immediately sent an emergency appeal to the state Congress in Saltillo, demanding that further debate on Article 13 be halted until Texas could weigh in on the matter. Lamenting "the death-blow that Texas receives with the constitution's article on slavery," political chief José Antonio Saucedo then forwarded a copy of Article 13 to Stephen F. Austin, imploring him to petition the state legislature on behalf of the colonists. They had to move quickly, urged Saucedo, to ward off an emancipation act that would destroy any hope for the rapid populating of Texas. "Otherwise," wrote an exasperated Saucedo, "all is lost." San Antonio's town council began drafting a petition to the state legislature that defended slavery as "*indispensable* to the prosperity of this Department," protesting that "the prospect of freeing the slaves" of Austin's settlers would be "an unjust abuse of the rights of the Colonists." Resurrecting arguments they had made in Mexico City in 1823–24, Tejano elites protested that northeastern Mexico would remain impoverished and ungovernable for the foreseeable future without slave-based agriculture driving Americans into Texas.[7]

Following the Tejano lead, Austin launched his own intense campaign to lobby the Saltillo legislature to back away from abolition. He began by composing a long petition that detailed all the horrible consequences (including a mass exodus of settlers back to the United States, the financial ruin of the state, and increased Indian wars) that Austin imagined emancipation would bring to the region. Yet the heart of Austin's protests—and the central theme of Tejano protests—was his prophesy that an attack on slavery would destroy any future American immigration, thereby crippling Mexico's ability to populate and control its northeastern frontier. "I made efforts to persuade rich men who owned slaves to emigrate because with them the country would make swift progress," Austin explained. "I told them that the Government would never take away slaves brought by them for their own use." "What would the world say," he demanded, "if in direct violation of that law and that guarantee, the Government were to take away that property from those colonists against their will?" Such an act would drastically undermine the new government's credibility, and "the mistrust which is certain to follow will destroy all hope of further emigration." Only by allowing the Americans to retain their slaves, he insisted, could the Saltillo Congress prevent "the total destruction of all new colonies . . . the annihilation of all hope of emigration in the future, and the consequent abandonment of this beautiful country."[8]

Austin and the Tejano leadership moved in unison, building on relationships forged during the Mexico City battles and their shared desire to promote American immigration. Both sides coordinated regularly about strategy, collaborating with Tejanos already in Coahuila in order to build pressure on the state legislators. Austin sent notes to Juan Antonio Padilla, a Tejano from San Antonio currently serving in Saltillo as the Coahuila-Texas secretary of state, urging Padilla to explain to Coahuilan legislators the dire consequences of abolishing slavery. "I do not think it possible," Austin wrote, "that the Honorable Congress will destroy us in this way if all these matters are explained."[9] Austin felt so strongly about the matter that he sent his younger brother, James "Brown" Austin, to San Antonio in order to confer in person with the Tejano leadership on the matter.[10] The Tejanos, in turn, welcomed Brown and kept the Austin brothers informed about the news coming out of Saltillo. Brown stayed in the home of the Seguín family while in San Antonio, and political chief Saucedo took it upon himself to brief the younger Austin on their ongoing proslavery lobbying efforts.

The rapid closing of Anglo-Tejano ranks revealed the shared commitment of men like Austin and Saucedo to defend slavery as a means for supporting American colonization. Yet it also revealed their practical response to the daunting new challenges of developing the region under the shadow of Coahuila. With only a single Texas representative in the Coahuila-Texas legislature, any revision of Article 13—or any other law or policy concerning Texas—would require all the political force that Anglos and Tejanos could collectively muster. Combining their efforts to lobby the Coahuilan Congress had become an unavoidable necessity, and both Anglo and Tejano leaders agreed that immediate action must be taken in order to prevent the prospect of emancipation from wreaking havoc on American immigration.

Rumors and Panic

As Austin and the Tejano elite moved to head off emancipation, rumors spreading among colonists in Texas soon demonstrated that their fears were well founded. In early August 1826, two settlers in Austin's colony learned of Article 13 and wrote a panicked letter to a fellow slaveholder living near Nacogdoches. Jesse Thompson and J. C. Payton sent the note to their friend, John Sprowl, warning that "theare is hardly any room for doubt on the subject of our having to relinquish the right of slavery." News of the constitution's proposed abolition article had somehow bubbled up within Austin's colony, convincing Thompson that he would be "entirely ruined" if he did not "make every arrangement so soon as practicable to be in the United States with my property." The men warned Sprowl so that he could make similar arrangements, but they also stressed the grave importance of Sprowl not spreading the news any further, "least the negroes get hold of it." If Texas slaves learned that the state legislature were about to declare them free, Thompson and Payton feared, enslaved men and women in the region might resort to violence to prevent their masters from returning them to enslavement in the United States.[11]

Yet word of impending emancipation spread like wildfire among the colonists' farms and plantations throughout the late summer and early fall of 1826. John Sprowl did such a poor job of keeping the secret that one settler sent a letter to Austin demanding to know what was happening with regard to slavery that had prompted Sprowl to declare publicly that soon "one half of your Colony and the people here would be out of the Country."[12] Outrage spread quickly among settlers "so much dissatisfied with the news that all thier slaves was to be set free," and some settlers turned their fury against Austin as the man who had once assured them that slavery was both legal and protected under Mexican law.[13] "Fathers tell me that I have reduced their children to a life of poverty," Austin moaned. "A weeping widow berates me for having robbed her of her only means of subsistence."[14] As the nearest and most visible representative of the Mexican government, Austin bore much of the brunt of colonist outrage over the prospect of losing their enslaved property.

By September 1826, boiling discontent among the colonists had Austin worried that he would not be able to keep his colony together. Convinced that emancipation was at hand, many settlers began preparations for returning to the United States. Others hoped to stay at least until they could harvest the cotton crops that represented their entire annual income. Austin cautioned San Antonio that "more than one half of these people are awaiting the decision of Congress in regard to their slaves, as they intend to leave the Country if their emancipation is decreed." Rumors also circulated that the region's Indians planned a full assault on the colonies that fall, and Austin warned the Tejano leadership that "if the slaves are emancipated the government must not depend upon the assistance of this militia" because there simply would not be enough Anglo colonists left in Texas to quell an Indian uprising.[15]

As Austin struggled to keep his colony together, Tejanos in San Antonio grew increasingly confident that Article 13 could be amended somehow to protect slavery among the Anglo colonies in Texas. Saucedo's inner circle estimated that compensating Anglo slaveholders for the loss of their property would cost the state $500,000, a sum too massive for the Coahuilan treasury to bear. Optimistic messages from Texas's representative in the state Congress, Baron de Bastrop, also indicated that they were making progress with state legislators as the baron worked to build a proslavery coalition. On reading the baron's latest dispatches from Saltillo, Brown Austin assured his brother that "if a favourable Slave Law is passed it will be attributed in a great measure to the *unremitted* exertions of the Baron."[16] Brown Austin's time among the Tejanos in San Antonio, indeed, had buoyed his own hopes that American settlers could retain the right to hold slaves in northern Mexico. "Try and Keep the Slave holders from going until they hear the result of the Slave question," Brown urged his brother Stephen. "Tell them they are safe yet—and there is little doubt but part of the laws will be favourable."[17]

While the Tejano leadership labored to block Article 13, fears of emancipation spreading among the Anglo colonists began appearing in newspapers across the United States. On October 10, 1826, the *Arkansas Gazette* printed an article reporting "the recent passage of a law by the Mexican Government for the emancipation of all the slaves in the province of Texas, and that orders had been received for carrying it into immediate effect." According to the newspaper, the devastating news had produced "the greatest consternation among the slave-holders" in Texas and prompted those with significant slaveholdings to begin immediate preparations for a return to U.S. territory. Small slaveholders, according to the story, had resolved in public meetings to resist Mexican attempts to enforce abolition "until they can gather this year's crop, after which they have determined to leave the country." While the *Gazette* article wrongly claimed that slavery had already been outlawed in northeastern Mexico, the story accurately captured the panic that had gripped the Anglo settlers in Texas since the first draft of the Coahuila-Texas state constitution began circulating among the colonists.[18]

The *Arkansas Gazette* had long served as an organ for anti-Texas propaganda, publishing over the years a steady series of articles calculated to discourage American settlers from migrating to Mexican territory. "We have always been opposed to the blind infatuation which has led hundreds of American citizens to emigrate to Texas," declared the paper's editor in one issue, and the newspaper devoted most of its anti-Texas ink to arguing that Mexico's government was an enemy of slavery.[19] Brown Austin singled out the *Gazette* in 1825 as the worst source of anti-Texas propaganda appearing in United States, complaining to his sister that the "paper has always evinced a most *Deadly hatred* towards the settlement of this Colony" by doing everything it could "to prevent any one from emigrating" to Mexican territory.[20] When rumors reached Arkansas that slavery had been outlawed throughout northeastern Mexico, the *Gazette*'s editor did not hesitate to print them in the pages of his newspaper.

With publication in the *Gazette*, the story of Mexico forcibly freeing the slaves of American settlers soon found its way into newspapers across the United States, and the news discouraged potential settlers. Travelers from Arkansas carried issues of the *Gazette* to trading hubs such as St. Louis, Missouri, and New Orleans, Louisiana, while other copies made their way through the mails to destinations farther east. By the beginning of November, the *Gazette*'s story had found its way to Kentucky, where the editor of the *Louisville Public Advertiser* reprinted the full article under the headline "Emancipation of Slaves at Texas."[21] Ten days later the story appeared in both Richmond, Virginia, and Washington, D.C., as copies of the *Advertiser* joined those already circulating of the *Arkansas Gazette*.[22] Tales of Mexican abolition soon made their way up the Atlantic seaboard. Reports showed up in Maryland within days of appearing in Virginia, and by the end of the week three newspapers in Massachusetts had reprinted the story.[23] Newspapers in Connecticut, New York, Rhode Island, and Vermont also published versions of the article, as editors filled the columns of their newspapers with stories borrowed from the pages of their competitors.[24] By reprinting the same story throughout November 1826, newspaper editors across the United States vastly amplified the reach of the *Arkansas Gazette*'s original article and made an alarming account of Mexican antislavery legislation available to tens of thousands of Americans.

The ongoing debates within the Saltillo legislature about the future of slavery in northeastern Mexico had thus become part of the debates in the U.S. press about the future of slavery in North America. During the early nineteenth century, antislavery activism among white Americans in the United States remained largely confined to discussions of state-sponsored projects—known collectively as "colonization"—to deport people of African descent to Africa. Such schemes had emerged as the most popular approach to antislavery in the country primarily because "colonization" offered a slow, voluntary, nonconfrontational method for solving the problems of race and slavery in American society. Yet the seeds for a more militant and confrontational antislavery movement had already taken root in the United States by the late 1820s, as moral and political concerns about the institution's future in the country continued to grow in certain—mostly northeastern—communities. Some of these burgeoning antislavery sentiments came from the evangelical revivals that swept across portions of the United States during the 1820s; some emerged from the dogged abolitionist efforts of free African Americans in northern cities. Perhaps most important was the dramatic rise of a politically powerful abolitionist movement in Great Britain during these years, which helped crystallize American antislavery thought. Although full-blown, emancipationist antislavery would not emerge as a significant political force in the United States until the early 1830s, a rising tide of antislavery sentiments had nonetheless taken root in portions of the United States during the late 1820s. By the time the *Arkansas Gazette*'s story reached the U.S. East Coast in 1826, several editors thus seized upon rumors of Mexican abolition as an opportunity to voice their general displeasure with both slavery and American slaveholders.[25]

The story found particular resonance with newspapers in the northeastern sections of the United States. Printing a summary of the story, the *Boston Commercial Gazette* argued that allowing Texas planters to return their slaves to the United States would make a mockery of the American creed "that all men are born free and equal" by turning the country into "a shelter for the oppressor and the slave-holder."[26] The *National Intelligencer* speculated that most slaves held in Mexican Texas probably had been "imported from Africa and Cuba, instead of the United States," which ought to block Texas slaveholders from removing them to the United States in violation of American law.[27] The *New York Daily Advertiser* mocked expatriate Americans who would seek refuge in U.S. territory from Mexican abolition laws for "setting a fine example of the principles of liberty, the rights of man, and respect for constitutional law."[28]

For some editors in the northeastern United States, the willingness of American slaveholders to abandon both the United States and Mexico whenever it proved convenient was tangible proof of their disreputable character.

The Saltillo Slavery Debates

While rumors spread across the United States about antislavery laws in Mexico, the Anglo-Tejano alliance worked feverishly to amend the proposed Article 13 of the new state constitution. Brown Austin traveled from San Antonio to the Saltillo capital in late September 1826, where he discovered that Baron de Bastrop's efforts to thwart Manuel Carrillo's antislavery coalition had produced mixed results. They might, explained the baron, be able to secure an exemption for Austin's existing colonists to retain ownership of slaves already held in Texas, but there would likely be no other concessions and "further introduction of slaves is out of the question."[29] Juan Antonio Padilla, the Tejano-born secretary of state in Saltillo, reinforced the baron's grim assessments. Padilla confessed that he was "afraid at present to do much" about the slave question because he had "no confidence in the members composing the Legislature."[30] Carrillo's antislavery faction of the Congress still outnumbered the baron's meager countercoalition, and its members had thus far proved largely unwilling to yield to Anglo-Tejano demands. "In another Legislature, a favourable Slave law might be procured," Brown Austin reported to his brother Stephen. "But the present one is composed of members so inimical to the interests of Texas, that the *most* that can be obtained is permission for the 300 families to hold their slaves."[31]

Brown Austin recognized that the political situation in Saltillo promised short-term relief to the American colonists while presenting more troubling long-term challenges. The possibility that slaveholders might be allowed to retain ownership of slaves already in Texas might help stave off an immediate exodus of settlers from the colonies. Yet Brown also knew that if new settlers were to be barred from bringing slaves into Mexican territory, empresarios such as Austin could no longer recruit slaveholders from the southern regions of the United States, which would ensure the slow withering of colonization efforts. The best the Anglo colonies could hope for, Brown Austin realized, was to convince the Saltillo legislature to extend the period of legally sanctioned slavery beyond the lifespan of those slaves already living in Texas. If they could somehow manage to stave off emancipation for a few more years, he reasoned, the Anglo-Tejano alliance might have an opportunity to gain more favorable laws from a future legislature.

Brown Austin decided to focus his lobbying efforts on convincing state legislators that the children of enslaved men and women in Texas should not be deemed free upon birth, detailing "every *reason* I can invent" for why freeing the children of Texas slaves would prove detrimental to the interests of the state and the slaves themselves. Attempting to play on the sentiments of antislavery legislators, Brown argued that freeing children too young—before they could develop skills with which to support themselves—would force those children to depend on handouts and thievery for survival, becoming "a Public pest and continually a subject of correction." Slaveholders would not support such children, Brown Austin pointed out, since "no Master will maintain a large family of young Negroes without receiving some compensation for it." The more humane alternative, he told legislators, would be to enslave those children until they reached at least fourteen years of age, when they would be "possessed of some useful branch of industry whereby they might gain a livelihood—instead of becoming *vagabonds*." Pitching enslavement as a benefit to the enslaved (years before such "positive good" defenses of slavery became common in the southern United States), Brown Austin and Baron de Bastrop lobbied every legislator who would listen to them.[32]

Their most important inroads came with a group of Coahuilan liberals based in the towns of Monclova and Parras, whose interests in promoting the economic development of northeastern Mexico exceeded their objections to chattel slavery. Led by José María and Agustín Viesca, this faction of the Saltillo legislature prized the rapid economic development of the region above all else, and its members had been deeply impressed by the power of the cotton trade to bring both American immigrants and foreign capital into northern Mexico during the early 1820s. The Viesca faction had been Bastrop's key ally in passing the 1825 state colonization law, and the baron appealed again to its desires to expand American immigration and investment in Texas. Sustaining slavery, Brown and Bastrop explained, was the singular key to sustaining American immigration, which was itself the key to securing a prosperous economic future by tying northeastern Mexico into the expanding global cotton market. Several of these Coahuilans—most notably the Viesca brothers and Victor Blanco, then serving as governor of the state—joined the Anglo-Tejano alliance.[33]

When Article 13 finally came up for debate on the floor of the state Congress in late November 1826, Austin and Bastrop remained unsure what their backroom wrangling of the past few months would bring. Brown was convinced that his recent work with legislators meant that "children born after the publication of the Constitution will not be freed under fourteen," and he remained optimistic that several members of Congress were "inclined not to free them under the age of 25 or 21."[34] Baron de Bastrop commended Brown's efforts, praising "how much he has worked to amend article 13," although the baron was more reserved in his own assessment of what Texas would likely gain from the revised slave law. All the legislators, with the exception of antislavery leader Manuel Carrillo, had given the baron their word "that they will vote so the slaves now in the state remain slaves."[35] Yet the further importation of slaves was certain to be banned, the baron observed, and the age at which children of enslaved parents would be freed remained a point of fierce debate. Although the Texans appeared on the verge of preventing the emancipation of slaves already in northeastern Mexico, it remained to be seen if they could also continue to enslave the children of their laborers.

The far-reaching consequences of the legislature's decision on Article 13 and the fierce lobbying of the Anglo-Tejano alliance prompted Governor Blanco to issue a last-minute appeal to antislavery legislators. On the day the legislature began formal debate on Article 13, Governor Blanco penned a lengthy opinion on the matter that he forwarded to Congress. The governor noted that the issue of slavery placed two fundamental rights into direct conflict—"liberty and property, which are the greatest interests in regularly organized societies"—yet his primary concern was the potential depopulation of northeastern Mexico, as immediate abolition seemed likely to plunge the Anglo colonies in Texas into chaos. Recent reports from San Antonio and Nacogdoches warned that factions of Anglo colonists were "conspiring against the authorities" to resist the freeing of slaves in the region, warnings that resonated with the governor.[36] He begged the Congress to avoid "disastrous results" by instead approving a course of gradual emancipation: permit masters to retain possession of slaves already in the state, while outlawing the slave trade and freeing the children of the enslaved.[37]

On November 30, 1826, Article 13 was read before the Congress—along with the petitions of Stephen F. Austin and the Tejanos in San Antonio— and opened for formal debate. José María Viesca, serving as president of the Congress, began the discussion by pointing out that the philanthropic goals of the article, while laudable and important, were nonetheless unattainable in light of the state's dismal financial condition. Although committed to the idea of universal emancipation in principle, the committee that drafted Article 13 also "always knew the impossibility of freeing the slaves in the state all at once because the funds of the state are very short for compensating the masters for their slaves' value." Because immediate emancipation was not possible, Viesca asked to hear the opinions of his fellow legislators about how best to handle revisions to the constitution's provisions regarding the future of slavery.[38] The informal agreements forged in backroom negotiations during the past several months were now to be tested on the floor of the Saltillo Congress, where the discussion would establish a formal framework for rewriting the constitution's most controversial article.[39]

Some Coahuilans doubted that the state's constitution was the best venue for handling issues as vexing as slavery and emancipation. Dionosio Elizondo, a liberal from northern Coahuila, offered his support for the abolition of the slave trade yet also came down hard against writing emancipation into the state constitution. Elizondo had been taken with the legal writings of Jeremy Bentham, an English jurist and philosopher, and proposed an approach to emancipation patterned after Bentham's arguments in favor of gradual abolition. Forcing emancipation on the Anglo colonies, Elizondo predicted, would be "a violent operation" that "would bring tremendous ills upon the state" by destroying vast amounts of personal property that had been imported under the protection of the national colonization law. Elizondo recommended that Congress instead "adopt softer means" of emancipation by passing a series of laws—such as limiting the right of slaveholders to pass slaves down to their heirs, and setting a standard price for compensating slaveholders for the freeing of a slave—that would eliminate the institution from the region gradually, and without onerous consequences for the state. Beyond outlawing the slave trade itself, Elizondo believed the absoluteness of the constitution made it a poor venue for undertaking the nuanced task of gradual emancipation. "Because the legislator cannot cut the tether of slavery all at once," Elizondo counseled, "he unties it little by little over time, and the march of liberty is no less safe for being slow."[40]

Because most legislators agreed that the constitution should forgo immediate emancipation, the discussion quickly moved toward the question of when to free the children of the enslaved. Viesca recommended that Article 13 be rewritten to ensure that slaves already in Texas would

Rare daguerreotype of the main plaza in Saltillo, Coahuila, taken during the 1847–48 U.S. invasion of northern Mexico. The Saltillo slavery debates likely took place in a building facing this plaza. (Collection of Western Americana, Beinecke Rare Book and Manuscript Library, Yale University)

remain enslaved for life and to include a six-month extension for American colonists to import new slaves after the publication of the constitution. Both suggestions met no challenges. As for the children of those enslaved men and women, Viesca proposed that they be held as slaves themselves until they were twenty-five years old, "when they can think with judgment and maturity." Viesca acknowledged that most legislators hoped to emancipate the children of slaves by the age of fourteen, but he spoke out against the idea by employing Brown Austin's argument that such a move would free children before they developed the ability to support themselves. "If you give them freedom at 14 years of age," reasoned Viesca, "it would not accomplish anything but to fill the state with corrupt men who will be parasites on society." Viesca had apparently been swayed by Brown's backroom arguments and now deployed the Texan's logic on the floor of the state Congress.[41]

True to Baron de Bastrop's prediction, the precise timing of emancipation for the second generation of Texas slaves proved a flashpoint of debate. Santiago de Valle, a representative from northern Coahuila, challenged José María Viesca's contention that twenty-five years was the proper age for freedom. "The children of slaves should not be made to suffer the enormous imprisonment of slavery for so long," asserted Valle, who offered his own proposal for how Article 13 might be rewritten. His version would free enslaved children at the age of fourteen, when, Valle believed, they would still be young enough to devote a few years of work toward purchasing the freedom of their parents. By making the children of slaves instruments for freeing their parents, Valle's plan promised a more rapid path toward full emancipation and a means for compensating slaveholders without depleting the state treasury. Dionisio Elizondo eagerly seconded the proposal as a clever scheme for enlarging the reach of freedom throughout Coahuila and Texas. Viesca, however, objected to the enterprise as wholly unrealistic, pointing out that Valle's proposal rested on the assumption that fourteen-year-olds would voluntarily take it upon themselves to work for the freedom of their parents. "If the children are ingrates," as Viesca argued that boys and girls just entering puberty were likely to be, "they would serve nothing to their parents."[42]

With no one willing to yield on the matter, Article 13 was sent back to the drafting committee for rewriting without a consensus on the age at which enslaved children would be freed. Most of the important details over how the revised state constitution would deal with slavery and freedom, however, appeared to be settled. Those already enslaved in Texas, legislators agreed, would remain the lifelong property of their masters. Yet slavery as an institution in the region was being placed on a slow road to extinction. Six months after the publication of the state constitution, the importation of slaves into Texas would become illegal. The Congress also agreed that children of enslaved parents in the region would eventually be freed, even if legislators continued to bicker over the age at which that should happen. This meant that the closing of the international slave trade to northeastern Mexico would be fundamentally different from what had happened in the United States. There would be no self-reproducing class of enslaved laborers in the Texas colonies, as had developed in the American South, to continue working the cotton fields of the Anglo colonists. The current generation of slaves in northeastern Mexico, the Saltillo Congress had decided, would be the last to be enslaved for life.

Rebellion and Rumors

As the Saltillo Congress considered rewriting Article 13, an uprising among Texas colonists dominated U.S. newspaper coverage of events in northeastern Mexico and revealed the extent to which the Saltillo debates had entangled questions of slavery and emancipation within the American imagination of Mexico's northern territories. The man at the center of the revolt, Haden Edwards, was a land speculator recently arrived from Mississippi who secured an empresario contract in 1825 from the Saltillo legislature. Covering much of the easternmost portion of Texas, the Edwards grant included the town of Nacogdoches and a motley band of French, Spanish, Mexican, and American squatters who had filtered in and out of the region over the course of several decades and now made their homes on lands near the U.S.-Mexican border. When Edwards arrived in Nacogdoches in the fall of 1825, he posted notices declaring that anyone already living within the boundaries of his grant must present valid titles for their land. Those who could not prove legal ownership, warned Edwards, would have their land confiscated and sold. Although many of these settlers had lived in the territory surrounding Nacogdoches for decades, most did not possess legal titles to their land. Edwards soon found himself locked in a fierce struggle with longtime residents of eastern Texas.[43]

Complaints about Edwards began pouring into San Antonio, where political chief Saucedo was already upset with the new empresario for declaring himself the military commander of eastern Texas. The situation deteriorated rapidly as Edwards's heavy-handed ways (at one point he annulled an election so he could install his son-in-law as mayor of Nacogdoches) continued to alienate Anglos and Tejanos alike, prompting the governor of Coahuila-Texas to inform Edwards that he had "lost the confidence of this government."[44] Reports of Edwards's ill behavior eventually reached the desk of the president of Mexico, Guadalupe Victoria, who revoked his empresario grant and ordered Saucedo to expel the American from Mexico. A disgruntled Edwards responded by riding into Nacogdoches in December 1826 at the head of a dozen armed men, who promptly took over the town. Edwards and his posse then launched a rebellion, declaring Texas to be the independent "Republic of Fredonia" and promising to throw off Mexican rule as "the yoke of an imbecile, faithless, and despotic government, miscalled a Republic."[45]

Stephen F. Austin saw in the Fredonian rebellion the potential destruction of recent Anglo-Tejano progress in carving out protections for slavery in the state constitution. Austin immediately sent messages to rebels he knew personally, pleading with them to abandon the rebellion. Arguing that "the people in your quarter have run mad or worse," Austin warned that the insurrection could extinguish all hope of preserving the right of Anglo colonists to hold slaves in northeastern Mexico. "The slave question is now pending in the Legislature, the constitution now forming," Austin seethed in his letter. "What influence are acts of this outrageous character calculated to have on the minds of the members and on the decission of the slave or any other question involving the interests and prosperity of the new Settlements?" Fearing that the Fredonian rebellion could give Manuel Carrillo's antislavery coalition control of the ongoing slavery debate in Saltillo, Austin urged the rebels to surrender themselves immediately to Mexican authorities as the "one way for you all to save yourselves and *only one*."[46]

News of the Fredonian rebellion soon made its way into the United States. The earliest rumblings of the revolt appeared in Louisiana's newspapers, first in villages near the U.S.-Mexican border and then in New Orleans.[47] Reporting on the rebellion in early January 1827, the *Louisiana Advertiser* in New Orleans interwove rumors of the uprising with unconnected reports that "slavery shall be abolished" in the new Coahuila-Texas constitution. The editor of the *Advertiser* made clear his own doubts that Mexican moves toward abolition had motivated the Fredonians, calling slavery "the pretended cause of the revolution," although he acknowledged that many in New Orleans believed the two were somehow related.[48] When copies of the New Orleans story arrived in New York City three weeks later aboard the brig *Arcturus*, they were rushed to the offices of local newspapers. The editor of the *New York Daily Advertiser* decided to reprint the New Orleans report of the rebellion, though he cut out the sections disclaiming slavery as a cause of the uprising as he fit the story into the space available for the next day's edition. As a result, the *Daily Advertiser* hit the streets on February 8, 1827, with an article that tightly interwove news of the Fredonian revolt with reports of the Coahuila Congress's attempts to outlaw slavery in northeastern Mexico.[49] As copies of the *Daily Advertiser* began circulating throughout the northeastern United States, where the story was subsequently reprinted by other newspapers, it was left to readers to somehow discern that the Fredonian rebellion and controversies over slavery in Texas were not related.[50]

Soon American newspaper editors began asserting that the Fredonians had revolted in order to preserve slavery within the Texas borderlands. When the *Niles' Weekly Register* published news of the rebellion on March 17, 1827, the newspaper reported that "the objection of the *Fredonians* to the Mexican government was, that it would not admit of *slavery*."[51] The

New York Observer published a similar piece, asserting that the rebellion "appears to have been occasioned by the new law prohibiting the importation of slaves into the Mexican dominions; or as some accounts say, abolishing slavery altogether."[52] The account in the antislavery *Observer*, which was reprinted throughout the northeastern United States, praised Mexico for embracing universal emancipation and chided the Fredonians as "advocates for the liberty of enslaving others."[53] At least one newspaper, confused by the various second- and third-hand accounts circulating, even reported that the Fredonians themselves had abolished slavery.[54] Mistaken though they were, by the spring of 1827 many U.S. newspapers had encouraged readers to imagine the revolt as an uprising of American slaveholders fighting to preserve the future of slavery in northeastern Mexico.

This sort of press was sure to dissuade potential colonists in the southern United States from considering migration. The disputes that led to the Fredonian rebellion were not themselves about slavery, and the revolt itself failed within a matter of weeks because so few Anglos rallied to its cause. Yet the timing of the insurrection, coming upon the heels of the Saltillo slavery debates, meant that many in the United States understood the uprising as a stand by Americans against Mexican antislavery legislation. Reports bandied about in U.S. newspapers of American slaveholders rebelling against Mexican abolitionism helped foment an image of the Texas borderlands as an unstable region where cotton planters clashed violently with the Mexican government. Such stories would prove highly effective at dissuading potential colonists in the southern United States from considering migration to Mexico, creating problems that American empresarios and Tejano leaders could not easily undo, no matter what the Saltillo legislature decided.

Constitution of 1827

As Americans read alarming reports about antislavery in Mexico, the debates over slavery's place in the Coahuila-Texas state constitution resumed in Saltillo. On January 31, 1827, the newly revised version of Article 13 was read before the Congress: "In the state no one is born a slave and six months after the publication of this constitution in each center of the state the introduction of slaves will not be permitted under any pretext."[55] The revisions represented a significant shift from the article's original thrust, in that it no longer promised to free slaves already present in northeastern Mexico. It would, however, end the importation of slaves following a six-month period, and promised freedom upon birth to the children of enslaved parents.

The proslavery bloc in Texas continued its relentless lobbying during the winter, focusing on selling the extension of slavery as a humanitarian effort. Before debate could resume on Article 13, the Congress read a new petition recently received from Stephen F. Austin that urged the Saltillo Congress to extend the period during which Anglos could import slaves as a means for expanding liberty and freedom. The enslaved men and women that American colonists brought to Mexico, Austin pointed out, were already enslaved in the United States. As such, "to extend the time for introducing slaves is not to make new slaves of free people" but would instead grant those slaves "the consolation of seeing their descendants freed." If the Saltillo legislature truly wanted to extend liberty in North America, he insisted, then it should permit colonists to continue importing new slaves into Texas because that would guarantee freedom to future generations and thereby "serve the cause of humanity." With similar reasoning, Austin pushed for the children of enslaved parents to remain slaves at least until they were twenty-five years old. Emancipated black people, he explained, would never attain high standing in society. Thus they needed to be trained "to be laborers and servants" in order to survive, and he could think of no better school for that than slavery. This was for the good of the enslaved, argued Austin, just as it had been for children in ancient Rome who were not free from the rule of their fathers until they reached their twenty-fifth birthday.[56] If adopted wholesale, Austin's proposals promised to push back emancipation in northeastern Mexico by at least thirty years, giving American settlers the time needed to develop the region's agricultural promise and perhaps secure more favorable slave laws from a future legislature.

Once debate over Article 13 resumed, however, it became clear that the Anglo-Tejano alliance had lost ground during the winter months as its proposal to enslave black children lost support among legislators. During the November 1826 debates, Dionisio Elizondo had argued for gradual emancipation and supported Santiago de Valle's proposal that the children of enslaved parents become free at the age of fourteen. In the months since, however, Elizondo had reconsidered the matter. The legislator from northern Coahuila now spoke forcefully against Valle's plans, arguing that the Congress should not endorse slavery any more than absolutely necessary. The source of Elizondo's shift in thinking, as he explained it, was his commitment to liberalism as the foundational framework of the state constitution. If the constitution was to be founded on "the gentle principles of the most liberal philanthropy," as Elizondo believed it should, that document could not embrace an institution that was fundamentally opposed to liberalism's principles. Slavery was the polar opposite of what he believed the new state constitution was meant to embody, and so Elizondo argued that if Article 13 endorsed enslaving anyone—even temporarily—it would undermine the concept of human liberty that served as the foundation of the constitution.[57]

Elizondo, and perhaps others, had also come to be frustrated by what he saw as the undue political influence wielded by American colonists in the rewriting of Article 13. The legislator recognized that the machinations of the Tejanos and Anglo settlers—and their alliance with the Viesca faction of the Saltillo Congress—had succeeded in blunting much of the immediacy of the abolitionist intent of Article 13. One of the greatest coups on that front, and especially frustrating to Elizondo, was the opening of a six-month window during which Texans could import new slaves into the state, who would then remain enslaved for life. "That, it seems to me, was very much arranged in consideration for the many individuals in Austin's colony," Elizondo noted with displeasure on the floor of the Congress. Although he wanted to make the constitution's ban on slave trafficking immediate, Elizondo recognized he could not overcome the political coalition supporting Anglo-Tejano efforts to allow further slave importations for at least a short period of time. Nevertheless, Elizondo made his disdain evident when he mocked Austin's arguments in favor of extending the six-month window to five years as an indirect means of increasing freedom. "Citizen Austin says that to delay the end of introducing slaves is not to create new slaves of free men," he announced to his fellow legislators. "The same would be a reason for us to never prohibit slavery, since until now everyone is aware that admitting new slaves is not to enslave free men."[58]

Because no other legislator appeared to support Texan proposals to extend further the period for legal slave importations, the debates continued to center on when to free the children of enslaved parents. Elizondo asked his fellow legislators to imagine themselves in the position of those unfortunate children, arguing that the Congress should do the right thing "even though the laws may demand means for maintaining and educating the orphaned." José María Viesca finally brought the impasse to an end by suggesting they defer to a future legislature the question of how to care for the freed children of the enslaved. Weary of the debate, and with few objecting to the central thrust of the revised version, the legislators finally approved Article 13. They published it in Saltillo with the completed constitution on March 11, 1827, and in its final form Article 13 remained unchanged from the revisions that had taken place between November 1826 and January 1827: "In the state no one is born a slave, and six months after the publication of this constitution in the centers of each part of the state neither will the introduction of slaves be permitted under any pretext."[59]

The position on slavery adopted by the 1827 Constitution of Coahuila and Texas was, at base, a compromise. Anglo colonists and the Tejano elite, through strenuous lobbying, had played a heavy hand in determining the final version of Article 13. By lining up strategic support in the Congress through Baron de Bastrop, the Anglo-Texans and Tejanos had managed to wield greater influence in the state legislature than their single representative could have managed alone, and thereby pressured the Saltillo Congress into making significant changes in the interest of Texas's long-term development. Bringing the Viesca faction of the state legislature into their proslavery alliance played a key role in that success, and the end result was an Article 13 far different from its original design: instead of immediately abolishing slavery outright, the constitution established a long-term framework for gradual abolition to come to northeastern Mexico. In the process, the constitution implicitly endorsed the continued lifelong enslavement of African people already in the region by making no provision for their freedom and by opening a six-month window for future slave importations. At least through the fall of 1827, settlers from the United States would be able to continue bringing enslaved people into northeastern Mexico under the protection of Mexican law.

Yet, despite its compromises, the Constitution's provisions leaned more heavily toward the goals of antislavery Coahuilans than they did the wishes of proslavery forces in Texas. While Anglo settlers had prevented the Mexican state from forcibly emancipating their slaves, the institution itself was still on a course to be eliminated from all of Coahuila and Texas. None of the legislators had supported the Texas petitions to extend the period for importing slaves, and within six months such trafficking would become illegal. Despite numerous attempts by the Anglo colonists—and even by some sympathetic legislators—to enslave black children born on Texas plantations, those children would be deemed free citizens of the state upon their birth. For Coahuilan legislators like Manuel Carrillo and Dionisio Elizondo, the original goal of immediate abolition in Article 13 had been traded away in exchange for antislavery provisions that committed the state to embracing freedom within a generation. For empresarios like Stephen F. Austin and the Tejano leadership in San Antonio, the constitution's slave provisions pitted important short-term gains against significant long-term challenges. While there would be no widespread confiscation of enslaved property by the state, Texas officials would be hard pressed to convince new settlers from the United States to move with their slaves to Mexican territory.

Seeds of Change

Knowing how close the Saltillo legislature had come to outlawing slavery entirely, Stephen Austin believed the final version of Article 13 represented the best compromise that American colonists could expect for the moment. In public, Austin worked to suppress simmering discontent among his colonists over the state's embrace of gradual abolition. When the new state constitution was published and read aloud in San Felipe de Austin in May 1827, Austin made a point of standing before the assembled settlers to extol the document's virtues. "The constitution is liberal and Republican," he assured them, "and its just and enlightened administration" promised that "the security of persons and property" would be "solemnly guaranteed" in Texas. Austin's only allusion to contentious issues such as slavery was to point out that "the power of Amendment" offered the colonists the ability to remedy any "evils or embarassments" that existed in the constitution.[60] In correspondence with relatives, however, Austin urged his extended family to migrate with their slaves to Texas before the importation ban could take effect. In one letter, Austin tried to reassure his brother-in-law, James Perry, that the new constitution's failure to effect immediate emancipation meant that enslaved property would continue to be protected by the Coahuila-Texas government. "Every thing you may have seen in the news papers relative to slaves being taken away from the settlers and freed is all false," he insisted.[61]

Austin's focus on the newspapers reflected his understanding that the fractious Saltillo slavery debates had already wrought painful effects on immigration from the United States, the evidence of which now arrived regularly in the mail. When James Davis rode into Nashville, Tennessee, in January 1827, he discovered reports in the local newspaper that Mexico "was about to prohibit the introduction of slavery." Davis had been driving several slaves toward Texas, hoping to establish a plantation in Austin's colony. But reading the newspapers had forced him to put his plans on hold in order to write Austin about the matter. "I have a strong inclination to live in the country," Davis told Austin, but he warned that the outlawing of slavery in Mexico would "be a bar to my removing to that delightful country." Davis hoped Austin could reassure him that the rumors were unfounded. "I have many relations and friends who wish to move with me," wrote Davis, and "the prohibition of slavery into your country will be a bar to most of them."[62] And Davis's concerned voice was just one among a growing chorus. "The manner in which the slave question is desided," warned Benjamin Milam, "will be a grait objection to the American population and I fear will put a Suden stop" to immigration from the United States.[63]

Austin, of course, had everything to lose if migration from the United States dried up. The appeal of Texas lands had attracted a steady stream of American families by the late 1820s, allowing Austin to expand his enterprise rapidly and secure three additional colonization contracts from Saltillo. "The settlers are beginning to reap the fruits of their labors," he observed. "They have opened extensive farms, and the produce of the soil far exceeds their most sanguine expectations. A number of cotton gins and mills are in operation and several more are building."[64] Even San Felipe de Austin, the empresario's makeshift capital along the Brazos River, had grown into a village "of forty or fifty wooden houses" with "nearly two hundred persons," and it now boasted two general stores that sold goods carted in from the United States.[65] Yet Austin recognized that the stability and future of his settlements hinged entirely on the continued movement of Americans into the region. Each new settler who carved out a farm or plantation along the banks of the Brazos and Colorado Rivers added to the security of the Anglo colonies by increasing their population and thereby making the region more appealing for future migrants. Each new family that arrived increased the value of Austin's enterprise by expanding the network of roads, trails, and ferry crossings that—along with the rivers—served as arteries of travel and trade. Losing that momentum of people and capital could easily reverse the hard-won development of his colony.

The abject failure of every other empresario in Texas demonstrated how fickle American migration into northern Mexico could be. During the 1820s, the Saltillo government issued contracts to more than two dozen would-be American empresarios, each of whom hoped to replicate Austin's success. Not one of them, however, ever managed to fulfill his contract. Haden Edwards had been the most spectacular of these failures, but he joined a long line of others—including Benjamin Milam, Sterling Robertson, Frost Thorn, Arthur Wavell, John Woodbury, and David Burnett—who never settled more than a handful of Americans in the territory. The closest to success was Green DeWitt, whose colony lay along the southwestern border of Austin's settlements. Yet by 1830 the entire population of DeWitt's colony amounted to a mere 377 people, and a year later the state legislature refused to renew his colonization contract.[66]

Austin achieved more than his competitors, in part, because he possessed a rare diplomatic talent for working effectively with both American settlers and Mexican officials that, when combined with his dogged work ethic, won him the public support he needed to build his settlement. But Austin also succeeded where others failed because as early as the mid-1820s his colony was seen by potential migrants as the most established one available and thus the most secure. When weighing all the risks that came with beginning a new life in Mexico, most Americans preferred the relative security of Austin's established colonies over the relative insecurity of any of the other less established empresario grants. A focus on security helped Austin by funneling more Americans migrants into his colonies, but it also revealed in stark detail just how easily U.S. perceptions of Mexico—particularly in regard to slavery—could shift and disrupt the movement of Americans.

Any disruption in migration, in turn, threatened the territory's expanding cotton industry. As Austin's colony grew during the late 1820s, so had the number of bales coming out of the Texas settlements. In 1827 the Mexican commander at Nacogdoches estimated that Anglo colonists shipped around 400,000 pounds of cotton annually to Louisiana—a number that meshed with similar estimates by Austin and other Mexican officials. By the end of the 1820s, Anglo farmers in Texas likely exported somewhere between 350,000 and 450,000 pounds of cotton annually, which meant that local production had roughly doubled in the handful of years since 1825. There was, in fact, virtually no other commerce in eastern Texas (the next most profitable industry was a small trade in animal hides) because Austin's settlers overwhelmingly poured their resources and capital into cotton.[67]

That growing cotton commerce continued to integrate the eastern portions of Texas ever more tightly into the global textile markets. Nearly

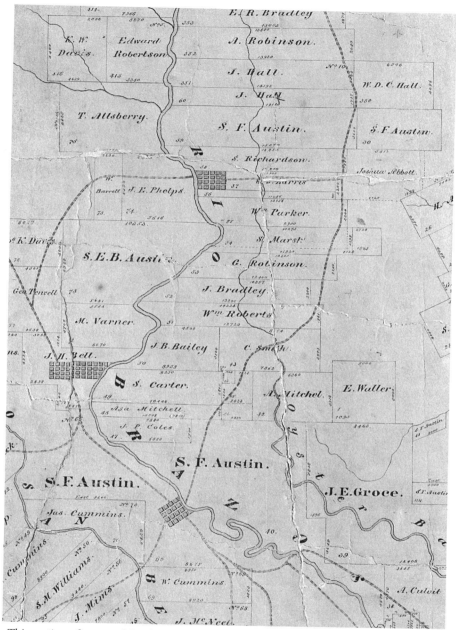

This section of a map of Stephen F. Austin's colony reveals how the growth of Anglo settlements followed the rivers and created new roads throughout eastern Texas. It also shows how Austin reserved large tracts for himself and his family. (Detail of "Connected Map of Austin's Colony, 1833–1837" [1892], #1944, Map Collection, Archives and Records Program, Texas General Land Office, Austin)

all of the cotton bales produced in Austin's settlements came down the Brazos and Colorado Rivers to the coast, where they boarded ships bound for New Orleans. Once aboard, the bales entered a complex trading system that swept cotton from the Gulf of Mexico into the textile factories of eager buyers on both sides of the Atlantic Ocean. Texas bales first made their way to the New Orleans port, where an agent for one of the local merchant houses (usually contacted in advance by the farmer) claimed them and arranged for each bale to be carted to a nearby warehouse. Working on behalf of the farmer, the New Orleans agent then had the cotton weighed, graded for quality, insured against loss, and properly stored. The merchant house, hoping for a quick sale, hustled to secure the best prices for the bales. Whenever they succeeded, the New Orleans firm took a cut—usually 2.5 percent of the profits—and sent a letter notifying the farmer of the sale and how much credit he now had on his account, which could then be used to settle debts, purchase new supplies, or send money wherever needed.

If the Anglo colonists looked to Saltillo and Mexico City for favorable laws, they depended just as heavily on New Orleans merchants for financing. The work of plowing, planting, maintaining gins, replacing equipment, harvesting, and generally keeping a farm in operation required a steady flow of funds. Settlers also needed access to goods they could not make themselves—such as baling line, barrels, cut lumber, saddles, rifles, hoes, and all manner of tools, as well as occasional luxury items like books and premade clothing. Louisiana merchants made these items available to Anglos in northern Mexico by extending lines of credit, which could be used to finance the supplies necessary to plant and harvest their fields. Those lines of credit, in turn, served essentially as liens on the farmer's cotton crop, to be repaid—with interest—at the next harvest. The system allowed merchants to make money on both the growing and selling of cotton. For farmers, there was no other way to secure the financing necessary for their farms or to secure goods for their families between harvests. And because almost no cash changed hands, the system made it possible to bring capital investments into a frontier territory where hard currency was never seen.[68] By trading in Texas cotton, merchants in New Orleans thus provided much of the financing that made it possible for Americans to migrate into northern Mexico.

Tejanos, too, continued to expand and rely on these same trade connections with New Orleans and markets in the southern United States. The small population of Tejanos living around Nacogdoches had become so deeply entangled with the Louisiana markets that one frustrated official from Mexico City grumbled that "accustomed to the continued trade with the North Americans they have adopted their customs and habits, and one may say truly that they are not Mexicans except by birth."[69] For Tejanos in San Antonio, a relative peace that prevailed with the Comanches and other tribes during the late 1820s had allowed them the security necessary to expand their trading runs to the U.S. border.[70] José Antonio Navarro passed through the Anglo colonies regularly on his purchasing trips to New Orleans, where he bought goods to sell in San Antonio and across northern Mexico. Yet one of the tangible benefits of the growing trade between Louisiana and Austin's colonies was that Navarro could now secure goods even without undertaking such an arduous journey, as Austin often served as a buying agent for Navarro and arranged for the purchase and shipping of goods on his behalf.[71]

Other Tejano merchants used the Anglo colonies and associations with Austin to their own economic advantage. Ramon Músquiz, who became political chief for Texas in 1828, maintained a close relationship with the empresario and—like Navarro—sometimes asked Austin to secure goods on his behalf (at one point he even asked Austin for prices on cotton gins, as his brother-in-law Victor Blanco was considering entering the cotton business himself). When Juan Seguín and Juan Martín de Veramendi traveled to New Orleans during the fall of 1826, they first made their way to San Felipe de Austin to pick up personal letters of introduction from Austin to various merchants in New Orleans.[72] Connections to Stephen F. Austin—who was well known among the New Orleans trade houses—apparently opened doors for Tejano merchants in the Crescent City, and the Seguín and Veramendi families took full advantage. When Tejanos arrived in New Orleans, they could see the piled-up bales of cotton along the waterfront that represented the heart of expanding U.S.-Texas commerce. As much as for the Anglos in Texas, those bales offered Tejanos the possibility of a prosperous future that integrated the Texas borderlands into an expanding and lucrative international marketplace.

If they watched cotton being sold in New Orleans, Tejanos like Seguín, Navarro, and Veramendi likely also saw Texas bales being loaded onto ships sailing out of the Gulf of Mexico. Many of those bales went to New York City, the primary port serving the growing manufacturing industry of the northeastern United States, and some made their way to France. But the great majority were bound for England, where Britain's manufacturing operation had become one of the largest in the world. English textile mills centered in Lancashire County processed raw cotton into a vast array of products—ranging from coarse calicoes to luxurious colorful cloths—that sold at high prices across Britain's expanding commercial empire. By the late 1820s, finished cotton goods made up fully half of the entire export trade coming out of Great Britain, which meant that British mills bought raw cotton on a massive scale. In 1830 they imported more than 263 million pounds of cotton, about 85 percent of which came from the southern United States. Indeed, by the early 1830s, English buyers purchased two-thirds of all bales sold in places like New Orleans. That meant that two of every three Texas bales sold in Louisiana markets eventually found their way aboard British ships steaming across the Atlantic. After a month at sea, the bales were unloaded at Liverpool—England's primary cotton port—and then shipped overland to mills towns like Manchester and Preston, where plants grown in Texas would be woven into English fabric to be sold in the Atlantic market.[73]

The intricate connections between these markets and the fights over slavery and migration in the Texas borderlands can be seen most clearly in how Stephen Austin reacted to a challenge to the U.S. cotton industry shortly after the Saltillo slavery debates. In May 1828 the U.S. Congress enacted a tariff aimed at protecting domestic manufacturing and industry in the northeastern states from competition with British-made goods. Furious cotton farmers in the southern United States immediately protested the measure, dubbing it the "Tariff of Abominations," out of fear that the British would respond by cutting back on imports of U.S. cotton. Reading about these debates in the newspapers, Austin became convinced that trade disputes between England and the United States could open the door for Texas farmers to displace U.S. planters as the primary cotton supplier to British textile mills. In lengthy proposals to the president of Mexico, his senator in the national Congress, the minister of foreign relations, the commandant of the eastern interior provinces, and the governor of Coahuila-Texas, Austin proclaimed that "Mexican cotton can fill the void in the English market caused by the exclusion of the United States" and suggested that "the arrival of a single ship in Liverpool loaded with good-quality Mexican cotton would have a huge influence." Now was the time, Austin urged, for the government to put policies into place to foster a highly profitable cotton industry that would benefit all of Mexico. "It seems to me that the Mexican nation can take great advantage of this fight between those two nations," the empresario advised, "if it can encourage the Mexican people to dedicate themselves to growing cotton."[74]

For Austin, Texas had an unprecedented opportunity to become a more appealing place to grow cotton than anywhere in the southern United States, opening the floodgates to a crush of American farmers eager for Mexican cotton lands. In a letter to the governor of Coahuila-Texas, Austin outlined three measures he believed necessary for Mexico to adopt in order to overtake the United States in supplying the British textile market: promote the rapid populating of Anglo colonies in Texas; allow for duty-free importation of cotton gins and baling equipment; and establish a trade agreement with England "favorable to the interests of the cotton farmers." The linchpin of Austin's plan, of course, was lifting existing restrictions on slavery in the region. "Only article 13 of our constitution is preventing many wealthy and powerful people from moving to Texas," Austin informed the governor. If the state government were to endorse slavery, thus opening northeastern Mexico to an exodus of disgruntled American farmers looking for a new place to grow cotton for export to England, Austin promised that "in a very few years the State of Coahuila and Texas will have more wealth and trade than any other state in the entire Mexican federation."[75]

Abolishing the Name

Yet antislavery Coahuilans moved instead to strengthen the region's prohibitions on slavery. José Francisco Madero, a liberal from northern Coahuila with close connections to the antislavery Elizondo family, led a renewed charge in the state Congress for stronger antislavery laws. "If all knew like me the hard and cruel treatment with which the Anglo Americans treat the slaves," Madero told his fellow legislators, "they would provide a means for saving them and perhaps would have written differently the second part of Article 13 of the constitution." Madero acquired his mistrust of American slaveholders from his travels to New Orleans, where he spent time along the docks of the largest shipping and slave-trading port in the southern United States. While in a New Orleans café one day, Madero overheard some Americans arguing that "negroes were the same as mules and should be treated as such." The comment stuck with Madero, who realized that Americans' famous devotion to liberty and freedom was entirely contingent upon race, and did not extend to "the unhappy men who only for being colored black have been sold as if they were things." "These ideas that so much degrade the men who proclaim so greatly liberalism," Madero thundered to his fellow legislators, "I do not think the colonists of Austin, the Colorado and Guadalupe have abandoned them on the other side of the Sabine."[76]

In concert with two fellow Coahuilans, Madero proposed a new law that would institute a five-hundred-peso fine for anyone caught exporting a pregnant slave back to the United States (owing to Madero's fears that Anglos would seek to avoid Article 13's requirements to free the children of their slaves) and mandated that whenever a master died that at least 10 percent of his slaves be freed by the state. The heart of this new law, however, was a requirement that each jurisdiction in Coahuila and Texas maintain a census of all nearby enslaved men, women, and children (which local authorities had to update every three months or face a five-hundred-peso fine) that would prevent Anglo slaveholders from hiding slaves in order to avoid the enforcement of gradual emancipation throughout the region. As they laid out their proposal, Madero and his compatriots drew heavily on the work of European philosophers, such as the French enlightenment thinker Charles-Louis Montesquieu (quoting extensively from the philosopher's arguments that in a democracy "slaves are contrary to the spirit of the constitution") and the abolitionist writings of British jurist Jeremy Bentham (whose proposals for gradual emancipation had surfaced during the Saltillo slavery debates and continued to hold weight among intellectuals in Coahuila). Despite strenuous objections from Texas—Austin protested that "the result would be to eliminate emigration in its entirety" and "the state of Coahuila-Texas will be reduced to ruin"—the passage of this law in September 1827 demonstrated the resilience of antislavery sentiment in certain quarters of northern Mexico.[77]

Authorities in Texas countered by simply refusing to comply, and the inability of the Coahuila-Texas state government to enforce such laws meant that the statute had essentially no effect on the lives of enslaved people or the operations of Texas plantations. When copies of the law arrived in San Antonio, the Tejano leadership had them duly published and forwarded to the centers of the Texas colonies in San Felipe de Austin and Nacogdoches.[78] Registrars were identified for taking the census of slaves in Texas, but neither the Anglo settlers nor the Tejano leadership apparently had any intention of following the law. By the summer of 1828, no census of the slaves in Texas had yet arrived in Saltillo, and the political head of Texas, Ramón Músquiz, forwarded a report to the governor of Coahuila-Texas detailing why. The report included two letters from Austin's colony explaining that the slave census had not been collected because local slaveholders did not speak Spanish (and thus did not know that reporting their slaves to local authorities was necessary) and because the planters all lived too far from one another to make visiting each plantation practical.[79] Without troops or any other means of enforcing the decree, there was little the Saltillo Congress could do. While the law remained in effect during the years that followed, there was no serious effort—from either the Tejano leadership in San Antonio or the legislature in Saltillo—to force the Anglo colonists to comply with its demands.

The damage came, instead, from the lasting effects such laws had on migration from the United States, and Stephen Austin received a constant stream of discouraging letters in San Felipe. A man named Henry Brown sent word from New Orleans that Mexico's continued embrace of abolitionism was preventing would-be settlers from making the journey. "If slavery was admitted there or the people Co[u]ld be satisfied that they would be safe in taking there slaves there," Brown explained to Austin, "the emigration would be grate."[80] Richard Ellis wrote a similar letter from his home in northern Alabama. "I have assertained beyond question," he informed Austin, "that 40 or 50 families would emigrate with me next fall to your country if they could introduce their slaves, many of them are large holders of that description of property." Although white Alabamans were eager to settle on cheap cotton lands in Mexico, recent battles between colonists and the Saltillo government over slavery had convinced many to abandon all thoughts of Texas. "Let me know if we will be allowed to bring in slaves under any circumstances," Ellis told Austin, emphasizing that everything "will depend on the *Slave Question*."[81]

With the possible failure of the American colonies looming, Austin gathered the leading settlers of his colony on March 31, 1828, to seek a way around the problem of emancipation. As they debated possible solutions, a consensus emerged to adopt the same scheme that Peter Ellis Bean proposed two years earlier in his letter from Mexico City. "Considering the paralyzed state of immigration to this Jurisdiction from the U.S. arrising from the difficulties encountered by Imigrants in bringing servants and hirelings with them," they declared at the end of their meeting, "this Body conceive it their duty to propose to the Legislature of this state" the need to pass a "Law whereby emigrants and inhabitants of this state may be secured in the Contracts made by them with servants or hirelings in foreign countries."[82] In other words, the Anglo council decided to try Peter Bean's suggestion that the way to avoid the abolition of slavery in northeastern Mexico was to call the institution something other than slavery. On its face, their proposal sounded innocent enough: they would ask the Saltillo legislature for a law guaranteeing that all labor contracts signed in foreign countries would be honored in Mexico. The underlying intent, however, was to create a legal loophole for U.S. slaveholders to force their slaves into lifelong labor contracts, thereby providing legal cover for slavery to continue in Texas under the name of indentured servitude. Such a ruse, they hoped, would circumvent existing antislavery statutes and open the region to renewed migration of masters and "servants" from the southern United States.

The Anglo colonists, in effect, planned to adopt the language of Mexican debt peonage as a means for protecting chattel slavery. Peonage had a long history in northern Mexico, stretching back into the Spanish era, and provided the majority of the labor needs for large ranches and haciendas in Coahuila. Mexican peasants who worked on these ranches invariably became indebted to their masters for room, board, medical care, clothing, and the like. In the process they became tied to the land as they worked endlessly to pay off their debts. While nominally free, these men and women lost control of their labor and their freedom to leave the ranch because their master came to control nearly every aspect of their lives, and often the lives of their extended families. Coahuila's most wealthy and powerful family, the Sánchez Navarros, used thousands of peons to run their expansive haciendas that sprawled out around Monclova, which collectively made up one of the largest ranching operations in North America. These peons often suffered forms of physical abuse and coercion (such as chaining, beatings, and whipping) not much different from practices on American plantations, although most Coahuilans nonetheless saw meaningful differences between peonage and chattel slavery. Austin's colonists, however, planned to blur those distinctions in order to provide legal cover for American slaveholders to continue coming into northern Mexico.[83]

Such an audacious plan needed the support of the Tejano elite in San

Antonio, who would have to make the case for the new law before the state Congress. Stephen Austin sent a draft of the proposal to political chief Ramón Músquiz, along with a letter explaining the desperate need for such a law. San Antonio's leading men shared the colonists' deep misgivings about the future prospects for Texas without American slavery driving its economy. "The evils that article 13 of our constitution have caused Texas are incalculable and as the representation that we have in the legislature is insignificant there is no hope to repair it," Músquiz lamented to Austin. So when the Anglo proposal for circumventing state slavery laws arrived in San Antonio, local Tejanos recognized a prime opportunity to resurrect their hopes for the continued economic development of Texas. Músquiz promised to send the proposal immediately to José Antonio Navarro and José Miguel de Arciniega, the two Tejanos who had replaced Baron de Bastrop in the Saltillo legislature, "so they can move forward in their work on such important matters."[84]

With many in the Coahuilan legislature as opposed to slavery as ever, Navarro and Arciniega knew their proposal would never make it through the Congress unless they concealed its true purpose. The Tejano legislators saw their chance in late April 1828, when the legislature became embroiled in fierce disputes over a bill introduced by conservatives to cut the state budget and centralize power in the state government. While their fellow legislators remained preoccupied, Navarro and Arciniega quietly brought their proposed contract law to the floor of Congress. The purpose of the bill, they told their fellow lawmakers, was to promote the migration of settlers from the free portions of "the United States of North America and principally those from Ohio." Many of these would-be colonists, according to the two Tejanos, needed to contract with men "hiring out their services for two, three or more years" in order to deal with the labor shortage in Texas. Yet, without a law guaranteeing that such contracts would be honored in Mexico, they argued, people from places like Ohio would not migrate to Texas. None of that was true, but their proposal raised no eyebrows among legislators already familiar with a peonage system that followed the same logic. The law passed as Decree 56 on May 5, 1828, providing legal sanction to the scheme hatched by Austin's colonists little more than a month before. Arciniega later explained that the law would never have passed if his fellow legislators had not been distracted by other debates at the time.[85]

Tejanos and Anglos moved quickly to seize the new law's potential for

Photograph of José Antonio Navarro, during his later years. (McArdle Notebooks, Texas State Library and Archives Commission, Austin, Texas)

reinvigorating the immigration of American slaveholders. José Antonio Navarro sent word directly to Austin about their legislative success. "It will sanction the law authorizing contracts made in foreign countries as you desired," Navarro told Austin, "and I have the satisfaction of telling you that it will go out in today's mail."[86] Austin wasted no time in drafting a template contract for American migrants to follow as they crafted legal agreements that would allow them to bring new slaves into Mexican territory. In Austin's example, the contract listed each slave's value and promised those same slaves their freedom after they paid their master for the cost of emancipating them. Because the contract set a slave's "wages" at $20 per year, it would take at least sixty years for a field hand worth $1,200 to be able to claim his freedom. But since the contract mandated that the costs of clothing, food, and housing also be deducted from the slave's wages, freedom would never come. The contract also bound the children of enslaved people to the same terms, although those children would not earn any "wages" toward freedom until either their eighteenth or twenty-fifth birthday. Austin's contract was nothing more than an attempt to redefine chattel slavery as debt peonage, with no meaningful distinction drawn between the two. Yet with the seal of a notary public from the United States on it, such a document would enable Americans to resume importing slaves into northeastern Mexico.[87]

Austin began sending letters to the United States explaining how to circumvent Mexican statutes against slave importations, presumably with copies of his sample contract. The empresario sent a note to Frost Thorn in New Orleans, who was thrilled at the news. "The entelligence I immediately made public," Thorn told Austin, "and am induced to believe the Law will be of great service to this Country. It has made a material change in the feelings of many valuable Emgrants and I will have it published in N. Orleans, that it may have publicity in the U.S." One such emigrant was Amos Edwards, who had recently arrived in New Orleans from his home in Russellville, Kentucky, where he owned ten enslaved men and five enslaved women. Edwards had been driving his slaves toward Texas, hoping to establish a plantation in one of the Anglo colonies, when he learned of the laws preventing the importation of new slaves into Mexican territory. Edwards had been worried about how he would secure his enslaved property, Frost reported to Austin, "but this Law at once places him at ease on the subject." More than likely, Edwards brought his slaves before a local official in New Orleans, where he promised to grant them freedom in exchange for enough labor to compensate him for their value.

With a contract in hand that protected him from emancipation, Edwards could then resume his journey into Mexico to establish his plantation.[88]

BY THE LATE 1820S, Anglos and Tejanos had succeeded in carving out a place for slave-based agriculture in northeastern Mexico, despite strong resistance to those efforts in the Coahuila-Texas Congress. When legislators in Saltillo moved to use the state Constitution as a tool for abolishing slavery, Anglos and Tejanos banded together in an alliance to pressure Congress into pulling back from state-mandated emancipation. Through petitions, protests, negotiations, backroom wrangling, and outright threats, they succeeded in pushing state legislators away from immediately freeing the enslaved people toiling on Texas plantations. Anglos and Tejanos had, in fact, managed to secure assurances that slaves already in Texas would remain enslaved for life, and even achieved the opening of a six-month window for the importation of new slaves into the region. It was a remarkable reversal of the original abolitionist design of Article 13 of the state constitution and helped prevent the widespread abandonment of the American colonies by Anglo planters already growing cotton in Texas.

Yet Anglos and Tejanos also understood that if Texas was ever to realize its full economic potential through cotton commerce, the region needed far more than a loophole underpinning the legality of the labor system that made that possible. Although Coahuilans such as Manuel Carrillo and Dionisio Elizondo had conceded certain liberties to American slaveholders in the short term, they held firm in their commitment to emancipate all enslaved people in the region within a generation. The Saltillo Congress had no ability to enforce those laws, which meant they had almost no effect on the operations of farms and plantations in eastern Texas. But it turned out that the debates themselves—because of their widespread coverage in U.S. newspapers—had been more important than the laws they produced, striking heavy blows against the stream of Americans moving into northern Mexico. With every story that Americans read about antislavery debates in Mexico, it became increasingly difficult for empresarios such as Stephen F. Austin to convince American farmers to establish cotton plantations in Mexico.

Although they could preserve a place for slavery in Mexico, Anglos and Tejanos in Texas had come to understand that they could not build a thriving cotton economy while in conflict with their government. In a letter to a friend in the United States, George Smyth noted that chattel slavery continued unabated on Texas plantations despite abolitionist laws passed in Mexico. "Mexico is said to be a government in which slavery is not tolerated," Smyth told his friend. "They have indeed abolished the name but not the Thing."[89] Yet that name turned out to be of greater consequence than American settlers or Tejano leaders expected. Slavery rested heavily on the understanding that the government stood behind the institution, and the cloud of uncertainty and insecurity that hung over Texas cotton fields had become simply too much for many Americans. The hopes of Anglos and Tejanos to take advantage of the American cotton economy had run headlong into the antislavery convictions of many Coahuilan politicians.

Three weeks after Decree 56 passed the Saltillo Congress, a glowing report appeared in the *New Orleans Halcyon and Literary Repository* about the future prospects of Mexican Texas. "Although little more than seven years have elapsed since the Austins' began their colony near the Rio Grande," reported the newspaper, "it now numbers from 12 to 15,000 souls." The agricultural potential of the region, according to the article, had no rival in North America. "The cotton lands yield astonishing crops of the finest cotton, tobacco and corn—innumerable herds graze on the elevated prairies—and the mountains are known to contain the precious metals." The government of Mexico was depicted as the benevolent patron of American settlers. "The colonists are to be exempt from taxes," crowed the report, "and the merchandize they may import will pay no duties." If anyone harbored doubts about the friendly nature of the Mexican government, the paper tried to reassure them: "The law of Mexico, prohibiting slavery, is evaded by having negroes bound to serve an apprenticeship of 99 years. There are several planters who number 50 or 60 of such apprentices." There was, it seemed, no limit to what could be accomplished under such favorable circumstances.[90]

The situation in northeastern Mexico was not quite as promising as the newspaper led its readers to believe. Migration to Austin's colony had never come close to the heights of fifteen thousand people claimed by the *New Orleans Halcyon*, and the article had likely been written by an American empresario hoping to entice new settlers into the Texas colonies. Although cotton production in the region had grown tremendously by the late 1820s—expanding in proportion to the increases in Anglo population—that industry was now threatened by the growing perception

among Americans that Mexico was a region overtly opposed to enslavement. More than a year after Decree 56 passed, Austin received a letter
concerning a would-be American settler who would not come to Texas
unless Austin wrote to him directly and explained how slaves "could be
introduced, and would be secure" as indentured servants in Mexico.[91] Ner-
vous about abandoning the protections of the United States, the American refused to believe that he could bring slaves into northern Mexico
unless he received assurances directly from Austin himself.

FOUR

Cotton, Slavery, and the
Secession of Texas, 1829–1836

When General Manuel de Mier y Terán arrived on the plantation of Jared Groce in January 1829, he marveled at the sheer size of the operation. Groce maintained an enslaved work force of more than a hundred people who planted and tended their master's fields, Terán observed in his diary, although "nowhere around the house are there cages, prisons, or any other sign that force is necessary to subordinate so many slaves." The general had reached the Texas farm at the end of the picking season, when mountains of raw cotton were being deseeded, processed, and baled for the market. Terán toured the grounds and delighted in the operations of the plantation's cotton gin, recording a detailed description of its mechanics, which had already cleaned 270,000 pounds—600 bales worth—that winter. Groce, like most Texas planters, planned to ship those bales down the Brazos River and on to New Orleans, where they would join cotton from the United States on its way to mills in England. The enterprise revolved around the deft direction of Groce, his son, and their overseer, whose coordinated management of the plantation's massive work force made such immense crop yields possible. The efficiency of the plantation impressed Terán, and its profitability could be seen in the "well dressed" figure of Groce himself.

Upon arriving at the picked-over cotton fields, however, Terán noted the harsh effects that such industry wrought on the Texas landscape. "Although the fields are largely cleared, around the land one sees hundreds of tree trunks that—having been cinched—no longer grow." In clearing their fields for cultivation, the Anglo colonists stripped the bark off each tree's trunk rather than chopping them down. Deprived of their ability to nourish themselves, the trees then slowly rotted away from within, leaving behind only withered stumps. What once had been vast forests thus became open fields ready for cotton seed, providing a visible marker of the transformation American colonization had brought to this section of northern Mexico in only a few years. Although they represented the industriousness of Anglo plantations, vistas of dying trees and rotting stumps struck Terán as a depressing sight. "Gross's fields have a melancholy appearance," the general noted, "because of the enormous skeletons of trees that still stand."[1]

General Terán's ambivalence about what had been lost in the making of Groce's cotton mirrored his growing concern about the trajectory of the Anglo colonies in Texas. Sent by Mexico's national government to inspect the boundary between the United States and Mexico, Terán toured eastern Texas during 1828 and 1829 as part of an unofficial mission to assess the conditions of the American colonies. The growing profitability of those settlements could be seen in piled-up bales of cotton—"industry in this colony is outstanding," noted Terán—and colonization had already enabled Mexico to bring many thousands of new settlers into one of its least populated territories. Yet the increasing dominance of Americans in a portion of Mexico that remained isolated from the rest of the country struck Terán as an insidious trend with potentially disastrous consequences for the Mexican Republic. Anglos-Texans heavily outnumbered Mexicans, Terán observed, and many of them seemed wholly unconcerned with following Mexican law. The general feared the continued Americanization of Texas would, if left unchecked, slowly strip away Mexican authority in Texas in the same methodical manner as the cinched trees rotting in colonists' cotton fields. Terán's tour of the Anglo colonies convinced him that Mexico City had to reassert its power along the northeastern frontier in order to save the territory for Mexico, prompting him to make a bold recommendation to the nation's president: "Settlement by North Americans should be suspended in the territory of Tejas."[2]

Following Terán's counsel, Mexico's national government attempted to reassert its authority in northeastern Mexico during the late 1820s and early 1830s, producing a series of heated clashes and disputes that eventually ended in the secession of Texas. During this period, Texas became swept up in violent political storms raging in Mexico City, as renewed struggles within the Mexican Republic between centralism and federalism reverberated into the country's far-northern territory. Beginning with a national attempt in 1829 to abolish slavery throughout Mexico, followed by a national ban on further immigration from the United States in 1830, Anglos and Tejanos in Texas felt increasingly threatened by Mexico

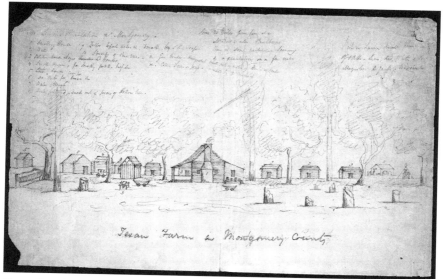

Texan Farm in Montgomery County. This 1843 pencil sketch by William Bollaert centers on the master's cabin, with slave cabins dotting the background. The two structures on the far right are a cotton gin and press, and the stumps in the foreground show how Anglos "cinched" trees in order to clear the land. (The Newberry Library, Chicago, Vault Oversize Ayers Art, Bollaert #49)

City during the first half of the 1830s. Subsequent clashes between Mexican troops and Anglo settlers pushed tensions still higher as the federal government established new military posts within the Anglo settlements. When Antonio López de Santa Anna moved in 1835 to overturn the federal Constitution of 1824 in favor of a centralized government based in Mexico City, Texas joined several other Mexican states in rebelling against the national government.

Questions of cotton and slavery lurked just beneath the surface of disputes surrounding what became known as the "Texas Revolution," as the fights over slavery and colonization that defined the 1820s soon bled into the battles of the 1830s. Everyone acknowledged the central role that plantation agriculture—and its entanglements with slavery—had played in bringing enough Americans into Texas by 1829 to give Mexican officials like Terán serious misgivings about Anglo colonization. Indeed, nearly every dispute between Anglo colonists and the governments in Mexico City and Saltillo during that time revolved around slavery, and Terán recognized the urgency that American settlers attached to the government's approach toward the institution and the cotton economy it supported.

"The most persistent goal for this colony is to obtain permission for the introduction of slaves," Terán wrote in his diary. "Without them they say that their settlement cannot prosper."[3]

The role that slavery played in the secession of Texas from Mexico has been a source of both consensus and conflict among scholars. Most historians argue that slavery played no significant part in bringing on the Texas Revolution and see the onset of the war instead as an almost inevitable clash of cultures between Americans and Mexicans who found themselves too different to remain long under the same government. In this interpretation, military clashes between Anglo settlers and the Mexican government during the early 1830s, followed by the revocation of the 1824 Mexican Constitution, produced the immediate spark for war, although the struggle itself emanated from a deeper problem: the cultural chasm separating Americans and Mexicans.[4] A handful of dissenting historians, however, particularly those who study Mexico, have argued the opposite, claiming that slavery played a central—perhaps defining—role in the outbreak of the revolution. Emphasizing the efforts of American settlers to thwart Mexican antislavery laws, these writers assert that Anglos rebelled from Mexico largely to avoid emancipationist legislation; and so they often dismiss the alarm voiced by Anglo settlers over threats to federalism in Mexico as merely "the pretext for the Texas Revolution" rather than as genuine concern.[5]

Both approaches focus on slavery as an end in itself for the colonists, rather than placing the institution within the larger context of what slavery was meant to support: the agricultural and economic development of Texas. In so doing, both miss how slavery was embedded in broader economic, social, and political changes sweeping across the territory during those crucial years, as tensions surrounding slave-based agriculture in Texas became part of larger battles raging in Mexico over state sovereignty and federalism.[6] Adopting a wider perspective, indeed, reveals how a complex tangle of cotton, slavery, and Mexican federalism—rather than any single factor—produced the fights that eventually led to the Texas Revolution. Officials in Mexico City, for example, sought to exercise a stronger hand in Texas during the 1830s precisely because the lure of Mexican cotton lands had brought so many Americans into the region, where those settlers continued to thwart antislavery laws and Mexican authority generally. Anglos and Tejanos, in response, pushed back against all efforts to rein in the authority of local officials or to limit the movement of people from the United States into the territory because they continued to believe that the prosperity of the region hinged on the immigration of Anglo farmers. These matters finally came to a head when they did because of a global boom in cotton prices during the early 1830s that led to a massive expansion in American migration into northern Mexico. The result was a doubling of the region's Anglo population in only four years that badly exacerbated tensions between those in Texas and dismayed authorities in Mexico City.

Anglos and Tejanos emerged as ardent federalists during this period because their experiences—forged largely in fights over slavery—had convinced them that only people within the Texas borderlands understood the urgent need for policies that would foster rapid economic development of the region. They both became deeply alarmed, therefore, by efforts in Mexico City during the 1830s to limit the sovereignty of individual states within Mexico. When a cabal led by Santa Anna then moved to centralize all authority in Mexico City, Texans rebelled in the name of federalism in order to defend their ability to control the development of the territory. Leaders in other parts of Mexico, such as Zacatecas and Yucatán, also rebelled against centralism in 1835 out of similar convictions about the importance of federalism and preserving local authority. The difference was that in Texas local control meant, among other things, empowering Anglos and Tejanos to foster the region's economic development by supporting slave-based agriculture.

By the mid-1830s, the cotton revolution in North America had brought far-reaching changes to northeastern Mexico, producing dramatic shifts in the region's population, politics, and economics that made Texas increasingly unlike the rest of the country. At precisely that same moment, however, struggles within the early Mexican Republic over state sovereignty finally devolved into civil war, throwing the entire nation into turmoil as authorities in Mexico City sought to rein in wayward places like Texas. It was at the intersection of those powerful forces in northern Mexico— where concerns over Mexican federalism became entangled in the vision that Americans and Tejanos held for Texas as a cotton empire—that we find the underlying causes of the Texas Revolution and the territory's break from Mexico.

President Guerrero and the Viesca Brothers

In the spring of 1829, Stephen F. Austin believed the political fortunes of his colonial enterprise were on the rise. Recent elections in Coahuila had shifted power in the state legislature toward the liberals of Monclova and Parras, the same men who had proved to be such staunch supporters of Anglo colonization during the writing of the Constitution of 1827 and had helped Anglos and Tejanos prevent the state from outlawing slavery outright. Led by the powerful Viesca brothers, José María and Agustín, this faction of the Saltillo legislature saw the development of the Anglo settlements in Texas as the key to ensuring foreign investment in northeastern Mexico and the rapid expansion of the territory's economy. They had become key partners of the Anglo-Tejano alliance, and so the rise of the Viesca faction of the state Congress renewed Austin's hopes for more active and sustained state support for slavery and cotton farming. José María Viesca, in fact, had recently been elected governor, and his brother Agustín served as the nation's prestigious minister of relations in Mexico City, providing Anglos and Tejanos powerful allies in their effort to cultivate favorable conditions for American migration into Texas.

Although many within the Saltillo Congress still staunchly opposed slavery, Austin now received a steady stream of encouraging letters from the state capital. Juan Antonio Padilla, the former secretary of state for Coahuila-Texas, reported that the Congress might annul some of the state's antislavery measures, and Ramón Músquiz, the political chief of Texas, sent notes concerning his ongoing efforts with Texas's representatives in Saltillo to repeal the antislavery laws. These reports, along with the growing influence of the Viesca brothers in state and national politics, emboldened Austin enough to ask the Tejano delegation in Saltillo to push for a suspension of the antislavery article in the state Constitution. "Texas cannot progress with the restriction of article 13 of the constitution," he wrote to José Antonio Navarro, "and I think a motion should be presented in September to suspend that article for ten years."[7] The rise of the Viesca faction had come at the same moment that controversies in the United States over the "Tariff of Abominations" began roiling the U.S. cotton market, producing what Austin believed was a perfect storm for migration. "The men now in power in this state wish to tolerate slavery," Austin observed with delight, and with the European market possibly turning from "the 'tarriffed cotton' of the U.S. to the fine long staple of Texas," conditions seemed ideal for a flood of American farmers to begin pouring into northern Mexico.[8]

And then everything changed. On September 15, 1829, President Vicente Guerrero declared an end to slavery throughout all of Mexico, promising to "free those who until today had been considered slaves."

Portrait of Agustín de la Viesca y Montes. With his brother José María, Agustín Viesca led the coalition of Coahuilans who allied themselves with Anglos and Tejanos to bring the cotton economy into Texas. (Image courtesy of Agustín L. Viesca)

Guerrero issued his proclamation as part of an annual September ritual, when Mexico's president would emancipate a handful of slaves in a ceremony commemorating the nation's independence from Spain. In years past, those fortunate enough to be freed had been purchased for the festivities by the government. By the late 1820s, however, so few enslaved people remained in central Mexico that officials in Mexico City struggled to find enough slaves for the ceremony. Guerrero, himself of Indian-African descent, decided in 1829 to turn the annual rite into a final end to the institution by freeing every slave throughout the republic. As for the owners of those emancipated slaves, Guerrero's order promised to compensate them "when the circumstances of the treasury permit it."[9]

The decree emerged from a combination of persistent antislavery sentiment in Mexico City and an unusual political situation brought on by a Spanish invasion of Mexican territory. Numerous legislators in the national Congress—much like their counterparts in the Coahuilan legislature—had remained dissatisfied with the survival of chattel slavery within the Mexican Republic following the passage of the 1824 Constitution. José María Tornel, a deputy in the Mexico City Congress, had led national efforts to force emancipation on the individual states in the years since (an effort directed at Texas, as the only portion of Mexico with a growing slave population) and presented a bill to Congress in 1827 demanding the outright abolition of slavery.[10] "It is not conceivable that a free Republic should subject some of its children to slavery," Tornel thundered, "let us leave such contradictions to the United States of North America."[11] Tornel's efforts at abolition, he later recalled, were calculated at establishing "a barrier between Mexico and the United States" by discouraging further immigration of Americans into Texas, although he had been unable to convince a majority of his fellow legislators to join him.[12] When Spain mounted an invasion of Mexico in July 1829, however, the Mexican Congress invested President Guerrero with emergency war powers, suspended the Constitution, and allowed him to rule the country by decree for the duration of the crisis. As Mexican forces fought Spanish invaders, Guerrero used his extraordinary power to issue a wide-ranging series of decrees aimed at strengthening the national government by expanding its authority. Tornel and others saw a remarkable opportunity, and convinced Guerrero to use his wartime powers to bypass Congress and mandate nationwide emancipation.[13]

News of the decree reached northeastern Mexico within a month of being published in Mexico City, although for most Coahuilans the emancipation order caused little concern. The mayors of the small villages of Longín, Allende, and Capellanía dutifully sent notices to the state capital in early October that they had received the decree and published it in their town squares.[14] When the mayor of Guerrero, Luis Lombraña, did the same, he included a list of those in his community affected by the decree. In a village of about 750 people, he noted, only two men and two women owned enslaved people. The decree had freed María Loreta, Josefa Ruiz, María de los Santos Garcia, Genobiba Garica, Rafael Garcia, and María Antonia, depriving each master of one slave, with the exception of Gertrudis Carrasco who had lost three. For the former slaves the degree was a life-changing event. But for most people in Guerrero, as for most Mexicans, slavery was an integral part of neither their economy nor their lives, and so the president's decree garnered little notice.[15]

In Saltillo and Texas, however, the emancipation order produced a firestorm that prompted state officials to defy the presidential directive. When the decree arrived in San Antonio, Ramón Músquiz refused to publish or enforce it. In an impassioned letter to Governor Viesca, Músquiz instead railed against "the fatal consequences that will result" if the decree were to go into effect and begged the governor to petition the president for an immediate exemption for Texas. Such a decree could not be enforced, Músquiz argued, because its violation of the property rights of slaveholders was unconstitutional. Yet the larger issue for Músquiz was his fear that abolition would effectively destroy the Anglo colonies by undercutting the labor system that drove plantations and farms in Texas. "It seems very harsh for the Supreme Government to now deprive them of their property and take from them what is most important to them for agriculture, cattle raising and other work in which they are engaged and which they cannot perform without the robust and almost tireless labor of this race of human species called blacks." Any effort by the national government to interject itself into such matters of state policy by emancipating the Texas slaves, Músquiz cautioned the governor, would badly undermine Anglo allegiance to Mexico. "There would be absolutely no respect for any authority," he warned.[16]

Knowing they had the support of the Viesca faction of the Saltillo legislature, nearly every prominent Tejano joined Músquiz in pressuring the state government to demand a repeal. José Antonio Navarro noted that "the best men in the State are opposed to such a Law," and sent Austin a letter assuring him that the leaders in San Antonio "have already written very strong things to the Government, and we have friends who can exert much influence in the annulment of such a law."[17] José María Balmaceda, one of the Tejano representatives in the Saltillo Congress, joined the growing chorus of opposition, lobbying his fellow legislators about "how much damage this causes for the State."[18] By his own account, Juan Antonio Padilla, the former Tejano secretary of state for Coahuila-Texas, became unhinged when the governor showed him the emancipation order. "I spoke with such vehemence," Padilla noted, that the governor "placed his confidence in me to draft a presentation to the Government regarding the matter." Padilla's protest, he acknowledged, "was very strong, and perhaps excessive," but he remained determined to oppose "with all my strength the publication and fulfillment of a tyrannical, cruel, illegal and monstrous order."[19] The outrage shared among the Viesca faction and the Tejano leadership emanated from their common fear that national intrusion into local matters of such delicacy and importance could bring wrenching instability to northeastern Mexico.

Despite efforts in San Antonio and Saltillo to keep the matter quiet, news of Guerrero's decree reached the Anglo colonies by November 1829 and set off waves of anguished protest. "We have receivd by last Mail a Decree Given by the excutive of our Governmt Liberating all the Slaves in its territory," wrote John Durst, a settler near Nacogdoches. As Músquiz, Padilla, and others had feared, Durst believed that the order to free all Texas slaves marked the end of American colonization in Mexico. "In the Name of God what Shall we do?" he asked Stephen F. Austin in a panicked letter. "We are ruind for ever Should this Measure be adopted." Durst had already barred the law's publication in Nacogdoches, working with local Mexican authorities to embargo the news for as long as possible. But he knew that rumors of government-mandated emancipation would soon reverberate across eastern Texas, and Durst turned in despair to Austin for guidance. "For Gods Sake advise me on the subject by the return of Mail," he begged the empresario.[20]

As word of the decree moved across farms and plantations, alarmed colonists talked openly about armed resistance in defense of their property. Near Nacogdoches, José Ygnacio Ybarvo denounced the law as "a catastrophe" and sent a warning to San Antonio that rumors of revolt appeared to be spreading among the colonists. Colonel José de las Piedras, the Mexican military commander in Nacogdoches, heard the same grumbling among the settlers and advised against any attempt to enforce the decree. "There is no inhabitant of this frontier who does not have some negroes," he cautioned in a letter to San Antonio, warning that without their slaves the settlers "would be reduced to the ultimate state of misery." The more pressing issue, feared the colonel, was that any effort to free slaves in Texas could push the colonists into outright insurrection, and he urged state officials to defy the national edict as a means of preserving regional stability. "Many have announced to me that there will be a revolution if the law takes effect," Piedras reported, and he believed the settlers would sooner abandon Mexico than the institution and the agriculture it supported. "Austin's colony would be the first to think along these lines," he warned. "It was formed for slavery and without it her inhabitants would be nothing."[21]

Even without enforcement, the decree destabilized Texas plantations by prompting some slaves to run away. In December 1829, three escaped Texas slaves—John, Robert, and an unnamed woman—staggered into the village of Guerrero in northern Coahuila. Luis Lombraña took the fugitives into custody and questioned them under oath for the state's official records. John understood some Spanish and served as the group's interpreter, explaining that they had escaped from their Anglo masters in order to seize the liberty promised them by President Guerrero. John and Robert, sixteen- and twenty-four-years-old respectively, described themselves as descendants of the Guinea region along Africa's west coast, although both had been born in New Orleans. At age twenty-five, the woman was a year older than Robert and also a native of New Orleans. All three came to Mexico as slaves of American settlers, toiling in Texas fields until news of Guerrero's decree arrived in the colonies. Although overjoyed when they "heard the order of the government that slaves were to be free," they had also learned that their Anglo masters planned to thwart the law by "sending their slaves to New Orleans to sell them." Terrified of losing their chance for freedom, John, Robert, and the woman set out together for the interior of Mexico to claim the "liberty granted them by the Supreme Mexican Government." Following their testimony, Lombraña granted their wish when he declared them free citizens of Mexico and forwarded the news to Saltillo.[22]

Governor Viesca was likely not pleased with Lombraña's report, since Viesca was doing everything he could to pressure the national government into granting Texas an exemption from the abolition decree. He had already sent a heated protest to his brother Agustín, the powerful minister of relations in Mexico City. Viesca asked his brother to intercede personally with the president, reminding Agustín that only slave-based agriculture in the Anglo colonies had succeeded in bringing both

200 PESOS SE OFRECEN,

PARA DOS NEGROS esclavos, que fugaron de su amo, en principios del mes de abril del pasado año de 1829—Uno de dichos negros se llama

WILL,

Cosa de 6 pies de alto, 31 a 32 años de edad, su color es muy negro y tiene una cicatriz en al frente. El otro se llama

ADAM,

Cosa de 5 pies 4 ó 5 pulgadas de alto, entre 24 y 25 años de edad, el dedo indice de la mano izquierda esta casi cortada, su color inclina a ser mulato, y tiene una mira acrimonia. Qualquiera persona que los entragara a su amo que vive cosa de 7 leguas abajo de esta villa, recibira dos cientos pesos ó cien pesos por qualquiero de ellos.
                                    JUAN RANDON.
Villa de Austin, el 6 de febrero de 1830.

$200 Reward.

RANAWAY from the subscriber, living on the Brazos, about 20 miles below this place, about the 1st of April, TWO NEGRO MEN, as follows:

WILL,

About 6 feet high, between 31 and 32 years of age; very black, has a smal scar on his forehead.

ADAM,

About 5 feet 4 or 5 inches high; between 24 and 25 years of age, has lost about one half of the fore finger on the left hand; a little inclined to be yellow; looks sour. Any person returning said negroes to the subscriber, shall receive the above reward, or one hundred dollars for either.
                                    JOHN RANDON.
Austin, Feb. 6, 1830—9tf

Advertisement in the *Texas Gazette* for the capture and return of Will and Adam, slaves who escaped a plantation on the Brazos River in 1829. (General Collection, Beinecke Rare Book and Manuscript Library, Yale University)

people and wealth into northeastern Mexico. If slavery were abolished in the region, the governor cautioned, "it is certain, I repeat, that this state must for many years set aside its ideas of advancement" since Anglo slaveholders "currently constitute the department's main vein of wealth and population." More pressing, the governor warned, was the likelihood that desperate Anglo settlers would resort to armed insurrection in order to protect their property and livelihoods. "I don't want to imply by this that said colonists have a turbulent and insubordinate nature," the governor wrote, "but we need to be aware of man's condition and the emotions of which he is capable when from one day to the next he is ruined as would happen to many of them when their entire fortune consists of the ownership of their Slaves." Exempting Texas from the abolition decree, insisted Viesca, was indispensable for ensuring the prosperity of Coahuila-Texas and silencing talk of revolution among the colonists.[23]

Mexicans in both Texas and Coahuila banded together to block President Guerrero's decree because they shared two central concerns. The most practical was their desire to foster a growing economy and thriving population in Texas, and the leadership in San Antonio and the Viesca wing of the Saltillo legislature both agreed that slave-based agriculture in the Anglo colonies provided the foundation for that development. Potentially more alarming, however, was their common realization that both local and state authorities lacked the power to force emancipation on the settlers or to quell a rebellion in the colonies. With Mexico's military presence in the region as scant as ever, one consequence of the growing American population in Texas was a corresponding contraction of the ability of Mexican officials to enforce their will in the region when it ran counter to the desires of the Anglo settlers. That troubled some Mexicans, such as General Manuel de Mier y Terán, who worried about the ability of Mexico to hold on to the region. For most Tejanos and the Viesca faction, however, the desire to foster the region's rapid development outweighed such reservations, and so they tended to share the perspective held by the Anglo colonists: Guerrero's order of emancipation threatened to disrupt the peaceful and prosperous growth of the settlements and cotton economy in eastern Texas.

Authorities in northeastern Mexico also found themselves united in opposition to Guerrero's decree because of their shared interest in preventing incursions by the national government into state sovereignty. The federal division of power between the national and state governments codified in the 1824 Constitution came under attack by the Guerrero government during August and September 1829, when the president began issuing orders under his extraordinary wartime powers. Such decrees were supposed to be directed toward stopping the Spanish invasion, but Guerrero seized the opportunity to issue orders aimed at strengthening the national government at the expense of the states. The more controversial measures included efforts to shore up the national government's perennially bankrupt treasury by selectively nationalizing property throughout the country and instituting a direct tax on the states to fund the national army. These proclamations set off storms of protest across the republic—prompting Jalisco, Guanajuato, San Luis Potosí, Michoacán, and Zacatecas to threaten to secede from the Mexican union—and every state in Mexico refused to comply with at least one of Guerrero's decrees. In San Antonio, Ramón Músquiz grumbled that "the most prudent men in this town" agreed that Guerrero's emancipation decree "crosscuts the sovereignty of the States in the most repugnant manner." The refusal of officials in northeastern Mexico to enforce the abolition decree thus joined numerous other protests rippling across Mexico in 1829, as moves toward centralism in Mexico City pushed states to defend their rights under federalism.[24]

Officials in Texas and Coahuila won their reprieve when President Guerrero issued an exemption for Texas in late 1829—almost certainly at the behest of Agustín Viesca—thereby excluding the abolition order from the only portion of Mexico where slavery retained a central role in society. News of the exemption arrived in the Anglo colonies in late December 1829, as both the political chief of Texas and the commandant of the Eastern Interior Provinces sent letters directly to Austin in hopes of calming the settlers.[25] The exemption quelled talk of revolution in Texas, although disputes over Guerrero's assaults on federalism continued to reverberate across the country. Public outcry over the president's use of his wartime powers gave rise to a rebellion that began in Jalapa and ended with Guerrero being forcibly ousted from office at the end of December 1829. Guerrero went into hiding in the mountains of southern Mexico, until he was eventually captured, tried for treason, and executed in February 1831. Nearly all of his decrees—including the one abolishing slavery —were subsequently annulled by Mexico's national Congress.[26]

Losing Control

The crumbling of Vicente Guerrero's presidency illustrated a corrosive problem within Mexican politics during the late 1820s and early 1830s: an increasingly unstable political scene in Mexico City where fierce debates over the proper balance between federalism and centralism—the balance of power between the states and the national government—threatened to embroil the entire country. The passage of the national Constitution in 1824 had temporarily settled such issues in favor of federalism and the states during the administration of Mexico's first president, Guadalupe Victoria, who served until 1828. Centralism continued to be widely shunned during this period, as people remembered the failed emperorship of Agustín de Iturbide. Yet federalism did little to solve many of the daunting challenges—particularly the nation's perennially bankrupt treasury—confounding the Mexican Republic, and when the peaceful transfer of power to a new administration failed to happen during the presidential election of 1828, renewed political instability overtook Mexico City. The election had pitted Manuel Gómez Pedraza, a former minister of war with centralist leanings, against Vicente Guerrero, a known federalist. When the tallied votes indicated that Pedraza would become Mexico's next president, Antonio López de Santa Anna launched a rebellion (ostensibly in defense of federalism) that succeeded in overturning the results and forcing Guerrero into the presidency. When Guerrero's administration was itself overthrown in another coup (also largely over questions of federalism) in less than a year, some leaders in Mexico City began searching for ways to strengthen the nation's central government in order to bring much-needed stability to the country.[27]

Under the administration of Guerrero's successor, Anastasio Bustamante, officials in Mexico City began a campaign to move the national government toward a more highly centralized system. Lucas Alamán, an intellectual giant of early Mexico and leading centralist, led the charge as Bustamante's secretary of relations, the most powerful post in the administration. Alamán had become convinced by the early 1830s that federalism was at the root of the dysfunction plaguing the national government. Fully aware that threats to state sovereignty had helped bring down Guerrero's government, centralists remained cautious in their efforts to expand the reach of the central government. Yet the painful succession of two coups and three different governments in Mexico City between 1828 and 1830—and the wrenching instability that accompanied such rapid shifts—had produced a growing sense of fatigue within the Mexican nation. Instead of peace and prosperity, Mexico had endured a series of revolutions and an invasion by Spain during the 1820s, all of which helped lurch the country toward bankruptcy. Federalism's failure to bring stability to the nation eroded much of the system's appeal for some Mexicans and thereby opened the door for the first time since Iturbide for a renewed push toward a more assertive national government. Under the leadership of Alamán, the Bustamante administration thus began centralizing power in Mexico City.[28]

Part of that renewed centralist policy was a crackdown on American migration into Texas, as Lucas Alamán attempted to reassert national control over the borderlands in northeastern Mexico. General Manuel de Mier y Terán's troubling reports on the Anglo colonies—with his ominous predictions about the steady erosion of Mexican authority in Texas—arrived in Mexico City only two weeks after the Bustamante administration took office. Alamán immediately convened a secret session of Congress to consider the general's warnings about "the urgency of taking prompt steps to prevent the shameful loss of the department of Texas." Terán painted a dire portrait: farming districts in eastern Texas were overrun with Americans whose expanding cotton trade with New Orleans tied the Texas economy more tightly to the United States than to Mexico. General Terán's central recommendation—that Mexico cut off further American immigration—confirmed suspicions Alamán already held about American intentions along the U.S.-Mexican border, and the minister pushed the national Congress to pass a measure aimed at reasserting its authority in northeastern Mexico. "Either the government occupies Texas *now*," noted one official familiar with Terán's report, "or it is lost forever."[29]

Adopting nearly all of Terán's recommendations, Mexico's national Congress enacted a law on April 6, 1830, aimed at strengthening Mexico City's control over Texas by undermining the American presence in the region. The law granted President Bustamante authority to establish new fortifications and military posts in Texas, to transport convict-soldiers from the interior of Mexico to the frontier, and to send national commissioners to the Anglo colonies with the power to make "whatever arrangements seem expedient for the security of the Republic." In order to encourage the migration of Mexican families into Texas, the law sanctioned levying new taxes on cotton shipments—which Mexico City recognized as the most profitable industry in Texas—to provide financial support to native Mexicans in settling in the region. The most controversial portions of the law, however, sought to end all immigration from the United States into Mexico. "It is prohibited that emigrants from nations bordering on this Republic shall settle in the states or territory adjacent to their own nation," read the law's eleventh article, which also suspended all ongoing empresario contracts "not already completed." Because the illegal importation of slaves as indentured servants supported American migration into Texas, the law also mandated that "the government of each state shall most strictly enforce the colonization laws and prevent the further introduction of slaves." The Law of April 6, 1830, was nothing short of a sweeping reassertion of national control over colonization in Texas by cutting off the Anglo settlements' connections to the United States.[30]

Coming on the heels of Guerrero's emancipation decree, news of the law sent Stephen Austin into the depths of depression. Austin had lost his brother and closest confidant, Brown Austin, to yellow fever only months before. The empresario himself was then struck down by malaria, which confined him to bed on the edge of death for nearly a month. When news of the Law of April 6 arrived, Austin found himself struggling along the edge of mental and physical exhaustion during one of the lowest periods of his life. Anastasio Bustamante, Mexico's president, tried to reassure Austin in a letter of his continued goodwill toward the colonies despite the new restrictions.[31] Austin was cordial in reply but minced no words in protesting that the purpose of the Law of April 6 "seems to be to destroy in one blow the happiness and prosperity of this colony which Your Excellency has always protected."[32] Austin sent similar missives to officials in northeastern Mexico, perhaps hoping for another stand by state officials against Mexico City, but received little back in terms of encouragement. "I do not know what to tell you," Ramón Músquiz told the empresario, "except to agree with your opinion and have the displeasure of informing you that it is now impossible to do anything to counteract the proposed law, which is bound to retard the growth of Texas."[33]

The national government's renewed efforts to halt the importation of new slaves into Mexico, particularly in the wake of Guerrero's emancipation decree, prompted an exhausted Austin to despair of ever securing favorable laws toward slavery from Mexico City.[34] The empresario could imagine various ways around most of the restrictions imposed by the law (he asked for and received permission, for example, to continue accepting Americans into his colony who were already en route to Mexico when the immigration ban passed). But Austin also recognized that Mexico City had attacked slavery as a means of undermining further American immigration into Texas, an ominous sign of the future. "The main object of the law of 6th of april," he concluded, "is to keep out turbulent and bad men vagabonds and Slaves."[35] Austin, in desperation, began experimenting with the idea of perhaps ending enslavement in Texas as a means of saving his colonial enterprise. "I have always been opposed from principle to slavery," he announced in a letter to Lucas Alamán, with obvious disregard for his previous endorsements of the institution. "As far as my influence extends I shall forever oppose slavery in Texas." Austin decided against sending the letter (apparently he was not yet ready to make such definitive statements publicly), but the empresario began testing the idea of a slave-free Texas in correspondence with friends. Slavery had been a necessary evil during the beginning of his settlement, he conceded, but the future prosperity of the region now necessitated "the perpetual exclusion of slavery from this country."[36]

Austin made clear that his newfound opposition to the institution did not come from any concern for people of African descent. His sudden reservations about slavery, he insisted, sprang instead from fears that the black population might one day outnumber and overtake the white population. The massive slave revolt of 1791–1804 that had overthrown French power on the Caribbean island of Saint-Domingue (modern-day Haiti) provided a terrifying example to white Americans like Austin of the dangers that came with a rapidly expanding black population. To illustrate, he asked some planters in Alabama to calculate the likely increase of both black and white populations in slave states by 1910. "Compare the two sums," he said, "and then suppose that you will be alive at the period above mentioned, that you have a long-cherished and beloved wife, a number of daughters, grand daughters, and great grand daughters." Although it would surely be in the economic interest of white Texans to preserve slavery, Austin warned that those same slaves might one day rise up against whites in a violent race war: "Satan entered the sacred garden in the shape of a serpent—if he is allowed to enter Texas in the shape of negros it will share the fate of Eden."[37]

Austin's flirtation with the idea of a slave-free Texas proved short-lived because he utterly failed to convince his fellow Americans. S. Rhoads Fisher, a recent emigrant from Pennsylvania, rejected the proposition as hopeless and unattainable fantasy. "Do you believe that cane and cotton can be grown to advantage by a sparce white population?" Fisher asked incredulously. "It is impossible!" Practically all of the settlers in Austin's colony, Fisher reminded him, "are from Slaveholding States—they have enrolled themselves in your register under the firm conviction that slavery would be tolerated, and they would be secure in the ownership of those brought by them." Although himself a nonslaveholder from the northern United States, Fisher simply could not imagine the cultivation of cotton or sugar cane without enslaved labor. "There is no country in the world where these articles are grown unless by the assistance of Slaves," he pointed out. And without slave-based agriculture driving a thriving economy in Texas, there would be no migration from the United States to sustain the colonies. "Therefore we must either abandon the finest portion of Texas to its original uselessness," concluded Fisher, "or submit to the acknowledged, but lesser evil of Slavery."[38]

Austin found he could not escape the logic of cotton that was so deeply imbued on his colonists, and so he quickly abandoned notions that Americans would consider growing cotton in Texas without their slaves. The settlers, he acknowledged, remained stubbornly fixated on acquiring "negros to make cotton to *buy more* negros," and nothing he said seemed capable of persuading them otherwise.[39] "It is in vain to tell a North American that the white population will be destroyed some fifty or eighty years hence by the negroes, and that his daughters will be violated and Butchered by them," Austin lamented to a friend. "To say any thing to them as to the justice of slavery, or its demoralizing effects on society, is only to draw down ridicule upon the person who attempts it."[40] By the spring of 1831, Austin had returned to lobbying for reopening Texas to slave importations, and he petitioned the Saltillo legislature to rescind its restrictions on such traffic.[41] "The wishes of my colonists have hurried me into this thing," he conceded in a letter from Saltillo, "but I am now in for the cuestion and there is no retreat."[42] Austin had run headlong into a problem he helped to create. Because he had built his colonial enterprise on the promise of cotton, Austin found he could not convince his set-tlers to abandon using slaves to grow it. "Nothing is wanted but money," Austin concluded of his colonists, "and negros are necessary to make it."[43]

Mexico's national authorities found they, too, could do little to prevent the continued influx of Americans into Texas with their slaves. Francisco Pizarro Martínez, the Mexican consul in New Orleans, sent letters to General Terán and Lucas Alamán detailing the steady flow of U.S. slaves into northeastern Mexico under the guise of indentured servitude. Over the course of four months during the spring of 1831, Martínez reported, at least sixteen slaveholders had transported 105 enslaved people into Texas. Every one of those planters had passed through New Orleans on his way into Mexico, taking his slaves to the office of William Lewis, a notary public in the city. Lewis wrote and notarized contracts that ostensibly freed the slaves, while also obligating them to serve their former mas-ters in Texas for anywhere from seventy to ninety years. Isaac Tinsley, for example, arrived at Lewis's office in March 1831 from Pikesville, Alabama, with six enslaved people—Chilch, Philip, and Phoebus, along with Pheo-bus's daughters Hannah, Milli, and Prinnilla—en route for Texas. Tinsley swore he had advanced his slaves $1,750 in exchange for their promise to accompany him to Mexico "and loyally serve him, his heirs, or to whoso-ever right it is, with great care in all that is relative to agriculture, farming, or household work for the term of 70 (seventy) years." Noadiah Marsh did the same with his slave Henry, as did John Dillard with his eighteen slaves, James Routh with his fifteen, Albert Miller with his six, and eleven other American migrants noted in Martínez's report.[44]

General Terán, serving now as the commander of the Eastern Interior Provinces, forwarded his own reports to Mexico City lamenting the inability of Mexican officials to slow the influx of illegal slaves into Texas. Terán detailed for Lucas Alamán the process by which colonists employed contracts to circumvent restrictions passed by the Coahuila-Texas Congress on slave importations. "By this means the introduction of slaves is so frequent," the general explained to Alamán, "that in three months two-hundred (200) of them were introduced through the Brazos River to the colony of Austin." Letters sent to the governor of Coahuila-Texas about the illicit importations had only prompted Governor Viesca to forward copies of the laws passed by Coahuila against the slave trade, which Terán dismissed as meaningless because the indentured servant ruse "made a mockery of the law." Because all slaves from the United States were of African descent, Terán suggested that Mexico consider outlawing the immigration of blacks "since nobody is able to verify" that any given black person coming into Mexico was in fact enslaved or free. Yet the general recognized that the underlying problem remained the perennially weak military and small native Mexican presence in Texas—unless Mexico City could overcome the decisive population advantage enjoyed by Anglos in the region, there was little the national government could do to stem the flow of Americans and their slaves into Texas.[45]

By the early 1830s, both Austin and Terán recognized that the determination of Anglo colonists to remake Texas into an outpost of the expanding Atlantic cotton economy made it tremendously difficult to control their movements and nearly impossible to dissuade them on the issue of slavery. Austin conceded to a friend in 1833 that there could be no retreat from slave-based agriculture in the development of the region. "Texas *must be* a slave country," he declared, "circumstances and unavoidable necessity compels it."[46] For Austin, that meant there could be no retreat from the expansion of American influence in the region. Manuel de Mier y Terán had reached similar conclusions, as the ongoing political battles within Mexico City over centralism and federalism convinced the general that instability within the national government meant the country would never be able to mount the concerted effort necessary to reestablish its authority in northeastern Mexico. In a letter to Lucas Alamán on July 2, 1832, Terán confessed his fear that Texas was already beyond redemption. "We are about to lose the northern provinces," the despondent general concluded. "What will become of Texas? Whatever God wills." Terán rose early the next morning and donned his full-dress uniform, slipping out at dawn for his usual morning walk. Alongside the ruins of the San

Antonio de Padilla Church, he braced his sword against the earth and drove it through his heart.[47]

Boom

Terán's suicide came at a moment of profound transformation, as a booming international cotton market during the early 1830s began driving unprecedented numbers of Americans into northern Mexico. Following the remarkable rise of cotton during the late 1810s, prices paid in New Orleans for the crop had remained steady and strong from 1821 to 1825. During the late 1820s, however, the market had steadily weakened until a pound of cotton in 1829 sold for about half what it had in 1821. Then, beginning in 1831, the global cotton market rebounded and began another remarkable rise. The price of cotton boomed as merchants in New Orleans, New York, and Liverpool paid more for the crop each year, until prices eventually reached fifteen-year highs by 1835. The dramatic rise in prices, in turn, led to a remarkable expansion in the crop's production as farms across the southern United States ramped up cotton exportations during those years by a full 37 percent.[48]

The expansion of cotton farming within Mexican Texas, however, outstripped anything in Mississippi or Alabama. Although we lack precise numbers, it appears that cotton production in the Anglo colonies increased during the 1831–35 boom from approximately 450,000 pounds annually to more than 3.15 million.[49] That represented an astounding 600 percent increase. Indeed, by 1834 Texas farmers were sending more cotton to New Orleans than their counterparts in Florida, and the spike in prices even convinced some Tejanos to try their hand at cotton farming.[50] Erasmo Seguín planted a crop at his ranch, Casa Blanca, during the spring of 1833, and asked Stephen Austin to send a cotton gin to San Antonio.[51]

A tremendous boom in American migration into northern Mexico followed on the heels of this spike in cotton prices and drove much of the massive expansion in local farm production. Despite the strident prohibitions that Mexico City had placed on immigration with the Law of April 6, Americans poured into Texas during the early 1830s in unprecedented numbers. The Anglo population of the region more than doubled during those four years, increasing from around 10,000 in 1830 to almost 21,000 in 1834, as the cotton boom made Mexican land more appealing.[52] For American farmers, lands in Texas continued to hold all the same advantages as lands in the Mississippi River Valley: rich soils, long growing season, and ready access to Gulf Coast shipping. What made Texas different was the cheapness of the land and the political instability that came with it. By abandoning the United States for northern Mexico, an American farmer was freed from using his limited capital to purchase land—he could, instead, leverage his assets into purchasing equipment, supplies, and even slaves. The trade-off, however, had always been the uncertainty and political instability that came with living in northern Mexico, particularly in regard to the future of slavery. While Austin's colonies had attracted many Americans, the risks had long outweighed the rewards for many other U.S. farmers during the 1820s. The global boom in cotton prices during the early 1830s shifted that logic by making the advantages of moving to Texas more alluring for thousands of Americans, who decided that life in northern Mexico was now worth the risk.

With the tremendous rise in the local American population came a rapid expansion in the economic infrastructure of eastern Texas, as Anglo merchants in Texas moved to capitalize on the growth in both population and cotton production. During the early 1830s, Thomas F. McKinney and Samuel May Williams built a warehouse at the mouth of the Brazos River, where they began buying cotton from the colonists and selling them goods imported from New Orleans.[53] Their hope was to wrest control of the increasingly lucrative Texas markets away from New Orleans: McKinney ran the day-to-day operations, while Williams provided political and economic connections. Having served as Stephen F. Austin's partner and lieutenant throughout the 1820s, Williams could draw on long-established relationships with nearly all the powerful planters in the region. More important, the extended Williams family bankrolled the new McKinney-Williams trade house. Much of the money that launched their operation came from Mobile, Alabama, where Williams's brother-in-law "seems desirous to monopolize the Texas Cotton."[54] A great deal of financing also came from Samuel's brother, Henry Williams, who owned a shipping firm in Baltimore. Building on these credit lines from the United States, McKinney and Williams hoped to build a commission house on the Texas coast that could rival the great merchant houses in New Orleans.

An 1834 report on conditions in Texas, prepared during an in-depth inspection tour by Juan Nepomuceno Almonte, revealed the extent to which cotton had come to dominate the region's economy. According to Almonte, the entire export trade coming out of Texas by the mid-1830s amounted to an annual value of $500,000. Cotton bales made up approxi-

McKinney's Warehouse, or Quitana, 1835. This rough sketch by Mary Austin Holley provides a rare view of the warehouse and cotton-trading hub established by the McKinney-Williams firm on the Brazos River during the mid-1830s. (Mary Austin Holley Papers, Dolph Briscoe Center for American History, University of Texas at Austin)

mately two-thirds of that trade, making the plant the most valuable commodity in northeastern Mexico. All that cotton production, moreover, was centered in Austin's colonies and the eastern portions of Texas, which allowed the Anglo-dominated sections of Texas to account for an overwhelming 96 percent of the region's export economy. Cotton, in other words, had drastically remade the economic landscape of the Texas borderlands by the mid-1830s, shifting economic power in the region almost entirely into the expanding Anglo settlements. And, as Almonte noted, "this trade is growing more each day, due to the large cotton harvests and the consumption that is growing with the continued emigration from the United States to Texas."[55]

Almonte's report also revealed how the cotton economy had reshaped the political landscape of Texas. The rush of American farmers into northeastern Mexico meant that, by 1834, the Tejanos around San Antonio made up only 15 percent of the non-Indian population of Texas. Everyone else lived in the Anglo-dominated eastern portions of the region, practically all of whom were recent immigrants from the southern United

States.[56] Anglos had outnumbered Tejanos in the territory since the mid-1820s, but the imbalance became remarkably lopsided during the cotton boom. Indeed, by the mid-1830s there were likely just as many—if not more—enslaved African Americans living in Texas as ethnic Mexicans.[57] Such remarkable population shifts had, in turn, created a powerful geographic split in the region. Anglo immigrants dominated and controlled the eastern territories between the Colorado and Sabine Rivers, while Tejanos remained clustered in western Texas, predominantly around San Antonio and Goliad. The two groups communicated, collaborated, cooperated, and traded. Yet they also lived in segregated regions—the Anglo East separated from the Tejano West—which helped ensure that, as a general rule, most Anglo settlers and ethnic Mexicans living in the Texas borderlands had few interactions with one another.

The burgeoning Anglo population, at times, led to clashes that pointed toward declining Tejano influence in the region. Enslaved men and women working on Texas farms frequently ran away from their Anglo masters, and some made their way to San Antonio. During the spring of 1832, Peter and his son Tom fled the Brazos River plantation of their master, Alexander Thompson, and made the arduous trek to San Antonio where they turned themselves into Tejano authorities. Músquiz took Peter and Tom into custody and made arrangements for their care, although what he intended to do with them remains unclear. Thompson, in the meantime, commissioned a posse of Anglo slave-catchers to reclaim the runaways, and in May 1832 seven Anglos thundered into San Antonio, captured Peter and Tom from the Tejanos, and then escaped back toward the Anglo East. Outraged by the brazen affront to Tejano authority, Músquiz ordered the arrest of the Anglo marauders and spent the better part of a year attempting to capture the men responsible. Thompson got his slaves back, but the Anglo colonists refused to turn over the slave catchers. The great population imbalance that cotton brought to the territory meant, among other things, that San Antonio's authority in the eastern portions of Texas had waned considerably.[58]

Support for the Anglo colonies nonetheless remained strong among Tejanos and members of the Viesca faction in Coahuila. Músquiz continued to send encouraging notes to Mexican officials about Texas cotton production—noting, in particular, that most of the Anglo cotton went to New Orleans and that such reciprocal trade should be supported.[59] Many Tejanos, moreover, continued to capitalize on the expanding trade networks that came with Anglo immigration (the arrival of the McKinney-

GRAPH I. Value of Texas Commerce by Department in 1834 (Source: Almonte, *Almonte's Texas*, 274)

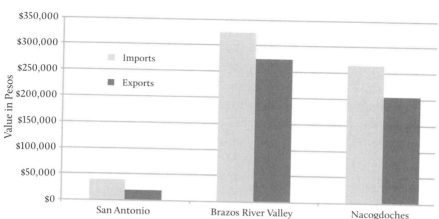

Williams trade house, for example, opened lucrative new opportunities) and some even began to acquire enslaved people from their Anglo neighbors. José Casiano, one of the most prominent merchants in San Antonio, asked Austin to purchase two enslaved African Americans for him during the early 1830s because, as he explained, their color ensured they would remain slaves for life.[60] Victor Blanco, the former governor of Coahuila-Texas and brother-in-law of Músquiz, pushed forward with plans to begin an Anglo settlement of his own in eastern Texas. Blanco had long hoped to profit from the influx of American capital into northern Mexico—at one point he had considered building a cotton gin in northern Coahuila—and by the early 1830s he was determined to become an empresario like Austin. Blanco had no intention of leaving his home in Monclova, as he planned to delegate to others the day-to-day logistics of settling Americans in Texas. For him, the venture was purely speculative and an opportunity to make money on the rising tide of Americans coming into the region.[61]

The Road to Revolt

Because cotton brought a massive population boom to eastern Texas at precisely the same moment that Mexico City began attempting to impose greater centralized control over northeastern Mexico, heated confrontations soon broke out between Anglo settlers and Mexican officials. Many of these disputes erupted at forts erected by the national government to enforce new tax collection measures. Since 1823, migrants into Texas had enjoyed a seven-year exemption from paying import and export duties. Such measures were intended to help colonists import the tools and materials needed for their new settlements, but they also helped foster the cotton industry by holding down the costs of shipping Texas bales to New Orleans and overseas markets. The Bustamante administration chose not to extend the exemption in 1830, in part because it planned to use tax revenues generated by cotton shipments to finance the establishment of new Mexican settlements in the region. The need to build new military fortifications and customhouses for the collection of those duties also provided a convenient excuse to increase the presence of national troops in the region. Unsurprisingly, these new outposts of Mexican soldiers and tax collectors—at the mouths of the Brazos, Colorado, and Trinity Rivers—quickly became flashpoints of conflict between the settlers and Mexico City. Clashes erupted at the new Anahuac fortification on Galveston Bay in the spring of 1832, followed by a bloody altercation at the new Velasco fort on the Brazos River, as Anglo colonists violently resisted any expansion of Mexico City's influence in the region.[62]

These initial fights between Texas settlers and Mexican soldiers did not generate a harsh backlash from national authorities because they happened to coincide with an ongoing upheaval in the interior of Mexico against the centralization policies of the Bustamante administration. Under the leadership of Santa Anna, another revolt in favor of federalism began in Veracruz in January 1832, this one seeking the resignation of President Bustamante for expanding the powers of Mexico City and undermining the 1824 federal Constitution. Numerous state legislatures—such as those in Tamaulipas, Jalisco, and Zacatecas—threw their support behind the uprising due to fears that continued concentration of power in Mexico City would undermine state sovereignty within the republic, and the anticentralist uprising quickly devolved into outright civil war between Mexican federalists and centralists. Because Anglos in Texas lashed out against Mexican soldiers at the same moment that Santa Anna's troops were forcing Bustamante from the presidency—finally overthrowing him in December 1832—authorities in Mexico dismissed these fights in Texas as simply another flare-up in Santa Anna's successful federalist campaign against Bustamante's centralists.[63]

The growing struggle between federalists and centralists across Mexico, however, soon embroiled Coahuila and presented daunting new challenges for Texans in securing favorable legislation for the Anglo colonies. Although the Anglo-Tejano alliance had forged powerful ties with sympathetic liberals and federalists within Coahuila, a power struggle within the state emerged during the early 1830s between conservatives based in Saltillo and the more liberal-minded federalists of the Parras and Monclova regions. Disputes between these two factions had long turned on questions of policy toward Texas—which invariably turned on questions of slavery and Anglo migration—and conservatives worked to enact new measures aimed at further restricting Anglo influence in the region. In April 1832 the conservative bloc passed a new state colonization law that closed the indentured servant loophole. "Servants and day laborers, hereafter introduced by foreign colonists" read the new law, "cannot be obligated by any contract to continue in the service of the latter longer than ten years." Beyond ending the last legal means for further importations of slaves into northeastern Mexico, the law demonstrated that Texans simply could not depend on political allies in Coahuila to ensure that legislation remained favorable to Anglo settlement. Battles between centralists and federalists in Coahuila became so heated during the mid-1830s that rival state governments emerged, with centralists passing legislation in Saltillo and federalists in Monclova.[64]

Such political turmoil within Coahuila and Mexico City convinced numerous Anglos and Tejanos that Texas must become its own state if the region were ever to realize the benefits of federalism. Some of their objections to the union with Coahuila remained unchanged from their original complaints in 1824—because Saltillo was so distant from either San Antonio or the colonies, it continued to be difficult for Texans to secure speedy action from the government on urgent matters. Yet their experiences during the years since the passage of the national Constitution convinced them that only the people living along the Mexican frontier understood the necessity of fostering the region's development by supporting Anglo colonization. Although Texans had found powerful allies in the Viesca faction of the state Congress, they had nonetheless failed to secure what Anglos and many Tejanos believed was indispensable in ensuring the region's economic success: unambiguous state support for slavery and Anglo colonization. And with the recent clashes between factions within the Saltillo Congress, it seemed unlikely that Texans would ever secure such legislation while still tied to Coahuila. Slavery, to be sure, was far from the only policy Texans hoped to defend through an embrace of federalism and separate statehood. But slave-based agriculture remained the foundational issue underlying disputes over colonization between those in Texas and leaders in state and national governments. It was, indeed, their endless fights over Texas policy during the 1820s with Mexico City and Saltillo—fights that almost invariably centered on slavery—that hardened both Anglos and Tejanos into such ardent federalists by the early 1830s.

Leaders in San Antonio and the colonies thus began petitioning for Texas to be granted more political autonomy within the Mexican Republic, only to be rebuffed repeatedly by Mexico City. The Anglos held conventions in 1832 and 1833 that demanded repeal of the Law of April 6 and the separation of the region from Coahuila. Many Tejanos did not approve of the Anglo conventions—which, under Mexican law, were illegal—yet they also began pushing for increased regional autonomy. Tejanos in San Antonio, for example, sent a memorial to national authorities in December 1832 protesting recent intrusions by Mexico City into state sovereignty that discouraged the immigration of Anglo "capitalists" from the United States. Tejanos in Nacogdoches and Goliad drew up similar petitions, threatening to exercise "the natural right of revolutionary measures against their oppression."[65] Stephen F. Austin even traveled to Mexico City in 1833 to plead Texas's case for separate statehood, although the empresario became dismayed when he could gain no traction on the issue. Despite the fact that committed federalists were in power in Mexico City—the new president, Santa Anna, was known as a champion of federalism—Austin was repeatedly told that statehood for Texas would have to wait. Deeply frustrated, the normally cautious Austin sent a letter to San Antonio urging Tejanos to form an independent state government even without approval from the national government. When Austin's rebellious letter found its way into the hands of Mexican authorities, the empresario was promptly thrown into prison on charges of sedition and treason.[66]

As Austin sat in jail, another seismic political shift in Mexico City—this time in favor of centralism—pushed numerous portions of Mexico into rebellion against national authorities. Responding to fears among many in the Mexican capital that the nation's experiment with federalism was spinning out of control, Santa Anna collected known conservatives and centralists in early 1835 into a new national congress that subsequently abolished the federal Constitution of 1824 and decreed that the states would be converted into military departments run by presidential appointees. Santa Anna thereby became the de facto ruler of Mexico, and the harsh return of centralist rule prompted several states, such as Zacatecas and Yucatán, to revolt against the new regime. At the same moment, a new contingent of national officials arrived in Texas to resume tax collections and increase Mexico's military presence within the region, actions that produced renewed conflicts between the Anglo settlers and Mexican army officials. Texas quickly found itself caught up in a violent civil war sweeping over Mexico, as the overthrow of federalism and the Constitution of 1824 sparked rebellions and revolts across the country. When Austin returned to the colonies in September 1835, recently released from prison in Mexico City, he threw his support behind those calling for armed resistance to centralism.

Fighting began in Texas in October 1835 when a group of Anglo-Texans opened fire on a Mexican cavalry unit near the hamlet of Gonzales. Within a month, a convention in San Felipe—headquarters of Austin's colonies— declared Texas in rebellion against Santa Anna's regime in Mexico City and called for a new Texas government. There was, however, no consensus among the rebels about what, exactly, they were fighting for. The majority of long-term Anglo settlers, particularly those who stood to lose extensive investments in cotton farms and plantations, resisted calls for outright independence and pushed instead for the restoration of the Constitution of 1824. A smaller group, composed largely of younger Anglos and recent arrivals from the United States—particularly those who had come during the 1830s cotton boom—pushed hard for Texas to declare independence, hoping to turn a rebellion against Mexico City into a rebellion against Mexico as a nation. Most Tejanos, for their part, saw the struggle as part of the broader centralist-federalist civil war raging within Mexico—and since most Tejanos counted themselves as ardent federalists, they threw themselves into the fight alongside the Anglos.[67] One of the most eager recruits was Juan Seguín, the twenty-eight-year-old son of Erasmo Seguín, who had grown up during the rapid transformations of the territory that had followed his father's efforts to tie the region to expanding Atlantic economic markets by supporting Anglo immigration. Juan, like most Tejanos, made his living through trade with New Orleans, and he had as much at stake as Austin or any other Anglo colonist in defending the continued development of the region. There was, indeed, a striking correlation between those Tejanos who had actively supported the importation of the cotton complex into Texas and those who joined the rebellion. Practically every prominent Tejano who had supported

Anglo colonization during the 1820s—such as José Antonio Navarro, Francisco Ruiz, and Juan Antonio Padilla—lined up alongside the Anglos against Santa Anna's centralist regime.[68]

Building a Rebellion

As the rebellion caught fire during the fall of 1835, leaders from across the colonies established a "General Council" charged with creating a new Texas government, even if no one could yet agree on whether that government would be for a new Mexican state or a newly independent nation. Members of the council soon organized a provisional congress and named a governor, appointed Sam Houston general of the incipient Texan army, and dispatched commissioners to raise war funds in the United States. The majority of their attention, by necessity, focused on military matters, and council members even managed to establish a navy of sorts. Yet the General Council was marked by deep division and discord, as competing factions within the rebel leadership quarreled endlessly about war aims and military strategy.[69]

There was, however, widespread agreement among rebel leaders that the financial stability of the region's next government would depend on cotton. A committee tasked in November 1835 with devising a strategy for financing the new Texas government recommended raising revenue by taxing multiple aspects of the cotton business. Land, naturally, would be the foundation for both the industry and future migration, and thus the most reliable tax base for the new government. "A direct tax on slaves," reported the committee, "comes next in order as a subject of certain revenue, and your committee recommends a tax of one dollar on all slaves in Texas over fourteen and under fifty years of age." After slaves, the committee recommended taxing shipments of goods exported out of Texas— also dominated by cotton—as the next most reliable source of revenue, followed thereafter by a tax charging planters "a duty of one quarter of a cent per pound for every pound of cotton exported out of Texas." Such measures, estimated the committee, could bring several hundred thousand dollars into the Texas treasury almost immediately, revenue that would only grow with increased immigration after the war. Although the committee's report was eventually tabled—most likely because Texas had not yet declared independence—it revealed the defining role that council members believed cotton would play in the new Texas.[70]

Another source of consensus among Texan rebels was that building a cotton nation demanded the construction of a much stronger legal framework for protecting slavery than had existed under Mexico. Despite its dysfunction in most other matters, the General Council quickly passed a measure outlawing immigration of free blacks into Texas to prevent "the infusion of dissatisfaction and disobedience into the brain of honest and contented slaves." Any free person of African blood who dared venture into Texas, they agreed, should be sold into slavery, and any whites who knowingly transported them into the region would be fined $5,000 and imprisoned.[71] Building unassailable walls around the institution was a consuming interest among Texas residents during the revolution, observed William Fairfax Gray, a Virginian touring Texas in 1835–36. "It is the opinion of all the *Texanos* with whom I have conversed on the subject," Gray noted in his diary, "that the new government of Texas must sanction the holding of slaves as property."[72]

Yet none of that would matter if the rebels could not field an army, and so the new Texas government turned to cotton merchants in order to finance its revolution. On the eve of the rebellion, Thomas McKinney had been working to arrange $200,000 in loans from New Orleans bankers, which he intended to use to "secure nearly all the cotton in the Country."[73] But as war began to engulf the region, the McKinney-Williams firm redirected its financial connections toward underwriting the Texas rebellion and army. Rather than cornering the 1835–36 cotton crop, the mercantile firm found itself instead loaning the rebels nearly $100,000 worth of war matériel, supplies, and services, including the use of several ships that would otherwise be carrying cotton bales. Recognizing what their contacts with wealthy trade houses in New Orleans could mean, the new Texas government also dispatched both McKinney and Williams to raise another $100,000 in emergency war funding from leaders in the Crescent City.[74]

Just as New Orleans merchants had financed Anglo colonization, the city's trade houses that profited so much from Texas cotton also provided the resources that made the Texas Revolution possible. In direct violation of U.S. declarations of neutrality in the conflict, American volunteers and supplies flowed from Louisiana into Texas, eliciting angry protests from Mexican authorities. When Texas dispatched three emissaries charged with raising $1 million in war loans from the United States, they soon secured pledges of several hundred thousand dollars from the merchant class in New Orleans. A few businessmen in the city openly opposed the Texas rebellion, largely because they feared the violence could imperil shipping in the Gulf of Mexico. Yet most residents of the city supported the Texas cause, not least because the rebellion promised lucrative new business opportunities. The Texas government offered generous land bounties to anyone who served in the Texas army. Even more enticing, the rebels offered to sell 300,000 acres of Texas farmlands at rock-bottom prices, producing a frenzy of speculation in the streets of New Orleans.[75]

As money and volunteers from New Orleans began flowing into Texas, the war finally erupted into savage violence. Following a long siege of the Mexican army in San Antonio, several hundred Texas rebels—about 150 of whom were Tejanos—stormed and captured the town in December 1835. Rather than use their victory as an opportunity to concentrate their forces, rebel Texas leaders continued to squabble among themselves as the Texas army and civilian government degenerated into near anarchy. At that same moment, Santa Anna streamed northward at the head of an imposing and disciplined Mexican army, intent on crushing all Texan resistance to his government. When Santa Anna's forces appeared on the outskirts of San Antonio on February 23, 1836, Texas rebels took refuge in the Alamo mission on the eastern edge of town. Thirteen days later, Santa Anna's army overtook the garrison in a bloody assault that killed every Alamo defender and hundreds of Mexican soldiers. Mexican troops then surrounded and captured another 350 Texas rebels at Goliad, who were subsequently marched into open fields and shot en masse. Recognizing that the rebels stood no chance without a larger army and the time needed to organize it, the commander of Texan forces, Sam Houston, ordered his men to fall back toward the Louisiana border. With the Texas army in full retreat, unbridled panic spread across eastern Texas.

Envisioning a New Nation

In the midst of such chaos and carnage, a new convention of rebels gathered at Washington-on-the-Brazos, a few miles upstream from San Felipe, and declared Texas independent of Mexico on March 2, 1836. Only the arrival of Santa Anna in San Antonio and the prospect of the Mexican army marching across Texas had managed to produce any sort of consensus among the Texas rebels. The declaration of independence, moreover, was a remarkable break from earlier discussions. The rebellion was no longer solely a revolt against centralism—it had become a war to make the Texas borderlands independent of Mexico. The men who made this decision were almost all Anglos—of the fifty-nine delegates at the convention, only two, José Antonio Navarro and Francisco Ruiz, were Tejano—and nearly half of those Anglos had arrived in Texas within the past two years, during the 1830s cotton boom. The rebels now had to lay the groundwork for a new country, and their first task was to write a constitution that would provide the foundation for the new Texas nation.[76]

In their rush to write an enduring national charter, the convention borrowed liberally from the U.S. Constitution and the examples of several western U.S. states, most notably Tennessee. Nearly all passages they considered for inclusion followed—often word for word—American models, although a few provisions were made for preserving certain Spanish legal traditions, such as community property laws.[77] Convention delegates paused, however, as they crafted the provisions on slavery, recognizing that the new government's approach to the institution would have lasting consequences for the region's development and—perhaps even more important—their efforts to secure international support for their new nation.

Reflecting Texans' experiences under Mexico, early drafts of the constitution contained several passages that defined in exacting detail how the property rights of slaveholders would be placed above the power of the state. Delegates recommended that the Texas Congress be stripped of any power to emancipate slaves or prevent the unlimited importation of enslaved people from the United States. Free blacks were, again, banned from living within Texas, and even slaveholders themselves were forbidden to free their own slaves unless they sent the emancipated to live outside the boundaries of Texas. Finally given the opportunity to establish their own laws concerning slavery, the convention delegates sought to replace the uncertainty that had hung over the institution during the Mexican era with unambiguous endorsements of the rights that slaveholders would enjoy under the new regime. The proposals met uniform approval, sparking no debate within the convention.[78] Beyond ensuring that slavery could never be challenged within the new Texas government, building a protective firewall around the institution served another central goal of the delegates: reassuring potential migrants from the United States that Texas would now be secured forever as slave country.

Questions of whether an independent Texas ought to engage in the international slave trade proved more complicated. Although both the United States and Mexico had outlawed the practice, a lively trade in enslaved Africans continued to be accessible to Texans willing to make the journey to Cuba, where farmers could purchase new slaves at roughly half the price they would pay at home.[79] During the early 1830s, a handful of Texas planters—such as Benjamin Fort Smith, Sterling McNeel, and Monroe Edwards—traveled to the Havana markets in search of cheap African labor. James Fannin, commander of the ill-fated Texan force at Goliad, imported more than a hundred enslaved Africans the year before the revolution. Such traffic had increased with the lawlessness that surrounded the outbreak of the rebellion, and the U.S. consul in Havana estimated that smugglers exported around a thousand Africans to Texas in 1836.[80] On the same day they declared Texas independence, delegates to the convention received word that Monroe Edwards, a Brazoria planter, had recently landed 171 African slaves on the Brazos River. "This traffic in African negroes is increasing daily," reported the customs official stationed on the Brazos, who asked how he should proceed.[81]

Although none of the delegates made any effort to prosecute ongoing importations by people like Monroe Edwards, all agreed that the new Texas government must issue an unequivocal declaration of opposition to the international slave trade as "abhorrent to the laws of God and the feelings of all civilized nations."[82] They recognized—much as Mexico had during the 1820s—that engaging in such traffic would bring international condemnation, making it impossible for Texans to secure the foreign assistance necessary to win their revolution. The African slave trade, observed one delegate, "has called forth the indignant condemnation of nearly the whole civilized world" and "it is to that civilized world that we now, in our present struggle look for sympathy, and hope from that sympathy to extract assistance." The ongoing efforts of Great Britain to abolish all such trade, in particular, appears to have weighed heavily on the minds of Texans at the convention. Whatever economic advantage Texas planters might derive from importing Africans, they recognized, would be badly outweighed by the diplomatic backlash Texas would then face from foreign powers. "We must be governed by the opinions of others," the delegates concluded, and so the convention recommended that Texas outlaw the African slave trade as "piracy," punishable by death.[83]

Fierce debates over land policy dominated the rest of the convention, as delegates fought one another over how best to protect their new government's most abundant resource.[84] Reports of the approach of Santa Anna's army, however, cut the discussions short, and the convention hurriedly issued a completed constitution on March 17, 1836. It was, on the whole, a framework built to replicate most of the political conventions of the United States, with specific adaptations—such as a prohibition on imprisonment for debt—geared toward encouraging future immigration. The final version provided for a president, bicameral congress, independent judiciary, and a bill of rights, all in the mold of U.S. examples. The provisions concerning slavery, however, had been crafted for the unique position of Texas, as the new charter moved well beyond what the United States or Mexican constitutions offered slaveholders.[85] At least on paper, the new Texas government promised to be the most protective slave regime in North America.

Retreat and Destruction

While the convention declared independence, news of the massacres at the Alamo and Goliad burned their way across the territory. With nothing between them and an approaching Mexican army—as Sam Houston continued pushing his ragtag forces eastward on a strategic retreat—Anglos and Tejanos began abandoning their homes in panicked droves, fleeing toward the United States. The mass exodus, later dubbed the "runaway scrape," became a stampede of terrified men, women, and children who left behind houses "standing open, the beds unmade, the breakfast things still on the tables, pans of milk moulding in the dairies."[86] The roads became choked with refugees, and torrential rains soon transformed overrun highways into muddy bogs—"nearly knee deep," one man observed—that no wagon could pass.[87] Tensions became nearly unbearable at the rivers, where families sometimes waited in line for days for their turn to ford swollen streams. Thousands of people piled up at the Brazos and Trinity Rivers; mounting desperation at the San Jacinto River crossing produced "almost a riot."[88] Indeed, it was along those riverbanks that Tejano families, such as the Seguíns and Menchacas, found themselves standing side-by-side with Anglo-Texans, each waiting their turn to be ferried to the other side in conditions that one participant called "hard beyond description."[89]

All the refugees feared the wrath of Santa Anna, yet many also feared other violence that could accompany his army into eastern Texas. Rumors of Indians raiding on the heels of the Mexican army flew throughout the region, terrifying settlers as they tried to escape eastward.[90] More pervasive, however, were fears among Anglo-Texans of a slave rebellion or that Mexican troops would "compel you to liberate your slaves." When Anglo authorities along the Brazos River plantations suspected rebellion among

View on the Guadalupe, Seguin, Texas. This 1853 watercolor by Sarah Ann Lillie Hardinge
depicts a typical Texas river crossing, which became scenes of terror and chaos in 1836
during the "runaway scrape" mass exodus to Louisiana. (Amon Carter Museum of
American Art Archives, Ft. Worth, Texas)

their slaves at the beginning of the revolution, they rounded up nearly
a hundred enslaved people who were either "whipd nearly to death" or
hung for their supposed conspiracy. And, indeed, the arrival of Santa
Anna's army marked the beginning of enslaved Texans running away
to freedom behind Mexican lines. When General José de Urrea's army
approached Victoria in April 1836, fourteen enslaved people fled to his
lines for protection.[91] As Santa Anna's men neared the plantation districts
along the lower Brazos and Colorado Rivers, slaveholders abandoned the
region in droves—including Stephen F. Austin's brother-in-law, James
Perry, who evacuated his slaves along with his family.[92] So many Anglo
planters began herding their slaves toward the United States that one
young woman, Dilue Rose, noted "there were more negroes than whites
among us" at the river crossings.[93]

Although they could not know it, Anglo planters had good reason to
worry that the Mexican army would liberate their slaves. On his way into
Texas, Santa Anna sent letters to Mexico City seeking official sanction
for freeing slaves as part of the eradication of the rebellion. "There is a
considerable number of slaves in Texas also, who have been introduced

by their masters under cover of certain questionable contracts, but who according to our laws should be free," he wrote to his minister of war in Mexico City. "Shall we permit those wretches to moan in chains any longer in a country whose laws protect the liberty of man without distinction of cast or color?"[94] Santa Anna's vision for redeeming northeastern Mexico would mean the end of chattel slavery in Texas, and likely Anglo colonization along with it.

Mexicans within the interior of the country certainly expected that the pacification of Texas would mean the end of slavery in northern Mexico. During the spring of 1836, plantation owners in southern Veracruz sent a letter to Mexico City requesting that any Texas slaves freed by the Mexican army be sent to their plantations in order to grow "cotton, coffee, cocoa, añil, cane, vanilla, tobacco, and everything which is sown." They proposed that ex-slaves from Texas be bound to Veracruz farms as indentured servants "for at least a term of 10 (ten) years," but remain bound in servitude for as long as they and their family members remained in debt to the plantation owners. A growing textile industry had emerged in central Mexico during the worldwide boom in cotton prices of the early 1830s, something Stephen F. Austin had noted during his last trip to Mexico City. These Veracruzanos, many of whom provided Santa Anna financial backing, apparently hoped that the 1836 Texan revolt would allow them to import a new crop of indebted peons. Much as the Anglos had hoped in 1827 to blur the lines between indebted peonage as practiced in Mexico and chattel slavery as practiced by the Americans, planters in Veracruz hoped to do the same in 1836. The fact that these laborers were already skilled in cotton farming only heightened their value.[95]

Everything, then, hinged on the outcome of the war. As Santa Anna marched into the Anglo colonies, Sam Houston maintained his strategic retreat. Impatient to end the rebellion, Santa Anna divided his army and surged ahead at the helm of a smaller force in an attempt to capture the Texas government. Sensing an opportunity, the Texas army suddenly stopped its retreat, turned, and began marching hard toward Santa Anna's pursuing troops. The two armies met on April 20, 1836, at the confluence of the San Jacinto River and Buffalo Bayou. The Texans arrived first, making camp in the shade of an oak grove along the banks of the bayou, while Santa Anna's men dug in about five hundred yards away, at the edge of a marshy lake. Following some brief skirmishing, both commanders fortified their positions and waited through a tense night. Santa

Anna received reinforcements the next morning—which gave the general 1,200 troops to Houston's 900—and positioned his men to repel any Texan assault. When none came by midday, Santa Anna allowed his men a much-needed rest.

In the late afternoon of April 21, Houston organized his men into two columns—at the far left rode nineteen Tejanos under the command of Juan Seguín—and ordered an all-out charge. Following one organized volley, the Texans overran the disorganized Mexican lines, and the fight soon devolved into a chaotic one-sided slaughter that continued until nightfall, when 630 Mexican soldiers lay dead on the field. The Texans lost only nine men. They had, moreover, captured another 700 Mexicans and entirely routed Santa Anna's army. When Santa Anna himself was captured the following day, Mexico lost the war for Texas, bringing the rebellion to a remarkable and unlikely end.[96]

NO MENACING NEW THREAT to slavery or colonization had emerged during 1835 and 1836 that pushed the people of Texas into revolution. In explaining their actions, the revolutionaries pointed instead to Santa Anna's overthrow of the federalist system under the Constitution of 1824 as the prime mover toward war. With the rise of centralism in the form of a dictatorship in Mexico City, they insisted, there could be no future for Anglo colonies or Tejano villages under a Mexican government that did not support their rights under federalism. As late as the first months of 1836, many rebels in Texas, both Anglos and Tejanos, wanted nothing more than the restoration of the 1824 Constitution—it was not until the arrival of Santa Anna's army on Texas soil that the revolt against centralism became widely embraced as a fight for independence. The destruction of the federal political system in Mexico during the rise of a Santa Anna dictatorship was, without doubt, the pivotal event in the outbreak of the Texas rebellion.

By 1836, however, questions of federalism in Texas could not be separated from the slave-based agriculture that supported growing colonies of expatriate Americans in the region. Tejanos and Anglos both embraced federalism as a means of supporting the development of northeastern Mexico though the rapid expansion of the American colonies. For the Tejano leadership in San Antonio, the success of those colonies represented the only means they had for fostering a robust economy and stable population in northeastern Mexico. For Anglos, the colonies offered them the opportunity to grow cotton on more land than they could ever hope to acquire in the United States. For both groups, supporting those colonies meant sustaining the cotton cultivation that made them profitable and attractive to American migrants. And if embracing federalism served as a means for Anglos and Tejanos to support the development of Texas into a cotton-based empire, then embracing federalism also meant supporting the slave-labor system that made such things possible.

It was, in fact, the power of that system to transform the Texas borderlands that brought the colonies into conflict with Mexico's national government during the late 1820s and early 1830s. Fears that growing American influence along the Mexican frontier might shear the region from Mexico prompted national officials to reassert the power of the central government. Interference began with the national emancipation decree issued by Vicente Guerrero in 1829, although more lasting problems developed under the centralization policies of Lucas Alamán during the Bustamante administration. Because the cotton boom of the early 1830s more than doubled the Anglo population of Texas at precisely the same moment that Mexico City attempted to end American colonization and increase the nation's military presence in Texas, a series of clashes emerged between colonists and Mexican officials that bred mistrust on both sides. Indeed, by demonstrating that an assertive national government would be highly disruptive to the ongoing development of Texas, Mexico City helped cement the strident devotion to federalism among colonists and Tejanos that led them to revolt against the centralist regime of Santa Anna.

The war also ended a standoff that had developed by the mid-1830s between the Texans and Mexican government over slavery and cotton's place in the future of northeastern Mexico. The governments in both Saltillo and Mexico City had demonstrated, through legislation passed during the 1820s and early 1830s, their commitment to ending slavery in Texas by cutting off the influx of new slaves into the region. Those efforts had been partially successful—fewer U.S. slaveholders ventured into Texas than would have if Mexico had openly embraced the institution—yet the government had also been unable to stop numerous other Americans from transporting their slaves into Mexican territory. At the same time, the efforts of Anglos and Tejanos to support slave-based agriculture had produced similarly mixed results. While authorities in Texas managed to find a way to keep slavery alive despite antislavery legislation, they also recognized that Texas could never develop a truly success-ful slave-based economy without the open support of the government. Matters related to slavery within Texas had thus settled into an endur-ing standoff by the eve of the Texas Revolution, with neither side able to control fully the institution's future. The events of 1835–36 resolved the matter in favor of proslavery forces, although it now remained to those who lived in Texas to determine what that would mean for the future of this borderland region.

PART III

Cotton Nation and Slaveholders' Republic

A very few years will find us an unincumbered, free, and a wealthy people, our independence recognized, and our commerce sought after by all the world.
—Telegraph and Texas Register, 1839

We are indeed in a most uncertain and precarious condition—without strength and, worse than all, without confidence in ourselves. . . . We are in collapse—perfectly prostrate and powerless.
—Washington Miller, personal secretary to
   Sam Houston, 1842

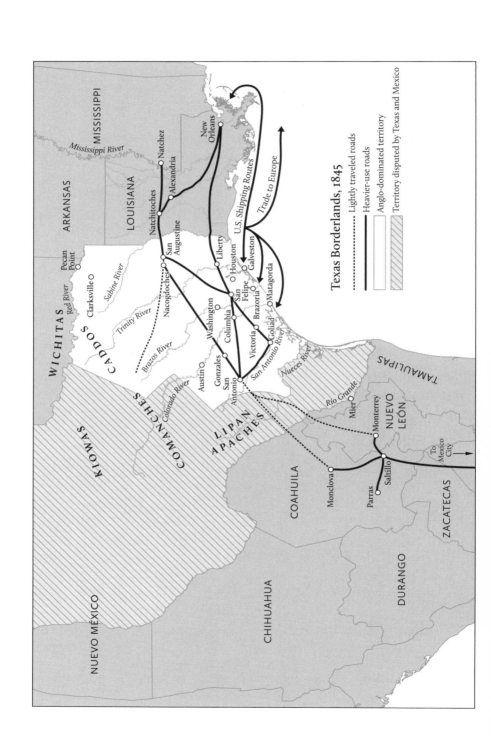

Texas Borderlands, 1845

.... Lightly traveled roads

──── Heavier-use roads

▢ Anglo-dominated territory

▨ Territory disputed by Texas and Mexico

FIVE

Creating a Cotton Nation, 1836–1841

As he made his way into Texas in April 1836, John Quitman found himself overwhelmed by the tide of terrified men, women, and children fleeing the region. Quitman, a wealthy cotton planter from Natchez, was serving as the governor of Mississippi at the outbreak of the Texas rebellion. Although people across the United States followed reports of the fighting in Texas with rapt attention during early 1836, the sheer number of expatriate Mississippians living in northern Mexico meant that the course of the war received special attention in the Magnolia State. In early April 1836, a traveler arrived in Natchez with news of the fall of the Alamo, along with reports that Santa Anna's armies were now marching toward the United States "with the design of inciting the slaves of Louisiana to freedom."[1] Outrage overtook the men of Natchez, and Quitman quickly organized a contingent of forty-five volunteers determined to join the Texan army. The makeshift militia then tore its way across Louisiana, picking up new recruits as it went, until at last it reached the Sabine River. Once across, the Mississippians rode headlong into a chaotic mass of Texas refugees scrambling to reach safety on the U.S. side of the border. "The road has been literally thronged by men women & children," Quitman wrote to his wife, Eliza, from his camp near Nacogdoches. "We have met at least one thousand."[2]

The throngs passing Quitman were part of the mass exodus of thousands of Texan settlers fleeing the violence of the revolution. When the decisive fight came on April 21, 1836, many of these refugees were near enough to the San Jacinto battlefield to hear the cannons. One young girl who heard them, Dilue Rose, would always remember how her father—convinced that the short duration of the cannonade signaled another defeat for the Texans—hurried his family along the road out of fear of the advancing Mexican army. Within days, Texan messengers heading east brought word of the defeat of Santa Anna's army and urged the refugees to turn back. Most refused, unwilling to abandon the road to the

United States and risk their families for what would likely prove to be another baseless rumor. A few settlers, including Dilue's family, did turn around and began the trek toward their abandoned homes.[3] Many others, like Quitman and his Mississippi volunteers, knew nothing for many days after the battle and assumed the region remained at war. Yet, in the aftermath of San Jacinto, the refugee tide started to slow as increasing numbers of people began turning back. And as people like Dilue Rose and John Quitman made their way across the post–San Jacinto landscape, they marveled at the decimation that so brief a war had brought to Texas.

The bloodied ground of San Jacinto—where both the Rose family and Quitman's troops arrived within days of the fight—embodied that destruction. When the wagon carting Dilue, her siblings, and her parents crossed the battlefield, Dilue recoiled at the "grewsome sight." The bodies of 630 dead Mexican soldiers had, by then, been rotting for five days where they had fallen, enveloping the area with the stench of decaying corpses. Although the Texans quickly buried their own, the Mexican dead were left to the elements until bones alone remained. When the Rose family camped that evening not far from the battlefield, Dilue and her siblings "could hear the wolves howl and bark as they devoured the dead."[4] Quitman arrived at the battlefield two days later and could hardly believe the carnage. "The ground is literally strewed with dead Mexicans," he reported to his wife.[5] Visitors who tired of battlefield gore could gawk at the more than 700 captured Mexican soldiers huddled in makeshift camps. In the chaotic and violent atmosphere that surrounded the battlefield, everyone recognized that the unlikely outcome of San Jacinto had irrevocably changed the relationship between Texas and Mexico. Yet what that would mean—for Texans, Mexicans, and Americans—remained entirely uncertain.

The decision of the rest of Santa Anna's defeated army to retreat toward the Mexican interior convinced many that the war was over and Texas would be free to determine its own fate. John Quitman, for his part, believed "that this victory decides the independence of the country," and immediately bought up thirteen thousand acres on speculation.[6] Certain that Texas would soon join the United States, Quitman began exploring the territory surrounding San Jacinto in hopes of purchasing more cheap land that he could then resell to the impending flood of Americans farmers.[7] Dilue Rose's father also thought the war had forever severed Mexico's claims to the region, although he believed that Texas would "become a great nation" rather than join the United States and soon set his family on the road to reclaim their farm.[8]

By the summer of 1836, Texan refugees began returning from the United States in hopes of resurrecting their homes and lives. When the Rose family finally reached their farm in early May, it had been ransacked. Mexican soldiers foraging for food had ripped up the floorboards of the house and scattered their belongings across the yard. Dilue's father recovered the plow he had hidden and set immediately to tilling his cornfields to ensure food for the coming season, while her mother directed the children in repairing the house itself. They also dug up a large blue chest they had buried just before their flight—filled with clothes, bedding, a few valuables—and before long the farm returned to working order. Their neighbors, too, soon trickled back into the neighborhood to reclaim abandoned homes. By the end of May, life had resumed enough of its normal cadence that Dilue's father and several other local farmers began building "a flat boat to ship their cotton to Brazoria."[9] Despite all that had been lost, the markets in New Orleans remained eager to purchase Texas cotton. In June 1836, only a month after returning home, the Rose family loaded new bales onto a flatboat bound for the Gulf Coast, knowing that the money that came from their sale would enable the family to rebuild.[10] Whatever Texas would become, it would remain cotton country.

Cotton, and its intertwined relationship to slavery, would shape the coming transformation of the Texas borderlands in the most fundamental ways. Some historians have noted, usually in passing, that the new Texas regime that emerged in 1836 endorsed slavery. What has remained so little understood, however, was how the devotion of Anglo-Texans to that institution brought with it remarkable burdens in global politics for the new Texas nation that would cripple the Texas government from the outset and isolate its people. Perhaps even less understood among scholars was how Anglo-Texan efforts to establish a slaveholders' republic served what they considered a greater end: rebuilding the region into a vast cotton empire that promised them a profitable future.[11] Cotton and slavery were inextricably linked in the minds of Anglo-Texans, who believed that the expanding economic power of their cotton fields would allow them to overcome whatever international objections might exist about their labor system. Anglo-Texans, as a result, came together during the mid-1830s to build a new nation based on what would turn out to be a flawed calculation—that the desires of the international community for

Texas cotton would force antislavery politicians in places like Great Britain and the United States into accepting Texas as a slaveholders' republic. They hoped, in other words, that being cotton country would protect them from abolitionists while also ushering in a new era of prosperity for Texas farmers.

The emergence of the Republic of Texas is best understood as an effort among Anglo-Texans to establish a haven for American cotton farmers in a world increasingly hostile to slave labor, foreshadowing similar efforts by the Confederates several decades later. Unlike the Confederacy, however, the Texans had some success—their sudden liberation from the threat of Mexican abolition, for example, brought a flood of eager Anglo farmers from the southern United States whose increased presence in Texas strengthened their hold on the region during the first few years after San Jacinto. Yet those same Texans also discovered, much to their dismay, that their heavy dependence on a single crop left them deeply vulnerable to the fluctuations of the global cotton market, which collapsed in spectacular fashion during the late 1830s. Being cotton country, it turned out, was not enough to overcome the great challenges—particularly the diplomatic burdens that came with their commitment to slavery—surrounding the Republic. The slow collapse of the Texas nation that followed would force Anglo-Texans to debate whether a country conceived as a cotton nation and dedicated as a slaveholders' republic could long endure. The answer would have consequences for more than just the Texas borderlands, setting off a fierce international struggle between Mexico, the United States, and Great Britain over the future of this particular corner of North America.

The break of Texas from Mexico also marked the beginning of a lasting shift in the relationship between Anglo-Americans and non-Anglos, as Tejanos and Indians found themselves increasingly pushed aside in the new Texas borderlands. Power in the region began to shift in disturbing ways with the last rifle shot at San Jacinto. Without the funds necessary to support several hundred prisoners of war, the Texas army began leasing out captured Mexican soldiers as "servants" to any Anglo willing to house, clothe, and feed them. The Rose family, along with most of their neighbors, soon acquired several Mexican prisoners to work their fields. "They all got Mexicans," Dilue recalled, "but it required an overseer to make them work."[12] If the line between using captured Mexican soldiers as servants or slaves became muddied for the Rose family, John Quitman apparently saw no such distinction in a post–San Jacinto Texas. In May

1836, as he prepared for the journey back to Mississippi, Quitman dashed off a short note to his wife, Eliza. Although he was still buying up land, Quitman wanted Eliza to know that he would be returning soon to "my beloved wife and children." In the meantime, he was sending her "a Mexican," who would be delivered in Natchez, Mississippi, by their friend, Mr. Ross. Quitman instructed Eliza "to have him sent over to the plantation," where she was "to make him a stock drover."[13]

Recognition and Annexation

In the months that followed San Jacinto, whatever order prevailed in Texas did not come from the new government or the army. The incessant dysfunction that plagued Texan leadership during the revolution continued unabated, so much so that by June 1836 there was virtually no functioning government in the region. Most people simply ignored what one settler deemed "perhaps the most imbecile body that ever sat judgment on the fate of a nation."[14] Refugees returning from Louisiana focused instead on rebuilding their homes and looked to the upcoming September elections for a permanent new government. If anything offered people like the Rose family some semblance of order amid such disarray, it was likely the familiar rhythms of the corn and cotton fields that resumed production that spring. Ships from New Orleans soon resumed their usual treks to the Texas coast, and in July 1836 Richard Royall loaded twenty bales from his Cedar Lane plantation on a New Orleans–bound schooner docked in Matagorda Bay.[15] James Perry, whose Peach Point plantation had survived the revolution unscathed, sent sixteen bales that summer to his agent in New Orleans, where their sale brought him $1,600.[16]

At the end of the summer of 1836, Texans held their first postwar election to select a permanent government. Sam Houston, now lionized as the "Hero of San Jacinto," won the presidency in a landslide, garnering 5,119 votes to the distant 743 cast for his closest opponent. Stephen F. Austin, who once stood at the center of Texas politics, garnered a mere 587 votes. When voters also unanimously approved the March 1836 Constitution and elected a slate of representatives for the new Congress, Texas emerged as the most unlikely creation: an independent slaveholders' republic, dominated by Anglo-Americans, dedicated to cotton, and built between the borders of the United States and the Republic of Mexico.[17]

It was hard to know how many people lived in the new Texas nation. The rapid movement of people shuttling back and forth across the U.S.-

Texas border during the war and its aftermath left the region's population in constant flux. The best sources suggest that by the fall of 1836 about 30,000 Anglo-Americans, 3,500 to 5,000 enslaved African Americans, 3,400 Tejanos, and approximately 14,500 Indians lived in the territory. The overwhelming desire of the majority of Anglo-Texans to make the region part of the United States, however, was unmistakable.[18] Some of this sentiment reflected the fact that many Anglos in the region still considered themselves Americans. Yet more practical reasons weighed on their minds, too. At its birth the Texas Republic was already $1.25 million in debt and lacked the infrastructure necessary for generating the revenue needed to run a government. Powerful Indian nations surrounded their western flank, and there were widespread fears that Mexico City would make good on its threat to launch an invasion to reconquer the country. Beyond solving these pressing challenges, joining the United States also promised tantalizing financial rewards to nearly everyone who owned land in Texas. If Texas were to become a U.S. state, most people assumed that the resulting flood of immigration would rapidly inflate Texas land prices, making everyone with a Mexican-era grant suddenly wealthy.

When Sam Houston assumed the Texas presidency in October 1836, he moved quickly to push annexation to the United States as the prime solution to the immense economic, political, and military challenges facing the new Republic. One of his first acts was to appoint Stephen F. Austin as secretary of state, hoping that Austin's reputation as the consummate diplomat would serve Texas well in such matters.[19] Yet simply gaining recognition from the United States was already proving difficult. Reports of the absolute mess that was the Texas government had already reached Washington, D.C., where the news undermined efforts at securing American assistance. Even before the September elections, Texas had dispatched two emissaries, James Collinsworth and Peter Grayson, to meet with President Andrew Jackson and members of the U.S. Congress on the possibility of bringing Texas into the Union.[20] Jackson, however, refused even to consider the matter until Texas "organized a more formal and regular government," and the U.S. secretary of state flatly refused to meet with them.[21] Houston sent a private appeal to Jackson, but such notes did little to counter the series of secret reports that Jackson received from an American agent stationed in Texas, who advised against recognizing Texas because Mexico would likely soon attempt to reconquer the province.[22] Citing the probability of a Mexican invasion, Jackson promptly sent a message to the U.S. Congress recommending that the

United States refuse to recognize Texas until "the course of events shall have proved beyond cavil or dispute the ability of the people of that country to maintain their separate sovereignty."[23]

Chastened, the Houston administration redoubled efforts to convince Americans that Texas could defend itself from Mexico and that annexation was in the best interest of the United States. Stephen F. Austin had already dispatched a new agent, William H. Wharton, who left for Washington, D.C., armed with laboriously detailed arguments about why Texas was "fully competent to sustain her independence, and fulfill the duties and obligations of an independent power."[24] Wharton also carried a set of secret instructions detailing the internal calculations of the Houston administration. To convince U.S. legislators to move quickly, Wharton was instructed to threaten American congressmen with the specter of an independent Texas in open competition with the southern United States, forging trade alliances with European powers based on "the great commercial advantages that will result to their nations from our cotton." The Texas diplomat, in other words, was to sell annexation as the only sure way for U.S. authorities to prevent Texas farms and plantations from becoming powerful economic rivals to the U.S. cotton industry. If such hard-nosed cajoling failed, Wharton was then to make good on those threats by approaching the ministers for Great Britain and France about recognizing Texas and establishing new trade relationships with the Republic.[25]

Austin planned to use Texas cotton as his central weapon in diplomatic negotiations with the United States and Europe, although he never lived to see the results. The new secretary of state caught a severe cold in the harsh December winds that rapidly worsened into pneumonia. Austin soon found himself too weak to leave the rented "shed room" that served as both his bedroom and office in the makeshift village of Columbia, where he suffered through the attempts of several local doctors to relieve and revive him. Eventually Austin slipped into unconsciousness. The former empresario, who did more than anyone to bring Americans into the Texas borderlands, died in the backroom of a ramshackle cabin on December 27, 1836.[26]

Yet the struggle for recognition went on, and from his perch in Washington, D.C., William Wharton reported that the real objection within the United States to recognizing or annexing Texas was the problem of slavery. U.S. secretary of state John Forsyth explained to Wharton that congressmen from northern states objected to the admission of Texas adding power to the cabal of southern slave states, and thus annexation would have to wait "probably for several years."[27] Although the place of slavery within the United States had been contested since the American Revolution, the challenge of balancing political power between slave and free states within the U.S. federal system had become increasingly difficult since the firestorm that erupted in 1819 with Missouri's petition to enter the Union as a slave state. Tensions between slave and free states grew increasingly heated during the late 1820s and early 1830s as various conflicts—fights over South Carolina's attempt to nullify a federal law, the emergence of a vocal U.S. abolitionist press, and a bloody slave revolt that erupted in 1831 in Virginia—pushed the volatile issue of slavery and the balance of power between the sections toward center stage in American politics. American southerners remained particularly incensed by tariff restrictions on importations from England, which they believed served the interests of northern manufacturers at the expense of cotton farmers in the southern United States. On the eve of Texas's rebellion from Mexico, the U.S. Congress became embroiled in a fierce battle over antislavery petitions, with several southern congressmen pushing a "gag rule" that prohibited the U.S. government from considering such proposals, and numerous northern congressmen protesting the gag rule as an open assault on free speech.[28]

Because Texas had declared itself unambiguously as slave country, the prospect of the United States' recognizing and annexing the Republic went straight to the heart of these controversies. The U.S. abolitionist press seized upon the revolt in Texas and the Republic's efforts to join the United States as clear evidence of a conspiracy among American slaveholders to steal as much of the continent as they could for slavery. "We regard the conduct of the Texians in the light of a REBELLION," screamed one northern newspaper, "and believe their object is to ESTABLISH AND PERPETUATE SLAVERY AND EXTEND THE SLAVE TRADE."[29] William Lloyd Garrison's the *Liberator* focused on Texas with searing intensity, publishing every anti-Texas speech, letter, and diatribe that Garrison could find.[30] Although most northerners were as apt as their southern counterparts to dismiss the arguments of abolitionists as fanatical rants, many northern congressmen—with former president John Quincy Adams in the lead—also stridently opposed incorporating Texas. Adams and others warned that annexing Texas would likely entangle the United States in a needless war with Mexico, but their main objection was to expanding southern strength in the U.S. Congress. Hoping to sidestep an intractable fight on the matter, members of both the outgoing Jackson and incoming Martin Van Buren administrations made it clear to Texas representatives that the United States would make no immediate moves toward annexation.[31]

Leaders in Texas understood these challenges. They had, however, also calculated that leveraging the political force of the Texas cotton trade would allow them to pressure the U.S. Congress into acting swiftly in their favor. In his conversations with American politicians, William Wharton had become convinced that publicly approaching European powers about establishing trade agreements with Texas would force a reluctant U.S. Congress to act. "This government cannot and will not consent to see an independent slave holding community existing contiguous" to the southern United States, Wharton predicted, since Texas would present "a formidable rivalry to the Cotton and Sugar growing interest of Louisiana and Missipi and the whole South."[32] James Pinckney Henderson, the new Texas secretary of state, wholeheartedly agreed, adding that the ability of Texas to supply cotton to textile mills "in the Northern States will more than compensate for the additional strength which its annexation will add to the political influence of the South."[33] Memucan Hunt, a Texas agent writing from Mississippi, urged Henderson to send "a secret agent to Great Britain" to secure recognition and a trade agreement. "The success in attaining which," he predicted, "will I believe guarantee our annexation to this country, for so ardent are the Southern States to procure the annexation of Texas to the Union that I believe the consequence of a failure to accomplish it, will produce a dissolution of the Union."[34] The Houston administration was betting, in other words, that being cotton country would allow Texas to overcome the political liabilities that came with also being slave country.

Texans were buoyed, too, by widespread public support they received from men and women in the southern United States. Editorials proclaiming support for the incorporation of Texas into the American Union appeared in newspapers across the South, and Thomas Richie's *Richmond Enquirer* emerged as a particularly strident voice in favor of joining Texas to the United States (which Richie called his "strongest wish, as well as the highest hope").[35] If some northerners fretted over the possibility of Texas adding to southern strength in the U.S. Congress, white southerners like Richie rejoiced at the same possibility. Southern excitement and sympathy for the Texan cause also came from the deep familial connections forged between the regions during the 1820s and 1830s, when nearly every Anglo immigrant into Texas came from the southern United

States.[36] In private, some southerners voiced concerns about a possible war with Mexico. Others fretted about what annexing Texas would do to land prices along the Gulf Coast. In South Carolina, Thomas Harrison urged his son James to sell as much of their land in Mississippi as possible, "for when Texas is opened to general enterprise" he expected an immediate drop in "the price of Mississippi lands."[37] From his home in Choctaw, Mississippi, Joseph Johnson predicted that opening Texas's "large territory of cotton growing country" to unrestricted American settlement would mean that land prices in Alabama and Mississippi "will decline at least one-third, if not one half."[38] Yet most southerners believed that widespread American migration into Texas would happen whether it joined the United States or not, and thus many threw their support behind securing the advantages that would come to the South from making Texas part of the Union.

Although southern political support helped secure U.S. recognition of Texas—which Andrew Jackson, in one of his last acts as president, made official in March 1837—it was not enough to spur the newly inaugurated Martin Van Buren into action on annexation. With an economic depression in the United States demanding his attention, Van Buren simply had no appetite for a possible war with Mexico and the all-out brawl within the U.S. Congress that could come with pushing forward on annexation.[39] And so the Texas government dispatched James Pinckney Henderson on a special mission to Great Britain in June 1837, calculating that widespread Anglophobia in the United States meant that any diplomatic or trade agreements that Henderson could forge in London would go a long way toward forcing the Van Buren administration to act.[40] Just as important, the desperately broke Republic needed to secure credit in order to have enough funds to run the Texas government, and London would be the most likely place to find willing creditors. And should Henderson somehow fail in Great Britain, he was then to proceed to Paris and open the same negotiations with the French.

If slavery posed a significant problem for Texans in their negotiations with the United States, Henderson had no doubt the institution would be the central obstacle to securing support from the British. By the mid-1830s, Great Britain had emerged as one of the most stridently antislavery governments in the world. Under the leadership of Quakers and Anglican evangelicals, abolitionist societies formed during the late eighteenth century had long petitioned their government to extricate the British Empire from the horrors of slavery. One of their first major victories came in 1807, when abolitionists pushed a law through Parliament out-lawing British participation in the Atlantic slave trade. The United States also banned the slave trade that year but the English proved far more dedicated to the cause than their American counterparts, and soon the British were using their status as the world's preeminent naval power to pressure other countries to follow suit. By the early 1830s, the abolitionist cause had gained so much force in Britain that in 1833 Parliament passed the Slavery Abolition Act, a sweeping plan of gradual emancipation that would free 800,000 slaves over five years.[41] When Henderson arrived in London in October 1837 as the representative of an avowed slaveholding republic, the Texas diplomat understood all too well that he would be asking for assistance from the country at the forefront of undermining New World slavery.[42]

England was also the world's leading consumer of raw cotton—import-ing more than 400 million pounds during 1837 alone—and Texas officials were once again betting that by offering access to their cotton fields they could overcome objections to their Republic's labor system.[43] A few days after reaching London, Henderson arrived at the office of British foreign secretary Lord Henry Palmerston to plead the case for British assistance. If England were to establish a formal relationship with the new Republic, Henderson explained, Texas would provide British manufacturers imme-diate access to "more good Cotton land, than was to be found in the whole United States." And because the Republic's economy focused exclusively on agriculture, a growing Texas population would be in perpetual need of purchasing manufactured goods, which would open another lucrative market for British exports. Palmerston, a seasoned diplomat, listened carefully to Henderson's arguments and asked in genial ways about the size and population of Texas. He then cut to the heart of the matter, ask-ing "rather archly" about the status of slavery in the new Texas Republic.[44]

In a tortured attempt to portray the Texas nation as a friend to Great Britain's antislavery efforts, the Texas diplomat found himself resort-ing to outright lies. It was true, Henderson conceded, that the Republic of Texas sanctioned slavery, but he blamed Mexico for the institution's endurance. Mexico, he argued, had repeatedly refused to outlaw slavery, and Mexicans had even "sanctioned the introduction of slaves into Texas from Africa." When Texas became independent in 1836, he explained, the new government had been trapped "in her present peculiar situation" and could not immediately abolish slavery simply because the country was not yet strong enough to do so. But the Texas government, he assured the British foreign secretary, "had remedied the evil as far as it safely could under the circumstances" by outlawing the international slave trade. Making Texas independent of Mexico, as Henderson told it, had thus been a great step forward in the global struggle for freedom, because "Mexico never had the ability or the disposition to put a stop to the African slave trade in Texas." It was an audacious and illogical argument, but Henderson feared that portraying Texas as anything less than an awkward friend of abolition would imperil his crucial mission in London.

Palmerston was not fooled. Henderson's efforts to rewrite history were roundly contradicted by the coverage that Texan efforts to thwart Mexican antislavery measures had received in British newspapers during the 1820s and 1830s. Mexican representatives in London, moreover, had outflanked the Texas diplomat by keeping Palmerston informed about Mexico City's perspective. Following Henderson's efforts to blame Mexico for sustaining slavery, Palmerston asked whether the Texas representative was aware that Mexico had passed a sweeping new antislavery law. In response to the secession of Texas, the Mexican national Congress had decreed that "slavery is hereby abolished, without any exception, throughout the Republic," and offered compensation to masters of the emancipated. Aimed directly at undermining the rebels in Texas, the law made clear that "the compensation spoken of in this article will not affect the colonists of Texas who have taken part in the revolution of that department."[45] Henderson said he was not aware of the law and then tried to change the subject by castigating the Mexican legislature. When Palmerston pointed out that Henderson "appeared to have a great contempt for the Mexicans," Henderson replied "that I thought their Character warranted my opinions."

The two-hour discussion had not gone well for the Texan. Promises of boundless cotton failed to elicit the enthusiasm that Henderson had hoped—the British already had a steady supply coming from the U.S. South—and the best that Palmerston would offer were general assurances that he "would as speedily as possible lay it before the Cabinet." Worse, Texan efforts to finesse the slavery problem had fallen so flat that Palmerston made a point to reiterate that the Republic's status as a slaveholding nation "would be a serious question to be considered in her Majesty's Cabinet" as it pondered recognition. Great Britain also remained deeply concerned that Texas might soon join the United States. Two weeks later, Henderson attempted to repair the damage by sending Palmerston a rambling letter that rehashed his arguments about the advantages of Texan cotton, the reasons why Mexico was to blame for slavery in the region, and he even went so far as to claim that Texans would move to abolish the institution in the near future. For good measure, he ended his appeal by framing the birth of the Texas nation as a step toward "extending the Anglo Saxon Blood, Laws and Influence in this South Western Region of the Western World" by sweeping aside the "weak, ignorant, and degraded race" of Mexicans who lived there.

None of it worked. The British declined to recognize the Republic, and the best Henderson could manage was an informal agreement permitting Texas ships to dock in British ports. Great Britain, however, was willing to do so only under the humiliating pretext that Texas was still part of Mexico, thus allowing the Republic to trade under England's existing treaties with Mexico.[46] The Republic's European gambit also brought no new pressure to bear on the U.S. government. When the Texas chargé d'affaires in Washington, D.C., submitted a formal petition for annexation to the Van Buren administration during the fall of 1837, the U.S. secretary of state promptly rejected it. The diplomatic calculations of the Houston administration had failed on nearly all counts, as Texan efforts to use cotton as a political weapon in securing annexation to the United States and to gain recognition from Great Britain both crashed against the politics of slavery. When Sam Houston appointed Anson Jones during the summer of 1838 as the permanent minister to the United States, he ordered Jones to withdraw the request for annexation.[47] Texans would have to build their own nation.

Barnyard Republic

As the Houston administration suffered repeated setbacks in foreign relations, the government's efforts within the Republic fared little better. Although Texan representatives in Washington, D.C., and London boasted about the effectiveness of the new Texan state, the truth was that Sam Houston's government barely functioned. Having secured nothing more than recognition from the United States, Texans found themselves attempting to build an effective state with almost no resources. Indeed, the failure of cotton diplomacy to overcome international objections to Texas's emergence as a slaveholders' republic quickly brought painful consequences to the new nation.

What bedeviled the Republic of Texas most was the lack of revenue, without which there could be no government. When Texan agents failed to secure loans in either the United States or Great Britain, Houston's administration had no choice but to begin taxing imported goods. The cash required to pay such tariffs, however, was almost nonexistent among Texas citizens, and so the measure's primary effect was to increase the appeal of smuggling along the U.S.-Texas border. And because the anemic Texas government could not afford the manpower needed to enforce tariff duties or slow smuggling along the border, the Republic then turned to levying taxes directly on its citizens. In June 1837 the Texas Congress decreed that every citizen would be required to pay a 1.5 percent tax on the value of certain personal property he or she owned, such as land, slaves, mules, and horses. Yet, again, the Texas government lacked the means to enforce such measures, and so during the first three years of the Republic at least a third of all property taxes simply went unpaid. Houston's administration finally resorted to issuing paper money—"to avoid the absolute dissolution of the government," Houston grumbled—and printed $500,000 in treasury notes in late 1837, followed by another $300,000 in 1838. Backed solely by the faith of the Texas government, the notes soon traded in New Orleans for only fifty cents to the U.S. dollar.[48]

The result was a government that existed largely on paper. Although the Texas Congress passed numerous laws aimed at instilling some measure of order on the fledgling nation—including an act prescribing the death penalty for at least fourteen crimes, including murder, arson, robbery, and stealing slaves—it was impossible to enforce such measures without more revenue.[49] Key government posts could not be paid and administration officials went without salaries during the first year of the Republic.[50] The Texas nation, in fact, could not even manage to run a functioning postal system, and mail service became so abysmal that many Texans hired private carriers to transport their correspondence safely to the United States.[51] Perhaps most telling, however, was the dreadfully understaffed condition of the Republic's General Land Office. The Land Office was charged with sorting through an avalanche of competing claims to tens of millions of acres granted under the Spanish, Mexican, and Republic of Texas governments, so the office could then validate and issue new land titles. The task was simply enormous. But so was the need to establish a reliable system for issuing clear land titles, which were indispensable for securing the holdings of Texas citizens, developing Texan agriculture, and encouraging potential immigrants. Yet the Texas Congress could initially afford to appoint only a single man, John P. Borden, to the task. And so Borden began organizing one of the most critical offices in the Texas government without any funding, supplies, or staff.[52]

The Republic, in turn, could not afford to maintain its meager military. Sam Houston soon shuttered the army by furloughing all but six hundred soldiers, and then cut all funding for the tiny Texas navy as an unsustainable expense. The Republic, as a result, became wholly incapable of controlling its coastline, and smugglers quickly seized the opportunity to increase shipments of enslaved Africans into both Texas and the United States. As early as the summer of 1837, the Republic had been reduced to begging the United States to send cruisers to patrol the Texas coast in response to reports of illegal slave importations. The U.S. secretary of state ordered an American naval squadron stationed in the Gulf of Mexico to begin patrolling near Texas in search of slaving ships from Cuba.[53]

Nothing better captured the frustrated ambitions of the early Texas Republic than the woes of its capital, Houston City. Hoping to capitalize on the rapid growth of the Republic by establishing a central trading hub of the Texas cotton industry, Augustus and John Allen laid out the town of Houston during the fall of 1836 with the promise that it would become "the great interior commercial emporium of Texas."[54] The two brothers began selling their new town lots even before they had been cleared or surveyed ("the labor of clearing the great space was done by negro slaves and Mexicans," recalled their nephew), and John Allen used his position in the Republic's legislature to help convince the Texas government to relocate to the as-yet-unbuilt town.[55] Only a few tents and a handful of houses greeted government officials when they arrived in early 1837, although the presence of the Texas Congress and president promised rapid growth of the hamlet. Within a year, several hundred people drifted into Houston City, as the town began to fill with newly constructed houses, hotels, and storefronts.[56]

Despite the Allen brothers' promises of grandeur, visitors who made their way through the Texas capital during these years derided Houston as a "detested, self-poluted, isolated mudhole of a city." Much like the Republic it governed, Houston City had been thrown up in haste on the hopes that annexation to the United States or expanding the cotton trade with Europe would ensure the region a prosperous future— only to see both those ambitions badly frustrated. Although older Texas towns, such as San Augustine, could boast homes built in Greek Revival elegance, nearly all dwellings in Houston City were "merely patched up shantees of rough boards," most without even the warmth of a chimney. The presidential "mansion" was a crude log cabin, until President Houston upgraded to an unheated clapboard shack that at least came with an attached shed. The Republic's Congress did not have it much better. "The building dignified by the name of *Capitol*," observed one unimpressed French visitor, "is merely a barn where the national legislature assembles."[57] Poor planning created horrendous health conditions in Houston City (locating the town site on swampland, for example, made dysentery, typhus, and cholera constant plagues), and the village so lacked both order and housing that prostitutes often plied their trade outdoors. Both the Texas nation and its capital city failed to live up to the lofty visions of its founders during the late 1830s. Kelsey Douglass, a representative of Nacogdoches in the Texas Congress, spoke for many when he deemed the Republic's capital "the most misera[b]le place in the world."[58]

El Dorado

Yet something continued to draw a growing stream of new migrants into the Republic of Texas, despite the spectacular failures of its government. Most came from the United States, where many imagined that Texas had a more functioning government than it did. Con artists in New York City, passing themselves off as representatives of the "Texian Consulate," began selling fake Republic of Texas passports to passengers boarding Texas-bound ships on the pretense that officials in Galveston would not allow foreigners to land without proper paperwork.[59] In truth, the Republic simply had no ability to monitor the growing influx of immigrants, which the *Telegraph and Texas Register* estimated amounted to "not less than thirty thousand" during 1837 alone.[60] Although migration had not yet reached such heights, the stream of new settlers could be seen in the ungainly growth of Houston City. For new arrivals in the Republic, the *Telegraph*'s editor offered a singular recommendation: "We advise them to go immediately into the country and commence farming; the fertility of the soil will amply reward their industry."[61]

The crush of American farmers making their way into Texas ensured rapid growth of the Republic during the late 1830s, a movement driven by a series of favorable circumstances that enabled Texas to undercut the land market in the southern United States. The birth of the Texas Republic coincided, remarkably, with the peak of the mid-1830s cotton boom, when prices paid in New Orleans and Liverpool reached heights not seen in a decade.[62] At that same moment, as cotton lands became more valuable than ever, the U.S. government suddenly stopped accepting credit (in the form of bank notes) as payment for public land. American farmers could now acquire new Gulf Coast acreage only if they had enough hard currency to pay in full, and very few did. When the Panic of 1837 then devastated the American economy, as the rush for payments in gold and silver collapsed banks from New Orleans to New York, hard times came to the United States. Farmers across the country found themselves bankrupt, as public lands slipped beyond their financial reach.[63]

In the new Texas nation, however, vast tracts of Gulf Coast territory remained available at rock-bottom prices. Texas newspapers overflowed with advertisements for land—offering everything from unimproved wilderness to fully established plantations, complete with cotton gins and enslaved work force—that could be had on easy credit for as little as $0.45 per acre.[64] And because the Republic had rewarded veterans of its army with generous land grants (in parcels of 320 to 1,280 acres, depending on their length of service), reams of cheap Texas land scrip circulated freely in the streets of Houston and New Orleans.[65] Thousands upon thousands of farmers, as a result, began abandoning the United States for the new Republic, prompting at least one New Orleans land agency to relocate its offices to Texas in order to take advantage of the movement.[66] A newspaper reporter stationed in Washington, D.C., marveled at the "tremendous rush" of planters and farmers making their way toward Texas, "where lands can be had for little or nothing, and where three crops of cotton can be made from one planting."[67]

Although Texas land had been consistently cheaper than comparable tracts in the United States since the early 1820s, the region's independence from Mexico made these lands newly attractive to American farmers. The potential insecurities of life under Mexican rule had long dissuaded many would-be American migrants. Yet the emergence of the Republic of Texas as an independent nation meant there was now little in terms of language, political structure, and population that distinguished Texas from most western U.S. states. The Republic's uniquely strident and unambiguous endorsements of slavery—and thus public repudiation of Mexico's previous attempts at abolition in the region—also greatly increased the value of Texas lands in the eyes of men and women from the southern United States. The vast majority of migrants making their way to Texas during the late 1830s hailed from the southern United States (Alabama, Tennessee, and Mississippi contributing the most), and the sheer volume of U.S. slaveholders making their way into the Republic prompted one British observer to predict in 1837 that "in twelve months from this time, the Slave population of Texas will probably be doubled."[68] The population of both slaves and slaveholders, in fact, tripled between 1837 and 1840, as American planters snatched up available lands throughout the Republic of Texas. Wealthier migrants tended to buy acreage within the bounds of the original Austin colonies or along the U.S.-Texas border, although farmers, slaveholders, and enslaved people poured into every county in the new Republic.[69] "Vast numbers are gone, going, or preparing to go, with their money and their domestic slaves, into the new *El Dorado*," marveled one New York City newspaper.[70]

Investors in both Texas and the United States rushed to capitalize on this migration. Land speculators across the United States tried to buy up Texas acreage. Although Missourian George Blaikie never planned to set foot in the Republic, he bought numerous Texas tracts with the intention of reselling them "to some Cotton Planters in the U States."[71] More adventurous investors staked out new towns along the region's major rivers, banking on their creations becoming trade centers and markets for nearby plantations. While the Allen brothers built Houston, dozens of other would-be cities—with such optimistic names as "Rome," "Pompei," and "Geneva"—sprang up across the Republic, often advertised for their access to the region's growing cotton industry.[72] Boosters of the recently incorporated village of Liberty, alongside the Trinity River, boasted of the town's proximity to "some of the richest cotton lands of Texas."[73] The founders of Richmond, a new village staked out on the banks of the Brazos River, promised potential merchants that "a steam boat will commence running regularly" that "will carry 300 bales of cotton and accommodate 40 passengers."[74] Rather than attempt to create a new town from nothing, one group of investors simply bought and began expanding the village of Columbia, because—as the group explained—its position on the Brazos River ensured that "from this point four-fifths of the cotton produced in West Texas is shipped."[75]

The rapid growth of Galveston during the late 1830s embodied many of the changes overtaking Texas. All but abandoned since the late 1810s, Galveston Island guarded the largest and closest natural harbor to the United States. Although ships from New Orleans regularly docked in the bay—at a pace of about one a month—to trade with farmers along the Trinity and Brazos Rivers, as late as 1836 there were only "two or three houses" and three large oak trees on the island itself.[76] With independence, however, traders and merchants fell over each other to establish shipping operations at the mouth of Galveston Bay. McKinney-Williams, the mercantile firm headed by Thomas McKinney and Samuel May Williams, transferred its base of operations in 1838 from the Brazos River to Galveston, where the firm soon constructed a massive three-story warehouse to store incoming merchandise and outgoing cotton bales.[77] Steamboats from New Orleans could reach the island within forty hours, and much of the growing tide of Americans making their way into the Republic flowed through Galveston.[78] By 1839, Galveston emerged as the largest town in Texas—swelling to more than three thousand residents— as it became the epicenter of the Republic's economy, boasting several commercial wharves and a thriving trade with New Orleans.[79] "Vessels are arriving daily and the harbor presents quite the appearance of an Atlantic port," observed Houston City's *Telegraph and Texas Register*, predicting that Galveston would become "the commercial Emporium of Texas."[80]

Even as the promise of agriculture drove much-needed migrants and money into Texas, no one seemed to know just how large the Republic's cotton trade was. The Texas government lacked the means to gather reliable numbers, so local newspapers offered their own estimates. One New Orleans paper reported in 1836 that Texas produced sixty thousand bales annually, while the *Telegraph and Texas Register* estimated the Republic's 1837 crop at fifty thousand bales.[81] Both estimates overshot their mark, yet the era's newspapers offered numerous anecdotes that reveal a significant trade coming out of Texas plantations. The *Telegraph* reported in 1837 that four brothers on the Colorado River managed to pick more than 850 pounds of cotton in a single day.[82] A ship that sank on a sandbar along the Texas coast in June 1838 went down with more than 640,000 pounds of cotton aboard.[83] Indeed, so many Texas bales were arriving on Louisiana docks that the New Orleans firm of Abell, Hammet & Co. invested in the construction of a new branch office on the Brazos River, where it proclaimed itself "prepared to receive and ship Cotton, to any port that may be required."[84]

What American merchants like Hammet & Co. sought most were partnerships with Texas farmers like James Perry, whose Peach Point plantation occupied prime acreage along the Brazos River. Planters needed lines of credit and ready access to supplies in order to keep their farms operating, and during the winter of 1838–39 Perry relied on the services of three different brokerage firms in New Orleans to do everything from securing parts for the repair of his cotton gin to sending money to his son's

This detail from *View of Galveston Harbor*, an 1843 pencil sketch by William Bollaert, offers one of the few surviving images of the Galveston waterfront that emerged during the late 1830s and early 1840s. The large buildings next to the docks housed mercantile firms that traded in Texas cotton. (The Newberry Library, Chicago, Vault Oversize Ayers Art, Bollaert #36)

boarding school in Kentucky.[85] These merchants, in turn, were happy to advance him credit because they wanted first claim to Perry's cotton bales and the commissions that would come with processing and selling them on the global market.

During the spring of 1839, Perry's enslaved work force picked the Peach Point fields, cleaned the bolls, and then baled them for export. When the schooner *Urbana* arrived on the Brazos River, Perry shipped his first fifty bales to New Orleans, where the firm of John A. Merle & Co. took possession of them as soon as they arrived on the docks. Working as Perry's agent, Merle & Co. ensured that his cotton was promptly weighed, pressed, and stored, while it haggled with potential buyers for the highest price available. Brokers paid all the numerous costs—including freight fees ($131.25), insurance premiums ($120.67), and storage and weighing fees ($18.75)—that came with shipping and selling a cotton crop. The largest expense facing Texas planters was the three-cent-per-pound tax that the United States government charged for importing foreign cotton into American ports. Paying U.S. importation duties cost Perry $768.51, fully two-thirds of his expenses in selling his fifty bales. When Merle & Co. finally sold Perry's crop for $3,165.76, the company collected its own brokerage and commission fees ($106.27) and then used Perry's profits to pay off $2,084.12 in debts that he had accumulated with various New Orleans firms.[86]

Merchants stood to profit as much from supplying Texas farms as they did from selling their crops. These mercantile firms thus traded in nearly every item imaginable, offering access to everything from rotgut whiskey to silk umbrellas.[87] Although some of that commerce served the needs of new towns like Houston and Galveston, most of the trade consisted of plows, seeds, tools, cotton gins, clothes, and other items needed by farmers like James Perry. Farmers, in turn, invariably had only their crops to offer in payment, which meant merchants had little choice but to deal primarily in cotton.[88] Despite persistent talk among enterprising investors, no sugar industry had yet taken hold in the region, likely because the upfront costs involved in establishing sugar plantations remained prohibitive for most. An 1840 guidebook offering advice for Texas-bound migrants noted that although "sugar cane, like most other crops, has heretofore received but little attention," cotton continued to thrive as "large numbers of the planters along the Brazos and elsewhere, are rearing considerable crops of that great staple of the south."[89] Cotton, indeed, often composed more than 90 percent of the Republic's entire export trade (small shipments of animal hides made up the country's second-most-valuable export).[90] There was a great deal of money to be made serving the needs of the growing number of farmers arriving in Texas, whether from land speculation, supplying the equipment for their farms, or marketing the cotton bales that came from their fields.

The *Ambassador*

Two Texas-based firms—R. G. Mills & Co., and McKinney-Williams—jockeyed for dominance of the Republic's cotton trade. The Mills brothers, Robert and David, ran their mercantile business out of the town of Brazoria, whose position along the Brazos River gave them ready access to some of the largest plantations in the Republic.[91] McKinney-Williams ran a similar operation out of Galveston, where the company's newly built warehouse and shipping wharf offered Texas farmers the most direct connection to New Orleans and other international ports. Although they operated within the Republic, such firms relied heavily on investors and financiers based in the United States for the capital needed to advance large sums of credit to local farmers. McKinney-Williams, for its part, operated essentially as a branch of the Baltimore shipping firm of Henry Williams (brother of Samuel Williams), who underwrote the majority of the McKinney-Williams credit lines.[92] Numerous other merchants, based mostly in Texas and New Orleans, also competed for a cut of the Republic's cotton, although none in Texas could match the financing and political muscle of the Mills and McKinney-Williams operations.

During the winter of 1838–39, McKinney and Williams leveraged nearly all their capital in a bold gamble to establish themselves as the preeminent traders of Texas cotton. Through its business connections in Baltimore, the firm arranged for a British trading house in Liverpool to send a ship— the *Ambassador*—to its wharf in Galveston, where the British merchants hoped to exchange a cargo of English-made goods for as much Texas cotton as the vessel could hold. If successful, the shipment promised to mark the beginning of direct commerce between England and Texas, opening lucrative new opportunities for both the Republic's farmers and McKinney-Williams. British manufacturers paid more for cotton than buyers in the United States, and bypassing American ports like New Orleans would allow Texas farmers to avoid costly U.S. import duties (which meant Texas farmers could pocket an extra four or five cents per pound, perhaps doubling their profits). Cornering the Republic's cotton market and becoming the gateway to European markets, Thomas McKinney believed, would allow the firm to "control to a great extent all the valuable business of the Country" and thereby make him and his partner tremendously wealthy.[93] "We will ship more cotton this season than any five merchants in Texas," he predicted, "and indeed the whole country begin to look to us as the channel through which their business must be done."[94]

Enticing British shippers to invest in regular voyages to Galveston, however, depended on filling the *Ambassador* with high-quality Texas cotton, and McKinney moved swiftly to secure the rights to every cotton bale he could acquire. He sent word to Houston City, where the *Telegraph* announced that "a vessel richly freighted with British manufactured articles is now on her way from Liverpool to Galveston." The newspaper, a longtime advocate for establishing direct commerce with Europe, trumpeted the news as the dawn of a new era for the Republic, "when our planters will no longer look to the ports of the United States for their supplies of manufactured articles, not for a market for their cotton, but directly to Europe."[95] The firm hoped that local farmers would feel much the same. McKinney and S. L. Jones, an employee of the company, began making their way up and down the Republic's rivers, traveling from farm to farm, where they tried to sell every planter on the profits to be had from shipping their crops directly to British buyers. Most farmers recognized the remarkable opportunity, and McKinney soon began collecting promises for processed bales. In exchange, McKinney provided letters of credit—essentially advances on the eventual sale of their crops—which farmers could then use either to purchase goods from his Galveston store or to pay off other debts.

While farmers lined up behind McKinney-Williams, other Texas merchants did their utmost to counter the operation out of fear of losing business. Robert Mills threw everything he had into undermining the purchasing trip of S. L. Jones, following the agent of McKinney-Williams as he traveled up and down the Brazos River. Once Jones left a farm, Mills swept in and condemned Jones as a liar, claiming that there was no vessel coming from England. When that failed, Mills denounced the credit lines of McKinney-Williams as worthless, and then offered to extend his own generous credit terms in an attempt to scare farmers into marketing their crops with him. None of it had much effect. "It is really amusing to see him pass about and following in my track," Jones reported, "endeavouring to persuade the Planters to let him have the Cotton" and "offering to leave all their debts lay over and make advances besides." McKinney, knowing the stakes, found Mills's propaganda less entertaining. "Damn him," wrote an incensed McKinney, "I will give him a dose that will sicken him." Mills flew into his own rage when McKinney-Williams began collecting cotton from farmers previously committed to Mills & Co., leading to at least one heated exchange between Mills and Jones. Although no one fought as hard as Mills, nearly every other merchant in the region shared his angst. "Merchants are leagued against us here," Jones reported from the Brazos, "as they say we want to monopolize the trade."[96]

The most daunting challenge facing McKinney-Williams, as it turned out, was the Republic's appalling transportation infrastructure. Given the distances to be covered and the condition of Texas's few roads, the only cost-efficient means for transporting 450-pound bales of cotton was shipping them downriver to the coast. Yet large sandbars at the mouths of most Texas rivers made it difficult to move sizable ships up the Brazos or Colorado, and the rivers ran so low during the winter of 1838–39 that even small vessels regularly scraped the bottom. McKinney and Williams nonetheless directed their company fleet to sweep up and down the Republic's rivers collecting bales. Their steamboat, the *Laura*, soon ran aground while descending the Brazos, forcing the firm to charter a small schooner to rescue its cargo. That new schooner, however, nearly sank when it also ran into the Brazos sandbar. McKinney-Williams managed to reclaim the *Laura*'s bales by resorting to keelboats, whose shallow draft finally got the bales over the Brazos sandbar and loaded onto Galveston-bound ships waiting along the coast. With the Republic's government unable to promote internal improvements, the lack of reliable infrastructure for transporting crops to market would remain a central challenge for firms like McKinney-Williams hoping to expand the Texas cotton industry.[97]

Yet McKinney-Williams also proved that the Texas industry could now operate on the world stage. During the winter of 1838–39, the firm had enticed British shippers into investing in a voyage to the Texas Republic, cobbled together more than $50,000 in financing from the United States, and collected more than 1,200 bales in Galveston (where the merchants anticipated the arrival of 500–700 more).[98] When the 400-ton *Ambassador* finally sailed into Galveston's harbor on February 25, 1839, it was a triumph for both McKinney-Williams and the Republic's cotton industry. "It proves incontrovertibly," noted one French observer, "the feasibility of direct trade between Europe and this country, a commerce which the American merchants, principally those of New Orleans, quite understandably were doing their best to discourage."[99]

Everyone seemed to agree that such trade offered tremendous hope to the Republic. Celebrations broke out along Galveston's waterfront, where—according to Houston City's *Telegraph*—the locals manifested "as much joy as if our Independence had been acknowledged at the court of St. James."[100] Sam Houston and other Texas dignitaries rode out to greet the ship, and then "made quite a frolic" during the festivities that followed.[101] Despite the faltering of the Republic's government, the steady migration of Americans into the region and the recent success of their cotton industry gave Texans renewed confidence in the prospects of their nation. "There never has been such a universal feeling in favor of raising cotton in Texas as at present," proclaimed McKinney, who had already received orders for six new cotton gins.[102] Many, indeed, believed that establishing direct trade with Europe would usher in a new era of diplomatic successes for the fledgling Republic. Anson Jones, who had recently returned from serving as the Texas minister to the United States, predicted great things would follow the *Ambassador*'s arrival in Liverpool. "You have sent the best possible negotiator for the Government to England," Jones told a crowd in Galveston, "a ship loaded with cotton, the staple production of the country."[103]

The Promised Land

Texans needed something to celebrate. The repeated failures of the Republic's cotton diplomacy—to gain annexation to the United States, win recognition from Great Britain, or even secure a loan to shore up the nation's shaky finances—had ensured that Sam Houston's administration became increasingly unpopular. Houston's other signature policy, an effort to establish peace with the region's Indians, also rankled most white Texans, who could not fathom why the president sought "treaties of peace and amity, and the maintenance of good faith with the Indians" rather than waging war against groups like the Comanches.[104] Houston staked out his peace policy, in part, for personal reasons—he had been adopted as a youth by a band of Cherokees, served as an Indian agent for the United States, and at one time lived with a Cherokee woman. But Houston's position was also the only practical option for his administration: the Republic's international isolation ensured that the nation's finances could not sustain any protracted Indian war. And so Houston hoped that diplomatic overtures to the region's tribes—including the Comanches, Wichitas, Apaches, Caddos, and Cherokees—would prevent hostilities between Anglo settlers and Texas Indians that the Republic simply could not afford.[105]

Yet the sheer volume of Americans pouring into Texas for cotton lands rapidly undermined Houston's peace policy. Tens of thousands of farmers making their way into eastern Texas soon encroached on lands already claimed by Cherokees, Shawnees, and Caddos, producing renewed conflicts between Anglos and Indians. And as expanding Anglo settlements along the Republic's western flank pushed ever closer to Comanchería, violent raids and bloody retribution became more frequent on both sides. Caddos, Cherokees, Tonkawas, Apaches, and even Comanches all eventually signed treaties of peace, although in practice the agreements did little to stem the violence. Indians in both eastern and western Texas continued to make intermittent raids on Anglo homesteads, while bands of Anglo-Texans attacked various tribes and threatened Indian landholders. Despite President Houston's animated lobbying on its behalf, the Texas Senate rejected a proposed peace treaty with the Cherokees after the Republic's Committee on Indian Affairs denounced the tribe as "the most savage and ruthless of our frontier enemies." Most tribes in eastern Texas, overwhelmed and overrun by the growing tide of Americans flooding into the territory, concluded that the Republic's government lacked both the will and the desire to protect them.[106]

Tejanos, too, were being crowded out in eastern Texas by the flood of Anglo-American farmers coming into the region. The old political elite in San Antonio continued to hold some influence within the new Republic, and a few prominent Tejanos—most notably José Antonio Navarro,

Francisco Ruíz, and Juan Seguín—won seats in the Texas Congress.[107] By the late 1830s, however, the few hundred Tejanos who lived in the area around Nacogdoches found themselves surrounded by new settlers from the United States who cared nothing about the role Tejanos had played in supporting Anglo migration during the 1820s. The arriving Anglos often made few distinctions between these longtime residents of eastern Texas and any other ethnic Mexicans. As early as September 1836, a group of "american citizens" petitioned the Republic's government to disfranchise "the Mexican Population residing in the Municipality of Nacogdoches" for being "the friends of our enemies and the enemies of our friends."[108] The measure failed, yet Tejanos faced increasing levels of harassment and violence that grew in proportion to the influx of new Anglos. Some Tejanos began to abandon eastern Texas in search of refuge for their families.[109] A few, such as Vicente Córdova of Nacogdoches, even joined forces with local Indians in armed resistance against Anglo-Texan settlers, leading a short-lived revolt in 1838 against the Texas government.

In the midst of these upheavals, Texans elected a new president and administration to lead the Republic. The Texas Constitution barred a president from succeeding himself, so Sam Houston's supporters offered voters an uninspiring succession of presidential candidates—two of whom committed suicide before the election—although no one who advocated a continuation of Houston's policies had any hope of winning. Mirabeau Lamar, a Georgia slaveholder and newspaperman who came to Texas during the revolution, quickly became the frontrunner for the presidency on a stridently anti-Houston platform. Whereas Houston had sought to join Texas to the United States and pursued policies of peace with Indian nations and Mexico, Lamar promised instead to build an enduring and independent Texan nation by waging war against the Republic's enemies. The abject failures of Houston's cotton diplomacy efforts meant that Lamar's promises of a new direction resonated with most Anglo-Texans, allowing the Georgian to win with an astounding 96 percent of the vote.[110] "He appears to be unanimously popular," noted the *New Orleans Picayune*, "and it is expected that almost everything will be changed for the better."[111]

In his inaugural address, Lamar outlined his vision for a vast new Texan empire that would one day stretch "from the Sabine to the Pacific." It would be a nation of farmers, he explained, who would look to "agriculture, commerce and the useful arts, as the true basis of all national strength and glory." Despite his outright rejection of nearly all Houston's individual policies, Lamar nonetheless shared his predecessor's overarching faith that Texas's growing agricultural industry—particularly cotton, "in the production of which she can have no rival"—remained the key to securing a vibrant future for the region's Anglo population. With "the richest soil in the world," and farms across the Republic "all in the state of high cultivation and improvement," Lamar made clear that his administration would seek to transform the Republic's great agricultural potential into the foundation for a thriving independent nation. His faith was likely buoyed by the ongoing boom in cotton prices during the late 1830s and the hope that direct trade with England would usher in a new economic era for the Republic. Unlike Houston, however, Lamar had determined that building a cotton empire in Texas meant the region could never join the United States. Annexation, he warned, would "prove as disastrous to our liberty and hopes, as the triumphant sword of the enemy."[112]

Lamar rejected annexation—and the United States—because he believed that any political union subjecting Texas to the influence of abolitionists would be disastrous. Many Texans, like Lamar, found themselves aghast at how antislavery activists in both the United States and Great Britain held up the Texas nation as the embodiment of everything detestable about slavery and slaveholders in North America. Condemnations of the Republic—as a haven for slave smugglers, slave breeders, and all the most craven aspects of the institution—provided regular fodder for the abolitionist press in both countries. One of the more dramatic attacks came from Benjamin Lundy, an abolitionist newspaperman who published a pamphlet lambasting the Texas Revolution as a conspiracy by U.S. southerners *"to wrest the large and valuable territory of Texas from the Mexican Republic, in order to re-establish the* SYSTEM OF SLAVERY; *to open a vast and profitable* SLAVE-MARKET *therein; and, ultimately, to annex it to the United States."*[113] Such charges soon became standard in antiannexation speeches on the floor of the U.S. Congress, as well as among antislavery politicos in London, who sought to stymie the ambitions of the new slaveholders' republic.[114] Such charges had, indeed, helped derail nearly all the Republic's early diplomatic efforts.

White Texans also watched with alarm as sectional struggles over slavery grew increasingly heated within the United States. Following the example of their English cousins, American abolitionists during the 1830s began sending petitions to the U.S. Congress (most of which sought to outlaw the slave trade in Washington, D.C.) protesting the American government's complicity in slavery. Southern representatives responded by passing resolutions that prohibited Congress from receiving or considering the petitions. Numerous northern politicians, with John Quincy Adams in the lead, denounced such gag rules as an assault on free speech and demanded that Congress receive the antislavery resolutions.[115] Vicious public battles ensued over the role of the U.S. federal government in supporting slavery, all of which made annexation far less appealing to white Texans. Many in the Republic, indeed, were appalled that northern politicians and newspapers jabbed at Texas slaveholders just as often as they did slaveholders in the southern United States. "If Texan liberty means nothing more than the liberty to enslave their fellow beings," wrote the editor of one Massachusetts newspaper, "we candidly confess that we care not how little of it they may ever possess."[116] President Lamar, in response, declared that he had no interest in bringing Texas into a country "in which a large portion of the inhabitants are alarmed for the safety of the very institution upon which her own hopes and happiness are based."[117]

Lamar, instead, imagined an expanding Texas empire that would serve as a refuge for North American slaveholders. In an earlier draft of his inaugural remarks, Lamar predicted that continued agitation by abolitionists in the United States meant "that a dissolution of the American Union must take place at an early day." The problem, he argued, was that slaveholders in the United States had no "guarantee stronger than the feeble & inefficient one afforded at present by the national constitution." The Republic of Texas, by contrast, offered slaveholders an unabashedly proslavery constitution. In Texas, there would be no abolitionist movement, no meddling northern politicians like John Quincy Adams, and thus no acrimonious debates about "the preservation of the institution of slavery, upon which our character prosperity and happiness as a free people must necessarily depend." And with no local manufacturing industry to protect, Texas would remain free "from the thralldom of tariff restrictions" that had so angered U.S. cotton planters. The Texas Republic could, in other words, offer slaveholders everything that the United States could not—a government fully supportive of slavery, dedicated to building the infrastructure and trade system necessary for a dynamic cotton economy—thereby making the Republic a sanctuary for American southerners hoping to escape the bane of abolitionism.[118] And the new president was hardly alone in such hopes. A few months before Lamar's inauguration, the *Telegraph and Texas Register* noted that the antislavery movement in the United States "operates as a powerful motive, on the

YOUNG TEXAS IN REPOSE.

Young Texas in Repose, circa 1845, published by R. Jones. This anti-Texas cartoon published in New York portrays the Republic of Texas as a not-fully-human slaveholder perched atop a badly whipped slave. The sombrero and Kentucky long rifle combine the Mexican and American influences, and his broken hand and ankle cuffs depict Texas as a fugitive from justice. (General Collection, Beinecke Rare Book and Manuscript Library, Yale University) part of many, to oppose the annexation of this country to the United States." The ironclad security of the institution in the Republic, bragged the *Telegraph*, meant that American slaveholders "will look to Texas as the Hebrews did to the Promised Land for a refuge and a home."[119]

Empire of the South

Lamar moved swiftly to clear out cotton country for Anglo farmers, and there was no room for Indians in his new Empire of the South. In his first message to Congress, Lamar called for "the prosecution of an exterminating war on their warriors, which will admit no compromise and have no termination except in their total extinction or total expulsion."[120] Following the lead of his native Georgia (which had also expelled Indians to clear ground for white settlements), Lamar dispatched hundreds of mounted troops to overrun Cherokee, Caddo, Shawnee, and Delaware homes in eastern Texas, forcing survivors to flee in terror to the United States.[121] After quickly decimating the small Indian presence in the East, Lamar authorized renewed campaigns against the Comanches in the West. Fierce violence ensued. Numerous raids by Texan militia on Comanche camps took a heavy toll on the nation, which responded in kind with brutal attacks on nearby Anglo farms. Several Comanche bands petitioned the Republic for peace, but a bloody melee erupted at the peace talks when Lamar's men attempted to arrest their Comanche counterparts.[122] The Comanches then retaliated with a massive raid along the Republic's southwestern flank in August 1840, burning the trade centers of Victoria and Linnville and stealing two thousand horses. A hastily assembled militia of several hundred Anglo-Texans, along with a handful of Tonkawa Indians, counterattacked in a bloody fight at Plum Creek that began a new sustained assault against the Comanches.[123]

As he had hoped, Lamar's vicious policy of driving out tribes in order to make way for cotton farmers succeeded in extinguishing the Indian presence in the eastern sections of the Republic. It also pushed back the Comanche presence in western Texas, as the tribe retreated farther up the Colorado River in the face of relentless violence. All of that came, however, at a tremendous price. Battles with Comanches decimated numerous Anglo farms and settlements along the Republic's western frontier, and Lamar's Indian wars cost the Republic $2.5 million that it simply did not have.[124] The Republic's failure in 1838 to secure a $5 million loan from the Bank of the United States—which Texan diplomats blamed on the "atmosphere of *abolitionism – fanaticism anti Texas & anti Slavery feeling*" in the northern United States—meant that Lamar's military campaigns pushed the Republic to the brink of bankruptcy.[125] The Indian wars, in other words, badly exacerbated the Republic's intractable financial problems that came with its international isolation as a slaveholding nation.

Lamar's administration, as a result, had no choice but to resurrect Sam Houston's original cotton diplomacy campaign in hopes that winning recognition in Europe would secure a desperately needed loan. Following his failure in London, Texas diplomat James Pinckney Henderson had moved on to Paris, where he expected a warmer reception. Not only was France the second-largest consumer of raw cotton in Europe, but the country was also embroiled in a heated dispute with Mexico over claims by French citizens against the Mexican government.[126] The moment appeared ripe for Texas to gain its first European ally, and Henderson made the same cotton-laden sales pitch in Paris as he had in London. By recognizing Texas, he explained, the French would gain access to "more land well adapted to the culture of cotton than is to be found in the whole United States," as well as an eager and growing market for selling French-made goods. Henderson entirely avoided talking about slavery, "deeming it most prudent to leave that subject untouched" after his debacle in England.[127]

The French proved to be far more concerned about the long-term stability of the Republic than its reliance on slavery. One report circulating in Paris lamented that the Texas government "exists only in the most rudimentary form" and its finances were "in the most deplorable condition," leaving the French Foreign Ministry to conclude that the survival of Texas "as an independent state is at best problematical."[128] France thus dispatched an emissary, Alphonse Dubois de Saligny, with orders to tour Texas and report to the king on its prospects. Saligny's dispatches back to Paris offered a glowing portrait of the country, urging the French government to establish a formal relationship with the Republic in order to take advantage of Texan commerce and trade, particularly before the British could. Texas would survive as a nation, he assured his superiors, because Mexico lacked the ability to reconquer the province and because American abolitionists would never allow it to be annexed to the United States. "Slavery is, as Your Excellency knows, the foundation stone of Texian society," Saligny explained.[129]

Satisfied that Texas could stand on its own, the French government decided to overlook the Republic's labor system in order to gain access to its cotton and markets. (Such news must have been a relief to Henderson, who had studiously avoided the topic while in Paris. When a French minister asked Henderson about slavery in Texas, the Texas diplomat retorted: "I will not even discuss that question.")[130] French negotiators of the treaty, however, adopted a hard line, demanding that French goods enter Texas ports at reduced tariff rates, even though they would grant no such favors in return on cotton imported from Texas. The lopsided terms made Henderson livid, but he also recognized that Texas could not afford to turn down any treaty opportunity. The Republic finally secured recognition from Europe on September 25, 1839, with the signing of a trade agreement with France.[131]

Yet recognition, it turned out, did nothing to help the struggling Republic secure financial assistance. Lamar appointed James Hamilton, the former governor of South Carolina and a prominent leader of the 1830s nullification movement, as a special agent to negotiate on behalf of Texas for a desperately needed $5 million loan. When Hamilton could raise no more than $400,000 in the United States, he turned to Europe. France, despite granting recognition, refused to lend any money to the Republic. Hamilton then made an extended pitch for financial assistance in London, but failed there, too. Hamilton blamed a soft money market in England and "unfounded prejudices against every Country tolerating domestic Slavery" for his inability to secure funds for Texas.[132] Appeals for assistance from the Netherlands and Belgium also produced nothing (although Hamilton did manage to secure recognition for Texas from Holland). With no other options available, the Lamar administration began printing reams of paper money, more than $2.7 million worth, backed only by the faith of the Republic. Before long, a Texas dollar would fetch only twelve cents on the streets of New Orleans.[133]

Many in Texas, including Lamar, recognized that Mexico's refusal to acknowledge Texan independence played an important role in discouraging nations from assisting the Republic. A frustrated Lamar sent an emissary, Bernard Bee, to Veracruz with an offer to pay Mexico $5 million in exchange for recognition. It was, however, a hopeless mission—no political party in Mexico could consent to Texas independence without losing all popular support, and a deep distrust on both sides over the slavery issue cast a shadow over all discussions. Bee nonetheless pressed the matter with Guadalupe Victoria, the former president of Mexico, who warned "that utter annihilation awaited us" unless Texas rejoined Mexico. Bee replied that reunification was impossible because "we were a different people" and "Texas was valueless without Slaves, and that under his constitution, Slavery could not exist." Victoria promised that the Mexican "Congress would assent to Texas holding them," but both sides simply talked past one another.[134] Mexico's ministers, in fact, took every opportunity in London and elsewhere to lambaste Texas as a slaveholders' haven, hoping that the Republic's commitment to slavery would help Mexico undermine Texan appeals for assistance in Europe.[135] Two other emissaries sent to Mexico by Lamar also failed to make any headway.

Yet it was the collapse of the cotton market that finally dashed Lamar's dream of transforming Texas into an empire for the South. Lamar's grand visions of expansion had been built explicitly upon the assumption that steady growth of the Texas economy would lift the nation—which, in turn, depended entirely on a continuation of the high prices that cotton commanded for most of the 1830s. The broad economic depression that devastated the United States following the Panic of 1837, however, soon engulfed the cotton market. The prices that New Orleans merchants could offer Texas planters began collapsing in 1839, and by 1842 the value of a bale of cotton had dropped by more than half.[136] Texas newspapers began carrying articles on the slowing cotton markets "which have proved so calamitous to the commerce of this country," and many Texans found themselves in desperate straits by the early 1840s.[137] Both farmers and merchants fell deeply into debt; prime lands along the Brazos River began selling for as little as twenty-five cents an acre.[138] Although the Republic's farms produced more cotton than ever—James Perry's plantation alone produced more than 250,000 pounds during the fall of 1840—the tailspin of cotton prices brought hard times to everyone.[139] "Times are worse than ever & they are still growing worse," reported one of James F. Perry's sons from the family's Peach Point plantation. "I dont know what we will do for money to pay our taxes."[140]

Voters across the Republic blamed the depression on Lamar's extravagant spending, although the truth was more complicated. In addition to the heavy expense of his Indian wars, Lamar had spent millions outfitting a new Texas navy (which he used mostly to harass the coast of Mexico), hiring a legion of new civil service employees (to staff a newly active government), and relocating the capital from Houston to a small hamlet (Waterloo, soon renamed Austin in honor of the empresario) on the far-western edge of Anglo settlement. Such unfettered spending, combined with the complete collapse of Texas currency under Lamar's watch, proved too much for most Texans. "In every quarter we hear constant lectures upon political economy, and reiterated complaints against the Government on account of national expenditures," observed Houston City's *Telegraph*.[141]

Lamar's reckless spending certainly made things worse. Yet the hard reality was that, no matter what Lamar did, the Republic of Texas remained far too dependent on trade with the United States to be able to escape the effects of the economic depression ravaging its northern neighbor. More than three-fourths of all Texas cotton still went to the United States during the early 1840s, and American ships made up 97 percent of the traffic coming into Texas ports.[142] Because Texas remained almost entirely a one-crop economy (cotton composed 95 percent of the Republic's exports as late as 1844), the nation proved deeply vulnerable to any price fluctuations in the market.[143] It was, in fact, the combination of cotton prices bottoming out in New Orleans and the profound weakness of Texas currency that accounted for the decimation of the Republic's economy during the early 1840s.

Collapsing Nation

The abysmal state of Texan affairs near the end of Lamar's term led, remarkably, to an unlikely breakthrough in diplomatic relations with England. British diplomats monitoring the Republic of Texas concluded that Mexico would never reconquer Texas, and France's decision to recognize the Republic left British manufacturers concerned about losing access to Texas cotton. For the British, bountiful access to cotton was a matter of grave national interest. English textile mills consumed 592 million pounds of raw cotton during 1840 alone, more than half the world's available supply. What made cotton king in England, however, was the fact that manufactured cotton products (such as clothing) accounted for nearly half of the United Kingdom's massive export economy. Yet most of Great Britain's raw cotton supply—82 percent—came from the southern United States, whose reliance on slavery consistently rankled powerful abolitionist elements within British politics. British leaders, as a result, continually searched for ways to develop free-labor sources of cotton. By the early 1840s, numerous British diplomats began suggesting that the growing desperation of the Texas Republic might present a unique opportunity. If Great Britain were to help stabilize Texas, went the theory, then perhaps it would have enough leverage to strong-arm Texans into abandoning slavery. In so doing, the English could secure a free-labor source of cotton that would enable them to abandon their reliance on the slave-holding American South, striking blows for both Britain's manufacturing economy and global abolitionism.[144]

Francis Sheridan summed up this perspective in a report he submitted to the British government during the summer of 1840. Following a tour of the Republic, Sheridan minced no words about the wretched state of the Texas government, where "the Authorities are as yet comparatively powerless." Yet, Sheridan noted, migrants fleeing the depression in the United States continued to pour into the region to claim their share of "the Cotton lands of Texas." If Great Britain offered recognition to the bedraggled nation, he reasoned, the English could "derive in a few years from Texas a full supply of cotton for her manufactures" that would allow them to "exclude every Bale of Cotton made in the [United] States." Sheridan's plan hinged on "the anxiety of the Texians that Great Britain should recognize their Republic," which he believed meant that England could make recognition contingent upon Texas moving toward abolishing slavery. In exchange for assistance to the struggling Republic, Sheridan argued, "Great Britain might make it a 'sine qua non' that Slavery should ultimately be altogether extinguished, and that, at no very distant period."[145]

Britain's foreign minister, Lord Palmerston, received other reports suggesting that England could transform Texas into a source of free-labor cotton, and by the fall of 1840 he had determined to recognize the Republic.[146] Palmerston approached James Hamilton (still in London on his never-ending quest to secure a loan for Texas) with an offer for a commerce treaty, and a second treaty wherein Great Britain promised to serve as a mediator for Texas in securing recognition from Mexico. London, however, would sign these pacts only on the condition that Texas also agree to a third treaty requiring the Republic to assist the British in suppressing the international slave trade. As part of its campaign against slaving ships, Great Britain had forged such agreements with numerous countries, and Palmerston clearly intended this to be an opening salvo in antislavery efforts with Texas. Hamilton did not hesitate, signing all three treaties in November 1840. Each then had to be approved by the Texas Senate and exchanged with London before they would be binding, and Hamilton lost no time in forwarding the first two treaties to Texas for immediate ratification.[147]

Yet, for reasons known only to him, Hamilton purposefully delayed sending the anti-slave-trade treaty to Austin. Perhaps Hamilton feared that proslavery interests in Texas would not accept any deal for recognition, even with Great Britain, that included an antislavery measure. More likely Hamilton hoped he could get the first two treaties approved and exchanged—thus securing British recognition—before Texas agreed to any antislavery pact. Whatever his motives, the Texas Senate gleefully approved the first two treaties when they arrived in Austin in January 1841, and promptly sent them back to London. The anti-slave-trade treaty, however, did not arrive until after the close of the legislative session, which meant it could not even be considered until Congress reconvened the following year. Hamilton, in the meantime, attempted to present the first two treaties for Parliament's approval, but Palmerston coolly informed him that nothing could be done until the Texas Senate also approved the anti-slave-trade treaty. The politics of slavery, once again, meant that British recognition of Texas would have to wait.[148]

Having been hemmed in by the collapse of international cotton markets and the Republic's ongoing isolation as a slaveholding nation, President Lamar launched a last desperate bid to rescue his dream of a Texan empire. Lamar had long schemed to send an expedition to Santa Fe in hopes of convincing New Mexicans to secede from Mexico and join the Texas Republic. While bringing New Mexico into the nation certainly fit Lamar's southwestern vision, his more practical goal was to rescue the Republic's finances by redirecting the lucrative trade along the Santa Fe Trail into Texas. And so, without approval from the Texas Congress, Lamar outfitted a 320-man expedition of soldiers, traders, newspapermen, and adventurers who began an arduous overland trek toward New Mexico in June 1841. New Mexicans, however, had no interest in joining Texas, and Governor Manuel Armijo placed the entire Texas delegation under arrest four months later when it finally straggled into Santa Fe. The Texas prisoners were then put on a forced march to Mexico City (several dying along the way), as the entire debacle became an international political embarrassment for the Republic and sparked outrage in both Texas and the United States.[149]

By then, however, Texans had turned once again to Sam Houston. In September 1841, following a bitter campaign marked by personal attacks on both sides, Houston won the presidency over David G. Burnet with nearly three-fourths of the vote. Burnet, who had served as vice president under Lamar, could not escape widespread disgust for the failures of the Lamar administration, and Houston's promises to save the Republic's finances and resurrect its economy helped return him to the helm of the troubled nation. "Old Sam H.," observed one Texan, "with all his faults appears to be the only man for Texas—He is still unsteady, intemperate, but drunk in a ditch is worth a thousand of Lamar and Burnet."[150] Such wild swings in leadership—from Houston to Lamar to Houston again—laid bare the increasing frustration of Texans about the future of their nation.

IN 1836, following independence from Mexico, most Anglo-Texans had looked forward to what seemed an irrepressibly bountiful future. With slavery's security in the region apparently assured, and global cotton prices reaching fifteen-year highs, both farmers and speculators flooded into the Texas borderlands during the late 1830s to seize their own piece of the region's vast potential. Whether the territory became part of the United States or remained an independent nation, most Texans—and many Americans—seemed to believe that profits from the region's rapidly expanding cotton fields would ensure Texas's future and success. Houston City's *Telegraph* captured this sentiment in a report on a bumper cotton harvest in eastern Texas. "Under such circumstances," predicted the newspaper, "a very few years will find us an unincumbered, free, and a wealthy people, our independence recognized, and our commerce sought after by all the world."[151]

Yet the hard lesson of the Republic's early years was that the political liabilities attached to being a slaveholding nation outweighed the economic advantages of being cotton country. The efforts of the Houston administration to deploy cotton as a diplomatic weapon crashed spectacularly in both Europe and the United States against the hard politics of slavery, leaving the new Republic without the resources necessary to build an effective state. The near-unanimous election of Lamar revealed widespread unease among Anglo-Texans about what such failures meant for the Republic. Voters had responded en masse to Lamar's promises of a new direction and vow to build a lasting slaveholders' republic for North America, but the collapse of cotton prices in the aftermath of the Panic of 1837 decimated the Republic's already teetering economy. Trade agreements with France did nothing to expand the cotton markets, and great Britain showed interest in Texas only when its dismal condition appeared to offer an opportunity to force the region to abandon slavery.[152] With Lamar's promises of empire collapsing around them, the rapid realignment of Anglo-Texans back toward Sam Houston betrayed their growing sense of bewilderment. Freeing the Texas borderlands from Mexican abolitionism, they discovered, did nothing to shield Anglo-Texans from the unease many countries felt about doing business with an avowed slave-holding nation.

Even as it floundered, the Republic's existence continued to transform the region. By undercutting the American land market, the Republic remained a magnet for Americans searching for cheap cotton lands and, by the early 1840s, for southerners escaping bankruptcy in the United States after the Panic of 1837. Swarms of new settlers overwhelmed the Indian and Tejano populations in eastern Texas, producing violence that forced eastern tribes and Tejano natives from their homes and communities. Rapidly expanding Anglo settlements and Lamar's Indian wars also challenged Comanche dominance along the western portions of the Republic. It was, in many ways, solely a matter of demographics that allowed Anglos to continue solidifying their dominance over the region. The draw of Texas cotton lands meant that tens of thousands of American migrants simply overran all the non-Anglo populations in the region.

Mass migrations of American farmers also meant that forced migrations of African Americans into Texas grew dramatically during these years. From 1837 to 1842, the enslaved population of Texas expanded from around five thousand to nearly twenty thousand men, women, and children.[153] That was a remarkable expansion by any measure, yet the raw numbers masked a troubling trend. Despite all the ironclad assurances of protection and security offered by the Texas government, wealthy slaveholders in the United States continued to shun the territory. Indeed, nearly all of the slaveholders who came to claim acreage in the Republic during these years were smallholders. Men of means in places like Mississippi, Alabama, or Louisiana recognized that the Republic's dysfunctional government could not enforce its own statutes, and so most made the calculation that the risks of relocating to Texas outweighed the benefits of cheap land. Smaller slaveholders, by contrast, were far more likely to seek out cheap Texas land because it allowed them to leverage their limited capital into more slaves and farming equipment than they could acquire in the southern United States, making the instability of Texas a more attractive gamble. The average slaveholder in the Republic of Texas, as a result, was poorer and owned fewer slaves than his counterpart in the United States, a trend that embodied many of the larger challenges facing the Texas nation.[154]

By the early 1840s, steady migration from the United States had allowed Anglo-Americans to solidify their command over the eastern sections of the Texas borderlands. Yet all their attempts to build a thriving cotton society continued to stagger beneath the political weight of Texas's labor system. With nearly $7.5 million in debt, cotton markets faltering, and rumors flying of a pending invasion by Mexico, the challenges facing the Republic in 1842 remained as fierce and daunting as the challenges of 1836. Sam Houston, upon regaining the presidency, had to consider how long Texas could survive as an independent nation.[155]

SIX

The Failure of the Slaveholders' Republic, 1842–1845

At dawn on March 5, 1842, a Mexican horseman riding under a white flag thundered into San Antonio. He was an advance scout for General Rafael Vasquez, the commander of an army of seven hundred Mexican soldiers that now stood on the outskirts of the town, and he brought a message from the general. Vasquez demanded the surrender of the village, promising to spare the lives of those who did not resist. Most of the townspeople had evacuated several days earlier—rumors of a possible Mexican invasion had been circulating for weeks—but a small force of around a hundred Texans remained under the command of John "Jack" Hays. Badly outnumbered, Hays and his men dumped more than three hundred kegs of gunpowder into the San Antonio River and then fled eastward on horseback. Vasquez's army marched into San Antonio without firing a shot and by afternoon had declared the restoration of Mexican sovereignty in Texas and raised the Mexican flag.[1]

News of the invasion spread panic across the Republic of Texas. A second Mexican force had also taken Goliad and Refugio, and escapees from both towns joined the stream of people fleeing San Antonio. Wild rumors "that an army of 30,000 Mexicans had cut up our forces" traveled with the terrified refugees, and settlers throughout western Texas began abandoning their homes in fear of an advancing Mexican force.[2] Even before they evacuated their families, some farmers—such as William and Andrew Maverick on the San Marcos River—sent their slaves on a forced march eastward in hopes of preventing the invading Mexican army from liberating Texas slaves as it had in 1836.[3] Early reports reached the Republic's tiny capital of Austin the next morning, when the Texas secretary of war declared martial law, ordered the closing of all saloons, and forbid anyone to leave town. Within days impromptu militias began forming in western villages like Gonzales, and soon several hundred Texans began making their way toward San Antonio. In Galveston and Houston, furious crowds jammed themselves into public meetings where they demanded that the Republic's government raise an army to repel the invaders. Many men volunteered for the fight, and one British observer marveled at how quickly Texans "sold their lots of land, some their Negroes, others their very houses, horses, oxen, etc., so as to raise funds" to fight off the Mexicans.[4]

In the meantime, Vasquez withdrew from San Antonio as quickly as he had come. Knowing that his small force would be unable to withstand an organized Texan assault, Vasquez spent only two days in the village, just long enough to sow chaos in western Texas and rest his troops for the return trip. The invaders were already gone by the time volunteers for the Texas militia began arriving in San Antonio. A small company of Anglos and Tejanos—including Juan Seguín, acclaimed veteran of the Texas Revolution and now mayor of San Antonio—attempted to pursue the Vasquez force. But the volunteers soon turned back for lack of enough men to launch a retaliatory strike.

The Vasquez raid laid bare the exceptionally dire circumstances that surrounded the Texas Republic after five years of failed cotton diplomacy. Politically isolated for its devotion to slavery, and persistently poor because of the ongoing slump in global cotton prices, the Texas nation by the mid-1840s was simply too weak to defend itself or its citizens. Although Mexico could not yet mount a full-scale reconquest of Texas, the sheer inability of the Republic's leaders to offer any sort of meaningful defense against such invasions exposed to the world just how incapable the Texas nation was of performing even the most basic functions of a government. The only thing keeping the nation alive by 1842 was the promise of the next cotton crop, and the Vasquez invasion threatened even that. Spring was the start of the planting season, and so most of the men scrambling toward San Antonio in makeshift militias had abandoned their farms in the process. President Sam Houston, in response, ordered Texan farmers to "*return to the cultivation of their fields*" rather than chase Vasquez back to Mexico, as the president worked to avoid the grave consequences that would follow if an army of Texas farmers failed to plant that year's cotton crops. "We can't be broke up in crop time," Houston confided in a friend.[5] With everything else about the Texas experiment in retreat or collapse, no one understood better than President Houston that the Republic could afford neither the cost of an army to confront

Vasquez nor the loss of the country's cotton crop that would result from chasing him.

It was this profound failure of Texas as a slaveholding republic and cotton nation that led to the unlikely annexation of the Texas borderlands to the United States. As the Republic flailed in isolation, British diplomats—who had observed all the weaknesses revealed by the Vasquez raid—moved quickly to capitalize on Texan struggles. Offering to mediate in the ongoing conflict between Texas and Mexico, the British began to explore whether Texas planters could be convinced to abandon slave labor in exchange for the support necessary to ensure the long-term success of their Republic. In return, London hoped to block the further expansion of the southern United States while also securing a much desired free-labor source of cotton that would allow them to wean their manufacturing industry away from its heavy reliance on American slaveholders in places like Mississippi and Alabama. The British were betting, in other words, that Texans would prove to be more dedicated to ensuring the survival of their new nation than preserving their labor system.

Yet the British badly misjudged Texan priorities. Anglo-Texans, as it turned out, could not imagine their portion of the Gulf Coast thriving without slave-based agriculture at its core. The underlying purpose of the Republic, in their eyes, was to support the development of an expanding cotton empire built atop thriving farms and plantations. And since that agricultural system depended upon slavery, they simply could not envision a future for Texas without the institution at its foundation. When the British increased their involvement in the flailing Republic during the early 1840s in hopes of convincing Anglo-Texans to abandon slavery as a means of saving their country, they fundamentally misunderstood the perspectives and priorities of Texas farmers. Yet that miscalculation by the British would have great consequences because it would lead both U.S. abolitionists and U.S. southerners also to believe that Anglo-Texans might indeed willingly abandon slavery. The result was a series of heated confrontations between Texas, Mexico, Great Britain, and the United States about the future of the territory that eventually forced the issue of annexation within Washington, D.C. If we ever hope to understand how Texas became the far-western outpost of the southern United States, we must first understand what the British did not: why Anglo-Texans chose to abandon their Republic and embrace slavery within the United States rather than save their nation under the guardianship of Great Britain.

The Vasquez invasion also demonstrated how the flood of Americans who came into Texas after 1836 in pursuit of cotton lands had rapidly eroded relations between Tejanos and Anglo-Americans. One of the primary goals of the Vasquez raid, it seems, was to discredit prominent Tejanos with the Anglo leadership of the Republic, and during his two days in San Antonio General Vasquez proclaimed that Juan Seguín was a spy for Mexico who was collaborating with the invading army. The general offered no proof of these claims, which seem highly unlikely since unmasking Seguín as a spy had no strategic value for Mexico. But sowing discord between Anglos and Tejanos did have value for Mexico, and Vasquez's charges rang true with some recently arrived settlers from the southern United States who made few distinctions between Tejanos and Mexican nationals. When Vasquez proclaimed Seguín to be a Mexican spy, some Anglo-Texans immediately turned on him. Demanding his arrest for treason, Anglo mobs soon drove Seguín out of San Antonio and forced him into hiding. Following several narrow escapes from bands of roving vigilantes, Seguín realized he would not survive long if he remained in Texas and decided that his only option was to seek refuge in Mexico. Riding along the same road that had guided Vasquez, Seguín crossed the Río Grande in May 1842. He was then promptly arrested by Mexican authorities, who threw him into prison as a traitor to Mexico for his role in the Texas Revolution.[6]

The rapid fall of Juan Seguín from Texan grace, from hero of the 1836 revolution to despised Mexican traitor, revealed how the founding of Texas as a cotton nation had led to a broad shift in attitudes among Anglo-Texans toward ethnic Mexicans. It also shone a bright light on the deep sense of vulnerability and desperation that now pervaded the embattled slaveholders' republic.

Mexico's Shadow

When Sam Houston regained the presidency of Texas, the greatest threat to the survival of the Republic was the continued freefall of its economy. Two years of aggressive military campaigns under Mirabeau Lamar meant that the Texas public debt had more than quadrupled, climbing from around $1.8 million to more than $7.5 million.[7] The Republic's political isolation meant it never secured any meaningful loans in the United States or Europe, and the lack of funds meant the Texas government could not afford the manpower needed to collect taxes and tariffs effectively. Not

Portrait of Juan N. Seguín,
1838, by Thomas Jefferson
Wright. (Texas State Preservation Board, Austin,
Texas)

that it would have made a difference; the collapse of the cotton market
during the late 1830s and early 1840s meant that few farmers could pay
their taxes anyway. In December 1840, the *Telegraph and Texas Register*
reported that eight Texas counties failed to send any taxes to the national
treasury during the past year, and two years later the Texas Congress had
to pass a sweeping law "for the relief of persons who are in arrears for
Taxes."[8] Printing paper money had produced only runaway inflation, and
by 1842 the Republic was—for all intents and purposes—bankrupt.

What little government had existed in Texas was now scaled back to
bones. The Texas Congress slashed government salaries, eliminated the
position of postmaster general, abolished the office of secretary of the
navy, and appropriated no money whatsoever for maintaining the small
Texas army.[9] The Republic also stopped issuing paper money, essentially

ceding all responsibility for currency to the cotton markets. Cotton bales had long served as the primary medium of exchange between farmers and merchants, but the Texas Congress now resorted to authorizing the cotton-trading firm of McKinney-Williams to issue its own private notes as legal tender. Unlike the Republic, McKinney-Williams backed its money with hard assets (such as improved land, slaves, and a saw mill), and as late as 1844 its money traded at ninety-five cents to the American dollar (while the Republic's currency never rose above half that amount).[10] Most telling of all, however, was the Republic's remarkable decision to stop making payments on either the principal or interest of its massive national debt, which all but ensured that securing a foreign loan would become nearly impossible.[11]

Such public weakness in Texas gave renewed hope to Mexican leaders, who had schemed since 1836 to reclaim the region. The fierce battles over federalism and centralism within Mexico that gave rise to the secession of Texas had continued full bore during the years after San Jacinto. Throughout the late 1830s and early 1840s, numerous rebellions and revolts throughout the country forced the government in Mexico City to spend dwindling resources on an escalating centralist-federalist civil war that continued to divide Mexicans. Bloody coups rocked Mexico City in 1840 and 1841, and by the early 1840s both Yucatán and Tabasco were in full rebellion from the nation, while federalists in northern Mexico attempted to establish the Republic of the Río Grande.[12] Amid such chaos, one of the only ways to rally together Mexicans of all backgrounds was to appeal to everyone's desire to avenge the stain on Mexico's national honor represented by San Jacinto. Indeed, the urgent need to reclaim Texas emerged during these years as a rare point of consensus among Mexicans. In 1837 a pamphleteer in Puebla demanded the reconquest of Texas as a national imperative and derided the Anglo-Texans as, in the words of historian Raúl Ramos, "inherently prone to enslaving people of other races and stealing land." Numerous other Mexican newspapers echoed the call, such as Chihuahua's *La Luna*, which urged Mexico City to send an army against Texas as both "the necessity of the present" and "the necessity of the future."[13]

Behind closed doors, however, most Mexican leaders recognized that internal instability and an empty treasury made it nearly impossible for the nation to mount an invasion of Texas. Mexico was as bankrupt as the Republic of Texas, running annual deficits of $18 million pesos and without the collateral or credit to borrow more money.[14] Although national

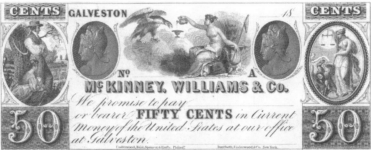

Fittingly, the Republic of Texas three-dollar note issued in 1840 featured a cotton plant in full bloom (top). When that currency became near worthless, the Republic authorized McKinney-Williams to issue its own promissory notes. (Rowe-Barr Collection of Texas Currency, DeGolyer Library, Southern Methodist University)

figures in Mexico City issued a steady stream of threats against the Texas Republic, the more pressing need to suppress rebellions within various Mexican states used up what little capacity Mexico had for making war. The most that members of Mexico's national Congress could muster was the passage of a law in April 1837 outlawing slavery throughout Mexico—which, as the text of the law made clear, they intended as a jab at the dependence of the Texas settlements on enslaved labor.[15] Mexican diplomats also used slavery as the centerpiece in their ongoing diplomatic efforts to undermine the chances of Texas's gaining international support and reminded European governments as often as they could of the Republic's dedication to the institution. Mexico's foreign secretary, for example, sent a blistering note in 1841 to Richard Pakenham, England's minister in Mexico, protesting Great Britain's proposed trade treaties with Texas as "an act amounting to a sanction and acknowledgement of Slavery."[16]

Adding urgency to the Texas question was a growing concern within Mexico that slaveholders in the United States were actively scheming to seize Texas, and perhaps other portions of northern Mexico, as a means of increasing their own political power within the U.S. Congress. Many Mexicans had interpreted the establishment of a slaveholders' republic in Texas—particularly after the protracted battles of the 1820s over the institution—as damning evidence of a conspiracy among U.S. slaveholders to wrest away Mexican territory. In the immediate aftermath of San Jacinto, Mexico's minister to the United States, Manuel Gorostiza, warned his colleagues in Mexico City of a broad slaveholders' conspiracy within the United States to seize northern Mexico. "The fundamental purpose of the plot," he wrote, "is to take possession of the entire coast of Texas, reunite it with the United States, make Texas into four or five slave states, in order to obtain by means of the new senators and representatives that these states name the preponderance in the Congress in favor of the South, therefore to sacrifice the interests of the North to those of the South and prepare for a separation from the North which sooner or later must happen, and is already believed to be near." The public fights over slavery and Texas annexation that raged throughout the late 1830s in both the U.S. Congress and American newspapers had only fueled those fears, and many Mexicans became fervent believers that the loss of Texas in 1836 had been engineered—somehow—by powerful slaveholding interests in the United States. Gorostiza urged his countrymen to remain vigilant against the designs of American southerners to seize portions of Mexico. "It is the same project as the *nulificadotes* of South Carolina," he warned, "on a bigger scale, and applied immediately to Texas."[17]

There was no such conspiracy among politicians in the southern United States during the 1830s and early 1840s. Mexicans, however, could find all the circumstantial evidence they wanted from abolitionist presses in the United States and Great Britain. *El Voto de Coahuila*, published in Saltillo, regularly reprinted anti-Texas editorials culled from various foreign newspapers. Throughout the 1840s, *El Voto* offered a steady stream of articles linking the loss of Texas to proslavery expansion efforts in the southern United States, quoting speeches by John Quincy Adams and making accusations of collusion between Sam Houston and Andrew Jackson. One of the remarkable consequences of the heated debates that took place within the United States during the late 1830s over annexing Texas—fights that invariably turned on slavery and American westward expansion—was how they made their way into Mexico, where they bolstered widespread fears of a U.S. slaveholder conspiracy to steal northern Mexico. Mexicans also blamed one another for the loss of Texas, as centralists and federalists each sought to use the controversy as a means for gaining political advantage over their rivals. But as they looked back on the 1836 secession of Texas and read wild accusations made over slavery and Texas in American newspapers, most Mexicans came to believe that powerful slaveholding forces within the United States were colluding to tear away Texas.[18]

Such fears added tremendous urgency within Mexico to reclaim Texas and helped produce the Vasquez raid in March 1842. Mexico then launched a second invasion in September 1842, when an army of twelve hundred under the command of General Adrian Woll captured and occupied San Antonio for nine days. Among the invaders was Juan Seguín, who had been offered a chance to escape prison in Mexico if he would agree to join Woll's expedition. Seguín accepted the proposal—earning him the enduring hatred of many Anglo-Texans—and forcing such a prominent Tejano to participate in the second invasion of San Antonio appears to have been another effort by Mexico to persuade Tejanos to abandon their support of the Texas Republic. Under enormous domestic pressure, the Houston administration then launched a retaliatory invasion of Mexico in November 1842, when seven hundred Texans marched out of San Antonio and looted an undefended Mexican village along the Río Grande. The expedition, however, fell apart when three hundred Anglo-Texans then attempted to sack the nearby town of Mier, where they were captured by a Mexican army of nine hundred. The defeat of the Texans at Mier sparked celebrations throughout Mexico amid renewed hope for reconquest of the renegade territory. "The triumph of arms against the perfidious Texans is glorious for the nation," crowed one Mexico City newspaper. "Soon the great and generous nation that has been insulted by that handful of adventurers will regain its territory and will have its laws and government respected."[19]

News of the disastrous Mier expedition ricocheted across the continent, bringing painful diplomatic consequences that further isolated the embattled Republic. During the winter of 1842 and spring of 1843, the Texas minister to the United States, Isaac Van Zandt, had worked feverishly to secure a new commercial treaty with the United States, the heart of which was a provision to eliminate the three-cent-per-pound tariff that American ports imposed on imported Texas cotton. Such tariffs constituted the largest expense facing Texas farmers shipping cotton to

New Orleans and had become an unsustainable burden for farmers in the Republic struggling through the global downturn in cotton prices.[20] Van Zandt had, somehow, managed to cobble together enough support in the U.S. Senate for an agreement to eliminate the tariffs. When news of the Mier expedition arrived in Washington, D.C., however, support for the treaty collapsed overnight as U.S. senators concluded that Texas might soon fall prey to an all-out Mexican invasion. Although the U.S. Senate did pass a stripped-down version of the treaty, the badly needed sections eliminating U.S. taxes on Texas cotton had been eliminated, which, Van Zandt reported, "to my mind amounts to a virtual rejection of the whole." He recommended that the Texas Senate not even consider approving the measure.[21]

Sorrow on Every Brow

Such news could not come at a worse time for Texas farmers. During the fall of 1842, violent storms and incessant rains blowing in from the Gulf of Mexico destroyed much of the Republic's cotton crops. High winds that came ashore with tropical storms during September meant that "in many fields the branches and stalks have been completely broken off and strewn about," reported the *Telegraph and Texas Register*. "In other places the bolls have been beat down by the rain, and are rotting by thousands."[22] Rivers across eastern Texas overflowed their banks, destroying farms, homes, and—according to one report—at least two-thirds of the cotton fields along the lower Brazos River.[23] Heavy storms returned during the fall of 1843, again decimating the region. "The rains that have fallen almost daily during the last five or six weeks," reported the *Telegraph* in October 1843, "have done immense injury to the corn and cotton crops throughout all the counties bordering on the coast."[24] In December 1843, the *Northern Standard* reported the "total failure of the cotton crop on the Brazos and Colorado, caused from heavy rains in the lower country."[25]

The near collapse of the Republic of Texas government also meant there would be none of the internal improvements so long desired by the region's cotton farmers. Inadequate roads and high sandbars at the mouths of most major rivers continued to make it difficult and expensive for planters to transport their crops to the market. With hardship pressing upon the country, the editor of the *Brazos Courier* could not understand why "no one has invested a dollar in any project to increase the facilities of transportation on the river," which he believed would surely expand the Republic's economy. "There are many of our farmers higher up on the river who would devote their attention entirely to raising cotton, were not for the difficulty of getting it to a shipping point so great."[26] Some private investors attempted to address the issue by building a railroad from the Brazos to Houston City. "So soon as the rail road shall be finished," they predicted, "it will have tributary to it a larger extent of rich cotton lands than any interior cotton growing country in the world."[27] The project, however, died from lack of funds, as the Texas government simply had no ability to support the effort. Several other would-be railroads met similar fates. The near impossibility of raising local investment capital ensured that no rail lines would ever be constructed in the Republic.[28]

Such intractable transportation problems continued to put Texas farmers at a painful disadvantage in a down cotton market. Because navigating Texas rivers remained so challenging, farmers had no way to predict when a boat might arrive nearby to pick up cotton for shipment, and so most planters simply piled their bales on the riverbanks where they remained exposed—for weeks or months—to the elements. Texas cotton, as a result, often arrived in the New Orleans markets in far rougher shape than its American competition, which meant the Republic's bales tended to draw lower prices.[29] Some Texas farmers gave up entirely on river transport and began hauling their bales to Houston on ox-drawn carts that could carry six bales each and charged a penny per pound.[30] Yet, for many, that was too expensive in a market where every penny mattered (the rate was approximately two to three times the usual charge for shipping bales by river). A few planters along the Brazos River resorted to making rafts out of cotton bales, wrapping each in a linen sheet that had been waterproofed with gum elastic. Using these "floater" bags, a hundred bales could be lashed together as a raft that moved downriver in as little as six inches of water.[31] Farmers along the Colorado River, meanwhile, experimented with new designs for keelboats capable of carrying cotton downstream in as little as five inches of water.[32]

The situation proved that investments in cotton were not always rational, and that people often could not shift as fast as the markets. Texas farmers found themselves stuck in cotton, even as prices tumbled. By 1843, prices reached painful thirty-year lows, with bales selling in New Orleans, New York, and Liverpool for less than half what they did at the birth of the Republic of Texas.[33] Such dismal markets made cotton practically unprofitable, and some newspapers in the Republic issued calls for local farmers to experiment with other crops (such as tobacco, indigo, rice, hemp, and silk), although few followed their advice.[34] Even if they wanted to transition to another crop, most Texas farmers struggling through the economic depression were simply too poor to make a change. Growing sugar, indigo, or rice required new equipment and infrastructure that practically no Texan could now afford, and so nearly all the region's farmers continued—sometimes despite their better judgment—to sow their fields with cottonseed. Cotton bales, indeed, made up 86 percent of the Republic's exports in 1843, with a small trade in animal hides the next closest in volume.[35] Hardly any of those bales, however, went to Europe. Buyers in England and France continued to get nearly all the cotton they needed from American ports, further depressing prospects for Texas farmers.[36]

The only part of the Texas economy that expanded was the rampant smuggling trade, which grew to new heights along the U.S.-Texas border. Much of this was driven by a combination of the weak cotton market and the inability of Houston's government to regulate the borders. Because the Republic had failed to secure a repeal of the U.S. duty on Texas cotton, many farmers carted their bales into Louisiana and shipped them to New Orleans as "American" cotton in order to avoid paying the three-cent tax. One English observer noted in his diary that thousands of "bales of Texas cotton annually goes by Red River to New Orleans" where "much of it passes for American cotton."[37] The Republic's customs agents assigned to the border reported even higher numbers—one estimated that twenty-five thousand bales went overland to Louisiana during 1843 alone—and they could do nothing about it. "The people of Eastern Texas are determined not to pay a tariff," reported one frustrated official, "and it is impossible to prevent smuggling to a considerable extent."[38] Smuggling, indeed, became the primary means by which local traders coped with the collapsing Texas economy. "Many of our merchants have become so exasperated," explained Houston City's *Telegraph*, "that they openly declare they feel under no obligations to obey the law, and will improve every opportunity to evade it."[39]

American merchants, for their part, took full advantage of the situation. Louisiana-based schooners began meeting Texas flatboats in the middle of the Sabine Lake, where they exchanged Texas cotton for American goods without regard for tariffs on either side. As one of the Republic's collectors explained, these U.S. ships sailed "well armed and equipped and ready for battle" because they knew Texas officials lacked the manpower and resources to challenge them.[40] When another agent of the Republic attempted to collect import duties from a U.S. steamship plying the Red River, the American crew instead kidnapped him, tied him "hand and foot," and then proceeded on with their shipments.[41] Texas diplomats lodged numerous complaints about such incidents with the U.S. government, but with little effect. Even in Galveston, the most regulated port in the Republic, customs collectors had to hire watchmen to guard the bay at night in order to prevent illegal shipments.[42] The result was, predictably, that the Republic became increasingly unable to collect import and export tariffs, which—because such taxes made up close to two-thirds of all revenue coming into the Texas treasury—further weakened an already reeling Texas nation.[43]

Reports of the Republic's tailspin appeared in U.S. newspapers, although many Americans received detailed accounts through letters sent by Texas citizens to their extended families back in the United States. Benjamin Shepherd, a twenty-five-year-old merchant, made his way to Galveston in 1839 to join a friend in establishing a new mercantile business on the island. For the next several years, Shepherd sent a steady stream of letters to his family in Virginia describing in painful detail the declining conditions in Texas. His early letters effused enthusiasm as he imagined a profitable future for himself through supplying the Republic's growing agricultural industry. There was no limit, he believed, to what Texans could do with "the most fertile land and the finest climate in North America." Within a year, however, the bottom dropped out of the cotton market and his business in Galveston began to suffer. The tone of Shepherd's letters to his Virginia family soon grew darker, although he continued to express "hope that ere long a change for the better must come."

Yet things did not improve, and Shepherd began grumbling that he heard "complaints every day of *hard times*" from customers in his store. Then, in 1842, the invasions by Mexico sent the country into panic and decimated his business. "This state of surprise is ruining every one," Shepherd groaned. "I am not quite ruined yet but one year more of such times I think will make me glad to leave the country." Following the debacle of the Mier expedition, Shepherd sent a long letter to family and friends in Virginia bemoaning the Republic's inept government, the refusal of Mexico to recognize the region's independence, and the incessant rains of 1842–43 that destroyed much of the region's cotton and made "the roads so bad that [crops] could not be brought to market." Now with an infant son to care for, Shepherd declared that he had seen enough of Texas. "If I had my choice," he wrote, "I would greatly prefer leaving here to staying." Shepherd never did leave—the failings of his business, ironically, left him too poor to move back to the United States—but his stark letters about the Republic's failures ensured that no one else from the Shepherd family followed him into Texas.[44]

Indeed, the flood of Americans coming to the Republic of Texas soon slowed to a trickle. The Republic had survived during the late 1830s solely because of the large and steady stream of American immigrants spurred on by the prospect of cheap cotton lands and the Republic's promises to provide more security for farmers—particularly on slavery—than Mexico had. By the early 1840s, however, much of that appeal had evaporated. The ineptitude of the Texas government and recent invasions by Mexico convinced most reasonable people that Texas could not defend itself or its citizens, while the simultaneous collapse of the cotton market badly undermined the appeal of Texas lands. Americans, as a result, simply stopped coming to Texas. Migration from the United States, the Republic's last source of growth and stability, had completely flatlined by 1842–43.[45]

Even Texans began abandoning some portions of the Republic. Although the small village of Austin remained the Texas capital, it had become a virtual ghost town in the aftermath of the Mexican invasions. A Tennessee newspaperman, Francis Latham, found Austin largely abandoned when he toured the capital during the summer of 1842. Part of this was because President Houston had moved most of the government—unofficially—to his namesake city. But locals told Latham that widespread fear of Indian raids and Mexican invasions along this "extreme frontier"—where the Texas government could do nothing to protect them—had chased away most everyone else.[46] No less than a third of all slaveholders abandoned the county surrounding Austin between 1842 and 1843 (taking with them two-thirds of the local enslaved population), most moving back east "where they can enjoy the blessings of security and peace."[47] Yet eastern portions of the Republic also showed troubling signs of decay. When a British visitor, William Bollaert, took a steamboat down the Trinity River, he saw impressive agricultural production piled up along the riverbanks. "There is much more cotton ready [for shipment] than boats," he observed.[48] But he also saw rotting remnants of the Republic's 1830s town-building boom as he sailed past abandoned villages that now stood as monuments to the Republic's unrealized potential. On one riverbank, Bollaert and his fellow passengers passed the town of "Carolina," which had twenty buildings—including a hotel—but no inhabitants. A few miles downstream they passed another failed town, "Rome," whose sole resident made cotton gins.[49]

These were ominous signs, particularly because any breakdown in the movement of Americans into Texas threatened to undermine Anglo-Texan ability to wrest the region away from local Indians. Although President Lamar's war policy had pushed back numerous native tribes, it was the rapid influx of Americans into the region that enabled Texans to force most Indian nations to the margins. If the demographic tide began to flow in the opposite direction, however, the Republic would become increasingly vulnerable to losing ground to Comanches, Wichitas, and numerous other tribes, particularly since Texas was now too broke to afford any meaningful military force. Upon regaining the presidency, Sam Houston moved quickly to resurrect his peace policy toward Indian nations and dispatched commissioners to the tribes with offers to sign lasting peace accords. Most tribes in eastern Texas readily agreed—Lamar's wars had decimated them, and formal treaties appeared to offer their only hope for security in eastern Texas since so many Anglo farmers now occupied their former lands. These Indians then resigned themselves to life beside their Anglo neighbors, and some supported themselves, in part, by picking Texan cotton.[50] Houston's emissaries encountered more resistance along the Republic's deteriorating western flank, where thinner Texan populations meant the tribes retained more autonomy and power. Wacos and Wichitas resisted talks for a long while, although they also finally signed peace treaties. As always, the powerful Comanches proved the most challenging, refusing even to meet with Texas representatives after the 1840 massacre of their peace emissaries at the council house in San Antonio. Years of war and disease, however, had reduced the Texas Comanches to around four thousand people, and—at the urging of various other tribes—the Comanches finally met with President Houston and signed a treaty at Tehuacana Creek in the fall of 1844.[51]

As both immigration and the Republic's government deteriorated, Anglo-Texans became increasingly anxious about controlling the region's enslaved population. During the early years following independence, the Republic's enslaved population had grown an astounding 420 percent—reaching nearly twenty thousand by 1842—as American farmers flooded into the region.[52] The Texas Congress, in response, passed various measures aimed at controlling these slaves, such as a law to outlaw interracial marriage and another disbarring "all negroes, mulattoes, Indians, and all other persons of mixed blood" from testifying against whites in Texas courts.[53] But as the Republic's economy bottomed out, taking down the government's ability to enforce its own measures, Anglo-Texas became increasingly concerned about whether their government could control the region's rapidly expanding slave population. Most of these concerns revolved around possible slave insurrections. Hoping to eradicate a potential source of such rebellions, the Lamar administration in 1840 ordered that all free blacks vacate Texas or face enslavement by the government.[54] Fearing "that an insurrection was contemplated by the slave population," Anglos in Nacogdoches began organizing nightly slave patrols.[55] In 1842 the mayor of Galveston outlawed the movement of any enslaved or free negroes on the island "after the hour of 8 o'clock at night," lest they conspire to revolt.[56] The inability of the Republic's government to function on even the most basic level left Texas slaveholders deeply concerned about their ability to control their slaves.

Just as threatening was the Republic's proximity to Mexico, which provided enslaved Texans more opportunities for escape than their counterparts in Alabama, Mississippi, or Louisiana. Numerous enslaved men and women ran from their Texas masters into Indian-dominated country in the West or southward toward Mexico, although their numbers have proved almost impossible to track.[57] Anyone reading the Republic's newspapers, however, found notices of slaves escaping to Mexico with alarming frequency.[58] A party of twenty-five slaves escaped their masters near Bastrop in December 1844, riding hard for Mexico on "the best horses that could be found." A posse of Anglo-Texans, headed by the sheriff of Gonzales County, managed to recapture several of the runaways, while the rest were reported "escaped to the Mexican settlements on the Rio Grande."[59] In an effort to curtail the traffic, the Texas Congress in 1844 began offering bounties for the capture of any runaway slave found west of San Antonio—promising fifty dollars for each, plus two dollars for every thirty miles covered.[60]

The fact that Mexico offered a haven to escaped slaves fed directly into Anglo-Texan fears about collusion among Mexicans, Indians, and African Americans. Newspaper accounts of runaways often speculated that Mexican agents, apparently hoping to destabilize the Texas Republic, were actively encouraging slaves to escape. When an Anglo farmer discovered a Mexican near his Brazos Valley plantation, he cut off the Mexican's ears and had him whipped for "enticing his slaves to run away with him to Mexico." The *Telegraph*, in reporting the incident, issued a warning to the Republic's planters to "be on their guard lest their slaves should be enticed away."[61] The proximity of Texas farms to both hostile Indians and Mexican invaders—and with no functioning government to defend them—made the region's farmers feel deeply vulnerable to slave revolts. The result was increased vigilante justice.[62] In March 1839, while pursuing a band of Mexicans and Indians, an Anglo-Texan posse captured "a negro by the name of Raphael." Under interrogation, Raphael testified that he had joined up with a roving gang of Mexicans and Indians in armed opposition to the Republic of Texas and "acknowledged himself a friend to their designs, and declared that he would continue to be." The audacity of this African American's "hostile attitude toward the Texans" convinced his captors that Raphael was beyond redemption. They shot him and then rode on.[63]

Such violence betrayed a growing sense of desperation within the Texas Republic. "We regret to see so much despondency prevailing in the country," grumbled the editor of Houston City's *Telegraph*. "We do not recollect a period since the establishment of the Republic when such general dissatisfaction and distrust have been manifested as now prevail. A general gloom seems to rest over every section of the Republic, and doubt and sorrow is depicted on almost every brow."[64] With little faith that Houston's government could save the country, many Texans began pinning their hopes for the future on intervention by a foreign power to change the Republic's fortune. "All would be gloom," observed the *Clarksville Northern Standard*, "if it were not for the prospect that the political horizon may lighten up during the next twelve months, and annexation with the United States, or commercial alliance with England, remove all our difficulties, and bring us once more, plentiful times, light hearts and merry faces."[65]

Great Britain's Shadow

As their nation crumbled around them, some in the Republic of Texas looked again toward Great Britain. Their long quest for British recognition succeeded in June 1842, when England's new foreign secretary, Lord Aberdeen, finally received from the Texas Senate a ratified copy of the last of the three treaties—the one requiring suppression of the African slave trade—negotiated by the two nations two years before.[66] Gaining official access to England's cotton markets offered hope that farmers might finally secure better prices for their bales and thus begin rebuilding the shattered Texas economy. Just as important, Great Britain seemed to be the only nation capable of forcing Mexico City to acknowledge Texas independence. As the world's largest consumer of raw cotton, the most powerful military force in the Atlantic, and the largest holder of Mexican debt, Great Britain was better positioned than any other nation to wield the economic and political power necessary to save the Republic of Texas from collapse.

Yet, by the mid-1840s, many Texans also harbored deep-seated suspicions of Great Britain's intentions, largely because the Republic's status as a slaveholding nation continually drew the ire of outspoken British abolitionists. An Irish member of the British Parliament, Daniel O'Connell, caused a row in 1839 when he called for the establishment of a colony of free blacks in northern Mexico, which, he hoped, would help destabilize and destroy "the piratical society called the State of Texas." "I have reason to be convinced," he told members of the British and Foreign Antislavery Society, "that the Mexican government will readily co-operate with any efficient society in England in order to carry it into effect."[67] In 1841 another group of antislavery activists in London began recruiting abolition-minded British laborers, hoping to send them as colonists to Texas in an effort to begin funneling antislavery voices and voters into the Republic.[68] Neither effort came to anything, yet the attention such proposals drew in both American and Texan newspapers demonstrated the growing alarm with which slaveholders living along the Gulf Coast viewed British intentions. The profound vulnerability of the Republic, as people on both sides of the Sabine River recognized, could make Texas an easy target for whatever influence Britons wished to have.

Some conspiracy-minded Texans began wondering aloud whether England might be in league with Mexico to bring down the Republic. The mysterious inability of British diplomats to persuade Mexico to acknowledge Texas independence fueled such suspicions. Her Majesty's Government failed twice in 1842 to convince Mexican leaders to accept proposals for the recognition of Texas, which struck many as odd since Mexico City nearly defaulted on British loans that year and needed British bondholders to restructure the debt in order to keep Mexico solvent.[69] If Great Britain truly wanted Texas recognized, it seemed that Mexico would have little choice in the matter.[70] The subsequent decision of the British foreign office to reject France's offer to join them in pressuring Mexico to recognize Texas did nothing to dispel such talk. Rumors even began circulating throughout the southern United States that antislavery

British financiers were supplying the Mexican army in hopes of destroying slaveholders in Texas.[71] Although no evidence emerges from England's voluminous diplomatic correspondence of any such conspiracy, paranoid Texans found enough circumstantial evidence to fuel their growing mistrust of the intentions of Great Britain.

The Republic's new chargé d'affaires to Great Britain and France, Ashbel Smith, saw anti-Texas conspiracies throughout England. Only a week after arriving in London, Smith sent back an alarmed report. "There are numerous and active enemies of Texas here," he warned, "consisting chiefly of the Anti-Slavery party and of persons interested in colonizing portions of the British territories abroad."[72] The most frightening evidence came in the form of two war steamships, the *Guadalupe* and the *Montezuma*, being constructed in English shipyards for the Mexican government. There could be no other purpose for these ships, Smith believed, than making war on the Texas Republic, and the Texan diplomat filed numerous protests with Lord Aberdeen on the matter. Yet Aberdeen refused to intervene, leaving Smith shaken by the prospect of British anti-slavery groups funneling money and weapons to the Mexican army. The people financing the building of these ships, he explained to the Houston administration, "are violent *anti slavery* men" whose "hostility to Texas as a *slave holding country* is extreme." Smith feared an alliance of Mexican nationalists and British abolitionists would, if left unchecked, guarantee future invasions of Texas. "We have now to contend with Mexico," Smith warned, "aided with British mercenaries and British money."[73]

Great Britain's selection for its first chargé d'affaires to the Republic, Charles Elliot, provided Texans little reassurance. Lord Aberdeen chose him for the post, in part, because Elliot was a highly seasoned diplomat recently returned from an assignment in China as the British chief superintendent for trade. Elliot also happened to be a committed abolitionist who had served as "protector of slaves" in Guiana during the early 1830s—an assignment that surely did not escape the British foreign secretary's notice. And, indeed, within weeks of arriving in Galveston, Elliot began hatching what he called "my scheme"—a plan to use British financing to abolish slavery in Texas and thereby transform the ailing Republic into a thriving free-labor nation. Like Francis Sheridan before him, Elliot believed that the increasingly desperate position of the Republic's planters meant that they could be convinced or coerced into emancipating their slaves, if England offered them suitable compensation. "Their circumstances make them a timid and needy people," he explained, "and ready enough to compound reasonably for a monied consideration." Free trade with Great Britain would then follow, guaranteeing English access to Texas cotton and economic prosperity for the Republic. Elliot had a few other small reforms in mind for the Republic—such as a revamped land distribution policy—but the core of his plan was quite simple: offer the Texans a clear choice between the collapse of their nation beneath the burdens of slavery or the salvation of their Republic by embracing emancipation.[74]

Securing abolition in Texas, Elliot believed, would set in motion far-reaching changes that could remake the whole of North America. He imagined free blacks and escaped slaves from the southern United States finding refuge in Texas, where they would be guaranteed civil and voting rights. This would, in turn, create an impenetrable barrier against the further westward expansion of slavery in the United States—"a bound marked, beyond which Slavery could not advance"—which Elliot hoped would destabilize the American South and lead to the eventual dissolution of slaveholding in all of North America. Elliot believed that foreign investment would then naturally flood into a slave-free Texas, which, in turn, might convince various provinces in northern Mexico to abandon Mexico City in order to join this newly prosperous free-labor nation. The end result, Elliot hoped, would be an expansive British-sponsored empire for liberty in North America that could serve as a bulwark against the growth and power of the United States. Conveniently, it could also provide free-labor cotton to England's massive textile industry. "The supply from Texas will exceed a Million of bales within 10 years," Elliot gleefully predicted.[75]

Although Elliot never received an endorsement of his scheme from Lord Aberdeen, the British diplomat did inspire at least one person to begin working for emancipation in Texas. In March 1843, a Massachusetts-born lawyer named Stephen Pearl Andrews joined Elliot on a boat traveling down Buffalo Bayou from Houston City to Galveston. Andrews, who ran a small law practice in Houston, had never approved of American slavery and found himself intrigued by the possibility of British investments in a slave-free Texas. On the ship to Galveston, the two men loudly discussed their shared interest in abolition, making "bitter & hostile opponents" of some of the other passengers. Once on the island, Andrews began promoting the idea of British-sponsored emancipation with an evangelical zeal, traveling door-to-door until, in his words, "the whole little city of Galveston was fairly seething with excitement." Andrews planned to make a public speech at the Galveston customhouse, where he would call for "a new constitution, to abolish slavery the government paying for the slaves that the British government would advance the money." Local businessmen, however, refused to allow it, and an armed posse forced Andrews off the island at gunpoint the following day. Word of his antics followed Andrews to Houston, where an angry mob surrounded his house and threatened to lynch him, forcing Andrews to flee with his family in the dead of night toward safety in the United States.[76]

Despite such damning reactions from Anglo-Texans to the mere suggestion of bringing abolition to the Republic, both Andrews and Elliot remained undaunted. After escaping the Houston mob, Andrews traveled to New York City and joined abolitionist leader Lewis Tappan on a ship headed for England, where they planned to attend the 1843 World Antislavery Convention in London. Armed with letters of introduction from Charles Elliot, Andrews and Tappan managed to secure a personal meeting with Lord Aberdeen, where they laid out a variation of Elliot's plan for British-sponsored emancipation in Texas. Although Aberdeen made no commitments, he apparently liked what he heard and promised that Great Britain "would employ all legitimate means to attain so great and desirable an object as the abolition of Slavery in Texas."[77] Aberdeen's encouragement made Texas the centerpiece of discussion the next day at the World Antislavery Convention, as delegates debated various proposals for bringing emancipation to the Republic. A general feeling pervaded the convention that the near-bankrupt Texas "cannot continue in its present state: it must either, by virtue of its annexation to the United States, become a slave-holding country, or it must have a distinct existence as a free state." And many delegates had somehow convinced themselves that Texans would gladly abandon slavery if it meant they could ensure the survival of their Republic. "My impression," testified Reverend A. A. Phelps, is "that the Texans would prefer an independent existence as a free state." Another delegate assured the assembly that he knew from his own travels throughout Texas that "emancipation was whispered throughout the country."[78]

Such impressions—based on a desire among abolitionists to believe that slavery was, somehow, not yet well entrenched within the Republic— defied reality and even reports coming back to London from the British consul's office in Galveston. During the summer of 1843, Lord Aberdeen asked for an in-depth report on the current state of slavery within the Texas Republic. He wanted a clear assessment of just how entrenched the institution was, requesting details about such things as the growth of the region's slave population, the quality of food and care that enslaved Texans received, the average lifespan of a Texas slave, and whether "the Laws and Regulations in respect to Slaves" had become "more or less favourable to them" under the Republic. Above all, however, the British foreign secretary wanted to know whether Anglo-Texans could be induced to embrace abolition and free labor in exchange for enough British support to ensure the survival of the Texas nation. "Is there in the State in which you reside," he asked, "a party favourable to the Abolition of Slavery? and what is the extent and Influence of such party?"[79] The request landed on the desk of William Kennedy, who served as consul in Galveston, and the report he sent back should have been sobering.

Kennedy noted the steady increase in the Republic's slave population, despite assertions among abolitionists to the contrary, and reported that enslaved people were treated generally as well as could be expected. "Opinion stigmatizes persons who maltreat their Slaves," he explained, "and the general tendency is to feed them sufficiently, and to use them without rigour." Yet the Republic's legal code afforded virtually no rights to the enslaved because, as Kennedy pointed out, Texans had purposefully strengthened the laws protecting slavery when they established the Republic. As to the commitment of Anglo-Texans to maintaining slavery, Kennedy confessed that he had seen nothing to suggest that Texans would ever abandon the institution. "The Manumission of Slaves is of rare occurrence," he reported, and even nonslaveholders in Texas fully supported the institution. "There is no professed or recognized section of Citizens in Texas," Kennedy concluded, "favourable to the Abolition of slavery."[80] To emphasize his point, Kennedy then forwarded Aberdeen a series of Texas newspaper articles denouncing abolitionism.[81]

Reports going the other direction, from London to the Republic, took on an increasingly alarmist tone. Ashbel Smith, the Texan minister to London, watched in dismay as Stephen Pearl Andrews and other anti-Texas abolitionists secured private meetings with high-ranking British officials. Smith took it upon himself to monitor the movements of such men and became so concerned that he even attended the World Antislavery Convention in order to take notes on the various schemes being bandied about for freeing Texas slaves. Most proposals Smith heard involved variations on Elliot's plan for leveraging British capital to force Texas emancipation, although a few proved more devious. Smith reported that a man "having relations with the British Govt." had approached him earlier with a strange proposal to divide Texas into two states—one slave, one free—separated by the Colorado River. The Texan diplomat quickly recognized the underlying intent ("the population which would flock into this 'free state' from Europe would be enabled to vote down the Slave holders," he observed) and warned the Houston administration about such designs. More alarming, however, were Smith's reports that some abolitionists talked openly of transforming Texas into "a sort of continental Hayti, populated chiefly by blacks" by making the Republic "a refuge for fugitive slaves from the United States."[82]

Believing that cold economic considerations drove British diplomacy, Smith saw far more at work than humanitarian concerns for the enslaved. Cotton, once again, figured prominently into the political calculus of the Republic's diplomats, as Smith reasoned that the English wanted Texas primarily for "commercial reasons, as a consumer of their manufacturers and a producer of cotton." The profound weakness of the Texan state thus provided a unique opportunity for the British to promote free labor, and Smith believed that "they are prepared to profit by our supposed difficulties." Smith had, indeed, become convinced that the need to promote free-labor cotton and sugar in the British colonies (where England had already enacted emancipation) drove many Britons to support policies aimed at undermining slavery in North America. Emancipation in Texas was, Smith reasoned, simply a first step for the British on the road toward bringing abolition to the American South—which would, in turn, allow England to shift global cotton production away from the United States and toward its own colonial investments. Any British attack on slavery in Texas, in other words, would be a British attack on slave-based agriculture across the entirety of North America, all intended to promote British economic interests. "The independence of Texas and the existence of Slavery in Texas," Smith concluded, "is a question of life or death to the slave holding states of the American Union."[83]

It was all too much, and the Texas diplomat confronted Lord Aberdeen about British intentions. In a long meeting at Aberdeen's office, Smith declared "that Texas will not make any change in her institutions concerning slavery" and denounced abolitionists like Stephen Pearl Andrews. "No disposition to agitate this subject existed on the part of the Government or any respectable portion of the citizens of Texas," Smith explained, and he warned that any attempt by the British to force the issue "would be derogatory to our national honor." Why, then, Smith demanded to know, did Aberdeen continue to encourage abolitionists agitating about Texas?

Aberdeen, in reply, attempted to assure Smith that Her Majesty's Government had absolutely no intention of interfering with Texas's internal institutions, including domestic slavery. At the same time, however, it remained standard British policy to encourage emancipation throughout the world, and the British minister made no attempt to hide the fact that the "abolition [of slavery] in Texas is deemed very desirable." Yet Aberdeen also assured the Texan that the British government would make no effort to target the Republic and "that they would not give the Texian Govt any cause to complain." Aberdeen apparently proved persuasive, because Smith left the British Foreign Office that day convinced that Her Majesty's Government was not directly behind the schemes of British abolitionists to destroy the Republic of Texas.[84]

Anglo-Texans, however, would soon have reason to doubt that. In August 1843 a leading proponent of British abolitionism, Lord Henry Brougham, confronted Aberdeen during a debate in Parliament, demanding to know what role the British government intended to play in ending slavery in the Republic of Texas. "If it were abolished," Brougham proclaimed, "not only would that country be cultivated by free and white labor" but "it must ultimately end in the abolition of slavery in America." Aberdeen, apparently caught off guard, tried to assure his legislative colleagues that "no one was more anxious than himself to see the abolition of slavery in Texas." Her Majesty's Government, he promised, would attempt to leverage the country's considerable political might— "as well as by every other means in their power"—toward pressuring the Texas Republic into abandoning the institution.[85] Meant to reassure the powerful abolitionist faction of the British Parliament, Aberdeen's comments seemed to imply that Great Britain would do whatever it took to force Texas to free its slaves. Splashed across London's newspapers, the Brougham-Aberdeen exchange soon made its way across the Atlantic where it was then reprinted in newspapers across North America.

The response within Texas was electric, raising virulent anti-British sentiment across the Republic. Newspapers in Houston and Galveston published scathing responses. Outraged that "our suspicions that the British government was secretly endeavoring to effect the abolition of slavery in Texas" had proved true, Houston City's *Telegraph* demanded that the Republic's Congress and president issue unequivocal declarations that Texas would never abandon the institution. For the *Civilian and Galveston Gazette*, however, there was simply no need to reiterate what should be clear to the world. "The institution of slavery is engrafted upon our Constitution, and interwoven with the very existence of the Government," explained the *Gazette*'s editor. "Its abolition would involve the overthrow of both, as well as bear along with it a train of evils, resulting not only in the destruction of the civil institutions of the country, but of all order and security both to person and property." Any illusions that British policymakers might hold that Anglo-Texans would willingly abandon the institution, both newspapers agreed, could only be based on "the repeated and glaring misrepresentations" of misguided men like Stephen Pearl Andrews. There was, they insisted, no white person within the Republic of Texas willing even to consider the prospect of British-sponsored emancipation.[86]

What terrified these editors was the prospect that such talk would undermine the further movement of Americans into the Texas borderlands. Many Anglo-Texans believed that even the mere mention of abolition would discourage migrants from the southern United States, much as it had during the Mexican era. "While it continues in agitation," fumed the *Telegraph*'s editor, "it will prove more injurious to Texas, than the war with Mexico, for all emigration from the Southern States will be effectively suspended." Abolitionists in England and elsewhere could, in that sense, inflict tremendous damage on the Texas nation simply by speaking loudly and often about forcing the weakened Republic to abandon slavery. The *Civilian and Galveston Gazette* made the same case in blunt terms. "Without slavery, there would be little or no cotton produced in the country," which, in turn, meant no more migration from the American South. "White men neither have been nor can be found to labor in its cultivation on the low, rich lands of Texas," warned the *Gazette*. Abandoning slavery, in other words, would mean abandoning cotton, which the editors believed would be tantamount to abandoning Texas. "If abolition is to be the price of British mediation," concluded the *Telegraph*, then Texans "will respectfully, but positively decline the proffered mediation."[87]

With its one-crop economy crippled by the steep downturn in global cotton prices, the Texas nation teetered along the edge of collapse by late 1843. Although Great Britain seemed more capable than anyone of saving Texas, the British appeared interested in the Republic only as a means for undermining North American slavery and pushed for Texans to transition toward free labor. Yet that was the one thing that the Republic's farmers were simply unwilling to do. Anglo-Texans, as a result, talked aloud about the need to end their experiment in nationhood, and newspapers across the Republic began calling for the United States "to come to the rescue, and restore Texas to her proper place with regard to the Mother Republic of America."[88]

The Houston administration had come to similar conclusions. Washington Miller, President Houston's personal secretary, wrote a painfully candid letter to Ashbel Smith that laid bare the dark thinking within the Republic's government. "We are in collapse," he confessed, "perfectly prostrate and powerless" and "worse than all, without confidence in ourselves."[89]

Nine-Tenths of the People

With almost no other options, the Houston administration launched a renewed push to convince the United States to annex the Texas borderlands. Its strategy was to overcome American resistance to annexation by emphasizing how the eminent collapse of Texas would leave the southern United States vulnerable to British influence. During the spring of 1843, the Texas minister to the United States, Isaac Van Zandt, met privately with U.S. president John Tyler and his cabinet, where he issued blunt warnings about England's intention to abolish slavery in Texas as a means of menacing slavery in the United States.[90] Houston's secretary, Washington Miller, followed up late that summer with a personal letter to President Tyler—almost certainly at the behest of Houston—warning that Texas would be unable to resist British influence much longer without direct American assistance.[91] And such efforts seemed to have the desired effect. In September 1843, Van Zandt got word that the Tyler administration wanted to discuss possible terms for bringing Texas into the American Union. In a long conversation with Tyler's newly appointed secretary of state, Abel Upshur, the Texas minister began secret negotiations for an annexation treaty. "For the great welfare, and prosperity of Texas, I believe nothing could contribute so much as her annexation to the United States," Van Zandt reported back with excitement to the Republic. "I left untried no means, which I thought calculated to advance or promote this object."[92]

Public debates among British abolitionists about how best to assail the weakened Republic had, it turned out, rattled politicos within the southern United States almost as deeply as they had Anglo-Texans. Duff Green, a Tyler administration insider and John C. Calhoun's son-in-law, had been in London during the same 1843 World Antislavery Convention that had so disturbed Ashbel Smith. Green, in response, fired off a series of alarmed reports to Washington, D.C., detailing the apparent British plot to dominate Texas as a means for quashing slavery throughout North America. Such reports confirmed a growing suspicion among John Tyler's closest advisers that Great Britain intended to assault the slave-based economy of the U.S. South as part of a larger strategy to encircle and stymie the further growth of the United States. The Tyler administration, therefore, responded immediately to suggestions from Texas to renew annexation talks, hoping to prevent Great Britain from using the implosion of the Texas Republic as a means for undermining the further development of the southwestern United States.[93]

And for the Tyler administration—just as for the Texans—the deep connections between cotton and slavery proved paramount. Both Duff Green and John C. Calhoun, for example, had become convinced that Great Britain's desire to stamp out slavery in North America sprang from base economic concerns about global cotton production. During his sojourn in London, Green discovered that England's colonies in the Caribbean and India—following the emancipation of British slaves during the 1830s—had failed to produce raw goods as cheaply as farms that relied on slave labor in the southern United States, Cuba, and Brazil. That meant, Green reported to Calhoun, that England's "war on slavery" was nothing more than a means to "increase the cost of producing the raw material" by her competitors and therefore "maintain her commercial and manufacturing superiority." Great Britain, in other words, wanted to assault American slavery as a way to undermine the U.S. South's dominance in the production of the raw cotton that was so vital to the British textile industry.[94] British efforts to turn Texas into a bastion of free-labor cotton therefore had terrifying implications for the fate of both slavery and cotton in the United States and demanded an American response. Annexing Texas would also allow the United States to secure a monopoly on North American cotton production, which the Tyler administration hoped would translate into a powerful economic weapon for challenging Her Majesty's Government.

Such anti-British logic helped the Tyler administration to frame the annexation of Texas as a matter of national interest for the United States, rather than as a sectional measure to protect the particular interests of the South. Playing on the virulent Anglophobia that pervaded the entire United States, Tyler's lieutenants worked to build public support for annexation as a matter of national security. In newspaper editorials and public speeches, they argued that annexing Texas was the only way for Americans to prevent the British from launching a western assault on U.S. interests, detailing the grave consequences sure to follow if England managed to gain control of Texas. And, remarkably, it worked. Northern politicians who might have otherwise opposed annexation as the expansion of U.S. slave territory suddenly found themselves eager to strike a blow against British encroachment and allowed the Tyler administration to quietly round up enough supporters to ensure the approval of an annexation treaty in the next session of the U.S. Senate. "I can make the question so clear," Upshur bragged to a friend, "that even the Yankees will go for annexation."[95]

Anglo-Texans monitored these debates in the United States with delighted interest, although neither they nor the general American public knew about the ongoing secret negotiations between Abel Upshur and Isaac Van Zandt. Beginning in January 1844, newspapers across the Republic of Texas jammed their columns with every wayward rumor about the rising possibility of an annexation treaty being presented to the U.S. Congress. Despite having nothing to offer its readers beyond pure speculation, Houston City's *Telegraph* nonetheless pronounced the prospects for annexation to be "exceedingly flattering" and—following a spate of encouraging rumors from the United States—reveled in the likelihood that two-thirds of the U.S. Senate would approve an annexation treaty.[96] Speculators on both sides of the Sabine began buying Texas bonds on the possibility of annexation, which some newspapers took as evidence of positive movement within Washington, D.C.[97]

It was, of course, the benefits that annexation could bring to Texas that interested people in the region most. And most Anglo-Texans had little trouble imagining what would likely follow. Annexation would end Mexican claims to Texas (because, many Texans imagined, Mexico would never challenge the U.S. Army), which would therefore bring renewed security and a massive new wave of American migration into the territory. A flood of new migrants, in turn, would greatly increase land prices (making numerous Texans rich in the process) and thereby help stabilize the region's reeling economy. New infusions of people and capital into Texas could then lead to long-sought internal improvements (new roads, railways, and improved river navigation) that would finally allow Texas cotton farmers to realize the territory's vast agricultural potential. All of these hopes hinged, however, on a single requirement: the development of Texas required the support of a competent government. The diplomatic shackles of being a slaveholders' republic had hobbled the Republic of Texas government from the start, weakening it until slumping cotton markets brought the nation to its knees. The United States, by contrast, protected slavery and provided full access to the global cotton market and could therefore offer Texas farmers everything the Republic could not, ensuring that by 1844 nearly every Anglo-Texan supported annexation to the United States. "We believe this to be the wish of nine-tenths of the people of Texas," observed Houston City's *Democrat*.[98]

The only notable pocket of resistance to annexation emerged within Galveston, where merchants feared that joining the American Union could imperil their shipping and trade businesses. Galveston remained the dominant shipping point for Texas, and practically all the Republic's cotton trade to Europe went through the island. And everyone in Galveston was well aware that becoming part of the United States would mean the end of Texas farmers' paying import taxes in order to sell their cotton through New Orleans. While that would be terrific news for Texas planters, it also meant that Galveston merchants would have to compete directly with New Orleans firms for dominance in the Texas cotton market. Many Galveston merchants feared that annexation would therefore put them at a painful disadvantage because they imagined that Texas farmers would shift their business to the better-established and internationally connected trade houses in New Orleans. The island's *Civilian and Galveston Gazette* emerged as the only prominent newspaper within the Republic to oppose annexation, deriding the proposal's "sudden and violent revolutions in the commercial regulations" as sure to "convulse and distract trade."[99]

Fueling this resistance was the fact that by early 1844 more European ships had begun docking in Galveston to pick up cotton, which meant that the island was the only portion of the Republic where the economy had finally begun to recover.[100] There was, observed the *Gazette*, "more money, and more general comfort, contentment and enjoyment at Galveston now than we have ever before witnessed."[101] And as the island's shipping business slowly picked up, the *Gazette* tried to argue that prosperity was also returning to the rest of the Republic. "Many a man has gone home this winter with one hundred or five hundred hard dollars in his saddle bags, the savings of his farm for a year, feeling more contented and carrying more happiness to his family than they experienced five or ten years ago."[102] That was, in fact, simply not true: the prices that Texas farmers received for their cotton remained at all-time lows in 1844, leaving them in desperate straits. The *Gazette*, however, seemed unaware that conditions within Texas had not improved beyond Galveston Island, and the newspaper argued that the ongoing failures of the Republic's bankrupt government were unlikely to impede future growth in the region. "We think that Government has little to do with the prosperity or adversity of the people," asserted its editor.[103]

A far different perspective pervaded the rest of Texas. The *Planter*, published in Brazoria and representing the heart of cotton farming in the Republic, laid out a stark case for annexation that represented the consensus view. The collapse of the Texas cotton economy during the early 1840s had devastated local farmers and cut off the flow of immigrants into the region, leaving people too poor to pay their taxes or support their families. The *Planter* laid the blame for these troubles squarely at the feet of the failures of the Republic's isolated government. It argued that annexation promised to bring levels of security and prosperity to the region that only competent governance could provide. "We want that confidence in the stability of our institutions—that reliance upon the protection of our government and laws—that belief in the security of life and property," which the Republic had never managed to achieve. "Give us then annexation," demanded the *Planter*, "and we start fair with the world—our unrivaled lands, and congenial climate will no longer be shunned by the honest and industrious emigrant, and the prudent man of money."[104]

The other factor driving consensus within the region was the growing fear that an independent Texas would remain forever weak, and thus vulnerable to the schemes of abolitionists. Persistent rumors about British intentions to destroy slavery within Texas continued to rattle Anglo-Texans, who lambasted such ideas at every turn. Never once did a single Texas public official or newspaper endorse the idea of striking any deal with Great Britain to abolish slavery in exchange for financial or military support, despite the fact that doing so could ensure the survival of the Texas Republic. Houston City's *Telegraph*, instead, continued to rail against British antislavery efforts, insisting that "we shall always oppose any foreign protection or assistance, that may be predicated upon the slightest interference with our domestic institutions."[105] Galveston's *Gazette* likewise rejected any proposition of abolition as "revolting to our pride and self-respect as a nation."[106]

Perhaps most telling, Mirabeau Lamar suddenly emerged as a proponent of annexation as a means for securing slavery in Texas. At his inauguration as the Republic's second president in 1838, Lamar had outright rejected the idea of annexation because he believed that joining the United States would expose Anglo-Texans to the deadly influence of American abolitionists. By the mid-1840s, however, Lamar had come to fear abolitionists in Great Britain even more, and he now urged his fellow Texans to join the United States because it represented the only sure way to preserve slavery in the region. "I paused in my opinions," he explained, "and turned to seek for my country a shelter from the grasp of British cupidity beneath the only flag under which her institutions could be saved."[107] For even the most ardent of Texas nationalists like Lamar, there was simply no reason to maintain their independence if it meant sacrificing slavery and the cotton economy in the process.

Annexation

Despite the nearly universal enthusiasm among Texas citizens, the Houston administration walked a taut diplomatic tightrope during annexation treaty negotiations. Its primary concern was ensuring that any public announcement of the agreement did not prompt a preemptive invasion by an outraged Mexico (a grave concern, particularly since Texas was even more vulnerable than it had been during the 1842 incursions), and Isaac Van Zandt insisted that the Americans provide military protection to the Republic while negotiations continued. Although Secretary Upshur offered as much reassurance as possible, President Tyler could not promise to fight a war against Mexico without approval from the U.S. Congress. Texas officials also feared what would become of their relations with England if the annexation gambit failed. Being publicly spurned for a second time by the United States would leave the tottering Republic almost entirely at the mercy of Great Britain and Mexico, and so the Houston administration carefully cultivated a public stance of general indifference on the matter. Sam Houston, indeed, continued to foster his close relationship with the British chargé to the Republic, Charles Elliot, which could help inoculate Texas against British reprisals should annexation fail. Houston's open flirtations with Great Britain also kept alive rumors in the United States that Texas might accept British assistance in exchange for emancipation—despite the protests of every Texas newspaper to the contrary—which added pressure to U.S. congressmen pushing for annexation.[108]

Because nothing about annexation was certain, Texas diplomats also worked on a backup strategy. In collaboration with a Louisiana congressman, Van Zandt managed to get another bill introduced into the U.S. House of Representatives to eliminate American taxes on cotton imported from Texas. New Orleans merchants had a great deal to gain from opening their port to a flood of Texan cotton, which made it easy to secure support from Louisiana's representatives. The Texas consul in New York City sought similar support during a special meeting of the city's chamber of commerce, although the chamber declined to involve itself. The Houston administration continued to push hard for removing barriers to exporting Texas cotton to the United States, knowing that increasing the profitability of those bales would—if annexation failed—provide the only means for reviving the Republic's economy.[109]

By the end of February 1844, Van Zandt and Upshur had nearly completed the annexation agreement. Just as important, the strategy of selling annexation to Americans as a means for countering the British had proved remarkably effective in lining up northern votes. Both men felt confident that at least two-thirds of the U.S. Senate would vote to approve, and Van Zandt's messages back to Texas became so encouraging that many of the Republic's newspapers predicted "the certainty of immediate annexation."[110] Then, on February 28, 1844, a massive explosion aboard the U.S. Navy's newest warship, the *Princeton*, changed everything. Both Upshur and Van Zandt had joined President Tyler that day—along with three hundred other guests—for a private tour of the ship and a demonstration of its powerful new weapons. When they fired the largest member of the *Princeton*'s battery, the "Peacemaker," at the end of the demonstration, the massive cannon blew apart in an awful explosion that killed Upshur and six others. President Tyler and Isaac Van Zandt survived, but both men realized instantly that Upshur's death would make the approval of any annexation treaty far more difficult.[111]

The fragile consensus built by Upshur in the U.S. Senate soon began to fall apart as heated tensions over slavery reemerged. President Tyler made John C. Calhoun his new secretary of state, and Calhoun quickly concluded the treaty with Texas. It was not everything the Republic's delegation had hoped for, but "it was deemed best to accede to the terms" before the opportunity slipped away.[112] President Tyler then forwarded the agreement to the U.S. Senate for approval in mid-April 1844. But only days before the Senate could begin debating the treaty, newly installed Secretary Calhoun sent a letter to the British minister to the United States, Richard Pakenham, that would decimate northern support for annexing Texas. Seething with anger over the possibility of Great Britain using Texas as a means for attacking slavery in the United States, Calhoun denounced British interference in North America and heralded the impending annexation of Texas as indispensable for protecting the future of American slavery.[113] Reprinted in newspapers across the United States, Calhoun's blistering proslavery remarks seemed to reveal annexation as nothing more than an effort to defend the sectional interests of the southern United States. With sectional tensions now inflamed, northern support for the treaty evaporated. On June 8, 1844, the U.S. Senate rejected the annexation treaty by a vote of 35 to 16, and the once jubilant mood in Texas turned dark. "The fruits of our negotiations have uniformly been a useless expenditure of public money, mortification and disgrace," fumed the *Telegraph*.[114]

The issue seemingly settled, both Texans and Americans turned to electing new presidents for their nations. Within the Republic, a short campaign pitted Anson Jones (Houston's handpicked successor) against Edward Burleson (the anti-Houston candidate) that said little about annexation and resulted in an easy victory for Jones.[115] Yet, within the United States, the Texas question came to dominate the presidential contest of 1844. The nominee for the Whig Party, Henry Clay, had come out early against annexation as certain to incite a war with Mexico and destabilize the American Union. Democrats, however, nominated the relatively unknown expansionist James K. Polk, who proclaimed that he would push to annex Texas and force the British out of the southern half of Oregon, reigniting annexation talk throughout the United States. Linking Texas with Oregon offered something to expansionists in both the North and the South, and it allowed the Democrats once again to argue for annexation as a matter of national defense against the encroachments of Great Britain. Polk's expansionist platform proved to have just enough appeal to bring him victory in November 1844, allowing him to edge out Clay by the slimmest of margins.

Calling Polk's narrow victory a mandate for annexation, President Tyler and the Texas delegation in Washington, D.C., put in motion another plan for bringing Texas into the United States. Tyler and Van Zandt had long discussed various fallback measures if the U.S. Senate failed to ratify the 1844 treaty, and they agreed to attempt to push a joint resolution for annexation through the U.S. Congress. An unprecedented method (and therefore legally questionable), a joint resolution would require only a bare majority in both houses rather than the clearly impossible two-thirds majority in the Senate. The U.S. Congress took up the matter when it reconvened in early 1845, and the House of Representatives passed the resolution on January 25, 1845, by a vote of 120 to 98. The wisdom of a joint resolution became apparent on February 27, 1845, when the U.S. Senate approved the measure by a razor-thin margin: 27 to 25. President Tyler wasted no time, signing the resolution on March 1 and sending an urgent dispatch to the Republic of Texas. The United States had, finally, approved annexation—it was now up to the people of Texas to decide if they would accept.[116]

When the resolution arrived, Texans saw that the terms offered by the United States had changed since the failed 1844 treaty. Texas would now enter the American Union as a state—and thus could write its own constitution in regard to slavery—but would remain responsible for the massive debt accumulated by the Republic's government. The United States was to take custody of all public buildings and forts, but Texas would be allowed to keep its expansive public lands (so the new state could pay down its debt). The state could also, if Texans approved, divide itself into as many as five states. More important than anything, however, was the promise by the United States to settle the boundary dispute between Texas and Mexico. Mexico still did not recognize Texas as an independent state and maintained that the Nueces River marked the region's southern boundary. Anglo-Texans continued to insist that Mexico had no claim to the territory and that the Río Grande marked the southern border of Texas. The United States now offered to enforce the perspective of the Anglo-Texans.[117]

Everything thus came down to whether Anglo-Texans wanted to join the United States, and their perspective on annexation had not changed much since the spring of 1844. Because most Texans expressed euphoria at the prospect, public meetings soon sprang up across the Republic urging the Texas government to accept the American offer as quickly as possible. Counties offered resolutions urging annexation for all sorts of reasons. Citizens in Montgomery County, for example, said they favored the measure as a means for ending the "onerous burthens" of U.S. taxes on imported Texas cotton. Most people, however, pointed toward a single defining reason for annexation: the Republic's painful experiment in nationhood had failed, and the U.S. government could now offer them the security in their slaveholdings and the protection for their farms needed to develop the full agricultural potential of the region. In an open letter to the people of Houston, Peter Gray explained why he could endure living in "a feeble Republic" no more. "By taking this step," he explained, "we secure to ourselves all the benefits for which governments are established, and for which we would otherwise have to struggle over a long, a rough and weary road."[118]

The only notable resistance came—once again—from Galveston, where cotton merchants feared that the island "will become a mere tributary to New Orleans, and eventually cease to flourish" if Texas joined the United States.[119] Benjamin Shepherd's mercantile shop had only recently "recovered from the effects of the incursions of Mexico in 1842," and so he worried that annexation would transfer the island's "immense commercial advantages" to ports in the United States and plunge him back into poverty.[120] The *Civilian and Galveston Gazette* continued to make similar predictions. Galvestonians, fretful about what annexation might mean for their trade business, likely took heart that one other Texas newspaper, the *National Register*, also argued against annexation.

Yet most Anglo-Texans felt otherwise, and the remarkable rise of xenophobia in the Republic during the fall of 1844 and spring of 1845 demonstrated why. Up until the mid-1840s, most Texas newspapers had applauded the tiny stream of immigration coming from Europe, particularly the small contingent of Germans who made their way into the western portions of the Republic. Following the failure of the 1844 annexation treaty, however, paranoia about British efforts to root out slavery in the region reached new levels, giving rise to wild rumors of abolition coming to Texas in the form of European immigrants. Because new arrivals could become voting citizens of Texas within six months, many Anglo-Texans feared that abolitionists would send enough new settlers into Texas to form an antislavery majority that could simply outlaw the institution at the ballot box. "They will come among us, with all that is different and foreign to the present people of Texas," including their deep distaste for "the institution of domestic slavery," predicted the *Red Lander*. "Every thing would go on quietly, until the new emigration had considerably the majority in numbers. Then would come the great convulsion." One man became so distressed that he published a public letter demanding that the Republic pass a law that would force all immigrants to sign an oath pledging to "never, directly, or indirectly, suggest, advise, vote for, or in any manner, endeavor to procure the Abolition of Slavery in Texas." The hysteria reached such heights by early 1845 that Houston City's *Telegraph* published a long editorial belittling such "churlish and illiberal prejudices," but to no avail.[121] In the aftermath of the failure of the 1844

annexation treaty, Anglo-Texans believed their hold on the Texas borderlands was more vulnerable than ever.

The offer by the United States in 1845 thus struck nearly all Anglo-
Texans as the only way to ensure the continued survival of their communities *and* the success of slave-based agriculture in the region. Although
they knew they could save their Republic by abandoning slavery, that
prospect held absolutely no appeal for people so intertwined in the global
cotton economy. During the summer of 1845, both houses of the Texas
Congress endorsed annexation—with only a single dissenting vote—and
Texans approved the measure in a public referendum by a lopsided vote
of 4,254 to 267 in October 1845. The voters also approved a new state constitution that they immediately forwarded to Washington, D.C. When
President James K. Polk signed the Texas Admission Act on December 29,
1845, Texas became the twenty-eighth state in the American Union.

Both Great Britain and Mexico had launched last-ditch efforts to thwart
annexation, but they could not overcome the tide of sentiment within
Texas favoring the United States. Probably because he spent nearly all his
time in Galveston, the British minister to Texas, Charles Elliot, remained
convinced that most Texans would reject annexation if Mexico finally
acknowledged their independence. Elliot undertook a daring secret mission to Mexico City, where he hoped to secure the recognition of Texas
independence that he believed would prevent the Republic from joining
the United States. Turmoil within the Mexican government delayed the
matter, but the Mexican Congress finally made an offer to acknowledge
Texas independence if the Republic promised to reject annexation. When
Elliot returned to Galveston, however, he discovered that his mission had
only confirmed suspicions among Texans of a covert British-Mexican alliance, stiffening their resolve to take shelter within the United States.[122]

The success of annexation elicited joy throughout many sections of
the United States, particularly in the slave states. Yet many Americans
nonetheless worried that their country had now locked itself into a war
with Mexico. The Mexican minister in Washington, D.C., Juan Almonte,
had warned the United States in 1844 that Mexico would consider the
annexation of Texas nothing less than an outright attack on Mexican sovereignty. And so, as Americans and Texans celebrated, Almonte severed
Mexico's diplomatic ties with the United States and returned to Mexico,
where he began preparations for the war he believed was sure to come.[123]

Migrations and Transformations

Following the annexation of Texas to the United States, momentous events came in a rush. President James K. Polk came into office determined to wrest California from Mexico, anxious to claim the rich Pacific coastline—and all the lucrative trade opportunities that would come with it—for the United States. The annexation of Texas did not make war between the United States and Mexico inevitable. It did, however, offer Polk the leverage he needed to force Mexico's hand in the matter, which he used to devastating effect. Polk dispatched a special envoy to Mexico City during the fall of 1845—even before annexation was complete—with an offer to pay up to $25 million in exchange for the territory between Texas and California. Mexico's leaders, deeply divided among themselves and unwilling to cede their far-northern territories to the United States, refused to receive the envoy. Polk, in response, ordered the U.S. Army to take up a position along the banks of the Río Grande, far beyond the Nueces River that Mexico considered the border of Texas. When the Mexican commander on the other side retaliated, the U.S. Congress declared war on May 13, 1846. Calls for volunteers for the U.S. Army brought a flood of eager young men into Texas, as the newest member of the United States became the staging ground for the American invasion of Mexico that began during the summer of 1846.[1]

Because the U.S. military knew almost nothing about the geography of northern Mexico, Texas Rangers became favored scouts for the advancing army. Benjamin McCulloch, a Ranger who had distinguished himself as a frontier scout and fighter, served as General Zachary Taylor's chief of scouts, leading reconnaissance missions across northern Mexico in preparation for the American advance. In late July 1846, McCulloch's company discovered that Juan Seguín was somewhere in the territories north of Monterrey, commanding a small Mexican cavalry unit known as the Escuadrón Auxiliar de Béjar. The Escuadrón consisted of displaced Tejanos who, like Seguín, had fled into northern Mexico during the years since 1836—pushed out by increasing Anglo violence against Mexican Texans—and in the process had been branded by Anglo-Texans as traitors for seeking refuge in Mexico. So when McCulloch's Rangers received word that Seguín and his Escuadrón had passed through a nearby village only days before, they moved fast. McCulloch sent a hurried note to General Taylor's chief staff officer declaring his intention to kill Seguín and his company. "It would be ridding the world of those that are not fit to live in it," he promised. Along the road to Monterrey, the Rangers then made an all-out pursuit of the Tejanos. The Escuadrón, however, learned of the approaching American force and, scattering into smaller bands, attempted to escape by riding through the night.[2] As the U.S. Army marched into northern Mexico, Anglo-Texans began to hunt Juan Seguín.

It was a remarkable turn of events, since the Seguín family had done more than almost anyone in Mexico to bring Americans into the Texas borderlands. It had been Juan's father, Erasmo Seguín, who rode from San Antonio to Louisiana in 1821 to throw open the gates of Texas to American immigration, the importation of the global cotton market, and all the opportunities that rapid development of the territory would mean for Tejanos. Erasmo had personally guided Stephen F. Austin into the region, and it was the unwavering political support of the Seguín family—as well as numerous other Tejano families—during the years that followed that had made Anglo immigration into the territory even possible. Just as important, Erasmo represented Texas during the 1823–24 constitutional debates in Mexico City, where he helped ensure that the 1824 national Constitution did not outlaw slavery in the new Mexican Republic. Working hand in hand with men like Austin, Erasmo brought cotton, slavery, and Americans into Texas as a means of expanding the population, economy, and prosperity of northeastern Mexico. He even tried his own hand, at least briefly, at becoming a cotton planter.[3]

Erasmo's son, Juan, grew up during this period of Anglo-Tejano alliance, when the Texas borderlands transformed from Indian country into an Anglo-Mexican state, and Juan's hopes for the development of Texas were much the same as his father's and Stephen F. Austin's. Like most Tejano leaders, Juan made his living through trade, making his first trips to the New Orleans markets during the late 1820s. And, like his father, Juan had become intimately aware of the connections between cotton commerce, American expansion into northern Mexico, and the economic opportunities available to Tejanos such as himself. He emerged by the mid-1830s as an ardent Texas federalist, throwing in his lot with the

Anglo-Americans during the 1835–36 rebellion, and became a celebrated veteran of the Texas Revolution. Juan then worked to build a place for Tejanos within the new Texas nation, serving in the Republic of Texas Senate where he chaired the committee on military affairs. The Seguíns, as much as anyone, had made possible the profound transformations that American immigration and cotton commerce brought to the region during the years before 1846.[4]

Yet the changes that Erasmo and Juan Seguín helped usher into the Texas borderlands began to spin out of their control by the early 1840s. The increasing flood of Americans making their way into the territory soon overran both Tejanos and Indians. Secession from Mexico stripped Tejanos of their unique political standing within the region (since they no longer could serve as power brokers between Anglo settlements and the Mexican government), rapidly eroding their status within the new Republic of Texas. The remarkable Anglo-Tejano alliance that had opened Texas to cotton development during the 1820s thus began to fray by the late 1830s and early 1840s, as conflicts between new Anglo settlers (nearly all of whom had no personal experience with earlier Tejano efforts to encourage American immigration) and ethnic Mexicans in Texas continued to rise. When tensions between the Texas Republic and Mexico reached a boiling point during the 1842 invasions, even Tejanos as respected as Juan Seguín found themselves living under hostile conditions. Tejanos became increasingly crowded out by the very forces they had brought into the territory, and the hunt for Juan Seguín was only the most poignant example of a larger trend overtaking the Texas borderlands.[5]

Benjamin McCulloch and his troops never did catch the Escuadrón, losing Seguín and his men in the chaparral. The Rangers returned to Taylor's army, which soon captured Monterrey and then Saltillo. In the meantime, Santa Anna had returned to power and—determined to repulse the American invaders—streamed northward in early 1847 at the head of a hastily assembled army. As Mexican forces neared the U.S. Army camps just south of Saltillo, Seguín and his company joined Santa Anna's army of nearly fifteen thousand. Soon thereafter, on February 23, 1847, Santa Anna slammed his exhausted troops into Taylor's much smaller—but far better positioned—forces at the Battle of Buena Vista. For several bloody hours, as Mexicans and Americans cut each other to pieces, McCulloch and his Texas Rangers fought on one side of the battlefield against Seguín and his Escuadrón on the other. Santa Anna's soldiers nearly carried the day, but eventually fell back under relentless battering by the American artillery. When Santa Anna retreated with his shattered army that night, the war for northern Mexico was lost. Within months another U.S. Army would land at Veracruz, where the Americans prepared for a final march toward Mexico City.[6]

UNDERSTANDING HOW Juan Seguín and Benjamin McCulloch found themselves on opposite sides of the battlefield at Buena Vista requires a long perspective. Three waves of migration were at the root of these great changes, and the first came during the early nineteenth century as the rise of a new economic boom in cotton textiles sent tens of thousands of Americans surging into the Gulf Coast territories of North America. The rush to establish cotton farms in places like Mississippi, Alabama, and Louisiana produced a dramatic reorientation of economic power within the territories bordering northern New Spain. Voracious new markets for horses emerged in the southwestern United States, prompting Indian nations—with the Comanches in the lead—to raid Spanish outposts in Texas and northern New Spain with unprecedented violence. Combined with the convulsions of the Mexican War for Independence, this migration of Americans to the Gulf Coast thus helped to decimate the already weak Spanish presence in the Texas borderlands. It also drew the region's Tejanos more deeply into the growing American markets in the southwestern United States as their last economic hope in an increasingly desperate situation. The result was, by the early 1820s, a willingness on the part of both Mexican officials and Tejanos to bring Americans—and thus the cotton frontier—into the Texas borderlands as a means of securing and developing the region.

A second migration followed during the 1820s and early 1830s, when the flood of Americans moving into the Gulf Coast began flowing into northern Mexico. This was, in one sense, simply a continuation of the southwestward movement of Americans in search of new cotton lands, as both New Spain and Mexico sought to redirect that migration of American farmers toward their own ends. Yet the timing of these events mattered enormously, because the moment that New Spain collapsed and Mexico became independent was also, remarkably, the same moment that the Panic of 1819 made U.S. cotton lands unaffordable for most American farmers. The particular geography of the Texas borderlands, in turn, also mattered a great deal. The region's position alongside the far-western edge of the U.S. cotton frontier, where it shared the same alluvial soils and ready access to Gulf Coast shipping that made Mississippi acreage so appealing, made the prospect of claiming farmland in a foreign country far more attractive to Americans than it might otherwise have been. Thousands of farmers and their families thus began abandoning the southern United States for new homes and opportunities in northern Mexico.

Yet this second migration was highly contested because it brought enslaved African Americans into Mexico. Nearly all Americans coming into Texas from the southern United States considered slavery to be the indispensable foundation for building a successful cotton economy, demanding—in a unified voice—the continued legality of the institution in northern Mexico. Mexicans, however, became deeply divided over the role that slave-based agriculture should play in the development of their nation and its northern frontier. During the 1820s and early 1830s, contentious debates about the future of slavery dominated discussions about American migration into Mexico, as Tejanos, Anglos, Coahuilans, and officials in Mexico City struggled in competing pro- and antislavery coalitions that fought one another to a standstill. Although antislavery Mexican legislators managed to pass abolitionist legislation at both the state and federal levels, they never succeeded in forcing Texans to abandon slavery. Yet neither could Anglos and Tejanos force state or national authorities in Mexico to embrace the institution, leaving its future in the Texas borderlands in perpetual limbo.

The result was a mixed migration pattern from the United States. Because chattel slavery remained tentatively legal in northeastern Mexico during the late 1820s and early 1830s, the Anglo colonies in Texas continued to attract Americans willing to trade security in their slaveholdings for access to far larger tracts of fertile land than they could ever hope to afford in the southern United States. At the same time, however, there were far more Americans who chose *not* to come to the Texas borderlands because tales of Mexican abolitionism—some real, some imagined—circulated regularly in U.S. newspapers of the era. The flow of information across North America through these newspaper networks turned out to have an enormous influence on the movement of Americans into northern Mexico, as shifting American perceptions about the Texas borderlands played a decisive role in shaping the ebb and flow of Anglo migration into the region. As the Anglo-Tejano alliance discovered, much to their frustration, even the mere rumor that Mexico might outlaw slavery was enough to discourage many Americans from considering new lives in northern Mexico.

The American colonies, therefore, never flourished as Tejanos and people like Austin believed they should. And the result was an escalating series of fights between Texans and Mexico City—as struggles over slavery and American migration became entangled in larger debates about federalism within Mexico—that led ultimately to the secession of Texas from Mexico in 1836. In trying to bring the American cotton frontier into northern Mexico, the Anglo-Tejano alliance came to a painful realization: they simply could not remake the region with slave-based agriculture if they did not also have the government's unabashed support for the institution that made that possible.

The Republic of Texas was to be that government, the first fully committed slaveholders' republic in North America. It was, in that sense, a nation uniquely suited to the mid-nineteenth century. At the same moment that the growing Atlantic cotton economy of the early 1800s had made such commerce more profitable than ever, the simultaneous rise of the antislavery movement—particularly in Great Britain and the northeastern United States—began threatening the use of slave labor as the engine of cotton production in North America. The Republic's founders, therefore, envisioned their nation as an elegant means for addressing the needs of mid-nineteenth century cotton farmers. By building a permanent firewall around slavery, they imagined their Republic as a refuge for North American planters against abolitionists in Mexico, Great Britain, and the northern United States. Unimpeded Texas farmers, they believed, would then be free to create a cotton empire along the Gulf Coast that would secure a profitable future for the new Texas nation.

The founding of the Texas Republic thus unleashed a third wave of American migration, as tens of thousands abandoned the southern United States for Texas during the late 1830s. Drawn by the Republic's promises of greater security for slavery than had existed under Mexico, as well as higher cotton prices during the early 1830s, Americans fell over one another in their rush to claim a piece of the Texas borderlands. The resulting population shifts helped cement Anglo-American control over the eastern portions of the territory by pushing both Tejanos and Indians to the margins. This third wave also brought a massive new forced migration of African Americans into the region. The enslaved population of Texas increased by more than 400 percent as American slaveholders flooded into the new El Dorado of North America during the late 1830s and early 1840s.

Yet the Texas nation failed for two overlapping and interconnected

reasons. First, its public commitment to defending chattel slavery isolated the Republic in an Atlantic world where the forces of antislavery
wielded increasing levels of political power. White Texans, much to their
surprise and chagrin, found their Republic unable to secure the recognition, trade agreements, military assistance, and loans they so desperately
needed. Second, the collapse of the cotton market in the aftermath of
the Panic of 1837 devastated the one-crop Texan economy, leaving the
Republic's government bankrupt and largely unable to defend the Texas
nation or its people. The appeal of Texas lands, as a result, plummeted
during the early 1840s, as did migration from the southern United States,
pushing the weakened Republic toward the edge of collapse. When Great
Britain sought to capitalize on that weakness as a means of increasing its
influence in North America, Anglo-Texans turned toward annexation to
the United States as the only viable avenue for saving their vision for the
future of the Texas borderlands.

Through it all, three broad forces—the Atlantic cotton economy, the
international debates over slavery, and the efforts of various governments
to control the Texas borderlands—had combined to shape these migrations and thereby transformed the shared edges of the United States and
Mexico in ways that brought momentous changes to the rest of North
America.

THE WAR BETWEEN THE UNITED STATES AND MEXICO that followed
would, in turn, remake both nations. When the U.S. Army finally marched
into Mexico City in September 1847, the war's end transferred fully half of
Mexico's national territory—nearly 530,000 square miles of land—to the
United States.

Within Mexico, such massive losses left behind deep-set instability that lasted for generations, and the humiliation of the war exacerbated the ongoing struggle between liberals and conservatives to define
Mexico's future. Throughout the late 1840s and 1850s, liberals blamed
the nation's defeat on the ruinous policies of conservatives, arguing that
the corruption and incompetence of both the church and the army had
robbed Mexico of the strength to defend itself. Conservatives countered
that the war was indisputable proof that the nation's experiment in federalism had failed and that only a centralized and strong-armed government could reestablish stability and prosperity in Mexico. Yet stability
and prosperity never came. Liberals controlled the national government
for the first few years after the war, until conservatives staged a coup in

1853 that brought Santa Anna back to power. A counterrebellion against Santa Anna's repressive government then followed in 1854, when liberals instituted their own repressive regime. By the late 1850s another bloody civil war erupted between liberals and conservatives—and although liberals emerged triumphant, their victory proved short-lived. French troops invaded a badly weakened Mexico in 1862 (on the pretext of collecting long overdue debt) and captured Mexico City, where they installed a puppet dictator, Ferdinand Maximilian. Mexico would remain under French occupation until 1867.[7]

The fallout from the transformations of the Texas borderlands also led to bloody internal strife within the United States, where fighting centered on questions of slavery's future in the nation. The acquisition of so much Mexican territory ignited violent new battles over whether slavery would be allowed to expand west, as northerners and southerners fought over the precarious balance of power between free and slave states in the U.S. national government. Heated debates broke out even before the end of the U.S.-Mexican War and only intensified when California petitioned in 1849 to enter the Union as a free state. During the years that followed, political fights surrounding the future of the territories taken from Mexico eroded nearly all the middle ground between pro- and antislavery forces in the United States. In 1854, a new political party emerged in the northern United States—the Republicans—whose sole purpose was to prevent the expansion of slavery into the West and thus the expansion of southern power in the U.S. Congress.[8] White southerners felt so threatened by 1860 that they demanded the Democratic Party nominate a stridently proslavery candidate for the presidency to oppose the Republicans. When the Democrats chose a moderate candidate instead, many southern states—including Texas—rebelled and nominated their own separate, proslavery candidate. In so doing, these proslavery southerners split the Democratic Party and all but ensured the triumph of the Republican candidate, Abraham Lincoln, in November 1860.

Convinced that Lincoln would move to abolish slavery throughout the United States, southern states soon began seceding from the United States. When Anglo-Texans seceded in February 1861, they explained that they did so because they opposed "the debasing doctrine of the equality of all men, irrespective of race or color" and thus left the United States as a means of "holding, maintaining and protecting the institution known as negro slavery."[9] The U.S. Civil War that followed was the bloodiest conflict in American history, claiming 750,000 lives. And because it freed 4 million men and women from bondage, the war fundamentally reordered American society. The vast territory taken from Mexico in 1848 had thus forced the United States to confront slavery's future on the continent and—ultimately—helped bring about a war that would end chattel slavery in North America.[10]

This was not the first time that Anglo-Texans had formed a nation to defend the institution of slavery. Indeed, we can find within the Republic of Texas of the 1830s and 1840s much of the same ideology that drove the formation of the Confederacy during the 1860s. In both, American farmers tried to build a nation unequivocally dedicated to supporting and fostering slave-based agriculture. They were each, in that sense, reactions by American farmers to the rise of antislavery movements in Europe and North America during the first half of the nineteenth century. And defending slavery was, for both nations, a means for ensuring what they saw as a greater end: the rise and success of an agricultural empire along the Gulf of Mexico based primarily in cotton. Because cotton commerce had remade the Gulf Coast of North America—thereby making slavery increasingly profitable—at precisely the same moment that abolitionists rose in political influence in the Atlantic world, American slaveholders became convinced that their future depended on the creation of explicitly proslavery governments. The rise of the Texas nation, then, reveals in stark detail how these international tensions over slave-based agriculture that led to the Confederacy had been shaping the worldview of American farmers and slaveholders long before the 1860s.

The Confederates lost their war for independence in 1865 and thus never had the opportunity to test the strength of their proposed nation. The Republic of Texas, however, survived for nearly a decade, offering a tantalizing glimpse into what might have been for the Confederacy. Much like the founders of the Texas Republic, Confederates believed the economic power of their cotton fields would provide the diplomatic leverage necessary to secure assistance from European powers that might otherwise cringe at collaborating with an avowed slaveholders' republic. Yet the tactic failed repeatedly for the Confederates during the 1860s, just as it had for Anglo-Texans during the 1830s and 1840s.[11] When the Confederacy cut off cotton exports to Europe, Great Britain and other nations invested heavily in the development of cotton farming in India, Egypt, and Brazil.[12] Worldwide production of cotton, as a result, expanded rapidly during the 1860s and 1870s, producing a global glut of cotton during the decades after the American Civil War that drove down crop prices. A pound of cotton sold during the mid-1890s fetched less than half of what it had during the mid-1850s, and the price continued to decline during the early twentieth century.[13] It seems more than likely, therefore, that an economic calamity similar to the one that helped bring down the infant Republic of Texas—the freefall of cotton prices during the late 1830s and early 1840s—would have hobbled an independent Confederacy during the late nineteenth century's worldwide tumble of cotton prices. Indeed, the travails of Texas lay bare some of the painful limits of the Confederate vision, suggesting that winning independence might have been only the first of the Confederacy's struggles for survival.

AT THE END of the U.S.-Mexican War, Juan Seguín rode up to an American fort along the Río Grande and asked the commander for permission to return to Texas. Looking "careworn & *thread-bare*," Seguín and his family wanted to come back to their home near San Antonio so they could begin rebuilding their lives. By the winter of 1848, the Seguín family had returned to San Antonio with little fanfare. In the aftermath of the Treaty of Guadalupe-Hidalgo, far fewer Anglo-Texans seemed concerned about Seguín's supposed collusion with Mexico during the 1842 invasions of Texas. Indeed, Juan soon became involved again in local politics, winning an election for justice of the peace in 1852 and later helped to found the Democratic Party in Bexar County. Yet enough angst continued to agitate against him that Seguín felt compelled to publish a memoir in 1858 emphasizing his contributions to securing Texas independence in 1836 and defending his actions during 1842.[14]

As it happened, Seguín returned to Texas just in time to witness another dramatic transformation. Following annexation and the close of the U.S.-Mexican War, Americans flooded into the newest addition to the United States in unprecedented numbers. During the three years from 1847 to 1850, more than 70,000 people came into Texas. During the decade that followed, another 400,000 followed. By the eve of the American Civil War, four out of every five Texans had arrived in the region only *after* it became part of the United States. Nearly all these new migrants hailed from other slaveholding states, and most came to grow cotton. The price of cotton had rebounded during the U.S.-Mexican War, marking the beginning of a new worldwide cotton boom that lasted throughout the entire 1850s. Texas farmers exported 58,000 bales in 1850. Ten years later, they shipped more than 431,000 bales. With the infusion of new capital into the region, a section of farmers along the Texas coast finally devel-

Photograph of Juan N. Seguín after his
return to Texas in the aftermath of the
U.S.-Mexican War. (McArdle Notebooks,
Texas State Library and Archives
Commission, Austin, Texas)

oped a small sugar industry. Yet cotton's reign as king remained unchallenged in Texas, and within a few decades the state would become the crop's leading producer for the entire United States—a position it has maintained ever since. Indeed, by the late 1850s, Texas had become the thriving economic powerhouse that the Seguín family hoped it would when they began supporting American immigration during the 1820s.[15]

Yet many of the groups that made the Americanization of the Texas borderlands possible also became its greatest victims. Although Indian raids during the 1810s in service of the U.S. cotton frontier had helped open Texas to Anglo-American settlement, the relentless waves of American immigration that followed then forced Native Americans to abandon the eastern sections of the state. Such waves of migration would continue to bludgeon the surviving native groups until, by the mid-1870s, even the once dominant Comanches sought refuge on reservations in Oklahoma.[16]

With those waves of Anglo-Americans came a massive forced migration of enslaved men and women, who were brought into the region to toil on the farms and plantations that made so many Anglo-Texans wealthy. When Marian, Richard, and Tivi escaped their Louisiana master and ran to Texas in 1820, they hoped the territory would offer them new lives in freedom. Yet during the decades that followed, Texas had instead become everything they had once hoped to escape. Nearly all the political battles that consumed the territory during the years between 1820 and 1860 had revolved around questions of whether white Texans would continue to own black Texans as property. And as Anglo-Texans consolidated their power within the region, the number of imported slaves grew at an astounding pace. By the eve of the U.S.-Mexican War, 25,000 enslaved people had been brought into Texas. On the eve of the American Civil War, the 182,000 enslaved African Americans in Texas made up nearly a third of the state's population.[17]

No one played a more active role in opening Texas to Anglo-Americans than the Tejano leadership in San Antonio. Yet Tejanos, too, found themselves forced to the margins of Texas society by the transformations they helped create. American-written histories of Texas soon began offering Anglo-centric explanations for how the Mexican Far North had become the American Southwest, and their pages had no room for the pivotal role Tejanos played in ushering the cotton empire into Texas. One of the most popular of these new histories, Henderson Yoakum's *History of Texas from Its First Settlement in 1685 to Its Annexation to the United States in 1846*, appeared in 1855 with a simple explanation. In Yoakum's telling, American civilization had redeemed the Texas wilderness from "ignorance and despotism" as, according to historian Laura McLemore, "the growth of Texas proved that American principles of government were superior to others."[18] Looking back with the hindsight of American victory in the region, Yoakum reimagined the history of the Texas borderlands as simply the slow unfolding of American destiny.

Some Tejanos pushed back against this "manifest destiny" interpretation. José Antonio Navarro, one of Stephen F. Austin's closest collaborators and a signer of the Texas Declaration of Independence, published a series of newspaper articles during the 1850s arguing that the history of Tejano sacrifice for Texas required that the Anglo-Americans "treat with more respect this race of men who, as the legitimate proprietors of this land, lost it together with their lives and their hopes." Yet nothing came of Navarro's anguished protests. Juan Seguín, for his part, eventually decided that there was no future for him in the region. Sometime during the late 1860s, at the close of the American Civil War, Seguín moved his family to a new home in northern Mexico.

He died there on August 27, 1890.[19]

APPENDIX I
The Texas Slavery Project

During its decade-long career as an independent nation, the Republic of Texas struggled to raise enough revenue to keep its government functioning. Beginning in 1837, the Republic instituted a nationwide tax that required all households to pay an annual fee for holding certain types of property, including horses, mules, cows, gold and silver pocket watches, pleasure carriages, and even wooden clocks.[1] The various items subject to taxes shifted over the years, but the Republic always taxed the two types of property in which most people invested their wealth: land and slaves. Each year, the county sheriff was tasked with recording the property holdings of every household in a tax book that was then forwarded to the Texas treasury office. These tax records thus provide a census of the taxable property reported by each county, including the number of enslaved people held by each slaveholder, during every year of the Republic of Texas. Although they represent an imperfect count of the slave and slaveholder populations, the tax rolls nonetheless provide the clearest window available into the fluctuating levels of slaveholding and wealth within the Republic of Texas as they shifted across both time and space.

These annual county-level tax assessments are available today in the Records of the Comptroller of Public Accounts, Ad Valorem Tax Division, County Real and Personal Property Tax Rolls, 1837–1900, Archives Division, Texas State Library and Archives (TSLA), in three forms: a positive-image microfilm collection (available in-house at the TSLA), a separate negative-image microfilm collection (available in-house at the TSLA and through Inter-Library Loan), and the original books held in the manuscripts division of the TSLA. The two microfilm collections appear to have been filmed at separate times, and each contains images of county records not available in the other. Some records remain illegible in both microfilm collections, while some were never microfilmed in either and thus are available only in the original manuscripts. Because of the fragility of the originals, the TSLA does not make them publicly available, although they were kind enough to grant me permission to consult the originals when necessary in order to complete assessments not possible with either microfilm collection (for which I am in their debt and tremendously grateful). Using all three sources, I have compiled as complete a count as possible of slaves and slaveholders living in the Republic of Texas from 1837 to 1845.

My database, along with mapping and graphing tools used to explore and analyze it, are publicly available on the *Texas Slavery Project* (http://www.TexasSlavery

Project.org), where the full dataset is also available for download. The database counts the total number of slaves, total number of slaveholders, and subcategories of slaveholders (those who owned 1–4 slaves, 5–9 slaves, 10–19 slaves, 20–49 slaves, and 50+ slaves) listed for each county in the surviving Republic of Texas tax records for every year between 1837 and 1845. My assessments of the movement and settlement patterns of slaveholders in Texas during this era, as well as where enslaved people lived in the Republic, are based on both that database and the digital tools that I used to analyze them.

Randolph B. Campbell demonstrated the value of these records when he used them to estimate the slave population in Texas during the Republic and U.S. statehood periods. (For Campbell's dataset, see *An Empire for Slavery*, 264–67.) My own database, however, differs in several respects from Campbell's. Campbell relied on the recapitulations (aggregated counts of the tax records complied by the tax assessors, which typically appeared at the end of the assessment for each county in a given year) filmed on the negative-image microfilm reels. Although these were usually accurate, the recapitulations paired in the microfilming (both the positive- and negative-image versions) sometimes were appended to the wrong county list. In other cases, the counts in the recapitulations did not match the numbers in the person-by-person assessments. To avoid these discrepancies, I created my database by examining the tax records of each county, using all three sources available, without relying on the recapitulations (except in a handful of cases when those are the only records that survive). This allowed me to count not only slaves but also slaveholders and subcategories of slaveholders with a granularity unavailable to Campbell. As a result, the numbers that appear in my database sometimes differ from those in Campbell's book. I do not, however, make any claim that my database is definitive or that discrepancies between what I counted and what Campbell counted are due to errors on his part. Errors surely remain in my counts, although I have made every effort to make my database as accurate as I could.

Even a perfect accounting of the extant tax records would represent an undercount of slaves and slaveholders in Texas during those years. The records for several counties during certain years, for example, have not survived. And, as Campbell noted, it appears that the county sheriffs allowed slaveholders to underreport the number of slaves they owned by 10 to 20 percent.[2] Perhaps planters understood they only had to report the number of slaves who performed valuable labor, excluding the very young and old. Other slaveholders simply chose to underreport since the weak Republic of Texas government could do little about it—the *Telegraph and Texas Register*, for example, openly grumbled that "some persons owning one or two hundred negroes, have given in only twenty or thirty" to the tax assessors.[3] As such, the numbers in the tax records should be considered approximations that show the minimum populations. Yet because these discrepancies also appear to have been rather uniform—that is, not confined to any particular area or time period—calculating the percentage of change over time in populations is likely to be more accurate than the raw numbers. In other words, if the slave population was underreported in the tax records in both 1837 and 1838 by about 15 percent, we can use the two numbers to calculate an accurate estimate of the percentage of increase between those two years. This has been my method for reporting changes in slave and slaveholder populations during the Republic of Texas era, as I use the percentages of change rather than the raw numbers whenever possible.

In order to get those percentages as accurate as possible, my online database also employs statistical methods for estimating data that are missing for lack of extant records in certain counties for certain years. This would be the case in a place like Robertson County, which has surviving information on the number of slaves and slaveholders living in the area for the years 1837–1840 and 1842–1845. Although there were certainly slaves and slaveholders in the county during 1841, the returns for that year are missing, and so I have generated a statistical estimate for 1841 based on the returns collected from the original records for the other years. To that end, I grouped together counties that exhibited similar population patterns and trends over time, using the arc of population shifts in particular counties to estimate changes for similar counties whose data were missing for a particular year. The population trends in some counties, however, seemed to have followed trends that differed from most counties, and in those cases I used the average of the preceding and subsequent years to estimate missing data. The results offer a better approximation of the slave and slaveholder populations—almost always with lower percentages of increase—than the raw counts, and therefore I have included these statistical estimates in my calculations of the percentages of increase in both specific counties and the Republic as a whole. The *Texas Slavery Project*'s online database marks when statistical estimates provided the source of information, and the search engine allows users to decide whether to include or exclude these statistical estimates in search results.

My analysis of the tax records also relies on a geographic information system (GIS) of slave and slaveholder populations in the Republic of Texas that I created using ESRI's ArcMap suite of tools. This GIS plots the slave and slaveholder populations in the Republic of Texas each year by county, accounting for shifts in the boundaries of those counties as the Republic's population expanded. To create the historical boundaries I relied on Luke Gournay's *Texas Boundaries: Evolution of the State's Counties*, and these geo-coded datasets are available on the *Texas Slavery Project* through a Flash-based mapping tool that translates ArcMap shapefiles into vector graphics. Anyone can use the *Texas Slavery Project*'s mapping tools to plot slave and slaveholder populations as they shifted across the Texas landscape during the Republic years, as well as click on the individual counties to access the raw data from the database. I have relied on these visualization tools for some of my spatial analysis of the evolution of the region, which I then paired with traditional archival sources in order to confirm meaningful patterns in how people moved across the Texas borderlands during this era.

TABLE I. Aggregate Slave and Slaveholder Populations, Republic of Texas, 1837–1845

Year	TOTAL SLAVE POPULATION		TOTAL MASTER POPULATION		MASTERS W/ 1–4 SLAVES		MASTERS W/ 5–9 SLAVES		MASTERS W/ 10–19 SLAVES		MASTERS W/ 20–49 SLAVES		MASTERS W/ 50+ SLAVES		AVE. # OF SLAVES PER MASTER
	Raw	Est.	Raw	Est.	Raw	Est.	Raw	Est.	Raw	Est.	Raw	Est.	Raw	Est.	
1837	3,097	3,711	596	706	412	481	106	129	51	65	23	27	4	4	4.61
1838	5,786	5,786	1,049	1,049	681	681	217	217	94	94	50	50	7	7	4.73
1839	7,147	8,739	1,367	1,572	913	1,025	272	321	131	153	51	70	6	9	4.95
1840	11,827	11,827	2,163	2,163	1,370	1,370	475	475	232	232	77	77	9	9	4.84
1841	12,746	14,431	2,092	2,401	1,265	1,469	456	524	261	288	91	98	19	19	5.57
1842	19,463	19,463	2,996	2,996	1,736	1,736	684	684	395	395	152	152	29	29	5.75
1843	19,613	19,613	2,998	2,998	1,741	1,741	679	679	390	390	158	158	30	30	5.85
1844	20,291	22,852	3,134	3,399	1,872	1,989	673	746	398	455	171	184	25	30	6.17
1845	24,401	24,401	3,651	3,651	2,118	2,118	824	824	463	463	212	212	34	34	6.23
% Increase:	687.89	557.53	512.58	417.14	414.08	340.33	677.36	538.76	807.84	612.31	821.74	685.19	750	750	

GRAPH 2. Slave and Slaveholder Population Increases, Republic of Texas, 1837–1845

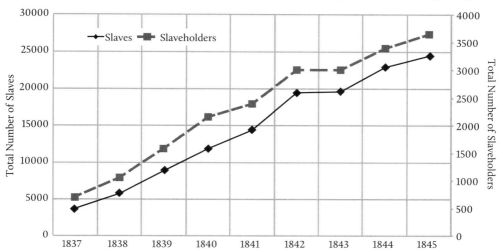

Cotton Prices and Trade

As my notes attest, I have relied on a wide range of sources for statistics on the growth of the cotton economy and international trade during the first half of the nineteenth century. Among the most useful for tracing global cotton prices and cotton production in the United States were Stuart Bruchey, *Cotton and the Growth of the American Economy*; James Watkins, *King Cotton*; and Douglass North, *The Economic Growth of the United States*. For cotton production in Mexico, see Alberto Ruiz y Sandova, *El Algodón en México*. On cotton's place within Great Britain and the British economy, see Thomas Ellison, *The Cotton Trade of Great Britain*; Ralph Davis, *The Industrial Revolution and British Overseas Trade*; and Michael Edwards, *The Growth of the British Cotton Trade*. For the global reach and power of the cotton economy, see Sven Beckert, *Empire of Cotton*.

For the transformations that cotton wrought on the southern United States—and the Mississippi River Valley in particular—see Harold Woodman, *King Cotton and His Retainers*; John Hebron Moore, *The Emergence of the Cotton Kingdom in the Old Southwest*; and Walter Johnson, *River of Dark Dreams*. For an analysis of how the global economics of cotton affected and altered politics within the United States, see Brian Schoen, *The Fragile Fabric of Union*.

All the statistics in table 2 and graph 3 are drawn from Stuart Bruchey, *Cotton and the Growth of the American Economy*, 7–32.

TABLE 2. Average Annual Price of Cotton, 1815–1845

YEAR	NEW ORLEANS (cents)	NEW YORK (cents)	LIVERPOOL (pence)
1815	27.3	21	20.7
1816	25.4	29.5	18.25
1817	29.8	26.5	20.12
1818	21.5	24	20
1819	14.3	24	13.5
1820	15.2	17	11.5
1821	17.4	14.32	8.23
1822	11.5	14.32	6.95
1823	14.5	11.4	7.21
1824	17.9	14.75	7.66
1825	11.9	18.59	10.1
1826	9.3	12.19	5.85
1827	9.7	9.26	5.79
1828	9.8	10.32	5.84
1829	8.9	9.88	5.32
1830	8.4	10.04	6.44
1831	9	9.71	5.38
1832	10	9.38	6.22
1833	11.2	12.32	7.87
1834	15.5	12.9	8.1
1835	15.2	17.45	9.13
1836	13.3	16.5	8.79
1837	9	13.25	6.09
1838	12.4	10.14	6.28
1839	7.9	13.36	7.19
1840	9.1	8.92	5.42
1841	7.8	9.5	5.73
1842	5.7	7.85	4.86
1843	7.5	7.25	4.37
1844	5.5	7.73	4.71
1845	6.8	5.63	3.92

GRAPH 3. Imports of Raw Cotton by Great Britain, 1815–1845

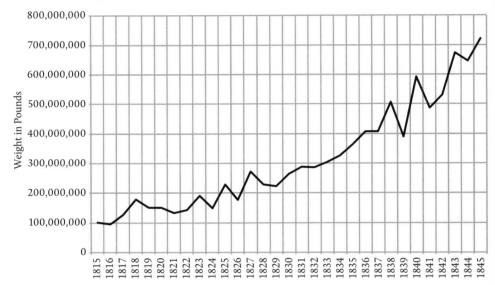

ACKNOWLEDGMENTS

I have been far more fortunate than I ever expected—or deserved—in the tremendous assistance and encouragement I received while writing this book. Whatever virtues these pages may hold are due to my wonderful family, friends, and colleagues who made this work possible. Whatever faults remain are mine alone.

The research and writing could not have happened without the sustained support I received from a number of institutions. The project began at the University of Virginia, where I was fortunate to work with a number of gifted historians. Gary Gallagher, Peter Onuf, and Richard Handler read early drafts of the manuscript, offered insightful commentary, and pushed me to think both broadly and deeply about my subject. The History Department, Southern Seminar, and Raven Society of UVA each provided fellowships for several indispensable research trips to archives in Mexico. At UVA, I was lucky to be surrounded by wonderful friends who also made tremendous critics, particularly Vanessa May and Patrick McDonough, Erik and Carrie Alexander, Calvin Schermerhorn, Scott Nesbit, Andrew Witmer, and Jaime Martinez. Members of the Southern and Early American seminars also cheerfully endured early incarnations of my ideas.

I feel particularly fortunate that I arrived at UVA at the outset of a new era in digital humanities, a coincidence that benefited this project immensely. At the Virginia Center for Digital History, Will Thomas (now of the University of Nebraska) helped guide me into the digital world, made it possible for me to develop the *Texas Slavery Project* (http://www.TexasSlaveryProject.org), and has continued in his support of my work at every stage. In developing that project, I also relied heavily on the insight, assistance, and goodwill of so many in Virginia's impressive digital humanities cohort. Scot French, Bill Ferster, Bill Covert, David Zimring, and Chris Gist, in particular, helped me to develop a digital research project that I could never have completed alone. The *Texas Slavery Project*, moreover, would not have been possible without a generous grant from the Summerlee Foundation of Dallas, Texas, for which I am deeply grateful.

I wrote early drafts of several chapters while serving as director of the Digital Scholarship Lab at the University of Richmond, where I worked with generous colleagues. I am particularly grateful to Nate Ayers, Kathy Monday, Eric Palmer, Troy Boroughs, Kevin Creamer, and Rob Nelson for their patience and goodwill.

At the University of North Texas, I have been lucky to be surrounded by talented scholars immersed in research on Texas and the U.S.-Mexican borderlands, all of whom have been as supportive as one could ever hope. Rick McCaslin, in particular, has been a wonderfully obliging chair, and Don Chipman provided insightful suggestions on an early draft of chapter 1. I benefited greatly from the research assistance of several talented graduate students at UNT—most notably Brad Folsom, Debbie Liles, Cameron Zinsou, and Mick Miller—all of whom tracked down obscure sources and citations. To my amazing fortune, UNT's library runs *The Portal to Texas History* (http://texashistory.unt.edu), the most comprehensive and impressive digital collection of primary sources on the history of Texas and the American Southwest available online. Simply put, this book would not exist without the amazing resources of the *Portal*, and I could not be more grateful for the tireless efforts of Cathy Hartman, Mark Phillips, Dreanna Belden, Tara Carlisle, Ana Krahmer, and innumerable others, who have made that digital archive possible.

Much of this book depends on material gleaned from archives in Mexico, and I have depended heavily on a number of people who made that research possible. Stan Green of Texas A&M International University shared his personal contacts among scholars in Mexico and lent his deep knowledge of the archives of Coahuila, enabling me to make every day count during my time in northern Mexico. Brian Owensby of the University of Virginia spent hours patiently orienting me in the archives of Mexico City, wrote letters of introduction, and even hand-drew maps of the archives and routes across the city. Rebeca Villalobos Alvarez and Rodrígo Diaz, both of the Universidad Nacional Autónoma de México, proved to be tremendous allies, going out of their way to help me prepare for a research trip to Coahuila. In Saltillo, Martha Rodríguez spared no effort to help me feel at home in an unfamiliar city and to make the most of my time in the archives, kindnesses that proved essential for completing this work. At the Archivo del Estado de Coahuila, Francisco Rodríguez went beyond what any researcher could expect, enabling me to benefit more than I ever hoped from the wealth of resources available in Ramos Arizpe.

I owe some of my deepest debts to my wonderful friend, Gerardo Gurza Lavalle of the Instituto Mora in Mexico City. A tremendously talented historian, Gerardo has become a dear friend of whom I have asked too much over the years. Even while balancing the full-time demands of his own scholarship and teaching, Gerardo graciously tracked down citations, sources, and information in various archives in Mexico City that proved invaluable to this study and which I would never have found on my own. At key moments Gerardo made all the difference, whether it was by helping me decipher incomprehensible handwriting, translating baffling passages and documents, providing insightful commentary on drafts of chapters, or simply offering moral support. He has been, at all turns, the embodiment of what a true scholar should be, and I could not be more grateful for his tremendous patience and generosity. It is an honor to call him a friend.

Within the United States, I benefited from the unwavering support of a number of key allies. My undergraduate adviser, Dale Baum, first introduced me to historical research and has continued to support my work over the years, reading the entire draft of the manuscript and offering insights that improved it immensely. Eric Walther, of the University of Houston, offered tireless support and generously shared his own research and insights. James F. Brooks and Bonnie Martin allowed me to work through various ideas as part of their "Uniting the Histories of Slavery in North America and Its Borderlands" symposia, and I am grateful to all the members of that group for their feedback. Luis Alberto Garcia of Southern Methodist University graciously shared sources and insights from his own research in northern Mexico. The Texas State Historical Association supported this project in innumerable ways over the years—most directly with a fellowship that allowed me to complete crucial archival research—and I am deeply indebted to Kent Calder, former executive director of the TSHA, for his support and warm friendship over the years.

Like all historians, I relied heavily on archivists and librarians at so many institutions, and I am deeply grateful to the staffs of all the archives—in both the United States and Mexico—cited in the notes. Brenda Gunn and John Wheat at the Dolph Briscoe Center for American History at the University of Texas, Donaly Brice and Jean Carefoot at the Texas State Library and Archives, and James Harkins and Mark Lambert of the Texas General Land Office all deserve special thanks for going far beyond the call of duty in tracking down manuscripts and resources. I also want to thank Ron Tyler and Andrés Tijerina for their kind assistance in tracking down images for the book, which I would never have found on my own, as well as Agustín L. Viesca for generously allowing me to reproduce an image of his famous ancestor. I am indebted to Larry, Betty Lou, and Kate Sheerin for allowing me to include an image from their family's remarkable collection of Theodore Gentilz paintings. And I am grateful to William J. Hill for giving me permission to use a painting from his wonderful Texas art collection for the book's cover, as well as everyone at the Museum of Fine Arts in Houston for making that possible.

Yet without time to write and rewrite—to craft my discoveries in the archives into paragraphs and pages—there could be no book. The William P. Clements Center for Southwest Studies at Southern Methodist University, a remarkable incubator for innovative scholarship, gave me that time through a fellowship that provided the gift of a year of uninterrupted writing. Nothing could mean more, and Andrew Graybill, Andrea Boardman, Ruth Ann Elmore, and Sherry Smith, as well as everyone else associated with the center, went out of their way to ensure that nothing stood between me and the project during my wonderful year at SMU. As they do for all their fellows, the center convened a workshop that brought together an array of talented scholars who collectively vetted the manuscript as a work-in-progress. Andrés Résendez, Alan Taylor, Gregg Cantrell, Sam Haynes, Stephanie Cole, Ed Countryman, Andrew Graybill, Sherry Smith, Katrina Jagodinsky, Joseph Abel, and Sascha Scott all provided me with far more constructive feedback than I had any right to expect, and much of those workshop discussions found their way into these pages.

Even after my fellowship year ended, the center's sustained support for my work has continued. Benjamin H. Johnson and Andrew Graybill brought the book into their David J. Weber Series in the New Borderlands History at UNC Press, and I feel particularly lucky to have had the chance to work with them on the project. Wonderful series editors, they vetted the manuscript, championed the project, and proved to be the best allies a writer could ever hope for. My editor at UNC, Chuck Grench, has been supportive and encouraging from the first, and I have been deeply grateful for the professionalism and assistance of everyone at the press.

There are two scholars to whom I owe special debts.

Edward L. Ayers left his deep imprint on this volume, where his influence is woven throughout the pages. It was my tremendous good fortune to collaborate closely with Ed on numerous projects at both the University of Virginia and the University of Richmond for several years, providing me the opportunity to observe firsthand a visionary historian at work. His insatiable curiosity, dedicated work ethic, and remarkable abilities as a writer set a standard that remains my bench-mark for what it means to be an engaged and innovative historian. But I owe Ed a far larger debt for his example as a selfless scholar who pushes himself and those around him to grapple honestly with the profound complexity of the past. I can never thank him enough for all the opportunities he has given me over the years, or for his example as a scholar, teacher, and writer. He is a terrific friend, and I often hear his Appalachian accent as I struggle to craft new pages, always reminding me to allow the past to speak with its own voice.

Randolph "Mike" Campbell was an inspiration before he became my colleague and close friend at UNT. Mike's groundbreaking work, *An Empire for Slavery: The Peculiar Institution in Texas, 1821–1865*, was the first book-length study to grapple with the dark legacy of slavery in the development of Texas. I began this project, in part, as a response to *An Empire for Slavery*, and because Mike's many other works had made me aware of the deep and lasting influence of the American South on the territories that became Texas. When I reached out to him during my earliest forays into the archives, Mike offered unalloyed encouragement, which has never faltered in the years since. He read multiple versions of the manuscript, provided invaluable advice, and endured my ceaseless questions, always with patience and cheer. Somehow I ended up in the office next to his at UNT, and I will always be grateful that I did.

Friends and family proved some of my greatest allies in the project. Kris Nelson and Eric Winzeler put up with me during numerous research trips, and Kris even joined me on a trip to Mexico City. My wonderful parents-in-law, Joseph and Mary Lou Castillo, offered their unwavering support in every way possible, whether it was during my frequent research trips, by providing me with a room in their house to write, or even on occasion finding original sources for my research. Christina and Audrey Parker always brought infectious joy with them whenever they came to visit, and I'm tremendously grateful to Cynthia and Matthew Jeter for their steadfast love and support. My talented sister-in-law, Charlotte Castillo, even provided crucial translation assistance on several primary sources, for which I am deeply grateful.

My parents, Tom and Kathy Torget, and my brother, Steve Torget, have done more than even I realize—all that is good in my life flows directly from my fiercely loving and supportive family. My dad is a tremendously talented and accomplished writer, whose grasp of the cadence of language and facility of expression are skills that I will never match. My admiration for his talent, self-discipline, and dedication to the craft have pushed me to be a better writer. My mom instilled my deep love of reading and kindled an abiding faith in myself, without which I could never have completed this work. She has been an enduring rock of support through it all. My brother lent his couch on innumerable research trips to Austin, where he kept my spirits high, listened to rough drafts of my ideas, and generally put up with far more than anyone should. Steve even did some research for his grateful brother that proved essential. My parents and my brother, moreover, read the entire manuscript, each of them providing me with voluminous notes that significantly improved the book.

In my life, none compare with Alexandra. She has endured far more than I could ever repay, inspired more than I could ever hope, and she alone understands what this work has meant and required of us both. She has been the first and best reader of every page, braved my long absences on research trips—and even longer ones into my office to write—without complaint, and tackled every challenge with cheer that belied the heavy burdens I placed on her. And for both of us, nothing lifted those burdens like our son, Antonio, and our daughter, Catalina. I began writing these pages the summer Antonio was born, and every day since—particularly the day Catalina arrived two years later—has been beautiful because of them. Their love and laughter filled our home with sunlight even on the darkest days.

NOTES

Abbreviations

ACEC	Archivo del Congreso del Estado de Coahuila, Saltillo, Mexico
AGEC	Archivo General del Estado de Coahuila, Ramos Arizpe, Mexico
AP	Eugene Barker, ed., *Annual Report of the American Historical Association for the Year 1919: The Austin Papers*, 3 vols. (Washington, D.C.: Government Printing Office, 1924, 1928; Austin: University of Texas Press, 1927)
BA	Béxar Archives, Dolph Briscoe Center for American History, University of Texas, microfilm edition
BDC-ROT	Ephraim Douglass Adams, ed., *British Diplomatic Correspondence concerning the Republic of Texas, 1838–1846* (Austin: Texas State Historical Association, 1918)
Blake	Robert Bruce Blake Research Collection, Dolph Briscoe Center for American History, University of Texas
Beinecke	Beinecke Rare Book and Manuscript Library, Yale University
CAH-UT	Dolph Briscoe Center for American History, University of Texas
CGG	*Civilian and Galveston Gazette*
DCROT	George Garrison, ed., *Diplomatic Correspondence of the Republic of Texas* in the *Annual Report of the American Historical Association for the Year 1908*, 3 vols. (Washington, D.C.: Government Printing Office, 1908–11)
Dublán y Lozano	Manuel Dublán and José María Lozano, *Legislación Mexicana o Colección Completa de Disposiciones Legislativas Expedidas desde la Independencia de la República* (Mexico: Imprenta del Comercio, 1876)
HOT	*The Handbook of Texas Online*, Texas State Historical Association, http://tshaonline.org/handbook
LOT	H. P. H. Gammel, *The Laws of Texas, 1822–1897*, 12 vols. (Austin: Gammel Book, 1898)
Mateos	Juan Antonio Mateos, *Historia Parlamentaria de los Congresos Mexicanos* (Mexico: J. V. Villada, 1877)
NA	Nacogdoches Archives, Texas State Library and Archives, Austin
PCRCT	Malcolm D. McLean, ed., *Papers Concerning Robertson's Colony in Texas*, 3 vols. (Ft. Worth: Texas Christian University Press, 1974–76); 15 vols., plus intro. vol. (Arlington: University of Texas at Arlington Press, 1977–93)
SFA	Stephen F. Austin
SHC-UNC	Southern Historical Collection, University of North Carolina
SMWP	Samuel May Williams Papers, Galveston and Texas History Center, Rosenberg Library, Galveston, Texas
TTR	*Telegraph and Texas Register*
TSLA	Texas State Library and Archives, Austin, Texas

Introduction

1. All information about Marian, Richard and Tivi in this and the following paragraphs comes from "Declaracion del Negro Esclavo Marian," April 24, 1820; "Declarar del Negro Esclavo Ricardo Moran," April 25, 1820; "Declaracion de la Negra Esclava, Tivi," April 25, 1820; all from Provincias Internas, volumen 187, expediente 9, Archivo General de la Nación, Mexico City, Mexico.

2. Ignacio Pérez to Antonio Martínez, December 3, 1819, in Gulick, in *The Papers of Mirabeau Buonapart Lamar*, 1:41; Martínez to Joaquín de Arredondo, December 10, 1819, in Martínez, *The Letters of Antonio Martinez*, 284.

3. For the journey of Kirkham and Austin, see "Declaracion de Xacobo Querkham," December 23, 1830; "Declaration of Moses Austin," December 23, 1820; as well as Jacques Villeré to Antonio Martínez, September 12, 1820, and Antonio Martínez to Joaquín de Arredondo, December 24, 1820, all in Archivo General de la Nación, Provincias Internas, Transcripts, tomo 251, box 2Q217, vol. 541, CAH-UT. For Martínez's endorsement of Austin's plan, see Martínez to Joaquín de Arredondo, December 26, 1820, in *PCRCT*, 1:301.

4. On cotton statistics, see Bruchey, *Cotton and the Growth of the American Economy*, 7–32. On the early British cotton trade, see Edwards, *The Growth of the British Cotton Trade*; Davis, *The Industrial Revolution and British Overseas Trade*. On the effects of cotton on the southwestern United States, see Moore, *The Emergence of the Cotton Kingdom in the Old Southwest*; Rothman, *Slave Country*; Schoen, *The Fragile Fabric of Union*; Johnson, *River of Dark Dreams*.

5. Population statistics drawn from the *Historical Census Browser*, Geospatial Center, University of Virginia (http://mapserver.lib.virginia.edu). For the origins of British abolitionism, see Brown, *Moral Capital*. For American views of British abolitionism, see Haynes, *Unfinished Revolution*. For the rise of Garrisonian abolitionism in the United States and its connections to the British movement, see McDaniel, *The Problem of Democracy in the Age of Slavery*.

6. There are innumerable books on this subject, but the best remains Potter, *The Impending Crisis*. See also McPherson, *Battle Cry of Freedom*, and Freehling, *The Road to Disunion*.

7. There is a small but expanding number of works examining the global context of the growth of cotton and slavery in North America, most notably Schoen, *The Fragile Fabric of Union*; Johnson, *River of Dark Dreams*; Beckert, *Empire of Cotton*.

8. By 1843, 85 percent of all England's raw cotton imports came from the southern United States and manufactured cotton products made up fully half of England's entire export economy. Cotton bales made up nearly 60 percent of all U.S. exports. For statistics on British cotton consumption and U.S. cotton exports, see Bruchey, *Cotton and the Growth of the American Economy*, 7–17.

9. The question of how capitalistic was the slave-based economy of the U.S. South was a consuming question in the field of American slavery during the second half of the twentieth century, represented best by the divide between the works of Eugene Genovese (most notably *Roll Jordan Roll*) and James Oakes (particularly *The Ruling Race*), as well as the debates surrounding Robert Fogel and Stanley Engerman's *Time on the Cross*. The general consensus now holds that American slavery was both capitalistic and widely adaptable, as recent scholarship has focused on the institution's aggressive expansion across the conti-

nent, a trend best seen in Ira Berlin's *Generations of Captivity* and Walter Johnson's *River of Dark Dreams*.

10. My thinking about the overlapping and often mutually reinforcing relationships between economic, political, social, and labor systems in the development of New World societies has been powerfully shaped by the writings of Robin Blackburn, particularly *The Making of New World Slavery*.

11. Works citing "manifest destiny" as the root of the American takeover of northern Mexico, particularly in regard to the coming of the U.S.-Mexican War, have a long history. See, for example, Weinberg, *Manifest Destiny*, and Merk, *Manifest Destiny and Mission in American History*. For a more recent example, see Winders, *Crisis in the Southwest*, particularly 71–73. Andrés Reséndez has commented insightfully on this point in "National Identity on a Shifting Border," 668–88, and in *Changing National Identities at the Frontier*, particularly 5–6.

12. Here I have been greatly influenced by the work of David Weber and Andrés Reséndez, who have both stressed the influential role of the Mexican state on the development of the Texas borderlands, as well as Will Fowler's work on the early Mexican nation. See, in particular, Weber, *The Mexican Frontier*; Reséndez, *Changing National Identities at the Frontier*; Fowler, *Mexico in the Age of Proposals*.

13. The most influential recent works are Pekka Hämäläinen's *The Comanche Empire* and Brian DeLay's *War of a Thousand Deserts*. Both Hämäläinen and DeLay argue that the collective political and military will of native groups—the Comanches, above all—played critical roles in the political decisions of both Mexicans and Americans during this era. DeLay, in particular, links the military, economic, and political violence of Indians in Texas to the political calculations of both Mexico and the United States on the road to the U.S.-Mexican War. Other recent works have also contributed to a new emphasis on native agency in the Texas borderlands, most notably Smith, *From Dominance to Disappearance*; Britten, *The Lipan Apaches*; Anderson, *The Indian Southwest*; Barr, *Peace Came in the Form of a Woman*. For an overview of recent developments in the literature on Indian nations in Texas, see Hämäläinen, "Into the Mainstream: The Emergence of a New Texas Indian History."

14. The most detailed work on the movement of American slavery into Mexico was done by Lester Bugbee during the 1890s and Eugene C. Barker during the 1920s. See Bugbee, "Stephen F. Austin's Views on Slavery in Early Texas," 405–8; Bugbee, "Slavery in Early Texas," 389–412 and 648–68; Barker, "The Influence of Slavery in the Colonization of Texas," 3–36; Barker, *The Life of Stephen F. Austin*. Bugbee and Barker both concluded that slavery was only peripheral—rather than central—to the movement of Americans into Mexico, an interpretation that has proven remarkably resilient and influential in the historiography of the U.S.-Mexican borderlands. In 1989, Randolph B. Campbell published the first book-length study on slavery in Texas, *An Empire for Slavery*. Campbell's work, however, concentrated almost entirely on the period after Texas joined the United States in 1845 and thus relied heavily on Bugbee and Barker for the period before annexation. Sean Kelley's *Los Brazos de Dios* is a community study of the lower Brazos River that focuses on plantation life in Texas, although it pays much more attention to the Mexican and Republic-era political contexts than previous work. A smattering of other article and thesis-length works have examined discrete aspects of slavery in preannexation Texas (a

detailed discussion of these works can be found in Torget, "Cotton Empire: Slavery and the Texas Borderlands, 1820–1837," 12–17).

15. If the literature on slavery in preannexation Texas remains underdeveloped, the work on cotton during that period is even more anemic. There is, for example, no volume dedicated to the subject, and discussions of the industry tend to be scattered across works devoted to other topics. The most thorough treatment of the influence of cotton on politics in Mexican-era Texas is the brief discussion in Andrés Tijerina's *Tejanos and Texas under the Mexican Flag*, 114–15. A similar discussion can be found in Gregg Cantrell's *Stephen F. Austin*. Hints of cotton's role in the preannexation Texas economy can be found in Hogan, *The Texas Republic* and Crane, "The Administration of the Customs Service of the Republic of Texas." Discussions of specific planting methods can be found in Silverthorne, *Plantation Life in Texas*, and Jones, *Texas Roots*. Some discussions of the mechanics of shipping cotton can be found in Puryear and Winfield, *Sandbars and Sternwheelers*. Descriptions of the operations of specific plantations can be found in Curlee, "A Study of Texas Slave Plantations, 1822 to 1865"; Jones, *Peach Point Plantation*; Kearney, *Nassau Plantation*; Kelley, *Los Brazos de Dios*. Some references to the cotton economy can also be found in biographies of figures particularly close to the industry, such as Barker, *The Life of Stephen F. Austin*, and Henson, *Samuel May Williams*.

16. Most histories that touch on American migration into Mexico during the 1820s and 1830s explain this phenomenon largely within the context of the availability of cheap Mexican land—see, for example, Campbell, *Gone to Texas*, 102. On the combined influence of the U.S. economy and the Mexican government, see Weber, *The Mexican Frontier*; Reséndez, *Changing National Identities at the Frontier*. Both Weber and Reséndez point toward trade between northern Mexico and the United States—particularly commerce on the Santa Fe Trail—as the dominant economic influence on the region, which then shaped the efforts of various levels of Mexico's government to control the territory. Neither addresses the problem of slavery or the role of the cotton economy as central factors, although a consideration of those contexts would bolster the main arguments of Weber and Reséndez.

17. See, for example, Weber, *The Mexican Frontier*, 122–57.

18. Ibid., 179–84.

Chapter 1

1. Juan Bautista de Elguézabal to the Commandant General, June 20, 1803, in Elguézabal, "A Description of Texas in 1803," 513–15. For the early history of San Antonio, see de la Teja, *San Antonio de Béxar*.

2. "General Census Report of the City of Bexar and its Missions: Barrios Valero, Sur, Norte, Laredo," January 1, 1820, in Leal, *Translations of Statistical and Census Reports of Texas*, reel 2, frames 650–730.

3. Information on the July 5, 1819, flood of San Antonio in this and the following paragraphs comes from Antonio Martínez to Joaquin de Arredondo, July 8, 1819, in Martínez, *The Letters of Antonio Martinez*, 241–43, and Antonio Martínez to Viceroy Juan Ruíz de Apodaca, July 8, 1819, in Martínez, *Letters from Governor Antonio Martinez to the Viceroy*, 34.

4. Martínez to Apodaca, July 8, 1819, in Martínez, *Letters from Governor Antonio Martinez to the Viceroy*, 34.

5. Information on the layout and neighborhoods of San Antonio come from "General Census Report of the City of Bexar and its Missions: Barrios Valero, Sur, Norte, Laredo," January 1, 1820, in Leal, *Translations of Statistical and Census Reports of Texas*, reel 2, frames 650–730, and de la Teja, *San Antonio de Béxar*, 31–48.

6. Decades later, Antonio Menchaca recalled that 28 people drowned in the flood (Menchaca, *Recollections of a Tejano Life*, 56).

7. Martínez to Apodaca, July 8, 1819, in Martínez, *Letters from Governor Antonio Martinez to the Viceroy*, 34.

8. See, for example, the two main collections of Martínez's writings from this period: Martínez, *The Letters of Antonio Martinez,* and Martínez, *Letters from Governor Antonio Martinez to the Viceroy.*

9. On complaints by governors who preceded Martínez, see, for example, Manuel Pardo to Arredondo, February 13, 1817, and March 27, 1817, in Blake, supplement vol. 10, 244–58; Almaráz, *Tragic Cavalier*.

10. Governor Juan Bautista de Elguézabal reported the population of La Bahía in 1803 at 618 (Elguézabal, "A Description of Texas in 1803," 514). A census in 1804 noted about 700 people living in the region ("Census of the Residents of the Real Presidio of La Bahía del Espíritu Santo," December 31, 1804, reel 1, frames 1487–1494, and "Census Report of the Presidial Company of La Bahía del Espíritu Santo," December 31, 1804, reel 1, frames 1499–1504, both in Leal, *Translations of Statistical and Census Reports of Texas*).

11. Weber, *The Spanish Frontier in North America*, 211–12. La Bahía was later renamed Goliad in 1829 as an anagram of "Hidalgo" in honor of Miguel Hidalgo, the priest who sparked the rebellion that would become the Mexican War for Independence.

12. On ranching in Spanish Texas, see Jackson, *Los Mesteños*.

13. Elguézabal reported the population of Nacogdoches in 1803 at 770 (Elguézabal, "A Description of Texas in 1803," 514); an 1804 census counted 789 people ("Census Report of the Town of Our Lady of Pilar de Nacogdoches," January 1, 1804, reel 1, frames 1392–1427, in Leal, *Translations of Statistical and Census Reports of Texas*); Harrison, "The Failure of Spain in East Texas," 192–95. According to Harrison, nearly 58 percent of slaveholders in Nacogdoches during the years between 1793 and 1809 were listed as French in the census, providing a sense of how deeply interconnected Nacogdoches was with French Louisiana in terms of economic and social exchange.

14. An American officer stationed in Natchitoches, Louisiana, noted in 1804 that the Spaniards in eastern Texas depended heavily on importations from western Louisiana, telling the Louisiana governor, William C. C. Claiborne, that "the inhabitants between here and there [San Antonio] do not raise Sufficient Provisions to carry them through half the year. If it were not for the Supplies they get from this District [Natchitoches] they would absolutely starve" (Townes, "Invisible Lines," 164 [because no page numbers are available in the dissertation manuscript on Proquest, this is my approximation]).

15. On the difficulty of estimating Texas Indian populations, see Meacham, "The Population of Spanish and Mexican Texas, 1716–1836," 344–66. Anderson's *The Conquest of Texas* estimates the 1820 population at 30,000 (4, 22). See also Elguézabal, "A Description of Texas in 1803," 515.

16. Padilla, "Report on the Barbarous Indians of the Province of Texas," 61–62.

17. On the failure of the Spanish missions in Texas, see Smith, *From Dominance to Disappearance*, 14–18; Weber, *The Mexican Frontier*, 53–56.

18. On seventeenth-century violence between the Spanish and various Indian groups, see Smith, *From Dominance to Disappearance*; Britten, *The Lipan Apaches*; Hämäläinen, *The Comanche Empire*; Anderson, *The Indian Southwest*; Weber, *The Spanish Frontier in North America*; Weber, *Bárbaros*. On the 1785 agreement between the Comanches and Spaniards, see Smith, *From Dominance to Disappearance*, 31–32; Hämäläinen, *The Comanche Empire*, 107–17. On the war of extermination that ensued against the Lipan Apaches, see Britten, *The Lipan Apaches,* ch. 4; Weber, *Bárbaros*, 148–51.

19. On the destructive force of the Comanches against Spaniards in Texas during the 1770s and 1780s, see Hämäläinen, *The Comanche Empire*, 98–100, 143. The Comanches agreed to the 1785 treaty, in part, because they were eager for access to Spanish trade in firearms, as well as the eradication of the Apaches.

20. Weber, *The Spanish Frontier in North America*, 228–34; Smith, *From Dominance to Disappearance*, 19–23, 35–36.

21. Weber, *The Spanish Frontier in North America*, 174–77; Smith, *From Dominance to Disappearance*, 34–40.

22. Smith, *From Dominance to Disappearance*, 73–94; Weber, *The Spanish Frontier in North America*, 292–95.

23. Ramos, "Finding the Balance," 49.

24. On racial and power categories in New Spain, see Weber, *The Spanish Frontier in North America*, 326–28; Elliot, *Empires of the Atlantic World*, 170–72; Tjarks, "Comparative Demographic Analysis of Texas, 1777–1793," 291–338 (especially 322–23).

25. Henderson, *The Mexican Wars for Independence*, 53–107. On the upheavals of the Mexican War for Independence, see Van Young, *The Other Rebellion*.

26. Chipman and Joseph, *Spanish Texas*, 246–47; Almaráz, *Tragic Cavalier*, 104–24; Navarro, *Defending Mexican Valor in Texas*, 66–71; McDonald, *José Antonio Navarro*, 21–23.

27. See, for example, Captain Isidro de la Garza to Manuel Salcedo, September 20, 1812, in Blake, supplement vol. 8, 38–41.

28. Chipman and Joseph, *Spanish Texas*, 247–50; Almaráz, *Tragic Cavalier*, 151–73. The question of whether the James Madison administration, as well as Louisiana's territorial governor, William Claiborne, actively encouraged the Gutiérrez-Magee expedition has long been the subject of debate by historians. The long-held consensus has been that James Monroe, as Madison's secretary of state, covertly encouraged the rebellion of Mexico against Spain (see Bradley, "Forgotten Filibusters," 146–65, and Brady, "Unspoken Words: James Monroe's Involvement in the Magee-Gutierrez Filibuster," 58–68). J. C. A. Stagg, however, argues that the Madison administration did not intend to encourage the rebellion. See Stagg, "The Madison Administration and Mexico," 449–80.

29. Warren, *The Sword Was Their Passport*, 66–68; Chipman and Joseph, *Spanish Texas*, 250–51; Almaráz, *Tragic Cavalier*, 175–79; McDonald, *José Antonio Navarro*, 28–29.

30. McDonald, *José Antonio Navarro*, 29–30; Menchaca, *Recollections of a Tejano Life*, 52–53.

31. Menchaca, *Recollections of a Tejano Life*, 53–54; Navarro, *Defending Mexican Valor in Texas*, 54–55. Menchaca remembered that eight people suffocated in overcrowded cells, while Navarro believed it was eighteen. "La Quinta," as a term Spaniards used for their restful country retreats, was selected by Arredondo for its irony.

32. On the confiscation of the property and homes of insurgents, see Christoval Dominguez Proclamation, August 28, 1813, in Blake, supplement vol. 8, 60. Many of these

homes remained abandoned and unused in San Antonio as late as 1819 (see, e.g., Martínez to Arredondo, September 14, 1817, and December 10, 1819, in Martínez, *The Letters of Antonio Martinez*, 56–57, 282–83). On the confiscation of firearms, see Martínez to Apodaca, August 1, 1817, in Martínez, *Letters from Antonio Martinez to the Viceroy*, 6.

33. Castañeda, *Our Catholic Heritage in Texas*, 6:117–20.

34. For Elizondo's field reports, see Ignacio Elizondo to Joaquín de Arredondo, September 2, 1813, and September 12, 1813, both in Blake, vol. 46, 355–61.

35. Anonymous, "Memoria de las cosas más notables que acaecieron en Bexar el año de 13 mandando el Tirano Arredondo, 1813," translated in Coronado, *A World Not to Come*, 427. José Antonio Navarro, writing in the 1850s, also recalled that about 105 refugees were shot at the Trinity River by Elizondo's men (Navarro, *Defending Mexican Valor in Texas*, 56–57). Antonio Menchaca recalled that Elizondo killed 279 men on the Trinity (Menchaca, *Recollections of a Tejano Life*, 55).

36. Castañeda, *Our Catholic Heritage in Texas*, 6:117–19; Ignacio Elizondo to Joaquín de Arredondo, September 12, 1813, in Blake, vol. 46, 360.

37. Bradley, "Forgotten Filibusters," 143–46. Louisiana's territorial governor, William C. C. Claiborne, estimated that at least 1,200 people fled Texas to the United States during the first few weeks following the defeat of the rebels (William C. C. Claiborne to L. B. Macarty, October 16, 1813, in Rowland, *Official Letter Books of W. C. C. Claiborne*, 6:272–73).

38. Arredondo even went so far as to dismantle the only military hospital in San Antonio when he left in late 1813 (see Martínez to Apodaca, May 1, 1820, in Martínez, *Letters from Governor Antonio Martinez to the Viceroy*, 43).

39. Haynes, *The Mississippi Territory and the Southwest Frontier*, 134.

40. Smith, *From Dominance to Disappearance*, 68.

41. Moore, *The Emergence of the Cotton Kingdom in the Old Southwest*, 5; Haynes, *The Mississippi Territory and the Southwest Frontier*, 12–13.

42. Schoen, *The Fragile Fabric of Union*, 45–46.

43. Unser, "American Indians and the Cotton Frontier," 315–16.

44. Moore, *The Emergence of the Cotton Kingdom in the Old Southwest*, 11–14.

45. Ibid., 8.

46. *Historical Census Browser*, Geospatial Center, University of Virginia (http://mapserver.lib.virginia.edu); Rothman, *Slave Country*, 182–83; Haynes, *The Mississippi Territory and the Southwest Frontier*, 133.

47. Howe, *What Hath God Wrought*, 128–31.

48. Hämäläinen, *The Comanche Empire*, 145–46; Kavanagh, *Comanche Political History*, 162. On Nolan's forays into Texas for horses to supply the southern United States, see Wilson and Jackson, *Philip Nolan and Texas*.

49. *Democratic Clarion & Tennessee Gazette*, May 19, 1812, in *PCRCT*, 1:152–55; Thomas Jefferson to William Dunbar, January 16 [1800?], in *PCRCT*, 1:19–20; Zebulon Pike published a journal in 1810 that included descriptions of massive horse herds he encountered during a journey across Texas, which in turn stirred speculation in the United States about Texas horses, including the *Democratic Clarion*'s story.

50. Anderson, *The Indian Southwest*, 252–53; Smith, *From Dominance to Disappearance*, 97–105; Hämäläinen, *The Comanche Empire*, 144–45, 184–86; Hämäläinen, "The Politics of Grass," 173–208.

51. Smith, *From Dominance to Disappearance*, 97–105. The Tejano ranches south of San

Antonio remained abandoned as late as 1819 (see Martínez to Arredondo, July 20, 1819, in Martínez, *The Letters of Antonio Martinez*, 247).

52. Governor of Texas to Arredondo, September 7, 1813, in Blake, supplement vol. 8, 61–63.

53. Kavanagh, *Comanche Political History*, 158.

54. Clayton, *The Indian Southwest*, 253–54. In August 1814, the governor of Texas reported that the Comanches had nearly destroyed "the livestock of the province" (see Benito de Armiñan to Arredondo, August 15, 1814, BA, reel 54, frame 122).

55. Jose Manuel Sambrano to Martínez, November 1, 1818, in Blake, supplement vol. 8, 212; Martínez to Arredondo, October 1, 1818, October 20, 1818, November 13, 1819, in Martínez, *The Letters of Antonio Martinez*, 181, 186, 280.

56. Kavanagh, *Comanche Political History*, 180; *PCRCT*, 2:211.

57. Schliz, "People of the Cross Timbers," 137; Smith, *From Dominance to Disappearance*, 103–9.

58. David Burnet to John Jamison, August 1818, in Burnet, "David G. Burnet's Letters Describing the Comanche Indians," 132.

59. Martínez to Apodaca (relaying a report sent to Martínez by Salvador Carrasco), January 27, 1818, in Martínez, *Letters from Governor Antonio Martinez to the Viceroy*, 12.

60. Unknown Writer, "Statement of News Gathered on the Frontier," March 15, 1821, Nacogdoches Archives Transcriptions, vol. 21, 5–6, NA, TSLA; Smith, *From Dominance to Disappearance*, 106.

61. The horses-for-guns exchange shows up regularly in the correspondence of both Spaniards and Americans during this era, as well as the newspapers of the United States. See, for example, Juan de Castañeda to Mariano Varela, June 30, 1816, in Blake, supplement vol. 8, 124; Martínez to Arredondo, May 31, 1818, in Martínez, *The Letters of Antonio Martinez,* 136; *National Intelligencer*, September 15, 1820; *Hallowell Gazette*, September 27, 1820; Anderson, *The Indian Southwest*, 232; Smith, *From Dominance to Disappearance*, 106.

62. Smith, *From Dominance to Disappearance*, 106–7.

63. Hämäläinen, *The Comanche Empire*, 186; Smith, *From Dominance to Disappearance*, 110.

64. This violence destroyed communities in the Río Grande Valley. An 1819 census in Laredo, a village along the Río Grande, noted that more than 80 percent of the ranches had been abandoned in the wake of the Indian raids from Texas (see Jackson, *Los Mesteños*, 550). Juan Antonio Padilla described the breadth of destruction wrought by the Indian raids into northern New Spain in his December 1819 reports on Texas (see Padilla, "Report on the Barbarous Indians of the Province of Texas"). For a description of Comanche raiding parties and their methods, see David Burnet to John Jamison, August 1818, in Burnet, "David G. Burnet's Letters Describing the Comanche Indians," 131–34.

65. *Natchez Republican*, reprinted in the *Washington Whig*, September 22, 1817 (emphasis in original).

66. Martínez to Apodaca, May 31, 1817, June 7, 1817, June 13, 1817, in Martínez, *Letters from Governor Antonio Martinez to the Viceroy*, 3–4; Martínez to Arredondo, May 30, 1817, July 25, 1817, August 12, 1817, in Martínez, *The Letters of Antonio Martinez*, 1–2, 30–31, 38.

67. Martínez to Apodaca, April 26, 1818, in Martínez, *Letters from Governor Antonio Martinez to the Viceroy*, 15.

68. Martínez complained regularly to his superiors about the frequency of desertions

among troops stationed in Texas. See, for example, Martínez to Arredondo, August 20, 1817, November 20, 1818, in Martínez, *The Letters of Antonio Martinez*, 42, 194.

69. Martínez to Arredondo, July 13, 1817, November 12, 1817, February 8, 1818, May 27, 1818, in Martínez, *The Letters of Antonio Martinez*, 20–21, 76–77, 103–4, 132–33; Martínez to Apodaca, May 23, 1818, in Martínez, *Letters from Governor Antonio Martinez to the Viceroy*, 18. Years later, Antonio Menchaca recalled how Tejanos during the late 1810s planted crops at the risk of their lives, often going into the fields "in squads of fifteen to twenty or more to look for their oxen, and while working had to keep their weapons with them" (Menchaca, *Recollections of a Tejano Life*, 57).

70. Martínez to Arredondo, July 23, 1817, in Martínez, *The Letters of Antonio Martinez*, 25; Diary of Operations of José Salinas, entry for November 18, 1819, in Blake, supplement vol. 8, 220; McDonald, *José Antonio Navarro*, 40–49. On contraband trade between Texas and Louisiana during the eighteenth and early nineteenth centuries, particularly in livestock, see Jackson, *Los Mesteños*.

71. Arredondo to Martínez, September 20, 1816, in Blake, supplement vol. 10, 222; Kavanagh, *Comanche Political History*, 179–80; Ramos, "From Norteño to Tejano," 99–100; McDonald, *José Antonio Navarro*, 15–16, 33–34.

72. Manuel Pardo to Arredondo, March 27, 1817, in Blake, supplement vol. 10, 254.

73. Declaration of Joseph Dailey to Manuel Pardo, May 7, 1817, in Blake, supplement vol. 8, 157; Martínez to Arredondo, June 26, 1818, April 1, 1819, October 23, 1819, November 13, 1819, in Martínez, *The Letters of Antonio Martinez*, 150, 217–18, 274, 280.

74. Martínez to Apodaca, January 26, 1819, in Martínez, *Letters from Governor Antonio Martinez*, 32.

75. Castañeda, *Our Catholic Heritage in Texas*, 6:139–40; Harris Gaylord Warren, "Aury, Louis Michel," *HOT*.

76. Downs, "The Administration of Antonio Martinez," 11–16; Bradley, "Forgotten Filibusters," 185–99; Castañeda, *Our Catholic Heritage in Texas*, 6:140–47; Chipman and Joseph, *Spanish Texas*, 252–53.

77. Beverly Chew to Secretary of the Treasury Crawford, August 1, 1817 (quotation), extracted in *Alexandria Gazette & Daily Advertiser*, December 24, 1817; Davis, *The Pirates Laffite*, 317–18, 339.

78. In 1820, the populations were in Alabama, 47,449 slaves out of 144,317 total people; in Mississippi, 32,814 out of 75,448; and in Louisiana, 69,064 out of 153,407. All numbers are taken from the *Historical Census Browser*, Geospatial Center, University of Virginia (http://mapserver.lib.virginia.edu/).

79. Deyle, *Carry Me Back*. On the slave trade in New Orleans, the largest slave port in the United States, see Johnson, *Soul by Soul*.

80. Beverly Chew to Secretary of the Treasury Crawford, August 1, 1817 (quotation), extracted in *Alexandria Gazette & Daily Advertiser*, December 24, 1817; Davis, *The Pirates Laffite*, 317–18, 339. Chew became so alarmed at the slave trafficking between Galveston and Louisiana that he appointed agents to monitor the plantations of suspected buyers and positioned other agents along the Sabine River to catch Americans coming into Louisiana with illegally purchased African slaves.

81. Chew to Crawford, August 30, 1817, reprinted in the *Orleans Gazette and Commercial Advertiser*, December 24, 1817; Davis, *The Pirates Laffite*, 361–62.

82. Chew to Crawford, October 17, 1817, reprinted in the *Orleans Gazette and Commercial Advertiser*, December 24, 1817. Chew forwarded reports he had received of smuggled Africans being herded through Louisiana, "bound for the Mississippi." For a similar report of the Texas-Mississippi trade, see the *Washington Review and Examiner*, August 31, 1818.

83. R. Jones Papers, "A Visit to Galveston Island in 1818," Galveston and Texas History Center, Rosenberg Library, Galveston, Texas.

84. Davis, *The Pirates Laffite*, 411–13, 450–51.

85. Smith, *From Dominance to Disappearance*, 96, 101.

86. For a detailed treatment of the early history of runaway slaves along the U.S.-Texas border, see Torget, "Cotton Empire: Slavery and the Texas Borderlands, 1820–1837," 49–52; Blyth, "Fugitives from Servitude"; Harrison, "The Failure of Spain in East Texas."

87. Deposition of Andrés, March 10, 1817, in BA, reel 58, frames 97–105.

88. Testimony of Juan José María Castro, Ennalt Calvin, and Yorca, in Felipe Roque de la Portilla to Arredondo, May 9, 1818, in BA, reel 60, frames 971–82. An English translation is available in Blake, supplement vol. 8, 183–93. On Arredondo's response to the testimony of the runaways, see Arredondo to Martínez, May 16, 1818, and Apodaca to Martínez, July 21, 1818, both in BA, reel 61, frames 1, 401.

89. See, for example, Martínez to Apodaca, May 28, 1818, August 6, 1818, August 14, 1818, December 10, 1818, in Martínez, *Letters from Governor Antonio Martinez to the Viceroy*, 19, 24–25, 29; Martínez to Arredondo, May 19, 1818, May 28, 1818 (quotation), September 8, 1818, in Martínez, *The Letters of Antonio Martinez*, 126–28, 134–36, 173–74.

90. Martínez to Arredondo, April 1, 1819, in Martínez, *The Letters of Antonio Martinez*, 217–218.

91. Martínez to Arredondo, August 18, 1818, in ibid., 163.

92. Martínez to Arredondo, November 12, 1818, in ibid., 194.

93. *Natchez Press*, reprinted in the *Boston Patriot*, August 9, 1819.

94. See, for example, *Louisiana Advertiser*, July 7, 1820.

95. Martínez to Arredondo, August 17, 1819, and September 5, 1819, in Martínez, *Letters of Antonio Martinez*, 252, 259–61; Castañeda, *Our Catholic Heritage in Texas*, 6:164–65.

96. Ignacio Pérez to Antonio Martínez, December 3, 1819, in Gulick, *The Papers of Mirabeau Buonaparte Lamar*, 1:34–44; Castañeda, *Our Catholic Heritage in Texas*, 1:164–68.

97. All information about Marian, Richard, Tivi, Samuel, and John comes from depositions they gave to Spanish authorities in Monterrey: "Declaración del Negro Esclavo Marian," April 24, 1820; "Declarar del Negro Esclavo Ricardo Moran," April 25, 1820; "Declaración de la Negra Esclava, Tivi," April 25, 1820; "Declaración del Negro Esclavo Juan Pedro," April 24, 1820; all in Provincias Internas, volumen 187, expediente 9, Archivo General de la Nación, Mexico City, Mexico. For Martínez quotation, see Martínez to Arredondo, December 10, 1819, in Martínez, *The Letters of Antonio Martinez*, 284.

98. Martínez to Apodaca, April 5, 1820, in Martínez, *Letters from Governor Antonio Martinez to the Viceroy*, 43.

99. Martínez to Arredondo, April 28, 1820, and June 19, 1820, in Martínez, *The Letters of Antonio Martinez*, 320–21, 336–37.

100. Martínez to Apodaca, April 5, 1820, in Martínez, *Letters from Governor Antonio Martinez to the Viceroy*, 43.

101. Martínez to Apodaca, November 26, 1820, in ibid., 48.

102. "Declaration of Xacobo Querkham," December 23, 1820, in Archivo General de la Nación, Provincas Internas, tomo 251, box 2Q217, vol. 541, CAH-UT. A somewhat inaccurate English translation of this document can be found in "Declaration of Jacob Kirkham," Nacogdoches Archives Transcriptions, vol. 18, 227–28, NA, TSLA.

103. "Declaration of Moses Austin" and "Declaration of James Forsythe," Archivo General de la Nación, Provincias Internas, tomo 251, box 2Q217, vol. 541, CAH-UT. English translations of these documents can be found in the Nacogdoches Archives Transcriptions, vol. 18, 224–27, 229–30, NA, TSLA.

104. On the easy terms for buying U.S. federal land before 1819, see Howe, *What Hath God Wrought*, 126–27; on the transformations in U.S. federal land policy post-1819, see Barker, *The Life of Stephen F. Austin*, 89–90.

105. The story of Austin meeting Bastrop, and Bastrop's intervention on his behalf, comes from Guy M. Bryan, the grandson of Moses Austin, who claimed to be quoting SFA on the subject. See Wooten, *A Comprehensive History of Texas, 1685–1897*, 1:442–43. The story seems reliable, given that Martínez had written several letters over the years singling out Bastrop for high praise—indicating that Bastrop would have been uniquely capable of convincing Martínez to reconsider hearing out the Americans. See, for example, Martínez to Arredondo, October 22, 1817, and April 25, 1818, in Martínez, *The Letters of Antonio Martinez*, 71–72, 120.

106. This material comes from the depositions of Kirkham, Forsythe, and Austin previously cited. For Kirkham's letter from the governor of Louisiana, see Jacques Villeré to Martínez, September 12, 1820, Archivo General de la Nación, Provincias Internas, Transcripts, tomo 251, box 2Q217, vol. 541, CAH-UT.

107. Castañeda, *Our Catholic Heritage in Texas*, 6:176–86.

108. Martínez to Arredondo, December 26, 1820, in *PCRCT*, 1:301.

109. Arredondo to Conde de Venadito, May 8, 1820, Spanish Collection, Bexar County Courthouse, San Antonio, Texas.

110. Ramos, "From Norteño to Tejano," 90–92 (quotation on 92).

111. Howe, *What Hath God Wrought*, 127.

112. For the application itself, see "Moses Austin's Application for Colonization Permit," December 26, 1820, in *AP*, 1:371–72. For Antonio Martínez's letter forwarding approval from Arredondo, see Martínez to Moses Austin, February 8, 1821, in Gracy, *Establishing Austin's Colony*, 33–34.

113. Moses Austin to Martínez, January 26, 1821, in *AP*, 1:377–78; Moses Austin to Baron de Bastrop, January 26, 1821, in *AP*, 1:379–80; Moses Austin to Felix Trudeaux, February 3, 1821, in *AP*, 1:381–82. The story of Kirkham abandoning Moses Austin and Richmond at the Trinity River comes from "Hardships of Travel," an undated note by the grandson of Moses Austin, Guy M. Bryan, in *AP*, 1:377. A few other details can be gleaned from another account written by Bryan (which he purported was based on information from SFA), in Wooten, *A Comprehensive History of Texas*, 1:442–43. On Moses Austin's death, see Cantrell, *Stephen F. Austin*, 87–89 (quotation on 88).

Chapter 2

1. Antonio Martínez to Felix Trudeaux, February 26, 1821, in Blake, supplement vol. 8, 243; Erasmo Seguín to Antonio Martinez, June 23, 1821, in Blake, vol. 10, 241–42; Austin,

"Journal of Stephen F. Austin on His First Trip to Texas, 1821," 286; McDonald, "Juan Martín de Veramendi."

2. Ayuntamiento of San Antonio to Antonio Martinez, May 1, 1821, in Blake, vol. 10, 228–36. On the Louisiana-Comanchería road, see Padilla, "Report on the Barbarous Indians of the Province of Texas," 55; Austin, "Journal of Stephen F. Austin on His First Trip to Texas, 1821," 290–91.

3. Ayuntamiento of San Antonio to Antonio Martinez, May 1, 1821, in Blake, vol. 10, 230–33.

4. Joaquin de Arredondo to Governor of Texas, March 29, 1821, Nacogdoches Archives Transcriptions, vol. 21, 9–12, NA, TSLA.

5. Erasmo Seguín to Antonio Martinez, June 23, 1821, in Blake, vol. 10, 241–42. On Tejano refugees in Louisiana, see *Louisiana Advertiser*, July 7, 1820, and Depositions of Ignacio Ibarvo, Vital Flores, Pedro Ibarvo, and Manuel Grande, in Blake, supplement vol. 8, 237–40.

6. Austin, "Journal of Stephen F. Austin on His First Trip to Texas, 1821," 286–88.

7. Ibid., 289–93.

8. Here I am pushing against one of the most dominant trends in the historiography of this region and era. Nearly every history that touches on American migration into Mexico during the 1820s and 1830s explains this phenomenon solely within the context of the availability of Mexican land. Randolph B. Campbell, in his recent history of Texas, offers the consensus view: "Anglo Americans poured into Austin's colony for a simple reason— cheap land" (Campbell, *Gone to Texas*, 102).

9. *New-York Gazette & General Advertiser*, September 3, 1821, quoting the *National Intelligencer*, August 30, 1821; see also the *Evening Post*, September 1, 1821, and the *Providence Patriot*, October 27, 1821.

10. Austin, "Journal of Stephen F. Austin on His First Trip to Texas, 1821," 296; Antonio Martínez to the Ayuntamiento of Bexar, July 17, 1821 and the Ayuntamiento of Bexar to Antonio Martínez, July 17, 1821, both in Nacogdoches Archives Transcriptions, vol. 21, 21–24, NA, TSAL.

11. SFA to Antonio Martínez, August 18, 1821, in *AP*, 1:407.

12. SFA to Joseph H. Hawkins, July 20, 1821, in *AP*, 1:402–4. SFA wrote a similar letter to John Sibley of Natchitoches, Louisiana, around the same time (see Cantrell, *Stephen F. Austin*, 95).

13. *Washington Gazette*, August 15, 1821, quoting from the *Argus*; *Arkansas Gazette*, September 29, 1821; *Edwardsville Spectator*, October 2, 1821; *St. Louis Enquirer*, September 22, 1821; *Richmond Enquirer*, November 20, 1821.

14. *Richmond Enquirer*, November 20, 1821; *Washington Gazette*, November 15, 1821.

15. Unser, "American Indians and the Cotton Frontier," 315–16.

16. *Mississippi State Gazette*, January 26, 1822, reprinted in the *Arkansas Gazette*, March 26, 1822.

17. *Mississippi Republican*, reprinted in the *Times, and Weekly Advertiser*, April 2, 1822.

18. See, for example, the *Mississippi State Gazette*, January 26, 1822, reprinted in the *Arkansas Gazette*, March 26, 1822.

19. Bruchey, *Cotton and the Growth of the American Economy*, 14–19.

20. *Louisiana Herald*, September 18, 1821, reprinted in the *Providence Patriot*, October 27, 1821.

21. Quotes from *Richmond Enquirer*, February 14, 1822. Versions of the story also appeared in the *Independent Chronicle & Boston Patriot*, February 16, 1822; the *City Gazette and Commercial Daily Advertiser*, February, 28, 1822; and the *Arkansas Gazette*, March 19, 1822, among others.

22. *Historical Census Browser*, Geospatial Center, University of Virginia (http://mapserver.lib.virginia.edu/).

23. Cantrell, *Stephen F. Austin*, 111–12.

24. For an overview of the challenges facing Mexico in 1821, see Henderson, *A Glorious Defeat*, 3–28. For an overview of Mexico's various provinces at the time of independence, see Green, *The Mexican Republic*, 6–30. Timothy E. Anna has also stressed the difficulty Mexico faced in integrating its various provinces and regions into a unified nation-state; see Anna, *Forging Mexico*, 98–138.

25. Weber, *The Mexican Frontier*, 11–14.

26. Reséndez, *Changing National Identities at the Frontier*, 29–37, 249; Weber, *The Mexican Frontier*, 5, 125–35.

27. "Dictamen Presentado a la Soberana Junta Gobernativa del Imperio Mexicano, por la Comision de Relaciones Exteriores," December 29, 1821, quoted in McElhannon, "Imperial Mexico and Texas, 1821–1823," 138.

28. *Historical Census Browser*, Geospatial Center, University of Virginia, (http://mapserver.lib.virginia.edu/). Census statistics on 1820 Arkansas comes from Taylor, *Negro Slavery in Arkansas*, 25. On Antonio Martinez's 1822 report on conditions in Texas, see Antonio Martinez to Gaspar Lopez, February 6, 1822, in *AP*, 1:472–75.

29. Hämäläinen, *The Comanche Empire*, 190–201.

30. Antonio Martinez to Gaspar Lopez, February 6, 1822, in *AP*, 1:475.

31. Quoted in McElhannon, "Imperial Mexico and Texas, 1821–1823," 138.

32. J. Reilly to Joseph H. Hawkins, April 26, 1822, in *AP*, 1:499 (quotation); Cantrell, *Stephen F. Austin*, 112–13; Janicek, "The Development of Early Mexican Land Policy," 92; Bolton, *Guide to Materials for the History of the United States in the Principal Archives of Mexico*, 350–61.

33. The original proposals and debates over them are available in Mateos, tomo I, 810–38. See also Janieck, "The Development of Early Mexican Land Policy," 91–103.

34. Número 80, "Bando aboliendo la esclavitud," December 6, 1810, in Dublán y Lozano, tomo I, 339–40.

35. Session of October 18, 1821, *Diario de las Sesiones de la Soberana Junta Provisional Gubernativa del Imperio Mexicano, Instalada según Previene el Plan de Iguala y los Tratados de la Villa de Córdova*, in Barragan, *Actas Constitucionales Mexicanas*, tomo I, 124. Azcárate may have seen the slavery issue tied to the influx of American settlers into Mexican territory, as he wrote a report on colonization for Lucas Alamán in 1823 emphasizing the dangers of American migration into Texas. See Azcárte to Alamán, August 4, 1823, Juan Francisco Azcárate y Lezama Correspondence with Lucas Alamán, Beinecke. For an example of antislavery rhetoric that referenced the ideals of the Mexican War for Independence, see the congressional debate of November 26, 1822, in Barragan, *Actas Constitucionales Mexicanas*, tomo VII, 64.

36. Henderson, *A Glorious Defeat*, 10. Gonzalo Aguirre Beltrán, whose work on the black population in Mexico remains the most comprehensive, reported Fernando Navarro y

Noriega's estimates during the early nineteenth century that the African population of Mexico stood at around 10,000 people in 1810 (Beltrán, *La Población Negra en México*, 232–34).

37. Lucas Alamán, for example, reported to the Chamber of Deputies in 1824 that "the English were demanding general emancipation as a precondition to diplomatic relations" (Green, *The Mexican Republic*, 119). On the financial influence of the British on early Mexico, see Tenenbaum, *The Politics of Penury*.

38. On Tejano trade with the southern United States, see Reséndez, *Changing National Identities at the Frontier*, 99–100, 117–22.

39. Francisco Ruiz to SFA, November 30, 1826, quoted in Weber, *The Mexican Frontier*, 176. On Navarro and Ruíz in Louisiana, see McDonald, *José Antonio Navarro*; on Casiano and Músquiz, see Reséndez, *Changing National Identities at the Frontier*, 99–100.

40. James Wilkinson to John S. Williams, December 1822, Manuscript WA MSS S-2091 W659, Beinecke; on Austin's lobbying efforts, see SFA to Edward Lovelace, November 22, 1822, in *AP*, 1:554–55.

41. Debates of August 20, 1822, in Mateos, tomo I, 831–38, 847–48. See also Janicek, "The Development of Early Mexican Land Policy," 102–4, 109; Barker, *The Life of Stephen F. Austin*, 65–66, 71–73.

42. For an analysis of the friction between Iturbide and the First Constituent Congress of Mexico, as well as the subsequent dissolution of congress and the eventual political fall of Iturbide, see Anna, *Forging Mexico*, 91–97.

43. SFA to Agustín de Iturbide, November 6, 1822, in *AP*, 1:548–52.

44. SFA to José Felix Trespalacios, January 8, 1823, in *AP*, 1:567.

45. SFA to Edward Lovelace, November 22, 1822, in *AP*, 1:555.

46. Debates of November 23 and 26, 1822, in *Diario de la Junta Nacional Instituyente del Imperio Mexicano*, reprinted in Barragan, *Actas Constitucionales Mexicanas*, tomo VII, 63–66; Mateos, tomo II, 25–29.

47. Debates of November 23 and 26, 1822, in *Diario de la Junta Nacional Instituyente del Imperio Mexicano*, reprinted in Barragan, *Actas Constitucionales Mexicanas*, tomo VII, 63–66; Mateos, tomo II, 25–29.

48. SFA to José Felix Trespalacios, January 8, 1823, in *AP*, 1:567.

49. Wright, "Father Refugio de la Garza," 78–80.

50. For the ideological battles between federalism and centralism in early Mexico, see Green, *The Mexican Republic*. For the development and evolution of Mexican liberalism, see Hale, *Mexican Liberalism in the Age of Mora*.

51. "Translation of the General Law of Colonization, No. 72," August 18, 1824, in *LOT*, 1:97–98.

52. This may have been influenced by desires to please the British, who at that moment were making large loans available to Mexico's Treasury. It may also have been an effort to restore the prohibitions on the slave trade lost with the repeal of the 1823 colonization law. The text of the law can be found in "Numero 412: Decreto de 13 de Julio de 1824—Prohibicion del comercio y tráfico de esclavos," in Dublán y Lozano, tomo I, 710. The July 13, 1824, law superseded a vague decree passed by the post-Iturbide Congress in October 1823 that stated, among other things, "Foreigners who bring slaves with them, will be subject to the laws established on the matter, or would henceforth be established" ("Numero 371: Decreto de 14 de Octubre de 1823," in Dublán y Lozano, tomo I, 684). Debates on the law can be

found in Mateos, tomo II, 838–40. For the Tejano response, see Juan Padilla to SFA, June 18, 1825, in *AP*, 1:1135–36. For a detailed treatment of the law and scholarly debates surrounding it, see Torget, "Cotton Empire: Slavery and the Texas Borderlands, 1820–1837," 110–11.

53. SFA to Erasmo Seguín, around January 1, 1824, in *AP*, 1:718–19.

54. Erasmo Seguín to Baron de Bastrop, March 24, 1824, in *AP*, 1:758. On the antislavery measure introduced in February 1824, see debates of February 21, 1824, and March 5, 1824, in Mateos, tomo II, 697, 707.

55. Although the federal structure of the 1824 Constitution suggested that the 1789 Constitution of the United States served as a model for Mexican legislators, the document in fact owed more to the example set by the Spanish Constitution of 1812. During debates in Congress, the model of the U.S. Constitution and American federalism came up regularly, demonstrating their influence on legislators (particularly federalists) in Mexico City. But the text of the 1824 Constitution followed the Spanish model far more closely than the U.S. model and even adopted whole sections of the Spanish text. In terms of influence and scope, the 1824 Constitution codified the embrace of federalism in the Acta Constitutiva (constitutive act) passed by the congress in January 1824. The Acta had already recognized the sovereignty of the individual states (something assumed but never addressed in the 1824 Constitution), set parameters for divisions of powers between the states and national government, and said nothing about the institution of slavery. Because the Constitution of 1824 built on the precedents of the Acta, the two documents should be considered in relation to one another rather than treated in isolation. See Anna, *Forging Mexico*, 141, 162–63.

56. The debates over combining Texas and Coahuila stretched out over most of a year, but some of the final discussions can be seen in the debates of May 7, 15, 18, 1824, in Mateos, appendix to tomo II, 229–303, 377, 388.

57. SFA proclamation, May 1, 1824, in *AP*, 1:781–82; Erasmo Seguín to SFA, August 11, 1824, in *AP*, 1:874.

58. Memorandum of Families Who Passed Through Nacogdoches, October 16, 1821–January 8, 1822, in Blake, supplement vol. 8, 252–53; Cantrell, *Stephen F. Austin*, 101, 133–36; Barker, *The Life of Stephen F. Austin*, 43–44, 98; SFA to Antonio Martinez, October 13, 1821, in *AP*, 1:419 (quotation).

59. For a description of the mechanics of nineteenth-century cotton production, and the role of nature in shaping it, see Fiege, *The Republic of Nature*, 100–138. See also Silverthorne, *Plantation Life in Texas*.

60. William Sheldon to SFA, October 15, 1825, in *AP*, 1:1223–24; Moore, *The Emergence of the Cotton Kingdom in the Old Southwest*, 11–13; on cotton in early Mexico, see Ruiz y Sandova, *El Algodón en México*.

61. Sarah Groce Birlet, "Life of Jared Ellison Groce One of the Old Three Hundred and his oldest son Leonard Wallace Groce," manuscript dated 1936, MSS #179, Woodson Research Center, Fondren Library, Rice University; Bertleth, "Jared Ellison Groce," 358–61. Both accounts were written by descendants of Groce, attempting to portray him in the best possible light, although they remain useful for the basic overview of Groce's migration to Texas.

62. Silverthorne, *Plantation Life in Texas*, 117.

63. Slaveholding, migration, and population statistics for 1825 come from Barker, "Notes on the Colonization of Texas," 149–51; Barker, *Life of Stephen F. Austin*, 98. Names of specific slaveholders come from "Census of the District of Collorado for the Year 1825," in *AP*,

1:1244. According to Barker, the 1825 census listed 443 slaves among the 1,800 inhabitants of Austin's colony. Sixty-nine families held those slaves, with 11 families holding 271 slaves (61 percent of the slave population) and 58 families holding 172 slaves (39 percent of the slave population). Of the migrants to Austin's colonies recorded from 1825 to 1831 (out of 902 applications, 864 noted places of origin with 806 from the United States), the states listed by Barker as providing the largest number of settlers were: Louisiana, 201; Alabama, 111; Arkansas, 90; Tennessee, 89; Missouri, 72; Mississippi, 56; New York, 39; Kentucky, 37; Ohio, 28; Georgia, 14; Pennsylvania, 14; Virginia, 13; New England, 20. As Barker points out, the point of departure for these colonists were usually western states (meaning that most of them had previously migrated from seaboard U.S. states) and therefore the list is not an indicator of the original birth state of the colonists. Large slaveholders, such as Groce, owned a significant portion of the colony's slaves, with 11 elite families in the colony holding an average of 25 slaves each. The majority of slave owners had far fewer, with most slaveholding families owning about 3 slaves.

64. Churchill Fulshear to SFA, November 22, 1824, in *AP*, 1:976.

65. SFA to Jared E. Groce, October 19, 1823, in *AP*, 1:701; Contract for Hire of Slaves, August 1, 1824, *AP*, 1:869–70.

66. SFA, "Criminal Regulations," in Gracy, *Establishing Austin's Colony*, 84–89; Barker, "The Government of Austin's Colony, 1821-1831," 228–30; McKnight, "Stephen F. Austin's Legalistic Concerns," 247-56.

67. SFA to Gaspar Flores, [answering letter of December 6, 1824], in *AP*, 1:984–85.

68. James Grant to SFA, March 23, 1824, in *AP*, 1:756; SFA to Colonists, [June 5, 1824?], in *AP*, 1:819–20; Archibald Austin to SFA, January 30, 1825, in *AP*, 1:1027–28; Nathaniel Cox to SFA, July 20, 1825, in *AP*, 1:1154.

69. SFA to Governor of Coahuila-Texas, December 20, 1824, in *AP*, 1:994–95; SFA to Congress of Coahuila-Texas, February 4, 1825, in *AP*, 1:1036–37.

70. SFA to Rafael Gonzales, April 4, 1825, in *AP*, 1:1006 (quotation).

71. SFA to Manuel de Mier y Terán, September 20, 1828, in *AP*, 2:116. At an average weight of 450 pounds each, 500 bales would equal 225,000 pounds of cotton.

72. Bruchey, *Cotton and the Growth of the American Economy*, 18.

73. SFA to Ceballos, September 20, 1828, in *AP*, 2:114–115; SFA to Manuel de Mier y Terán, September 20, 1828, in *AP*, 2:116.

74. Silverthorne, *Plantation Life in Texas*, 117–20.

75. SFA to Supreme Executive Power of the Republic, November 6, 1824, in *AP*, 1:935.

76. Articles of Partnership between J. E. B. Austin and John Austin, November 22, 1825, in *AP*, 1:1234.

77. "Life of Jared Ellison Groce One of the Old Three Hundred and his oldest son Leonard Wallace Groce," by Sarah Groce Birlet, [MS 179], Woodson Research Center, Fondren Library, Rice University.

78. Moore, *The Emergence of the Cotton Kingdom in the Old Southwest*, 178–79.

79. J. E. B. Austin to Emily Perry, June 15, 1826, in *AP*, 1:1358.

80. SFA to Gaspar Flores, [answering letter of December 6, 1824], in *AP*, 1:984.

81. Charles Douglas to SFA, February 25, 1825, in *AP*, 1:1047.

82. James Phelps to SFA, January 16, 1825, in *AP*, 1:1020.

83. Randall Jones to SFA, June 4, 1824, in *AP*, 1:809.

84. For examples of negative stories about Texas taken from real events, see *Edwardsville*

Spectator, June 1, 1822 (quotation); *Connecticut Mirror*, September 1, 1823; *Arkansas Gazette*, June 28, 1825. For examples of negative stories about Texas with little or no basis in fact, see *Baltimore Patriot*, July 11, 1822, reprinting from the *Floridian*; *Arkansas Gazette*, August 6, 1822, reprinting from the *Nashville Clarion*; *Carolina Centinel*, September 14, 1822, reprinting from the *Louisianan*; *Arkansas Gazette*, August 13, 1822; *City Gazette and Commercial Daily Advertiser*, November 9, 1822. For examples of positive stories about Texas, see *City Gazette and Commercial Daily Advertiser*, June 27, 1822; *National Daily Journal*, April 21, 1825; *Ohio State Journal and Columbus Gazette*, October 13, 1825, reprinting from the *Kentucky Whig* (quotation); *Niles' Weekly Register*, October 15, 1825; *Louisiana State Gazette*, December 30, 1825 (quotation).

85. *Louisianan*, reprinted in the *Carolina Centinel*, September 14, 1822.

86. *Natchitoches Courier*, September 6, 1825, quoted in *Arkansas Gazette*, November 8, 1825 (emphasis in original).

87. For examples of anti-Texas messages, see *Arkansas Gazette*, April 30, 1822; June 25, 1822; August 6, 1822; August 13, 1822; September 17, 1822; November 5, 1822; February 17, 1824; September 7, 1824; June 28, 1825; November 29, 1825.

88. *Arkansas Gazette*, September 17, 1822.

89. *Arkansas Gazette*, June 25, 1822.

90. *Arkansas Gazette*, August 13, 1822; September 17, 1822.

91. For articles that repeated the *Gazette*'s claims about Mexican antislavery laws, see *American Repertory & Advertiser*, October 22, 1822; *Baltimore Patriot*, November 7, 1822 (quotation); *City Gazette and Commercial Daily Advertiser* , November 21, 1822; *Edwardsville Spectator*, October 12, 1822; *Republican Star and General Advertiser*, November 5, 1822.

92. *Louisiana Advertiser*, reprinted in the *Arkansas Gazette*, May 13, 1823; *Kentucky Whig*, reprinted in the *Ohio State Journal and Columbus Gazette*, October 13, 1825; *Daily National Journal*, April 21, 1825. Slave population percentages from 1820 come from the *Historical Census Browser*, Geospatial Center, University of Virginia, (http://mapserver.lib.virginia.edu/). The proportion of the enslaved population in the states cited were Missouri (15 percent), Tennessee (18 percent), Kentucky (22 percent), Alabama (32 percent), Georgia (44 percent), Louisiana (45 percent), and Mississippi (44 percent). In addition, Austin's colony in Texas had approximately the same percentage as Maryland (26 percent).

93. For the settlement patterns of SFA's colonists, see "Connected Map of Austin's Colony, 1892 Copy," #1944, Texas General Land Office, Austin, Texas. On the establishment of San Felipe, see Cantrell, *Stephen F. Austin*, 147–49, 195–96.

94. SFA to Mateo Ahumada, September 10, 1825, in *AP*, 1:1198.

95. Smith, *From Dominance to Disappearance*, 124–33.

96. 1825 Census of Coahuila y Texas, "Informoe del C. Gobernador Interino del Estado leído ante este Congreso," Leyes, Decretos y Acuerdos (1827), Primer Congreso Constitucional, Primer Periodo Ordinario, Comision de Gobernacion, legajo 1, expediente 2, ACEC. The total population for Texas was listed at 4,405, with 1,800 in Austin's colony, 1,562 in San Antonio, 543 in La Bahía (Goliad), and 500 in Nacogdoches. On Comanches and Tejanos during early 1820s, see Smith, *From Dominance to Disappearance*, 122–24; Hämäläinen, *The Comanche Empire*, 190–201.

97. "Colonization Law of the State of Coahuila and Texas," March 24, 1825, in Gracy, *Establishing Austin's Colony*, 50–58.

98. SFA to Gaspar Flores, [answering letter of December 6, 1824], in *AP*, 1:984.

99. SFA to Gaspar Flores, [answering letter of December 6, 1824], in *AP*, 1:984–85 (quotation); SFA memorial to Coahuila-Texas legislature, December 22, 1824, in *AP*, 1:999; SFA to Rafael Gonzales, April 4, 1825, in *AP*, 1:1066; SFA to Rafael Gonzales, June 25, 1825, in *AP*, 1:1138; SFA to Rafael Gonzales, August 20, 1825, in *AP*, 1:1180; SFA bill and argument concerning slavery, August 18, 1825, in *AP*, 1:1170–80.

100. *Louisiana State Gazette*, November 14, 1825.

Chapter 3

1. Peter Ellis Bean to SFA, July 5, 1826, in *AP*, 1:1368–69. On Bean's winding path through Mexico and early Texas during the years before 1826, see Jackson, *Indian Agent*.

2. José Antonio Saucedo to SFA, June 29, 1826; Baron de Bastrop to Robert Leftwich, about May 30, 1826; both in *PCRCT*, 2:613, 2:596–97.

3. Coahuila y Texas Congressional Session of November 30, 1826, Congreso Constituyente, 1824–1827, Actas de Primera Sesión Ordinaria, Agosto 15, 1824 a Marzo 22, 1827, ACEC. The text of the initial draft of Article 13 can also be found in SFA to the Coahuila y Texas State Congress, August 11, 1826, in *AP*, 1:1407.

4. Article 11 of the Coahuila-Texas Constitution, which embodied these ideals, read: "Every man who resides within the limits of the state, although but transiently, shall enjoy the imprescriptible rights of liberty, security, property and equality; and it is the duty of said state to preserve and protect by wise and equitable laws, these universal rights of men." See the "Constitution of State of Coahuila and Texas, 1827," in *LOT*, 1:424.

5. Baron de Bastrop to Robert Leftwich, May 30, 1826, in *PCRCT*, 2:595–97.

6. On Coahuila's small enslaved population, see Robles, *Coahuila y Texas*, tomo I, 230–31. According to Robles, the total population of Coahuila (not including Texas) in 1828 stood at 66,131, making enslaved people about one-thousandth of 1 percent of the region's total population (Robles, *Coahuila y Texas*, tomo I, 327–28). On liberals and conservatives in early Mexican politics, see Green, *The Mexican Republic*. On political divisions within Coahuila and Texas, and the ideological leanings of various regions of the state, see Janicek, "The Development of Early Mexican Land Policy," 189–95; Tijerina, *Tejanos and Texas under the Mexican Flag*, 113–36.

7. J. E. B. Austin to SFA, August 22, 1826, in *AP*, 1:1430; José Saucedo to SFA, July 14, 1826, in *AP*, 1:1371; José Saucedo to SFA, July 27, 1826, in *AP*, 1:1390.

8. SFA to Coahuila y Texas State Legislature, August 11, 1826, in *AP*, 1:1406–9.

9. SFA to Juan Padilla, August 14, 1826, in *AP*, 1:1418–20; SFA to Ayuntamiento of San Antonio de Béxar, August 14, 1826, in *AP*, 1:1422.

10. J. E. B. Austin to SFA, August 22, 1826, in *AP*, 1:1430–34.

11. Jesse Thompson and J. C. Payton to John Sprowl, August 11, 1826, in *AP*, 1:1405–6.

12. James Gaines to SFA, August 21, 1826, in *AP*, 1:1428–29.

13. Samuel Norris to SFA, September 5, 1826, in *AP*, 1:1448.

14. SFA to Coahuila y Texas State Legislature, August 11, 1826, in *AP*, 1:1409.

15. SFA to José Saucedo, September 11, 1826, in *AP*, 1:1452.

16. J. E. B. Austin to SFA, August 22, 1826, in *AP*, 1:1430–34 (emphasis in original).

17. J. E. B. Austin to SFA, September 3, 1826, in *AP*, 1:1446.

18. *Arkansas Gazette*, October 10, 1826, reprinted in the *Connecticut Courant*, November 20, 1826.

19. *Arkansas Gazette* quoted in the *Democratic Clarion & Tennessee Gazette*, August 20, 1825. The *Tennessee Gazette* story was quoted in Barker, *The Life of Stephen F. Austin*, 97, n. 29.

20. J. E. B. Austin to Emily M. Perry, October 28, 1825, in *AP*, 1:1229–30 (emphasis in original).

21. *Louisville Public Advertiser*, November 1, 1826.

22. *Richmond Enquirer*, November 10, 1826; *Daily National Journal*, November 10, 1826.

23. *Republican Star and General Advertiser*, November 14, 1826; *Boston Commercial Gazette*, November 16, 1826; *Salem Gazette*, November 17, 1826; *Haverhill Gazette & Essex Patriot*, November 18, 1826.

24. *Providence Patriot, Columbian Phenix*, November 18, 1826; *Connecticut Courant*, November 20, 1826; *Norwich Courier*, November 22, 1826; *Newport Mercury*, November 25, 1826; *African Repository and Colonial Journal*, November 1826, vol. 2, issue 9, p. 291; *Vermont Chronicle*, December 1, 1826.

25. Davis, *Inhuman Bondage*, 231–67. See also McDaniel, *The Problem of Democracy in the Age of Slavery*, and Blackburn, *The American Crucible*.

26. *Boston Commercial Gazette*, November 16, 1826.

27. *National Intelligencer*, quoted in *African Repository and Colonial Journal*, November 1826, vol. 2, issue 9, 291.

28. *New York Daily Advertiser*, quoted in the *Newport Mercury*, November 25, 1826.

29. J. E. B. Austin to SFA, September 23, 1826, in *AP*, 1:1461–62.

30. J. E. B. Austin to SFA, October 10, 1826, in *AP*, 1:1474–75.

31. J. E. B. Austin to SFA, September 23, 1826, in *AP*, 1:1461–62 (emphasis in original).

32. J. E. B. Austin to SFA, October 10, 1826, in *AP*, 1:1474 (emphasis in original).

33. Tijerina, *Tejanos and Texas under the Mexican Flag*, 113–16.

34. J. E. B. Austin to SFA, October 10, 1826, in *AP*, 1:1474.

35. Baron de Bastrop to SFA, November 18, 1826, in *AP*, 1:1505.

36. Coahuila y Texas Congress to Vice-Governor, October 16, 1826, El Libro de Decretos y Ordenes de 1824 a 1826, Hacienda, ACEC. The letter from the alcalde of Nacogdoches had been forwarded to San Antonio, where José Saucedo then forwarded it to Saltillo, along with his own letter on the matter. These warnings may also have been prompted in part by the growing problems in Haden Edwards's colony, although they specifically reference Article 13 of the draft constitution.

37. "Governor's Opinion Concerning Slavery," November 30, 1826, in *AP*, 1:1523–25.

38. José María Viesca speech, November 30, 1826, Congreso Constituyente, 1824–1827, Actas de Primera Sesión Ordinaria, Agosto 15, 1824 a Marzo 22, 1827, ACEC.

39. There has been no comprehensive study of the slavery debates that raged in Saltillo during the late 1820s. Several works, usually those focusing on Tejanos, have referenced various aspects of the general debates in the Coahuila-Texas legislature. For example, Tijerina, *Tejanos and Texas under the Mexican Flag*, 114–18, touches briefly on the issue of slavery and Tejano support for the institution in the Saltillo legislature. The few works that mention the debates rely primarily on SFA's correspondence, rather than the records of the debates themselves (which are available today in the ACEC in Saltillo, as well as in transcript form at the CAH-UT in Austin).

40. Dionisio Elizondo speech, November 30, 1826, Actas de Primera Sesión Ordinaria, ACEC. Elizondo's approach to abolition was influenced by the writings of Bentham that

Pierre Dumont made available as French translations, particularly *Traté de legislation civile et pénale*, which was published in 1802. *Traté de legislation* contained several passages outlining possible approaches to abolition that are nearly identical to what Elizondo proposed in this speech. Bentham's influence with other legislators in the Coahuila-Texas Congress as can be seen in the September 11, 1827, debates, when Bentham was again quoted on the floor of the state congress. See Madero, Gonzalez, and Tijerina to the Coahuila y Texas Congress, September 11, 1827, Congreso del Estado Coahuila, Leyes, Decretos y Acuerdos (1827), Primer Congreso Constitucional, Primer Periodo Ordinario, Comision de Gobernación, legajo 1, expediente 43, decreto 18, ACEC.

41. Viesca speech, November 30, 1826, Actas de Primera Sesión Ordinaria, ACEC.

42. Valle, Elizondo, and Viesca's speeches, November 30, 1826, Actas de Primera Sesión Ordinaria, ACEC.

43. A thorough recounting of the Fredonian Rebellion can be found in Barker, *Life of Stephen F. Austin*, 168–202, and Parsons, "The Fredonian Rebellion."

44. Blanco quoted in Barker, *Life of Stephen F. Austin*, 188.

45. "The Fredonian Declaration of Independence," December 21, 1826, in *LOT*, 1:109.

46. SFA to John Williams and B. J. Thompson, December 14, 1826, in *AP*, 1:1532–33 (emphasis in original). Austin wrote a similar letter to Thompson ten days later, arguing again that "the Slave question is now pending before the Legislature and many other questions of great interest to the new settlers what effects are such mad proceedings likely to have on the decision of those questions?" See SFA to B. J. Thompson, December 24, 1826, in *AP*, 1:1538–40.

47. Articles about the rebellion appeared in New Orleans newspapers in January 1827, citing Natchitoches as the source of information. See, for example, the *Newport Mercury*, February 17, 1827, which quoted from a January 13, 1827, article published in New Orleans, which itself quoted "intelligence from Natchitoches." That same January 13 article from New Orleans became the basis of information for a wide number of reports on the Fredonian Rebellion that appeared in newspapers across the United States. The *Alexandria Messenger*, for its part, carried a story on the Fredonian Rebellion in its December 22, 1826, issue, which was subsequently reprinted in the *Portsmouth Journal of Literature and Politics* (January 27, 1827), the *New Hampshire Patriot and State Gazette* (January 29, 1827), the *Republican Star and General Advertiser* in Maryland (January 30, 1827), the *New Hampshire Sentinel* (February 2, 1827), and the *Vermont Gazette* (February 6, 1827), among others.

48. *Louisiana Advertiser*, January 12, 1827.

49. *New York Daily Advertiser*, February 8, 1827, reprinted in the *Pittsfield Sun* (Mass.), February 15, 1827.

50. See, for example, the *Pittsfield Sun* (Mass.), February 15, 1827, and the *New Hampshire Sentinel*, February 23, 1827.

51. *Niles' Weekly Register*, March 17, 1827.

52. *New York Observer*, date unknown (most likely mid-April 1827), reprinted in the *Farmer's Cabinet*, April 21, 1827.

53. See, for example, the *Farmer's Cabinet*, April 21, 1827; *Berkshire Star*, May 3, 1827; *Vermont Chronicle*, April 20, 1827; *Vermont Watchman and State Gazette*, May 1, 1827.

54. *Farmer's Cabinet*, February 17, 1827. Two months later, the *Farmer's Cabinet* printed another article claiming that the Fredonians had revolted because the Mexican government had outlawed slavery.

55. Sessions of January 2–31, 1827, Actas de Primera Sesión de Ordinaria, ACEC.

56. SFA to the Coahuila-Texas Legislature, November 20, 1826, in *AP*, 1:1507–10.

57. Debates of January 31, 1827, Actas de Primera Sesión Ordinaria, ACEC.

58. Ibid.

59. Debates of January 31, 1827; session of March 11, 1827; Actas de Primera Sesión Ordinaria, ACEC.

60. SFA on the State Constitution, May 29, 1827, in *AP*, 1:1648–49.

61. SFA to James F. Perry, May 26, 1827, in *AP*, 1:1645–46.

62. James Davis to SFA, January 30, 1827, in *AP*, 1:1598.

63. Ben Milam to SFA, March 27, 1827, in *AP*, 1:1622.

64. Austin, "Descriptions of Texas by Stephen F. Austin," 102.

65. Sánchez, "A Trip to Texas in 1828," 271.

66. Henderson, "Minor Empresario Contracts for the Colonization of Texas, 1825–1834," 298–300; Craig Roell, "DeWitt's Colony," *HOT*.

67. Mateo Ahumada to Anastacio Bustamante, April 1, 1827, cited in Reséndez, *Changing National Identities at the Frontier*, 41. Ahumada reported that Anglos exported around 16,000 *arrobas* of cotton in 1826 (an *arroba* being a weight measurement equivalent to around 25 pounds). In 1828, SFA estimated his colony exported 500 bales; in 1831, he estimated that exports reached 1,000 bales annually (SFA to Terán, September 20, 1828, in *AP*, 2:116; SFA to N. A. Ware, July 24, 1831, in *AP*, 2:681). In 1829, Manuel de Mier y Terán noted that Jared Groce had produced 600 bales on his plantation alone (see Mier y Terán, *Texas by Terán*, 144). Bales weighed 450 pounds each on average.

68. For an analysis of the finances of cotton, see Woodman, *King Cotton and His Retainers*.

69. Sánchez, "A Trip to Texas in 1828," 283.

70. Smith, *From Dominance to Disappearance*, 136–37.

71. McDonald, *José Antonio Navarro*, 70.

72. J. E. B. Austin to SFA, August 22, 1826, in *AP*, 1:1433.

73. For cotton statistics, see Bruchey, *Cotton and the Growth of the American Economy*, tables on 8–10, 12–13, 16–17.

74. SFA to Manuel Ceballos, September 20, 1828, in *AP*, 2:110–15 (second quotation); SFA to Manuel de Mier y Terán, September 20, 1828, in *AP*, 2:116–18; SFA to Minister of Relations, October 7, 1828, in *AP*, 2:122–28 (first quotation); SFA to José María Viesca, February 16, 1829, in *AP*, 2:168–72. For background on the tariff controversy in the United States, and the perceptions of American southerners that they could lose their position as the dominant source of cotton for the Atlantic economy, see Schoen, *The Fragile Fabric of Union*.

75. SFA to José María Viesca, February 16, 1829, in *AP*, 2:168–72.

76. José Madero speech to the Coahuila y Texas Congress, July 7, 1827, legajo 1, expediente 43, decreto 18, Congreso del Estado Coahuila, Leyes, Decretos y Acuerdos (1827), Primer Congreso Constitucional (PCC), Primer Periodo Ordinario, Comision de Gobernacion, ACEC. On Madero's liberal principles and connections to the Elizondo family, see Janicek, "The Development of Early Mexican Land Policy," 192; 256–57, n. 8.

77. Madero, Gonzalez, Tijerina to the Coahuila y Texas Congress, September 11, 1827, Congreso del Estado Coahuila, Leyes, Decretos y Acuerdos (1827), legajo 1, expendiente 43, decreto 18, PCC, Primer Periodo Ordinario, Comision de Gobernacion, ACEC; "Austin's

Argument against Law Regulating Slavery," November 8, 1827, in *AP*, 1:1719–20. In their speech, Madero, Gonzales, and Tijerina quoted from Montesquieu's *The Spirit of the Laws*, book 15, chaps. 1–2. Andrés Tijerina argues that this motion came from conservatives in the Saltillo legislature (see *Tejanos and Texas under the Mexican Flag*, 116) although Madero's leading role indicates it emerged instead from the liberal wing of the state Congress. For an English translation of the final version of the law, see "Decree No. 18," September 15, 1827, in *LOT*, 1:188–89.

78. A copy of Decree 18 arrived in San Antonio in November 1827, and Decree 35 arrived in January 1828. See José Antonio Saucedo to Governor of Coahuila y Texas, November 24, 1827, Fondo Jefatura Política de Bexar, caja 6, expediente 17, AGEC, and Ramon Músquiz to the Governor of Coahuila y Texas, January 5, 1828, Fondo Jefatura Política de Bexar, caja 7, expediente 18, AGEC.

79. Ramón Músquiz to the Governor of Coahuila y Texas, July 18, 1828; Tomás M. Huta to Ramón Músquiz, June 27, 1828; Unknown to Ramón Músquiz, June 27, 1828; all in Fondo Jefatura Política de Bexar, caja 8, expediente 81, AGEC.

80. Henry S. Brown to SFA, March 21, 1828, in *AP*, 2:27.

81. Richard Ellis to SFA, January 3, 1828, in *AP*, 2:2–3 (emphasis in original).

82. Entry of March 31, 1828, in Barker, "Minutes of the Ayuntamiento of San Felipe de Austin, 1828–1832," 311.

83. The literature on debt peonage in Mexico is vast, but a helpful overview can be found in Knight, "Mexican Peonage: What Was It and Why Was It?" 41–74. For an in-depth examination of peonage as practiced in Coahuila, see Harris, *A Mexican Family Empire*.

84. Ramón Músquiz to SFA, April 17, 1828, in *AP*, 2:31.

85. "Decreto 56," Primer Congreso Constitutcional, Segundo Periodo Ordinario, 1827–1828, Gobernacion, legajo 4, expediente 15, Decreto 56, ACEC; Miguel Arciniega to SFA, May 17, 1828, in *AP*, 2:41–42. For the full text of the law, see "Decree No. 56," May 5, 1828, in *LOT*, 1:213.

86. José Antonio Navarro to SFA, May 17, 1828, in *AP*, 2:41. Political Chief Músquiz had sent a similar note two days before (see Músquiz to SFA, May 15, 1828, in *AP*, 2:38).

87. The substance of Austin's template contract is available in Bugbee, "Slavery in Early Texas," 411–12.

88. Frost Thorn to SFA, July 22, 1828, in *AP*, 2:74. All information about Amos Edwards comes from Thorn's letter and the 1820 U.S. federal census (roll 26, p. 27), available on Ancestry.com.

89. George Smyth to John Gallagher, June 1, 1830, George Washington Smyth Papers, CAH-UT.

90. *New Orleans Halcyon and Literary Repository*, May 25, 1828, reprinted in the *Rhode-Island American and Providence Gazette*, June 20, 1828. Reprints of this article also appeared in Baltimore, Maryland (*Niles' Weekly Register*, July 19, 1828) and Cooperstown, New York (*Watch-Tower*, July 7, 1828) in July 1828.

91. Samuel May Williams to SFA, June 9, 1829, in *AP*, 2:222.

Chapter 4

1. Entry for January 31, 1829, in Mier y Terán, *Texas by Terán*, 144–45. Terán listed 600 bales, which generally weighed 450 pounds each.

2. Manuel de Mier y Terán to Guadalupe Victoria, March 28, 1828, in ibid., 29–38.

3. Entry for April 27, 1828, in ibid., 56. Terán urged keeping restrictions on slavery in place as a way of limiting American immigration into Mexico, warning that "if these laws were rescinded (may God forbid), in just a few years Tejas would be a powerful state that would rival Louisiana in production and wealth" (see Terán to Guadalupe Victoria, June 30, 1828, in ibid., 99).

4. The earliest work in this vein was Barker, "The Influence of Slavery in the Colonization of Texas," and has remained a dominating strand in the literature. Randolph Campbell's *An Empire for Slavery: The Peculiar Institution in Texas, 1821–1865*, for example, reinforced Barker's central conclusions, arguing that "Anglo-Americans were simply too different from Hispanic-Americans to accept Mexican government indefinitely" and that "protecting slavery was not the primary cause of the Texas Revolution, but it certainly was a major result" (48–49). For a discussion of the persistence of Barker's "clash of cultures" thesis among historians in explaining the Texas Revolution and the creation of the Republic of Texas, see Lack, "In the Long Shadow of Eugene C. Barker."

5. Vázquez, "The Texas Question in Mexican Politics, 1836–1845," 310 (quotation). Other works that cite slavery as a central issue in the 1835–36 rebellion include Fowler, *Santa Anna of Mexico*, 163; Vázquez, "The Colonization and Loss of Texas: A Mexican Perspective," 76; Taylor, *In Search of the Racial Frontier*, 37–45.

6. The best work remains Paul Lack, who has argued that concerns about protecting slave-based agriculture in Texas—coupled with fears among Anglos about what the shift from federalism to centralism in Mexico could do to undermine that system—played a central role in bringing on the Texas Revolution (see Lack, "Slavery and the Texas Revolution," and Lack, *The Texas Revolutionary Experience*, 238–52). No scholar, however, has tied concerns over slavery to the broader development of the region brought by the cotton economy, and how the far-reaching changes in population and power in the territory that followed helped lurch Texas toward war in 1835.

7. Juan Antonio Padilla to SFA, January 24, 1829, in *AP*, 2:162; Ramon Músquiz to SFA, May 28, 1829, in *AP*, 2:219; SFA to José Antonio Navarro, July 23, 1829, in *AP*, 2:234.

8. SFA to William H. Wharton, April 24, 1829, in *AP*, 2:210–12.

9. Número 703, "Decreto del gobierno en uso de facultades extradinarias—Abolicion de la esclavitud en al República," September 15, 1829, in Dublán y Lozano, tomo II, 163. On the tradition of emancipating slaves as part of celebrations of Mexico's independence during the 1820s, and the scarcity of enslaved people in central Mexico by 1826, see Ward, *Mexico in 1827*, 27–28.

10. Sessions of January 4, and January 8, 1827, in Mateos, tomo IV, 19–21.

11. Tornel speech of January 4, 1827, quoted in Fowler, *Tornel and Santa Anna*, 57.

12. Tornel y Mendívil, *Breve Reseña Histórica de los Acontecimientos más Notables de la Nación Mexicana*, 85–86.

13. On Guerrero's presidency, see Harrell, "Vicente Guerrero and the Birth of Modern Mexico, 1821–1831," 292–360 (particularly 343–44, regarding the emancipation decree); Vincent, *The Legacy of Vicente Guerrero*, 176–208; Green, *The Mexican Republic*, 162–74.

14. José de Jesús Ramos to the Governor of Coahuila-Texas, October 3, 1829, Fondo Siglo XIX, caja 10, fondo 9, expediente 1; José Felán to the Governor of Coahuila-Texas, October 16, 1829, Fondo Siglo XIX, caja 11, fondo 1, expediente 15; Juan Nepomuceno Ramos Valdés

to the Governor of Coahuila-Texas, October 26, 1829, Fondo Siglo XIX, caja 11, fondo 4, expediente 11; all in the AGEC.

15. Luis Lombraña to the Governor of Coahuila-Texas, October 18, 1829, Fondo Siglo XIX, caja 11, fondo 3, expediente 5, AGEC. Guerrero was about 200 miles from San Antonio, and held about 756 people. See Robles, *Coahuila y Texas*, 1:329 and 2:73. In Guerrero, Gertrudis Carrasco and Josefa Rodríguez were angry about their slaves being freed by the state and sought to be compensated by the national government. See, for example, Unknown to the Ministro de Hacienda, March 30, 1830, Fondo Siglo XIX, caja 5, fondo 5, expediente 10 and Document on Petition of Josefa Rodríguez and Gertudis Carrasco, June 30, 1830, Fondo Siglo XIX, caja 8, fondo 1, expediente 15; both in AGEC. News of the decree was slow to reach some of the more remote villages in Coahuila (see, e.g., Pedro Apolinario Martínez to the Governor of Coahuila-Texas, January 26, 1830, Fondo Siglo XIX, caja 2, fondo 4, expediente 7, AGEC).

16. Ramón Músquiz to the Governor of Coahuila-Texas, October 25, 1829, in *AP*, 2:273–75.

17. José Antonio Navarro to SFA, October 29, 1829, in *AP*, 2:277–78.

18. On Balmaceda's involvement in pushing for an exemption for Texas from the 1829 emancipation decree, see Ramón Músquiz to SFA, October 29, 1829, in *AP*, 2:278–80. Balmaceda and the other representative in the Saltillo Congress, Rafael Antonio Manchola, were tightly aligned with the Viesca wing of the Coahuila-Texas Congress, holding powerful positions in the Saltillo legislature while José María Viesca served as governor. See Tijerina, *Tejanos and Texas under the Mexican Flag*, 126.

19. Juan Antonio Padilla to SFA, November 26, 1829, in *AP*, 2:291.

20. John Durst to SFA, November 10, 1829, in *AP*, 2:285 (quotations). On efforts by Tejanos to keep news of Guerrero's emancipation decree from the Anglo colonists, see Ramón Músquiz to SFA, October 29, 1829, in *AP*, 2:278 and José Antonio Navarro to SFA, October 29, 1829, in *AP*, 2:277–78.

21. José Ygnacio Ybarvo to Ramón Músquiz, November 10, 1829, and José de la Piedras letter of November 9, 1829, related in Antonio Elozua to Ramón Músquiz, November 23, 1829; both were enclosed in Ramón Músquiz to the Governor of Coahuila-Texas, December 7, 1829, Fondo Jefatura Política de Bejar, caja 13, expediente 15, AGEC.

22. Luis Lombraña to the Governor of Coahuila-Texas, December 19, 1829, Fondo Siglo XIX, caja 12, fondo 8, expediente 11, AGEC.

23. José María Viesca to Agustín Viesca, November 14, 1829, in *AP*, 2:286–88. Viesca kept the leadership in San Antonio appraised of his efforts to secure an exemption for Texas; see Ramón Músquiz to the Governor of Coahuila-Texas, December 7, 1829, Fondo Jefatura Política de Bejar, caja 13, expediente 16, AGEC.

24. Ramón Músquiz to SFA, November 12, 1829, *AP*, 2:285–86 (quotation). For a discussion of the decrees passed by Guerrero aimed at expanding the reach of the national government at the expense of the sovereignty of the states, and the reaction of those states, see Harrell, "Vicente Guerrero and the Birth of Modern Mexico," 330–47.

25. On news of the exemption reaching Texas, see Manuel de Mier y Terán to SFA, November 20, 1829, in *AP*, 2:290; Ramón Músquiz to SFA, December 24, 1829, in *AP*, 2:303–4; SFA to Manuel de Mier y Terán, December 29, 1829, in *AP*, 2:306. The official exemption for Texas was dated December 2, 1829 (see Agustín Viesca to Governor of Coahuila-Texas, December 2, 1829, Fondo Siglo XIX, caja 12, fondo 7, expediente 4, AGEC), and arrived in San Antonio by January 3, 1830 (see Ramón Músquiz to the Governor of Coahuila-Texas,

January 3, 1830, Fondo Jefatura Política de Bejar, caja 14, expediente 4, AGEC). Because the letter from Terán to SFA about the exemption was dated November 20, 1829, it seems likely that Guerrero decided to exempt Texas from the decree even before most of the protests from Coahuila-Texas arrived in Mexico City and sent word to Terán before he issued the official exemption. Perhaps Guerrero had always intended to exempt the region, but it seems more likely that officials in Mexico City with sympathies for either the Anglo settlements, Tejanos, or Viesca wing of the Saltillo Congress interceded with the president in the matter. Because the December 2, 1829, exemption letter to Governor José María Viesca came from his brother, Agustín Viesca, it would seem likely that Agustín Viesca played a key role in securing the exclusion of Texas from the emancipation decree. Coahuila was not included in the exemption—only the department of Texas.

26. Although Guerrero's 1829 emancipation decree is nearly always cited by U.S. historians as the date when Mexico outlawed slavery, Mexico did not in fact outlaw the institution until 1837. When Guerrero exempted Texas from the effects of the law in 1829, he exempted the only part of Mexico where chattel slavery remained prominent. After Guerrero's overthrow in late 1829, and subsequent trial for treason and execution in 1831, Mexico's national legislature enacted a law abrogating "all the laws, decrees, regulations, ordinances and orders" issued by Guerrero under his wartime powers. The Congress exempted from annulment a number of laws passed by Guerrero, but the decree abolishing slavery was not among them. For the law abrogating Guerrero's 1829 decrees, including the abolition of slavery, see the Law of February 15, 1831, "Declaraciones Relativas a los Actos del Gobierno General en Virtud de Facultades Extraordinarias," in Arrillaga, *Leyes, Decretos, Bandos, Reglamentos, Circulares y Providencias de los Supremos Poderes y Otras Autoridades de la República Mexicana*, tomo de 1831, 37–38. Government-sanctioned slavery did not come to an end in Mexico until 1837, when the Mexican Congress abolished the institution "without any exception" as a response to the success of the Texas Revolution in 1835–36. See Number 1848, April 5, 1837, "Ley.—Queda abolida la esclavitud en la República, sin excepcion alguna," in Dublán y Lozano, tomo III, 352.

27. For an overview of the story of Guerrero's installation into the presidency over the rightfully elected Pedraza, see Green, *The Mexican Republic*, 154–61. For an in-depth discussion of Santa Anna's role in the pro-Guerrero revolt, see Fowler, *Santa Anna of Mexico*, 107–16.

28. For an overview of the intellectual background to renewed efforts at centralism under the Bustamante administration, see Green, *The Mexican Republic*, 189–229.

29. Constantino de Tarnava to the Minister of War, January 6, 1830, quoted in Howren, "Causes and Origins of the Decree of April 6, 1830," 407–13 (first quotation on 407; second 411, emphasis in original). See also Mier y Terán, *Texas by Terán*.

30. Law of April 6, 1830, translated in Howren, "Causes and Origins of the Decree of April 6, 1830," 415–17. The original Spanish can be found in Dublán y Lozano, tomo II, 238–40.

31. Anastascio Bustamante to SFA, March 20, 1830, translated in Howren, "Causes and Origins of the Decree of April 6, 1830," 419–20.

32. SFA to Anastascio Bustamante, May 17, 1830, quoted in Cantrell, *Stephen F. Austin*, 221. On Austin's depression, see ibid., 214–17.

33. Ramón Músquiz to SFA, April 29, 1830, Thomas W. Streeter Collection of Texas Manuscripts, Beinecke.

34. On SFA's approach to the April 6, 1830, law, see Cantrell, *Stephen F. Austin*, 222–27.

35. SFA to Thomas F. Leaming, June 14, 1830, in *AP*, 2:418.

36. SFA to Lucas Alamán, May 18, 1830, in *AP*, 2:384 (SFA noted on the manuscript: "Copy of letter not sent"); SFA to Henry Austin, [June 1830?], in *AP*, 2:405.

37. SFA to Richard Ellis, et al., June 16, 1830, in *AP*, 2:422; SFA to S. Rhoads Fisher, June 17, 1830, in *AP*, 2:427.

38. S. Rhoads Fisher to SFA, August 23, 1830, in *AP*, 2:469–70.

39. SFA to Edward Livingston, June 24, 1832, in *AP*, 2:795 (emphasis in original).

40. SFA to Thomas F. Leaming, June 14, 1830, in *AP*, 2:415.

41. See, for example, Manuel de Mier y Terán to SFA, March 1831, in *AP*, 2:635. Terán declined to endorse SFA's proposal.

42. SFA to Samuel May Williams, April 16, 1831, in *AP*, 2:645.

43. SFA to Edward Livingston, June 24, 1832, in *AP*, 2:795.

44. For the communication between Mexican officials relative to the illegal importation of slaves from New Orleans to Mexico, see Declaration of Isaac Tinsley, March 5, 1831; William Lewis to Manuel de Mier y Terán, May 13, 1831; Francisco Pizarro Martínez to Lucas Alamán, May 30, 1831; Declaration of Noadiah Marsh, June 2, 1831; Martínez to Alamán, September 24, 1831; Terán to Martínez, August 15, 1831; Martínez to Terán, September 1831; Martínez to Terán, September 24, 1831; Terán to Alamán, December 22, 1831; Terán to Alamán, January 19, 1832; all in "Correspondence Relative to the Introduction of Slaves into Texas," legajo 7, expendiente 56, Secretaria de Fomento, Transcriptions from Mexico City, vol. 316, box 2Q169, CAH-UT. The CAH-UT transcriptions were completed by University of Texas researchers working in Mexico City during the early twentieth century when these documents were part of the "Fomento, Colonizacion e Industria" archive described by Herbert Bolton in his *Guide to Materials for the History of the United States in the Principal Archives of Mexico*. The holdings of the Fomento archive were apparently redistributed at some point to other archives in Mexico City. In addition to the CAH-UT transcripts, these particular documents can be found today on microfilm under "Texas: Correspondencia relative a la importación de esclavos a aquel territoria, 1831," Primera Serie de Papeles Sueltos, roll 47, 51-7-56 (microfilm), in the Biblioteca Nacional de Antropología e Historia, Mexico City, Mexico.

A copy of the indenture contract signed by John Miller, who was among the sixteen slaveholders named by Martínez in his report, can be found in Indenture Agreement with John Miller, May 10, 1831, Claude Elliot Memorial Collection, Special Collections, M. D. Anderson Library, University of Houston. Miller lived in Alabama before making his way to Mexico, and his indenture agreement bound George (40 years old), Charlotte (38 years old), and her seven children—Mary (17), Sambo (13), Peter (9), Sally (8), Anna (5), Fanny (3), and David (1)—to serve Miller for 90 years.

45. "Correspondence Relative to the Introduction of Slaves into Texas," legajo 7, expendiente 56, Secretaria de Fomento, Transcriptions from Mexico City, vol. 316, box 2Q169, CAH-UT. Some of the traffic included slaves stolen from Louisiana plantations, and Terán found himself embroiled during the summer of 1831 in a dispute between Ezekiel Hayes and Patrick Henry Herndon over an enslaved woman named Sarah, whom Hayes claimed had been stolen by Herndon and then illegally transported to Texas. On the Hayes-Herndon dispute, see Francisco Pizarro Martínez to Lucas Alamán, May 30, 1831, and Ezekiel

Hayes to Terán, May 30, 1831, both in "Correspondence Relative to the Introduction of Slaves into Texas"; and also Ezekiel Hayes to Terán, May 30, 1831, in *AP*, 2:662.

46. SFA to Wily Martin, May 30, 1833, *AP*, 2:981 (first quotation, emphasis in original). For a more detailed analysis of SFA's views on slavery, see Torget, "Stephen F. Austin's Views on Slavery in Early Texas."

47. Morton, *Terán and Texas*, 178–83.

48. Bruchey, *Cotton and the Growth of the American Economy*, tables on 16–18.

49. In 1831, SFA estimated that his colony produced 1,000 bales annually (SFA to N. A. Ware, July 24, 1831, in *AP*, 2:681). In 1834, Juan Almonte estimated that the colonies produced 7,000 bales annually (Almonte, *Almonte's Texas*, 251, 258). Even if SFA's and Almonte's estimates were both above the mark, they nonetheless point toward a tremendous expansion in cotton production in Texas during the early 1830s.

50. Miller, *New Orleans and the Texas Revolution*, 217.

51. SFA to Samuel May Williams, May 9, 1833, in *AP*, 2:966; Berlandier, *Journey to Mexico during the Years 1826 to 1834*, 298.

52. On the population increase of 1830–1834, see Weber, *The Mexican Frontier*, 177, and especially 342, n. 65.

53. Elliott Gregory to Samuel May Williams, February 19, 1834; Thomas McKinney to Williams, March 27, 1834, April 7, 1834, June 2, 1834; Robert Williams to Samuel May Williams, April 24, 1834; Walter White to Samuel May Williams, December 22, 1834; all in SMWP.

54. Elliott Gregory to Samuel May Williams, April 24, 1832, in SMWP.

55. Almonte, *Almonte's Texas*, 240, 251, 258, 274, 258 (quotation).

56. Ibid., 234, 245, 253.

57. Almonte estimated there were around 2,000 enslaved people in Texas by 1834, although that appears to be an underestimate. Following the chaos of the 1836 Texas Revolution, there were at least 3,700 enslaved people counted in the 1837 tax rolls of the Republic of Texas (see appendix 1), and contemporaries estimated that around 5,000 enslaved people lived in Texas in 1836 (see Campbell, *An Empire for Slavery*, 54–55). As such, it is highly likely that in 1834–36 there were more enslaved people in Texas than the 3,100 Tejanos who Almonte recorded living in San Antonio and Goliad.

58. José Antonio de la Garza to Músquiz, May 23, 1832, BA, reel 150, frames 203–5; Músquiz to Alcaldes of Goliad and Austin, May 24, 1832, BA, reel 150, frames 218–21; Antonio Elozúa to Alejandro Treviño, May 26, 1832, BA, reel 150, frame 249; Instructions to Gaspar Flores, Músquiz to Green DeWitt and Ezekiel Williams, Músquiz to José Antonio de la Garza, Músquiz to Gaspar Flores, all May 27, 1832, BA, reel 150, frames 263–71; Ezekiel Williams and Green DeWitt to Músquiz, May 30, 1832, BA, reel 150, frames 339–41; Músquiz to José Antonio de la Garza, June 1, 1832, BA, reel 150, frames 452–56; Músquiz to Alcalde of Austin, Músquiz to Chief of Gonzales Police, both June 6, 1832, BA, reel 150, frames 608–14; Ezekiel Williams to Músquiz, Miguel Arciniega to Músquiz, both June 12, 1832, BA, reel 150, frames 719–25; Horatio Chrisman Affidavit, July 4, 1832, BA, reel 151, frame 355; Juan José Ruiz to José Antonio de la Garza, July 21, 1832, BA, reel 151, frames 769–71; Ezekiel Williams to Músquiz, August 10, 1832, BA, reel 152, frames 489–90; Juan Seguín to Manuel Jiménez, May 17, 1833, BA, reel 156, frames 416–22.

59. Músquiz to Unknown, January 30, 1831, BA, reel 138, frames 369–71.

60. José Casiano to SFA, August 4, 1831, in SMWP. Casiano continued purchasing black slaves as late as 1841; see Reséndez, "Ramón Músquiz," 135.

61. Músquiz to SFA, June 30, 1826, in *AP*, 1:1365; SFA to Victor Blanco, October 24, 1826, in *AP*, 1:1481–82; SFA to Samuel May Williams, January 9, 1831, in *AP*, 2:581–83.

62. On the disturbances at Anahuac, see Henson, *Anahuac in 1832*, and Henson, *Juan Davis Bradburn*. On the disturbances at Velasco and Nacogdoches, see Campbell, *Gone to Texas*, 118–22.

63. For examples of the colonists employing the language of federalism in defense of their rebellions, see July 18 and July 27, 1832, in *Communications Forwarded from San Felipe de Austin relative to late events in Texas*, published in Mobile, Alabama in 1832, MS# Zc52 832co, Beinecke. On Santa Anna's uprising against the Bustamante administration, see Fowler, *Santa Anna of Mexico*, 133–42.

64. "Decree No. 190," April 28, 1832, in *LOT*, 1:193 (quotation). The Monclova faction continued to openly support Anglo colonization in Texas, petitioning the national government for the repeal of the Law of April 6, 1830; see, for example, "Este Congreso pide al de la Unión, la degrogración por anticonstitucional de la Ley de 6 de abril de 1830," April 29, 1833, Cuarto Congreso Constitucional, 1832–1833, Primer Periodo Ordinario, Hacienda, legajo 2, expediente 53, ACEC. On the efforts of conservatives in Saltillo to tighten restrictions on Anglos in Texas, see Tijerina, *Tejanos and Texas under the Mexican Flag*, 127–29. For the Saltillo-Monclova split, see Soto, "La disputa entre Monclova y Saltillo y la independencia de Texas."

65. Tijerina, *Tejanos and Texas under the Mexican Flag*, 131–32 (quotation 132); de la Teja, "The Colonization and Independence of Texas: A Tejano Perspective," 87–95.

66. Barker, *The Life of Stephen F. Austin*, 432–59; Cantrell, *Stephen F. Austin*, 271–73.

67. There were, to be sure, a handful of Tejano centralists scattered across the region—such as Vicente Córdova in Nacogdoches, Carlos de la Garza near Goliad, and Angel Navarro in San Antonio—who opposed the war and distrusted the intentions of the Anglo settlers, although they found themselves the minority voice.

68. Lack, *The Texas Revolutionary Experience*, 3–74; Ramos, *Beyond the Alamo*, 133–66; Reséndez, *Changing National Identities at the Frontier*, 149–70.

69. On the General Council, see Lack, *The Texas Revolutionary Experience*, 53–74.

70. Report of the Committee on Finance, November 27, 1835, "Journal of the Proceedings of the General Council," in *LOT*, 1:593–97.

71. Report of the Committee on State and Judiciary, January 1, 1836, "Journal of the Proceedings of the General Council," in *LOT*, 1:720–22; "An Ordinance and Decree to Prevent the Importation and Emigration of Free Negroes and Mulattoes into Texas," January 5, 1836, in *LOT*, 1:1024–25.

72. Gray, *The Diary of William Fairfax Gray*, 56–57.

73. Thomas McKinney to Samuel May Williams, October 5, 1835, SMWP.

74. Henson, *Samuel May Williams*, 80–87; Bevill, *The Paper Republic*, 102–3.

75. Miller, *New Orleans and the Texas Revolution*, 61–70, 130–41, 180.

76. On the 1836 convention, see Lack, *The Texas Revolutionary Experience*, 75–95.

77. On Spanish and Mexican provisions included in the Republic of Texas Constitution and legal system, see Stuntz, *Hers, His, and Theirs*, 133–45.

78. General Provisions for Constitution of Republic of Texas, March 9, 1836, "Journals of the Convention at Washington," in *LOT*, 1:872–73.

79. On the importation of enslaved Africans during the 1835–1837 era, see Barker, "The African Slave Trade in Texas," 152–56; Torget, "Cotton Empire: Slavery and the Texas Borderlands, 1820–1837," 262–66; Kelley, "Blackbirders and Bozales," 408–13.

80. Kelley, "Blackbirders and Bozales," 410–13.

81. William S. Fisher to Henry Smith, March 2, 1836, quoted in Barker, "The African Slave Trade in Texas," 153.

82. General Provisions for Constitution of Republic of Texas, March 9, 1836, "Journals of the Convention at Washington," in *LOT*, 1:874.

83. Report of S. Rhodes Fisher on African Slave Trade, March 15, 1836, "Journals of the Convention at Washington," in *LOT*, 1:895–96; George Childress Proviso, March 9, 1836, "Journals of the Convention at Washington," in *LOT*, 1:874.

84. Lack, *The Texas Revolutionary Experience*, 90–95; Siegel, *A Political History of the Texas Republic*, 32–34.

85. For the full text of the 1836 Constitution, see *LOT*, 1:1069–85.

86. Smithwick, *The Evolution of a State*, 90.

87. John Quitman to Eliza Quitman, April 15, 1836, Quitman Family Papers, SHC-UNC.

88. Harris, "The Reminiscences of Mrs. Dilue Harris," 163.

89. De la Teja, *A Revolution Remembered*, 88–89; Jenkins, *Recollections of Early Texas*, 41.

90. Smith, *From Dominance to Disappearance*, 158–59.

91. Lack, "Slavery and the Texas Revolution," 187, 191, 194–95.

92. Cummins, *Emily Austin of Texas, 1795–1851*, 131–32.

93. Harris, "The Reminiscences of Mrs. Dilue Harris," 164.

94. Antonio López de Santa Anna to José María Tornel, February 16, 1836, in Jenkins, *The Papers of the Texas Revolution*, 4:358.

95. "Request by the Hacendados of Orizaba and Cordoba," April 16, 1836, legajo 10, expediente 87, Secretaria de Fomento, Transcriptions from Mexico City, vol. 311, box 2Q168, CAH-UT; SFA to Samuel May Williams, December 31, 1834, in *AP*, 3:36 (quotation); SFA to James Perry, February 6, 1835, in *AP*, 3:41; SFA to Samuel May Williams, April 4, 1835, in *AP*, 3:60; Tenenbaum, *The Politics of Penury*, 70–72; Fowler, "Joseph Welch: A British Santanista," 37.

96. At Houston's direction, Santa Anna sent orders to the rest of the Mexican army to retreat and General Vicente Filisola obeyed, taking his forces south of the Rio Grande. It was Filisola's retreat—based on his unwillingness to endanger the life of Santa Anna by continuing the campaign against Texas—that truly ended the war.

Chapter 5

1. John Quitman, 1837 narrative, Quitman Family Papers, SHC-UNC (quotation); May, *John A. Quitman*, 78; Walther, *The Fire-Eaters*, 91.

2. John Quitman to Eliza Quitman, April 14, 1836, Quitman Family Papers, SHC-UNC. Quitman had already been in contact with Sam Houston during the early months of 1836, when Houston asked Quitman to join the fight in Texas (see Sam Houston to John Quitman, February 12, 1836, in Claiborne, *Life and Correspondence of John A. Quitman*, 1:139–40).

3. Harris, "The Reminiscences of Mrs. Dilue Harris," 167–68.

4. Ibid., 171.

5. John Quitman to Eliza Quitman, April 29, 1836, Quitman Papers, SHC-UNC.

6. Ibid.

7. John Quitman to Henry Quitman, May 28, 1836, and July 31, 1836, Quitman Papers, SHC-UNC. Before returning to Mississippi, Quitman had secured 20,000 acres for $3,000 (15¢ per acre), which he estimated would resell for $400,000 ($20 per acre) once Texas joined the United States.

8. Harris, "The Reminiscences of Mrs. Dilue Harris," 178.

9. Ibid., 177–79 (quotation on 179).

10. Ibid., 179.

11. Remarkably, there has been no sustained scholarly treatment of the Republic of Texas since a handful of works came out during the 1940s and 1950s, none of which focused on the issues of slavery and the cotton economy. See Schmitz, *Texan Statecraft*; Hogan, *The Texas Republic*; Siegel, *A Political History of the Texas Republic*.

12. Harris, "The Reminiscences of Mrs. Dilue Harris," 178–79 (quotation on 179). This practice appears to have been fairly widespread (see, e.g., David Burnet to James Moran, August 18, 1836, Thomas Jefferson Holbrook Papers, TSLA). For a thorough overview of the treatment of Mexican prisoners of war in the aftermath of the Texas Revolution, see Henson, "Politics and the Treatment of the Mexican Prisoners after the Battle of San Jacinto," 189–230 (esp. 212–13).

13. John Quitman to Eliza Quitman, May 5, 1836, Quitman Papers, SHC-UNC.

14. L. A. McHenry to [John Hardin McHenry], June 17, 1836, quoted in Lack, *The Texas Revolutionary Experience*, 106.

15. Receipt for Cotton Shipment, July 20, 1836, Texas Manuscripts, Special Collections, M. D. Anderson Library, University of Houston.

16. John Merle to James F. Perry, June 30, 1836; Account of Cotton Sale, John A. Merle & Co., August 4, 1836, James F. Perry Papers, Records of Ante-bellum Southern Plantations (microfilm), CAH-UT.

17. On the 1836 election, see Siegel, *Political History of the Republic of Texas*, 55.

18. In the September 1836 elections, nearly every voter cast his ballot—3,277 to 91—in favor of annexing Texas to the United States.

19. Sam Houston Inaugural Address, October 22, 1836, in Wallace, Vigness, and Ward, *Documents of Texas History*, 123; Haley, *Sam Houston*, 166–73.

20. David Burnet to James Collinsworth and Peter W. Grayson, May 26, 1836, in *DCROT*, 2:89–91.

21. Haley, *Sam Houston*, 168–69. John Forsythe, the U.S. secretary of state, refused Collinsworth and Grayson on the grounds that the Texas agents' credentials lacked the official seal of the Republic of Texas, which was necessary to prove that they represented the new Texas government (Texas did not yet have a seal).

22. Williams and Barker, *The Writings of Sam Houston*, 2:42.

23. Andrew Jackson, "Special Message," December 21, 1836, quoted in Haley, *Sam Houston*, 175.

24. SFA to William H. Wharton, November 18, 1836, in *DCROT*, 1:127–35 (quotation on 128).

25. SFA to William H. Wharton, November 18, 1836 (secret instructions), in *DCROT*, 1:135–40 (quotation on 137).

26. Cantrell, *Stephen F. Austin*, 363–64.

27. William H. Wharton to SFA, January 6, 1837, in *DCROT*, 2:168–72.

28. On the contested nature of slavery in the early U.S. republic, see Mason, *Slavery and Politics in the Early American Republic*; Hammond, *Slavery, Freedom and Expansion in the Early American West*; and Hammond and Mason, *Contesting Slavery: The Politics of Bondage and Freedom in the New American Nation*. On the political controversies of slavery in the U.S. Congress during the 1820s and 1830s, see Freehling, *The Road to Disunion*, particularly chs. 8–10, 14–19.

29. *Buffalo Spectator*, reprinted in the *Liberator*, April 23, 1836.

30. The number of these pieces that appeared in the *Liberator* are too numerous to cite individually, but a good sampling from this period can be found in the *Liberator*, April 2, April 16, April 23, April 30, May 7, July 2, September 3, September 17, October 15, December 24, 1836; January 2, February 11, February 18, March 4, March 18, April 14, April 28, May 19, June 16, June 23, 1837. For similar anti-Texas rhetoric, see the *Colored American*, May 6 and June 10, 1837.

31. Silbey, *Storm over Texas*, 11–14.

32. William H. Wharton to SFA, January 6, 1837, in *DCROT*, 2:168–72.

33. James Pinckney Henderson to Memucan Hunt, December 31, 1836, in *DCROT*, 2:161–65.

34. Memucan Hunt to James Pinckney Henderson, April 15, 1837, in *DCROT*, 2:208–11.

35. See, for example, the *Richmond Enquirer*, November 11, December 6, December 13, December 22, 1836; *Niles' Weekly Register*, December 31, 1836 (typescript copy in James Hamilton Jr. Papers, SHC-UNC); *New Orleans Picayune*, July 23, 1837.

36. For examples of familial connections between U.S. southerners and people in the Republic of Texas, see Mary S. Watts to Ann Teates, April 24, 1836, in Correspondence of the Breckinridge, Gamble, and Watts Families, Albert and Shirley Small Special Collections Library, University of Virginia; Henrietta Wacherhagen to Eliza Quitman, June 12, 1836, Quitman Family Papers, SHC-UNC.

37. Thomas Harrison to James Thomas Harrison, April 10, 1836, and August 28, 1836, James Thomas Harrison Papers, SHC-UNC.

38. Joseph Gales Johnson to George W. Haywood, May 13, 1836, Ernest Haywood Collection of Haywood Family Papers, SHC-UNC.

39. Siegel, *A Political History of the Texas Republic*, 77–78; Morrison, *Slavery and the American West*, 14–15.

40. See, for example, Republic of Texas Senate Debates of May 12, 1837, in *TTR*, May 16, 1837. For anti-British sentiment in the United States during this era, see Haynes, *Unfinished Revolution*.

41. Davis, *Inhuman Bondage*, 233–38. For the origins of British abolitionism, see Brown, *Moral Capital*. For American views on British abolitionism, see Haynes, *Unfinished Revolution*, particularly ch. 8.

42. See, for example, the instructions that Henderson received before he left on his mission for England, which consisted primarily of tactics for how to deal with British objections to Texas's status as a slaving nation: R. A. Irion to James Pinckney Henderson, June 25, 1837, in *DCROT*, 3:308–9.

43. In 1840 England imported more than 53 percent of the world's cotton supply, their nearest competitors for the crop being the United States (which imported 17 percent) and France (13 percent). See Bruchey, *Cotton and the Growth of the American Economy*, 8–10.

44. My account of the meeting between Henderson and Palmerston in this and the

following paragraphs is drawn from James Pinckney Henderson to R. A. Irion, October 14, 1837, in *DCROT*, 3:812–20; James Pinckney Henderson to R. A. Irion, November 5, 1837, in *DCROT*, 2:821–29.

45. Número 1848, "Abril 5 de 1837—Ley.—Queda abolida la esclavitud en la República, sin excepcion alguna," in Dublán y Lozano, tomo III, 352. The law of April 5, 1837, rather than the oft-cited September 1829 presidential decree, ended legalized slavery in Mexico.

46. J. Pinckney Henderson to Robert Irion, January 5, 1838, and November 12, 1838, in *DCROT*, 3:840–42, 3:1235.

47. Siegel, *A Political History of the Texas Republic*, 85–91; Schmitz, *Texan Statecraft*, 57–61. Henderson reported that he believed the main objection within the British government to recognizing Texas was slavery.

48. "An Act to Raise Revenue by Direct Taxation," June 12, 1827, in *LOT*, 1:1319–22; Miller, "A Financial History of Texas," 20–69 (Houston quotation on 67); Siegel, *A Political History of the Texas Republic*, 78–80.

49. "An Act Punishing Crimes and Misdemeanors," December 21, 1836, in *LOT*, 1:1247–55.

50. Miller, "A Financial History of Texas," 20.

51. Hogan, *The Texas Republic*, 61–66.

52. John P. Borden to the Senate and House of Representatives, October 7, 1837, November 6, 1837, and November 7, 1837, all in Letters Sent by Commissioner of General Land Office, vol. 1, Archives and Records, Texas General Land Office, Austin, Texas. Borden would bring a staff member, Thomas Western, into the Land Office by December 1837, and a few other staff members in 1838. The Land Office, however, would remain so badly understaffed that Borden resigned in 1840.

53. Memucan Hunt to John Fosyth, July 18, 1837; Forsyth to Hunt, July 24, 1837; Hunt to Forsyth, July 28, 1837; Forsyth to Hunt, July 31, 1837; all in *DCROT*, 1:248–51.

54. *TTR*, August 30, 1836.

55. Hardin, *Texian Macabre*, 96–97 (quotation). Hardin's book provides one of the most detailed descriptions available of early Houston; see especially 78–120.

56. Ibid., 94, 143–45, 149; Hogan, *The Texas Republic*, 119.

57. "Memorandum on Texas" to French Department of Political Affairs, May 8, 1838, in Barker, *The French Legation in Texas*, 1:44.

58. Hardin, *Texian Macabre*, 95–99, 104–6, 111, 114; Hogan, *The Texas Republic*, 28–31, 129.

59. *TTR*, October 14, 1837.

60. *TTR*, February 17, 1838.

61. Ibid.

62. During the 1830s cotton boom, the average price paid per pound in New Orleans, New York, and Liverpool peaked in 1835 and then remained steady until 1838–39, when the price began dropping precipitously through the early 1840s. See Bruchey, *Cotton and the Growth of the American Economy*, 7–38.

63. On the Specie Circular and the 1837 Panic see, McGrane, *The Panic of 1837*.

64. See, for example, the numerous ads in *TTR*, March 10 and March 31, 1838.

65. Siegel, *A Political History of the Texas Republic*, 71.

66. *TTR*, December 29, 1838.

67. *New York Journal of Commerce*, reprinted in the *Niles' Weekly Register*, March 18, 1837.

68. Jos. T. Crawford to Richard Pakenham, May 26, 1837, Records of the Foreign Office of

Great Britain, 1837–1847, TSLA. On the geographic patterns of U.S.-Texas migration during these years, see Lathrop, *Migration into East Texas, 1835–1860*, 39.

69. My analysis of the migration and settlement patterns of slaveholders and their slaves during the Republic of Texas period is based on the Republic's annual tax assessments, which can be found in the Records of the Comptroller of Public Accounts, Ad Valorem Tax Division, County Real and Personal Property Tax Rolls, 1837–1900, Archives Division, TSLA. See appendix 1.

70. *New York Journal of Commerce*, reprinted in the *Niles' Weekly Register*, March 18, 1837 (emphasis in original).

71. George Blaikie to James F. Perry, June 3, 1836, and July 28, 1836, James F. Perry Papers, Records of Ante-bellum Southern Plantations (microfilm), CAH-UT.

72. Bollaert, *William Bollaert's Texas*, 314.

73. *TTR*, October 4, 1837.

74. *TTR*, May 30, 1837.

75. *TTR*, September 30, 1837.

76. *TTR*, August 19, 1837.

77. Thomas McKinney to Samuel May Williams, July 16, 1838, SMWP; Henson, *Samuel May Williams*, 105.

78. *TTR*, March 31, 1838 (40-hour distance).

79. Anson Jones, "Remarks at a Public Dinner," June 29, 1839, in Jones, *Memoranda and Official Correspondence Relating to the Republic of Texas*, 294.

80. *TTR*, February 17, 1838.

81. *New-Orleans Commercial Bulletin*, January 15, 1836; *TTR*, February 17, 1838.

82. *TTR*, November 4, 1837.

83. *Southern Patriot*, June 18, 1838. The *Patriot* reported that 1,424 bales were aboard which, when multiplied by an average of 450 pounds per bale, comes to 640,800 pounds.

84. *TTR*, March 31, 1838.

85. John A. Kerle to James F. Perry, March 31, 1838; James Reed & Co. to Perry, November 7, 1838; Perry to John Merle & Co., January 5, 1839, all in James F. Perry Papers, Records of Ante-bellum Southern Plantations (microfilm), CAH-UT.

86. "Sales Account of 50 Bales," John A. Merle & Co., February 9, 1839; Merle & Co. to Perry, February 15, 1839, both in ibid. Perry's 50 bales weighed 26,659 pounds and sold for 11$\frac{7}{8}$¢ per pound.

87. For a sampling of the wide assortment of trade goods available from Texas merchants, see the *Morning Star*, January 7, 1840.

88. See, for example, the advertisement of C. P. Green & Co. in the *TTR*, June 24, 1837.

89. Anonymous, *Texas in 1840*, 116–17.

90. Cotton made up 86 percent of the Republic's exports in 1843, and 95 percent in 1844, with animal hides composing the next largest category of export goods. See Crane, "The Administration of the Customs Service of the Republic of Texas," 227–30.

91. Hogan, *The Texas Republic*, 102–3; Marie Beth Jones, "Robert Mills," *HOT*. The Mills brothers would later shift their base of operations toward Galveston.

92. Thomas McKinney to Samuel May Williams, July 28, 1838, November 3, 1838, SMWP.

93. Thomas McKinney to Samuel May Williams, October 13, 1838, SMWP.

94. Thomas McKinney to Samuel May Williams, November 3, 1838, SMWP.

95. *TTR*, November 17, 1838. Francis Moore, Jr., the editor of the *TTR*, had long been an advocate of establishing a direct commerce with Great Britain (see, e.g., *TTR*, March 7, 1837).

96. All quotes from S. L. Jones to Samuel May Williams, January 31, 1839, except McKinney quote, which is from Thomas McKinney to Samuel May Williams, January 27, 1839, both in SMWP.

97. S. L. Jones to Samuel May Williams, January 31, 1839; Thomas McKinney to Samuel May Williams, February 22, 1839, SMWP.

98. Thomas McKinney to Samuel May Williams, January 1, 1839, and February 22, 1839, SMWP.

99. Alphonse Dubois de Saligny to Louis Mathieu Molé, March 8, 1839, in Barker, *The French Legation in Texas*, 1:63.

100. *TTR*, February 27, 1839.

101. Samuel May Williams to Anson Jones, March 11, 1839, in Jones, *Memoranda and Official Correspondence Relating to the Republic of Texas*, 145.

102. Thomas McKinney to Samuel May Williams, February 22, 1839, SMWP.

103. Anson Jones, "Remarks at a Public Dinner," June 29, 1839, in Jones, *Memoranda and Official Correspondence Relating to the Republic of Texas*, 294–95.

104. Sam Houston Inaugural Address, October 22, 1836, in Wallace, Vigness, and Ward, *Documents of Texas History*, 124.

105. Smith, *From Dominance to Disappearance*, 161–62.

106. Ibid., 162–66; Everett, *The Texas Cherokees*, 86–88.

107. Ramos, *Beyond the Alamo*, 170–76.

108. Lack, "The Córdova Revolt," 93–95.

109. Tijerina, *Tejanos and Texas under the Mexican Flag*, 138.

110. On the election of Lamar, see Siegel, *A Political History of the Texas Republic*, 92–98. Lamar received 6,995 votes; Robert Wilson (the pro-Houston candidate) received only 252.

111. *New Orleans Picayune*, December 18, 1838, quoted in Siegel, *The Poet President of Texas*, 52.

112. Inaugural Address of Mirabeau Lamar, December 10, 1838, in Gulick, *The Papers of Mirabeau Lamar*, 2:316–23.

113. Lundy, "The War in Texas, 1836," (emphasis in original).

114. See, for example, "The Texas Question—Extracts from J. Q. Adams' Speech," printed in the *Liberator*, July 20, 1838; for an example of this rhetoric in Great Britain, see Scoble, *Texas: Its Claims to Be Recognized as an Independent Power by Great Britain*.

115. On the gag rule battles in the United States, see Freehling, *The Road to Disunion*, 1:308–52.

116. *Dedham Patriot* (Dedham, Mass.), in the *Liberator*, May 17, 1839.

117. Inaugural Address of Lamar, in Gulick, *The Papers of Mirabeau Buonapart Lamar*, 2:320.

118. Lamar, "Notes for the Inaugural Address on the Annexation of Texas," December 10, 1838, in Gulick, *The Papers of Mirabeau Buonapart Lamar*, 2:324–27. Lamar's inaugural address cannot be fully understood without being read in tandem with these "notes," which provide explicit details on topics that Lamar addresses only vaguely in the inau-

gural address. A good example would be Lamar's allusions in his inaugural to unspecified defects in the U.S. Constitution, which—in his notes—he makes clear stem from the lack of "*sucerity* [security] which is to be furnished by that Government for the preservation of the institution of slavery." Previous to his inauguration, Lamar received a succession of letters from men in the U.S. South voicing many of these same opinions. See, for example, James Hamilton to Lamar, November 3, 1838, in Gulick, *The Papers of Mirabeau Buonapart Lamar*, 2:274–78.

119. *TTR*, October 13, 1838.

120. Mirabeau Lamar to the Republic of Texas Congress, December 21, 1838, in Gulick, *The Papers of Mirabeau Buonapart Lamar*, 2:352–53.

121. Smith, *From Dominance to Disappearance*, 168–74.

122. Hämäläinen, *The Comanche Empire*, 215–17; Smith, *From Dominance to Disappearance*, 174–75.

123. Brice, *The Great Comanche Raid*, 27–48; Anderson, *The Conquest of Texas*, 187–89; Smith, *From Dominance to Disappearance*, 175–76.

124. Lamar's Indian wars cost the Republic more than $2.5 million, whereas the previous Houston administration had spent $190,000 on Indian affairs; see Miller, "A Financial History of Texas," 25.

125. A. T. Burney and Samuel May Williams to Henry Smith, October 8, 1838, in Connor, *Texas Treasury Papers*, 1:133–37.

126. In 1840, the French consumed 116 million pounds of cotton (13.5 percent of world consumption), ranking them only behind England (53.5 percent) and the United States (17 percent); see Bruchey, *Cotton and the Growth of the American Economy*, 8. On the Franco-Mexican dispute that became known as the "Pastry War," see Costeloe, *The Central Republic in Mexico, 1835–1846*, 144–48.

127. J. Pinckney Henderson to Robert Irion, June 2, 1838, in *DCROT*, 3:1206–17; "Memorandum of Department of Political Affairs," October 15, 1838, in Barker, *The French Legation in Texas*, 1:48–49.

128. "Memorandum on Texas," prepared for Louis Mathieu Molé (French prime minister and foreign minister), May 8, 1838, in Barker, *The French Legation in Texas*, 1:39–47.

129. Dubois de Saligny to the Duke of Dalmatia, June 24, 1839, in ibid., 95–103 (quotation on 99). Saligny was not terribly accurate in his reports to the French government, turning in highly inflated accounts of the economic and political successes of the Republic.

130. J. Pinckney Henderson to Secretary of State, July 26, 1839, in *DCROT*, 3:1256–64.

131. J. Pinckney Henderson to David Burnet, October 16, 1839, in *DCROT*, 3:1265–66. The Texas Senate ratified the treaty with France on January 14, 1840.

132. James Hamilton and A. T. Burnley to James Starr, October 3, 1840, in Connor, *Texas Treasury Papers*, 2:550.

133. Miller, "A Financial History of Texas," 23, 70.

134. Barnard Bee to James Webb, May 24, 1839, in *DCROT*, 2:447–49.

135. Juan Nepomuceno Almonte to the Minister of Foreign Relations, Dispatch #8, June 15, 1838, Correspondencia diplomática de la Legación de México en Inglaterra, 1835–1848, L-E-1641; Ministry of Foreign Relations to Richard Pakenham, February 9, 1841, Sucesos entre México y los Estados Unidos de América, 1838–1841, L-E-1065 (2); Thomas Murphy to the Minister of Foreign Relations, Dispatch #1, January 15, 1841, Correspondencia

diplomática de la Legación de México en Inglaterra, 1835–1848, L-E-1641; all in Archivo Histórico de la Secretaría de Relaciones Exteriores, Mexico City, Mexico.

136. Bruchey, *Cotton and the Growth of the American Economy*, 30.

137. *TTR*, November 6, 1839.

138. Moses Austin Bryan to James F. Perry, September 30, 1840, James F. Perry Papers, Records of Ante-bellum Southern Plantations (microfilm), CAH-UT.

139. William J. Bryan to James F. Perry, October 7, 1840, ibid.

140. Moses Austin Bryan to James F. Perry, August 5, 1840, ibid.

141. *TTR*, July 15, 1840.

142. From January 1 to September 20, 1841, Galveston exported 3,657 bales (worth $130,593); 2,798 went to U.S. ports ($100,993) and 859 went to England ($29,600) (see Crane, "The Administration of the Customs Service of the Republic of Texas," 85–86). During that same six-month period, 285 ships arrived from the United States, 4 from England, 2 from Sweden, 1 from France, and 1 from Cuba (see *TTR*, June 9, 1841).

143. Crane, "The Administration of the Customs Service of the Republic of Texas," 229–30.

144. Adams, *British Interests and Activities in Texas*, 27–31, 52–58. For statistics on British cotton consumption, see Bruchey, *Cotton and the Growth of the American Economy*, 7–12.

145. Francis Sheridan to Joseph Garraway, July 12, 1840, in *BDC-ROT*, 18–26. For the diary Sheridan kept during his sojourn in Texas, see Sheridan, *Galveston Island, or A Few Months Off the Coast of Texas*.

146. James Hook to Lord Palmerston, April 30, 1841, in *BDC-ROT*, 29–39.

147. Schmitz, *Texan Statecraft*, 148–49.

148. For Hamilton's rambling explanations for his delay in sending the anti-slave-trade treaty, see Hamilton to Abner Lipscomb and Hamilton to Mirabeau Lamar, both January 4, 1841, in *DCROT*, 3:921–29. On the long journey of that treaty to Texas, see A. T. Burnley to David Burnett, February 21, 1841, in *DCROT*, 3:931–36. On Palmertson's refusal to accept the treaties without the anti-slave-trade pact, see Hamilton to J. S. Mayfield, May 18, 1841, in *DCROT*, 3:937–39.

149. The Santa Fe Expedition has been well documented, the classic account being Kendall, *Narrative of the Texan Santa Fe Expedition*. For an analysis of contemporary discussions of the expedition among Mexicans, Americans, and Indians, see Reséndez, *Changing National Identities at the Frontier*, 197–236.

150. James Morgan to Colonel Webb, January 29, 1841, quoted in Siegel, *A Political History of the Republic of Texas*, 182. On the final election tally, see Haley, *Sam Houston*, 227.

151. *TTR*, July 10, 1839.

152. During the year ending July 31, 1843, the Republic exported only $260 in goods to France (see Crane, "The Administration of the Customs Service of the Republic of Texas," 227–28).

153. For all slave and slaveholder population statistics during the Republic era, see the *Texas Slavery Project* (appendix 1). For the 1837 enslaved population in Texas, see Campbell, *An Empire for Slavery*, 54–55.

154. Making comparisons between the slaveholdings of Texans and their U.S. counterparts is difficult, largely because the United States census did not count the slaveholdings of individual planters during the 1830s or 1840s. As a rough means of comparison, however,

the average slaveholder in the United States in 1850 owned around 8 slaves, while in Texas in 1842 the average was 5.7 slaves. For a sampling and breakdown of the 1850 slaveholding statistics in the United States, see Oakes, *The Ruling Race*, 245–50. For all Texas slaveholding statistics, see appendix 1.

155. On the Republic's debt, see Miller, "A Financial History of Texas," table 4 on 391.

Chapter 6

1. This and the following paragraphs about the Vasquez raid are drawn primarily from Joseph Nance's exhaustive account, *Attack and Counterattack*, particularly 10–12, 24–31, 37.

2. Ibid., 34–35.

3. Maverick, *Memoirs of Mary A. Maverick*, 50.

4. Bollaert, *William Bollaert's Texas*, 27–35 (quotation on 34); Nance, *Attack and Counterattack*, 61–62.

5. Houston to Edwin Morehouse, March 18, 1842, and Houston to Robert Irion, April 14, 1842, both quoted in Haley, *Sam Houston*, 243 (emphasis in original).

6. Nance, *Attack and Counterattack*, 37–38; de la Teja, *A Revolution Remembered*, 94–97.

7. Miller, "A Financial History of Texas," 393.

8. *TTR*, December 16, 1840. On the inability of farmers to pay their taxes, see Henry Austin to James F. Perry, December 26, 1842, James F. Perry Papers, Records of Ante-bellum Southern Plantations (microfilm), CAH-UT; J. C. Brooke to Shaw, May 8, 1843, in Connor, *Texas Treasury Papers*, 3:924–25; "An Act For the relief of persons who are in arrears for Taxes," in *LOT*, 2:744.

9. Miller, "A Financial History of Texas," 22–26.

10. "An Act to Authorize the Firm of McKinney, Williams and Company to issue their Notes for Circulation as Money," in *LOT*, 2:598–600; Hogan, *The Texas Republic*, 101. On cotton serving as primary means of barter, see *TTR*, November 23, 1842.

11. *TTR*, April 19, 1843.

12. Vázquez, "The Texas Question in Mexican Politics, 1836–1845," 315, 332; Costeloe, *The Central Republic in Mexico, 1835–1846*, 160–63; Henderson, *A Glorious Defeat*, 117–18, 123–24.

13. Ramos, *Beyond the Alamo*, 180–81 (quotations); Vázquez, "The Texas Question in Mexican Politics, 1836–1845," 320–22; Costeloe, *The Central Republic in Mexico, 1835–1846*, 240–41.

14. Henderson, *A Glorious Defeat*, 114.

15. Número 1848, "Abril 5 de 1837—Ley.—Queda abolida la esclavitud en la República, sin excepcion alguna," in Dublán y Lozano, tomo III, 352.

16. Pakenham to Palmertson, June 10, 1841, quoted in Adams, *British Interests and Activities in Texas*, 64.

17. Manuel Gorostiza to the Minister of Foreign Relations, Dispatch #34, July 12, 1836, Sucesos entre México y los Estados Unidos de América relacionados con Texas y otros estados Limítrofes, 1836, L-E-1062, Archivo Histórico de la Secretaría de Relaciones Exteriores, Mexico City, Mexico.

18. *Alcance al Voto de Coahuila*, March 19, 1842; July 16, 1842; March 4, 1843; March 12, 1843; May 11, 1844, all in Fondo Periódico Oficial, AGEC.

19. *El Siglo Diez y Nueve*, January 6, 1843, quoted in Haynes, *Soldiers of Misfortune*, 80–81.

For Seguín's account, see de la Teja, *A Revolution Remembered*, 97–100. For an analysis of Seguín's situation, see Ramos, *Beyond the Alamo*, 188–89. For an exhaustive account of Woll's invasion, see Nance, *Attack and Counterattack*, 297–408.

20. Morgan L. Smith to Anson Jones, November 7, 1843, in Jones, *Memoranda and Official Correspondence Relating to the Republic of Texas*, 268–69.

21. Isaac Van Zandt to Anson Jones, March 13, 1843, in *DCROT*, 2:132–36 (quotation on 133). For Van Zandt's description of the centrality of cotton to the Texas economy, see Van Zandt to William Archer, January 10, 1843, in *DCROT*, 2:139–48.

22. *TTR*, September 21, 1842.

23. *TTR*, September 21, 1842; February 1, 1843; *Texas Times*, November 2, 1842.

24. *TTR*, October 11, 1843. See also *TTR*, September 13, 1843; *CGG*, December 16, 1843.

25. *Northern Standard*, December 16, 1843. See also Emily Perry to Stephen Perry, November 26, 1843, James F. Perry Papers, Records of Ante-bellum Southern Plantations (microfilm), CAH-UT.

26. *Brazos Courier*, July 14, 1840.

27. *TTR*, August 5, 1840.

28. Hogan, *The Texas Republic*, 74–75.

29. James Reed & Co. to James F. Perry, August 17, 1837; John A. Merle & Co. to James F. Perry, February 15, 1839; both in James F. Perry Papers, Records of Ante-bellum Southern Plantations (microfilm), CAH-UT.

30. Hogan, *The Texas Republic*, 67–68.

31. *Texas Times*, April 22, 1843; "Memorandum of Mrs. Hannah Adriance Munson," cited in Creighton, *A Narrative History of Brazoria County*, 178.

32. *Texas National Register*, July 10, 1845.

33. Bruchey, *Cotton and the Growth of the American Economy*, 14–17, 29–30.

34. *TTR*, August 5, 1840 (tobacco); June 14, 1842 (silk); March 8, 1843 (hemp); October 11, 1843 (indigo); October 25, 1843 (rice). On the unprofitability of cotton in Texas by 1843, see entry for December 16, 1843, in Bollaert, *William Bollaert's Texas*, 286.

35. Crane, "The Administration of the Customs Service of the Republic of Texas," 227–28.

36. Of the 171 ships that arrived in the Galveston port during the twelve months ending July 31, 1843, only 3 came from France, 4 from England, and 2 from Germany (see ibid., 67).

37. Entries for November 1843 in Bollaert, *William Bollaert's Texas*, 271.

38. William Holman to Secretary, January 31, 1843, quoted in Crane, "The Administration of the Customs Service of the Republic of Texas," 205. On reports of 25,000 bales, see 206.

39. *TTR*, November 23, 1843.

40. William Dashiell to Secretary Ochiltree, February 20, 1845, quoted in Crane, "The Administration of the Customs Service of the Republic of Texas," 185–86.

41. Jesse Benton to Anson Jones, May 1, 1843, in *DCROT*, 2:182–83. On other complaints by the Republic to the United States on smuggling, see G. W. Terrell to Isaac Van Zandt, August 28, 1842, in *DCROT*, 2:601–3.

42. Crane, "The Administration of the Customs Service of the Republic of Texas," 52.

43. The Texas Republic collected about 58 percent of its revenue from such tariffs (see Crane, "The Administration of the Customs Service of the Republic of Texas," 3).

44. Benjamin Shepherd to Mary Kent Shepherd, April 19, 1839, October 18, 1841; Benjamin Shepherd to Martin Baskett Shepherd, February 17, 1840, April 9, 1842, October

18, 1842, February 3, 1843; all in the Papers of Martin Baskett Shepherd, Accession #4241, Albert and Shirley Small Special Collections Library, University of Virginia. For ads from Shepherd's store, see the *Morning Star*, January 6, 1840, and *CGG*, January 18, 1840.

45. On the downturn in U.S. migration to the Republic, see Lathrop, *Migration into East Texas, 1835–1860*, 61, fig. 3; and the 1842–43 slave and slaveholder populations on the *Texas Slavery Project* (see appendix 1).

46. Latham, *Travels in the Republic of Texas, 1842*, 23–24.

47. *TTR*, August 3, 1842; on 1842–1843 population statistics for Travis County, see the *Texas Slavery Project* (appendix 1).

48. Entry for January 23, 1844, in Bollaert, *William Bollaert's Texas*, 313.

49. Entry for January 25, 1844, in ibid., 314–15.

50. William Bollaert observed that Coushatta Indians "occasionally assist the planters in their vicinity to pick cotton" (see ibid., 315); apparently some Tonkawas did the same (see Smith, *From Dominance to Disappearance*, 189). On Houston's renewed peace policy, and its success among tribes in eastern Texas, see Smith, *From Dominance to Disappearance*, 177–80.

51. Smith, *From Dominance to Disappearance*, 180–89; Hämäläinen, *The Comanche Empire*, 217–18.

52. See the population data on the *Texas Slavery Project* (appendix 1).

53. "An Act Establishing the Jurisdiction and Powers of the District Courts," December 22, 1836, in *LOT*, 1:1265–66; "An Act to Legalise Certain Marriages," June 5, 1837, in *LOT*, 1:1293–95.

54. "An Act Concerning Free Persons of Color," February 5, 1840, in *LOT*, 2:325–27. Sam Houston later nullified the law against free blacks; see Haley, *Sam Houston*, 240.

55. *TTR*, September 15, 1841.

56. *CGG*, April 16, 1842.

57. On enslaved people escaping into Mexico, see Tyler, "Fugitive Slaves in Mexico," 1–12; Schwartz, *Across the Rio to Freedom*; Sean Kelley, "'Mexico in His Head,'" 709–23.

58. See, for example, the *National Vindicator*, November 25, 1843, and February 10, 1844.

59. *TTR*, January 15 and 22, 1845.

60. "An Act Supplementary to 'An Act Regulating the Sale of Runaway Slaves,'" in *LOT*, 2:950–51.

61. *TTR*, June 15, 1842.

62. On the connections between insecurity among Texas slaveholders and increasing levels of violence, see Carrigan, "Slavery on the Frontier," and Carrigan, *The Making of a Lynching Culture*.

63. On Raphael's capture and execution, see *TTR*, April 17, 1839; Jenkins and Kesselus, *Edward Burleson*, 187–90; Wilbarger, *Indian Depredations in Texas*, 156–57.

64. *TTR*, August 3, 1842.

65. *Northern Standard*, December 2, 1843.

66. Adams, *British Interests and Activities in Texas*, 97.

67. Daniel O'Connell Address to Members of the British and Foreign Antislavery Society, October 11, 1839, reprinted in the *Liberator*, December 6, 1839. For the effect of O'Connell's speech on Texas diplomats, see Ashbel Smith to Anson Jones, July 2, 1843, in *DCROT*, 3:1099–1103.

68. Narrett, "A Choice of Destiny," 289.

69. Adams, *British Interests and Activities in Texas*, 118 (on earlier English efforts to persuade Mexico to recognize Texas, see 28–31, 59, 65); Tenenbaum, *The Politics of Penury*, 68.

70. See, for example, Ashbel Smith to Anson Jones, July 2, 1843, in *DCROT*, 3:1099–1103.

71. Ashbel Smith to Anson Jones, May 17, 1842, in *DCROT*, 3:957; Nance, *Attack and Counterattack*, 138–39.

72. Ashbel Smith to Anson Jones, May 17, 1842, in *DCROT*, 3:957.

73. Ashbel Smith to Isaac Van Zandt, January 25, 1843, in *DCROT*, 3:1103–8.

74. Charles Elliot to Addington, November 15, 1842, in *BDC-ROT*, 127–30.

75. Charles Elliot to Addington, November 15, 1842, in *BDC-ROT*, 127–30; Charles Elliot to Aberdeen, [late September or early October] 1843, in *BDC-ROT*, 266–67.

76. Stern, "Stephen Pearl Andrews," 491–508.

77. Ashbel Smith to Anson Jones, July 2, 1843, in *DCROT*, 3:1099–1103.

78. *Proceedings of the General Anti-Slavery Convention*, 297–98.

79. Aberdeen to William Kennedy, May 30, 1843, in *BDC-ROT*, 199–200.

80. William Kennedy to Aberdeen, September 5, 1843, in *BDC-ROT*, 254–61. Kennedy had secured his appointment in Texas, in part, because he had suggested to the British Foreign Office that he could help persuade members of the Texas legislature to consider embracing British-sponsored abolition (see Adams, *British Interests and Activities in Texas*, 74).

81. Kennedy to Aberdeen, September 6, 1843, in *BDC-ROT*, 261–62.

82. Ashbel Smith to William Daingerfield, June 28, 1843, in *DCROT*, 3:1098–99; Ashbel Smith to Anson Jones, July 2, 1843, in *DCROT*, 3:1099–1103; Ashbel Smith to Isaac Van Zandt, January 25, 1843, in *DCROT*, 3:1103–8.

83. Ashbel Smith to Anson Jones, July 2, 1843, in *DCROT*, 3:1099–1103; Ashbel Smith to Isaac Van Zandt, January 25, 1843, in *DCROT*, 3:1103–8.

84. Ashbel Smith to Anson Jones, July 31, 1843, in *DCROT*, 3:1116–19.

85. *TTR*, October 11, 1843.

86. *CGG*, October 7, 1843; *TTR*, October 11, 1843.

87. *CGG*, October 7, 1843; *TTR*, October 11, 1843.

88. *TTR*, December 27, 1843.

89. Washington Miller to Ashbel Smith, December 8, 1842, Ashbel Smith Papers, CAH-UT.

90. Isaac Van Zandt to Anson Jones, March 13, 1843, in *DCROT*, 2:132–38.

91. Washington Miller to John Tyler, September 16, 1843, cited in Haynes, *Unfinished Revolution*, 238.

92. Isaac Van Zandt to Anson Jones, September 18, 1843, in *DCROT*, 2:207–10.

93. The classic account is Merk, *Slavery and the Annexation of Texas*. For more recent treatments of the perspective within the Tyler administration, see Freehling, *The Road to Disunion*; Crapol, *John Tyler*; Haynes, *Unfinished Revolution*.

94. Duff Green to John C. Calhoun, January 24, 1842, in Jameson, *Correspondence of John C. Calhoun*, 842–43; Schoen, *The Fragile Fabric of Union*, 185–87; Hietala, *Manifest Design*, 64–70.

95. Crapol, *John Tyler*, 196–97 (quotation); Haynes, *Unfinished Revolution*, 240–41.

96. *TTR*, January 24 and 31, 1844.

97. *TTR*, February 21 and April 3, 1844.

98. *Houston Democrat*, quoted in the *CGG*, February 24, 1844. The Texas Congress passed a joint resolution in favor of annexation with overwhelming support (unanimous in the Texas House, with only two dissenting votes in the Texas Senate), which was promptly forwarded to Washington, D.C.

99. *CGG*, June 15, 1844. See similar statements in the February 10, March 23, and April 20, 1844 issues, as well as Galveston's *Weekly News*, May 11, 1844.

100. Crane, "The Administration of the Customs Service of the Republic of Texas," 74.

101. *CGG*, March 16, 1844; see also issue of May 1, 1844.

102. *CGG*, March 23, 1844.

103. *CGG*, March 16, 1844.

104. *Planter*, February 10, 1844.

105. *TTR*, February 7, June 13, June 19, June 26, 1844 (quotation).

106. *CGG*, May 25, 1844.

107. Mirabeau Lamar to T. P. Anderson et al., November 18, 1845, in Gulick, *The Papers of Mirabeau Buonapart Lamar*, 4:113.

108. Isaac Van Zandt to Anson Jones, January 20, 1844, in *DCROT*, 2:239–43; Haynes, *Unfinished Revolution*, 235.

109. Isaac Van Zandt to Anson Jones, January 2, 1844, in *DCROT*, 2:236–38; Mr. Bower to Van Zandt, January 31, 1844, in *DCROT*, 2:256–57.

110. *Northern Standard*, March 2, 1844 (quotation); *TTR*, February 14, 1844.

111. Isaac Van Zandt to Anson Jones, March 5, 1844, in *DCROT*, 2:261–62; Crapol, *John Tyler*, 207–9.

112. Isaac Van Zandt and J. Pinckney Henderson to Anson Jones, April 12, 1844, in *DCROT*, 2:269–73.

113. Calhoun to Pakenham, April 18, 1844, in Wilson, *The Papers of John C. Calhoun*, 18:273–78.

114. *TTR*, July 10, 1844.

115. Siegel, *A Political History of the Texas Republic*, 234–41.

116. Isaac Van Zandt and J. Pinckney Henderson to Anson Jones, April 12, 1844, in *DCROT*, 2:269–73; Crapol, *John Tyler*, 219–22.

117. "The Resolution Annexing Texas to the United States," March 1, 1844, in Wallace, Vigness, and Ward, *Documents of Texas History*, 146–47.

118. *TTR*, April 23, April 30, May 7, May 21, 1845.

119. *TTR*, April 23, 1845.

120. Benjamin Shepherd to Martin Baskett Shepherd, March 22, 1845, Papers of Martin Baskett Shepherd, Accession #4241, Albert and Shirley Small Special Collections Library, University of Virginia.

121. *Red Lander*, quoted in the *TTR*, November 6, 1844; *TTR*, July 24, 1844, and January 22, 1845. For other examples, see also *TTR*, May 29, July 10, 1844, and Narrett, "A Choice of Destiny."

122. Haynes, *Unfinished Revolution*, 254–58.

123. Harris, "The Public Life of Juan Nepomuceno Almonte," 180; Schroeder, *Mr. Polk's War*; Brack, *Mexico Views Manifest Destiny*.

Epilogue

1. The best treatment of the U.S. diplomacy and events of 1845–46 that produced the U.S.-Mexican War remains Pletcher, *The Diplomacy of Annexation*. For the Mexican perspective during the events of 1844–46 and the outbreak of the U.S.-Mexican War, see Vázquez, "The Texas Question in Mexican Politics, 1836–1845"; Santoni, *Mexicans at Arms*; Brack, *Mexico Views Manifest Destiny*.

2. Benjamin McCulloch to Captain Bliss, July 23, 1846, quoted in Wilkins, *The Highly Irregular Irregulars*, 64–65. For examples of Texas newspapers calling Seguín a traitor to Texas, see the *Northern Standard*, January 30, 1845, and *TTR*, February 5, 1845. On Seguín and the *Escuadrón*, see de la Teja, *A Revolution Remembered*, 48–50; Wilkins, *The Highly Irregular Irregulars,* 64–70.

3. SFA to Samuel May Williams, May 9, 1833, in *AP*, 2:966.

4. For an overview of Juan Seguín's life, see de la Teja, *A Revolution Remembered*.

5. For a detailed analysis of the decline of Tejano power in Texas following 1836, see Ramos, *Beyond the Alamo*, 167–204.

6. Eisenhower, *So Far from God*, 180–91; de la Teja, *A Revolution Remembered*, 50; Wilkins, *The Highly Irregular Irregulars*, 128–29.

7. Fowler, *Santa Anna of Mexico*, 291–318; Henderson, *A Glorious Defeat*, 182–86.

8. There are innumerable books on this subject. The best remains Potter, *The Impending Crisis*. See also McPherson, *Battle Cry of Freedom*, and Freehling, *The Road to Disunion*.

9. "A Declaration of the Causes Which Impel the State of Texas to Secede from the Federal Union," February 2, 1861, in Wallace, Vigness, and Ward, *Documents of Texas History*, 194–96.

10. Gary Kornblith has argued that the annexation of Texas and the resulting U.S.-Mexican War served as the fundamental pivot toward the U.S. Civil War and its aftermath (see Kornblith, "Rethinking the Coming of the Civil War"). For Civil War dead, see Hacker, "A Census-Based Count of the Civil War Dead." For the consequences of the war, see McPherson, *Battle Cry of Freedom*, and Foner, *Reconstruction*.

11. Schoen, *The Fragile Fabric of Union*, 264–67; Owsley, *King Cotton Diplomacy*.

12. Beckert, "Emancipation and Empire," 1405–38.

13. Bruchey, *Cotton and the Growth of the American Economy*, 16–17; Watkins, *King Cotton*, 24.

14. De la Teja, *A Revolution Remembered*, vii, 50–51.

15. On populations, see Campbell, *Gone to Texas*, 205; on cotton prices, see Bruchey, *Cotton and the Growth of the American Economy*, 16–17; on Texas cotton production, see Watkins, *King Cotton*, 23, 213; on Texas sugar, see Kelley, *Los Brazos de Dios*, 114–21, 207. On the role of cotton in Texas after the Civil War, see Foley, *The White Scourge*.

16. Smith, *From Dominance to Disappearance*, 154–252.

17. On 1845 enslaved population, see the *Texas Slavery Project* (appendix 1). On 1860 population, see Campbell, *Gone to Texas*, 205.

18. McLemore, *Inventing Texas*, 70 (quotation); Yoakum, *History of Texas from Its First Settlement in 1685 to Its Annexation to the United States in 1846*.

19. Navarro, *Defending Mexican Valor in Texas*, 76 (quotation). For rising Tejano-Anglo tensions in post-1848 Texas, see Ramos, *Beyond the Alamo*, 205–30; on Seguín's return to Mexico, see de la Teja, *A Revolution Remembered*, 52–56.

Appendix 1

1. "An Act to Raise Revenue by Direct Taxation," June 12, 1837, in *LOT*, 1:1319–22.
2. See, for example, Campbell, *An Empire for Slavery*, 54–58.
3. *TTR*, February 22, 1843.

BIBLIOGRAPHY

Archival Manuscripts

Albert and Shirley Small Special Collections Library, University of Virginia
    Correspondence of the Breckinridge, Gamble, and Watts Families
    Papers of Martin Baskett Shepherd
Archivo del Congreso del Estado de Coahuila, Saltillo, Mexico
    Congreso Constituyente, 1824–1827, Actas de Primera Sesión Ordinaria, Agosto 15, 1824
    a Marzo 22, 1827
    Cuarto Congreso Constitucional, 1832–1833, Primer Periodo Ordinario
    El Libro de Decretos y Ordenes de 1824 a 1826
    Leyes, Decretos y Acuerdos
    Primer Congreso Constitucional, Primer Periodo Ordinario
    Primer Congreso Constitucional, Segundo Periodo Ordinario
Archivo General de la Nación, Mexico City, Mexico
    Gobernación
    Provincias Internas
Archivo General del Estado de Coahuila, Ramos Arizpe, Mexico
    Fondo Jefatura Política de Bexar
    Fondo Periódico Oficial
    Fondo Siglo XIX
Archivo Histórico de la Secretaría de Relaciones Exteriores, Mexico City, Mexico
    Correspondencia diplomática de la Legación de México en Inglaterra, 1835–1848
    Sucesos entre México y los Estados Unidos de América relacionados con Texas y otros
    estados Limítrofes, 1836
    Sucesos entre México y los Estados Unidos de América, 1838–1841
Beinecke Rare Book and Manuscript Library, Yale University
    Assorted Individual Archival Letters (not part of larger manuscript collections)
    Communications forwarded from San Felipe de Austin relative to late events in Texas,
    published in Mobile, Alabama, 1832
    Henry Raup Wagner Collection of Texas Manuscripts
    Juan Francisco Azcárate y Lezama Correspondence with Lucas Alamán
    Thomas W. Streeter Collection of Texas Manuscripts
Bexar County Courthouse, San Antonio, Texas
    Spanish Collection
Biblioteca Nacional de Antropología e Historia, Mexico City, Mexico
    Primera Serie de Papeles Sueltos, roll 47, 51-7-56 (microfilm)
    Texas: Correspondencia relative a la importación de esclavos a aquel territoria, 1831
DeGolyer Library, Southern Methodist University
    Rowe-Barr Collection of Texas Currency
Dolph Briscoe Center for American History, University of Texas

    Archivo General de la Nación, Provincias Internas, Transcripts

    Ashbel Smith Papers

    Béxar Archives (microfilm)

    Eugene Campbell Barker Papers

    George Washington Smyth Papers

    Groce Family Papers

    James F. Perry Papers, Records of Ante-bellum Southern Plantations (microfilm)

    Lester G. Bugbee Papers

    Mary Austin Holley Diary

    Robert Bruce Blake Research Collection

    Secretaria de Fomento, Transcriptions from Mexico City

Galveston and Texas History Center, Rosenberg Library, Galveston, Texas

    Gail Border Jr. Papers

    R. Jones Papers

    Samuel May Williams Papers

M. D. Anderson Library, Special Collections, University of Houston

    Claude Elliot Memorial Collection

    San Jacinto Collection

    Texas Manuscripts

The Newberry Library, Chicago, Illinois

    William Bollaert's pencil sketches of Texas, Edward E. Ayers Collection

Robert J. Terry Library, Texas Southern University

    Heartman Collection, Texas Slave Trade Document Series

Southern Historical Collection, University of North Carolina, Chapel Hill

    Ernest Haywood Collection of Haywood Family Papers

    James Hamilton Jr. Papers

    James Thomas Harrison Papers

    Quitman Family Papers

Texas General Land Office, Austin, Texas

    Letters Sent by Commissioner of General Land Office

    Map Collection

Texas State Library and Archives, Austin, Texas

    Nacogdoches Archives Transcriptions, Nacogdoches Archives

    Records of the Comptroller of Public Accounts, Ad Valorem Tax Division, County Real and Personal Property Tax Rolls, 1837–1900

    Records of the Foreign Office of Great Britain

    Thomas Jefferson Holbrook Papers

Woodson Research Center, Fondren Library, Rice University

    Groce Family Correspondence

    Sarah Groce Birlet, "Life of Jared Ellison Groce One of the Old Three Hundred and His oldest son Leonard Wallace Groce" manuscript

    Thomson Family of Texas Papers

Newspapers

UNITED STATES AND MEXICO

African Repository and Colonial Journal (Washington, D.C.)
Alcance al Voto de Coahuila (Saltillo, Coahuila)
Alexandria Gazette & Daily Advertiser (La.)
American Repertory & Advertiser (Burlington, Vt.)
Argus (Frankfort, Ky.)
Arkansas Gazette (Arkansas Post, Ark.)
Baltimore Patriot
Berkshire Star (Mass.)
Boston Commercial Gazette
Boston Patriot
Carolina Centinel (New Bern, N.C.)
City Gazette and Commercial Daily Advertiser (Charleston, S.C.)
Colored American (New York, N.Y.)
Connecticut Courant (Hartford, Conn.)
Connecticut Mirror (Hartford, Conn.)
Daily National Journal (Washington, D.C.)
Democratic Clarion & Tennessee Gazette (Nashville, Tenn.)
Edwardsville Spectator (Edwardsville, Ill.)
Evening Post
Farmer's Cabinet (Amherst, N.H.)
Hallowell Gazette (Hallowell, Maine)
Haverhill Gazette & Essex Patriot (Mass.)
Independent Chronicle & Boston Patriot
Kentucky Whig (Lexington, Ky.)
Liberator (Boston, Mass.)
Louisiana Advertiser (New Orleans, La.)
Louisiana Herald (Alexandria, La.)
Louisianan (Monroe, La.)
Louisiana State Gazette (New Orleans, La.)
Louisville Public Advertiser (Ky.)
Mississippi Republican (Natchez, Miss.)
Mississippi State Gazette (Natchez, Miss.)
Nashville Clarion (Tenn.)
Natchez Press (Miss.)
Natchez Republican (Miss.)
Natchitoches Courier (La.)
National Daily Journal (Washington, D.C.)
National Intelligencer (Washington, D.C.)
New Hampshire Patriot and State Gazette (Concord, N.H.)
New Hampshire Sentinel (Keene, N.H.)
New-Orleans Commercial Bulletin
New Orleans Halcyon and Literary Repository

New Orleans Picayune
Newport Mercury (R.I.)
New-York Gazette & General Advertiser (New York, N.Y.)
Niles' Weekly Register (Baltimore, Md.)
Norwich Courier (Conn.)
Ohio State Journal and Columbus Gazette
Orleans Gazette and Commercial Advertiser (New Orleans, La.)
Portsmouth Journal of Literature and Politics (N.H.)
Providence Patriot (R.I.)
Pittsfield Sun (Mass.)
Republican Star and General Advertiser (Easton, Md.)
Rhode-Island American and Providence Gazette
Richmond Enquirer (Va.)
Salem Gazette (Mass.)
Southern Patriot (Charleston, S.C.)
St. Louis Enquirer (Mo.)
Times, and Weekly Advertiser (Hartford, Conn.)
Vermont Chronicle (Bellows Falls, Vt.)
Vermont Gazette (Bennington, Vt.)
Vermont Watchman and State Gazette (Montpelier, Vt.)
Washington Gazette (Washington, D.C.)
Washington Review and Examiner (Washington, D.C.)
Washington Whig (Washington, D.C.)
Watch-Tower (Cooperstown, N.Y.)

TEXAS

Brazos Courier (Brazoria)
Civilian and Galveston Gazette (Galveston)
Morning Star (Houston)
National Vindicator (Washington)
Northern Standard (Clarksville)
Planter (Columbia)
Telegraph and Texas Register (Houston)
Texas National Register (Washington)
Texas Times (Galveston)
Weekly News (Galveston)

Digital Scholarship and Online Databases

Chronicling America: Historic American Newspapers, Library of Congress and the National Endowment for the Humanities, http://chroniclingamerica.loc.gov

The Handbook of Texas Online, Texas State Historical Association, http://tshaonline.org/handbook

Historical Census Browser, Geospatial Center, University of Virginia, http://mapserver.lib.virginia.edu

Mapping Texts: Visualizing Historical Newspapers, University of North Texas and Stanford University, http://mappingtexts.org

The Portal to Texas History, University of North Texas Libraries, http://texashistory.unt.edu

Texas Slavery Project, http://www.texasslaveryproject.org

Published Primary Sources

Adams, Ephraim Douglass, ed. *British Diplomatic Correspondence concerning the Republic of Texas, 1838–1846*. Austin: Texas State Historical Association, 1918.

Almonte, Juan N. *Almonte's Texas: Juan N. Almonte's 1834 Inspection, Secret Report and Role in the 1836 Campaign*. Edited by Jack Jackson and translated by John Wheat. Austin: Texas State Historical Association, 2003.

Anonymous. "Memoria de las cosas más notables que acaecieron en Bexar el año de 13 mandando el Tirano Arredondo, 1813," transcribed and translated by Raúl Coronado. In *A World Not to Come: A History of Latino Writing and Print Culture*, 417–33. Cambridge, Mass.: Harvard University Press, 2013.

Anonymous. *Texas in 1840, or the Emigrant's Guide to the New Republic.* New York: William W. Allen, 1840.

Arrillaga, Basilio José, ed. *Leyes, Decretos, Bandos, Reglamentos, Circulares y Providencias de los Supremos Poderes y Otras Autoridades de la República Mexicana*. Mexico: Imprenta de J. M. Fernández de Lara, 1834.

Austin, Stephen F. "Descriptions of Texas by Stephen F. Austin," edited by Eugene C. Barker. *Southwestern Historical Quarterly* 28 (October 1924): 98–121.

———. "Journal of Stephen F. Austin on His First Trip to Texas, 1821," edited by Eugene C. Barker. *Quarterly of the Texas State Historical Association* 7 (April 1904): 286–307.

Barker, Eugene C., ed. *Annual Report of the American Historical Association for the Year 1919: The Austin Papers*. 3 vols. Washington, D.C.: Government Printing Office, 1924, 1928; Austin: University of Texas Press, 1927.

———. "Minutes of the Ayuntamiento of San Felipe de Austin, 1828–1832." *Southwestern Historical Quarterly* 21–24 (January 1918–July 1920).

Barker, Nancy, ed. *The French Legation in Texas*. Vol. 1, *Recognition, Rupture, and Reconciliation*. Austin: Texas State Historical Association, 1971.

Barragan, José, ed. *Actas Constitucionales Mexicanas (1821–1824)*. Mexico: Instituto de Investigaciones Jurídicas. Universidad Nacional Autónoma de México, 1980.

Bentham, Jeremy. *Traté de legislation civile et pénale*. Paris: Pierre Dumont, 1802.

Berlandier, Jean Louis. *Journey to Mexico during the Years 1826 to 1834*. 2 vols. Austin: Texas State Historical Association, 1980.

Bollaert, William. *William Bollaert's Texas*. Edited by W. Eugene Hollon and Ruth Lapham Butler. Norman: University of Oklahoma Press, 1956.

Burnet, David G. "David G. Burnet's Letters Describing the Comanche Indians." Edited by Ernest Wallace. *West Texas Historical Association Year Book* 30 (October 1954): 115–40.

Claiborne, John F. H., ed. *Life and Correspondence of John A. Quitman, Major-General, U.S.A., and Governor of the State of Mississippi*. 2 vols. New York: Harper & Brothers, 1860.

Connor, Seymour, ed. *Texas Treasury Papers: Letters Received in the Treasury Department of the Republic of Texas, 1836–1846*. 4 vols. Austin: Texas State Archives and Library, 1955.

de la Teja, Jesús F., ed. *A Revolution Remembered: The Memoirs and Selected Correspondence of Juan N. Seguín*. Austin: State House Press, 1991.

Dublán, Manuel, and José María Lozano, eds. *Legislación Mexicana o Colección Completa de Disposiciones Legislativas Expedidas desde la Independencia de la República*. Mexico: Imprenta del Comercio, 1876.

Elguézabal, Juan Bautista. "A Description of Texas in 1803," edited and translated by Odie Faulk. *Southwestern Historical Quarterly* 66 (April 1963): 513–15.

Gammel, H. P. H., comp. *The Laws of Texas, 1822–1897*. 12 vols. Austin: Gammel Book Co., 1898.

Garrison, George, ed. *Diplomatic Correspondence of the Republic of Texas*. In the *Annual Report of the American Historical Association for the Year 1908*. 3 vols. Washington, D.C.: Government Printing Office, 1908–11.

Gulick, Charles, Jr., et al., eds. *The Papers of Mirabeau Buonapart Lamar*. 6 vols. 1920–27; reprint, Pemberton Press, 1968.

Gracy, David B., II, ed. *Establishing Austin's Colony: The First Book Printed in Texas, with the Laws, Orders and Contracts of Colonization*. Austin: Pemberton Press and Jenkins, 1970.

Gray, William Fairfax. *The Diary of William Fairfax Gray*. Edited by Paul Lack. Dallas: Southern Methodist University Press, 1997.

Harris, Dilue. "The Reminiscences of Mrs. Dilue Harris." *Quarterly of the Texas State Historical Association* 4 (1900–1901): 85–127, 155–89.

Holley, Mary Austin. *Mary Austin Holley: The Texas Diary, 1835–1838*. Edited by J. P. Bryan. Austin: University of Texas Press, 1965.

Jameson, John Franklin, ed. *Annual Report of the American Historical Association for the Year 1899: Volume II, Fourth Annual Report of the Historical Manuscripts Commission, Correspondence of John C. Calhoun*. Washington, D.C.: Government Printing Office, 1900.

Jenkins, John Holland. *Recollections of Early Texas: The Memoirs of John Holland Jenkins*. Edited by John H. Jenkins. 1958; reprint, University of Texas Press, 2008.

Jenkins, John H., ed. *The Papers of the Texas Revolution, 1835–1836*. 11 vols. Austin: Presidial Press, 1973.

Jones, Anson. *Memoranda and Official Correspondence Relating to the Republic of Texas, Its History and Annexation*. 1859; reprint, Rio Grande Press, 1966.

Kendall, George Wilkins. *Narrative of the Texan Santa Fe Expedition*. New York: Harper & Brothers, 1844.

Latham, Francis. *Travels in the Republic of Texas, 1842*. Edited by Gerald S. Pierce. Austin: Encino Press, 1971.

Leal, Carmela, trans. and ed. *Translations of Statistical and Census Reports of Texas, 1782–1836, and Sources Documenting the Black in Texas, 1603–1803*. 3 reels of microfilm. San Antonio: Institute of Texan Cultures, 1979.

Lundy, Benjamin. "The War in Texas, 1836." Reprinted in Lundy, *The Life, Travels and Opinions of Benjamin Lundy*. 1847; reprint, Augustus M. Kelley, 1971.

Martínez, Antonio. *Letters from Governor Antonio Martinez to the Viceroy Juan Ruíz de Apodaca*. Edited by Félix D. Almaráz Jr. San Antonio: Research Center for the Arts and Humanities, University of Texas at San Antonio, 1983.

———. *The Letters of Antonio Martinez: Last Spanish Governor of Texas, 1817–1822*. Edited and translated by Virginia H. Taylor. Austin: Texas State Library, 1957.

Mateos, Juan Antonio. *Historia Parlamentaria de los Congresos Mexicanos*. Mexico: J. V. Villada, 1877.

Maverick, Mary. *Memoirs of Mary A. Maverick: A Journal of Early Texas*. Edited by Rena Maverick Green and Maverick Fairchild Fisher. San Antonio: Maverick, 2005.

McLean, John R., and Malcolm D. McLean, eds. and trans. *Voices from the Goliad Frontier: Municipal Council Minutes, 1821–1835*. Dallas: William P. Clements Center for Southwestern Studies, Southern Methodist University, 2008.

McLean, Malcolm D., ed. *Papers Concerning Robertson's Colony in Texas*. 3 vols., Ft. Worth: Texas Christian University Press, 1974–76; 15 vols. plus intro. vol. Arlington: University of Texas at Arlington Press, 1977–93.

Menchaca, Antonio. *Memoirs of Antonio Menchaca*. Edited by Frederick C. Chabot. San Antonio: Yanaguana Society, 1937.

——— . *Recollections of a Tejano Life: Antonio Menchaca in Texas History*. Edited by Timothy Matovina and Jesús de la Teja. Austin: University of Texas Press, 2013.

Mier y Terán, Manuel de. *Texas by Terán: The Diary Kept by General Manuel de Mier y Terán on His 1828 Inspection of Texas*. Edited by Jack Jackson and translated by John Wheat. Austin: University of Texas Press, 2000.

Navarro, José Antonio. *Defending Mexican Valor in Texas: José Antonio Navarro's Historical Writings, 1852–1857*. Edited by David McDonald and Timothy Matovina. Abilene, Tex.: State House Press, 1995.

Padilla, Juan Antonio. "Report on the Barbarous Indians of the Province of Texas," December 27, 1819. In Mattie Hatcher, trans., "Texas in 1820." *Southwestern Historical Quarterly* 23 (July 1919): 47–60.

Proceedings of the General Anti-slavery Convention Called by the Committee of the British and Foreign Anti-slavery Society and Held in London from Tuesday, June 13th, to Tuesday, June 20th, 1843. London: John Snow, 1843.

Rowland, Dunbar, ed. *Official Letter Books of W. C. C. Claiborne, 1801–1816*. 6 vols. Jackson: Mississippi State Department of Archives and History, 1917.

Sánchez, José María. "A Trip to Texas in 1828." Translated by Carlos Castañeda. *Southwestern Historical Quarterly* 29 (April 1926): 249–88.

Scoble, John. *Texas: Its Claims to Be Recognized as an Independent Power by Great Britain; Examined in a Series of Letters*. London: Harvey and Darton, 1839.

Sheridan, Francis C. *Galveston Island, or A Few Months Off the Coast of Texas: The Journal of Francis C. Sheridan, 1839–1840*. Edited by Willis W. Pratt. Austin: University of Texas Press, 1954.

Smithwick, Noah. *The Evolution of a State, or Recollections of Old Texas Days*. 1900; reprint, University of Texas Press, 1994.

Stevens, Kenneth R., ed. *The Texas Legation Papers, 1836–1845*. Ft. Worth: Texas Christian University Press, 2012.

Tornel y Mendívil, José María. *Breve Reseña Histórica de los Acontecimientos más Notables de la Nación Mexicana*. 1852; reprint, Mexico City, 1985.

Walker, Robert. *Letter of Mr. Walker, of Mississippi, Relative to the Annexation of Texas*. Washington, D.C.: Washington Globe, 1844.

Wallace, Ernest, David M. Vigness, and George B. Ward, eds. *Documents of Texas History*. Austin: Texas State Historical Association, 2002.

Ward, Henry. *Mexico in 1827.* London: Henry Colburn, 1829.

Wilbarger, J. W. *Indian Depredations in Texas.* 1889; reprint, Eakin Press, 1985.

Williams, Amelia, and Eugene Barker, eds. *The Writings of Sam Houston, 1813–1863.* 8 vols. Austin: University of Texas Press, 1938–43.

Wilson, Clyde, ed. *The Papers of John C. Calhoun.* Columbia: University of South Carolina Press, 1988.

Yoakum, Henderson. *History of Texas from Its First Settlement in 1685 to Its Annexation to the United States in 1846.* New York: Redfield, 1855.

Weber, David J., ed. *Troubles in Texas, 1832: A Tejano Viewpoint from San Antonio with a Translation and Facsimile.* Dallas: Wind River Press for the DeGolyer Library of Southern Methodist University, 1983.

Secondary Sources

Adams, Ephraim Douglass. *British Interests and Activities in Texas, 1838–1846.* Baltimore: Johns Hopkins University Press, 1910.

Almaráz, Félix, Jr. *Tragic Cavalier: Governor Manuel Salcedo of Texas, 1808–1813.* College Station: Texas A&M University Press, 1971.

Anderson, Gary Clayton. *The Conquest of Texas: Ethnic Cleansing in the Promised Land, 1820–1875.* Norman: University of Oklahoma Press, 2005.

———. *The Indian Southwest, 1580–1830: Ethnogenesis and Reinvention.* Norman: University of Oklahoma Press, 1999.

Anna, Timothy E. *Forging Mexico, 1821–1835.* Lincoln: University of Nebraska Press, 1998.

Barker, Eugene C. "The African Slave Trade in Texas." *Quarterly of the Texas State Historical Association* 6 (October 1902): 145–58.

———. "The Government of Austin's Colony, 1821–1831." *Southwestern Historical Quarterly* 21 (January 1918): 223–52.

———. "The Influence of Slavery in the Colonization of Texas." *Mississippi Valley Historical Review* 11 (June 1924): 3–36.

———. *The Life of Stephen F. Austin, Founder of Texas, 1793–1836: A Chapter in the Westward Movement of the Anglo-American People.* 1925; reprint, New York: Da Capo Press, 1968.

———. "Notes on the Colonization of Texas." *Mississippi Valley Historical Review* 10 (September 1923): 141–52.

Barr, Alwyn. *Texans in Revolt: The Battle for San Antonio, 1835.* Austin: University of Texas Press, 1990.

Barr, Juliana. *Peace Came in the Form of a Woman: Indians and Spaniards in the Texas Borderlands.* Chapel Hill: University of North Carolina Press, 2007.

Bauer, K. Jack. *The Mexican War, 1846–1848.* 1974; reprint, Bison Book, 1992.

Beckert, Sven. "Emancipation and Empire: Reconstructing the Worldwide Web of Cotton Production in the Age of the American Civil War." *American Historical Review* 109 (December 2004): 1405–38.

———. *Empire of Cotton: A Global History.* New York: Knopf, 2014.

Beltrán, Gonzalo Aguirre. *La Población Negra en México.* 1946; reprint, Mexico City: Fondo de Cultural Económica, 1972.

Berlin, Ira. *Generations of Captivity: A History of African-American Slaves.* Cambridge, Mass.: Harvard University Press, 2003.

Bertleth, Rosa Groce. "Jared Ellison Groce." *Southwestern Historical Quarterly* 20 (April 1917): 358–61.

Bevill, James. *The Paper Republic: The Struggle for Money, Credit and the Independence of the Republic of Texas.* Houston: Bright Sky Press, 2009.

Blackburn, Robin. *The American Crucible: Slavery, Emancipation and Human Rights.* London: Verso, 2011.

——— . *The Making of New World Slavery: From the Baroque to the Modern, 1492- 1800.* London: Verso, 1997.

Blyth, Lance. "Fugitives from Servitude: American Deserters and Runaway Slaves in Spanish Nacogdoches, 1803–1808." *East Texas Historical Journal* 38 (2000): 3–14.

Bolton, Herbert E. *Guide to Materials for the History of the United States in the Principal Archives of Mexico.* Washington, D.C.: Carnegie Institution of Washington, 1913.

Brack, Gene. *Mexico Views Manifest Destiny, 1821–1846: An Essay on the Origins of the Mexican War.* Albuquerque: University of New Mexico Press, 1975.

Bradley, Edward. "Forgotten Filibusters: Private Hostile Expeditions from the United States into Spanish Texas, 1812–1821." Ph.D. diss., University of Illinois at Urbana-Champaign, 1999.

Brady, Kevin. "Unspoken Words: James Monroe's Involvement in the Magee-Gutierrez Filibuster." *East Texas Historical Journal* 45 (2007): 58–68.

Brice, Donaly E. *The Great Comanche Raid: Boldest Indian Attack of the Republic of Texas.* Austin: Eakin Press, 1987.

Britten, Thomas. *The Lipan Apaches: People of Wind and Lightning.* Albuquerque: University of New Mexico Press, 2009.

Brown, Christopher Leslie. *Moral Capital: Foundations of British Abolitionism.* Chapel Hill: University of North Carolina Press, 2006.

Bruchey, Stuart. *Cotton and the Growth of the American Economy: 1790–1860.* New York: Harcourt, 1967.

Bugbee, Lester. "Slavery in Early Texas." *Political Science Quarterly* 13 (September 1898): 389–412; 14 (December 1898): 648–68.

——— . "Stephen F. Austin's Views on Slavery in Early Texas." *Texas Magazine* 13 (May 1897): 405–8.

Campbell, Randolph B. *An Empire for Slavery: The Peculiar Institution in Texas, 1821–1865.* Baton Rouge: Louisiana State University Press, 1989.

——— . *Gone to Texas: A History of the Lone Star State.* 2nd ed. New York: Oxford University Press, 2012.

Cantrell, Gregg. *Stephen F. Austin: Empresario of Texas.* New Haven: Yale University Press, 1999.

Carrigan, William. *The Making of a Lynching Culture: Violence and Vigilantism in Central Texas, 1836–1916.* Chicago: University of Illinois Press, 2004.

——— . "Slavery on the Frontier: The Peculiar Institution in Central Texas." *Slavery and Abolition* 20 (August 1999): 63–86.

Castañeda, Carlos E. *Our Catholic Heritage in Texas, 1519–1936.* 7 vols. 1950; reprint, Arno Press, 1976.

Chipman, Donald E., and Harriett Denise Joseph. *Spanish Texas 1519–1821*. Rev. ed. Austin: University of Texas Press, 2010.

Coronado, Raúl. *A World Not to Come: A History of Latino Writing and Print Culture.* Cambridge, Mass.: Harvard University Press, 2013.

Costeloe, Michael. *The Central Republic in Mexico, 1835–1846:* Hombres de Bien *in the Age of Santa Anna*. Cambridge: Cambridge University Press, 1993.

Crane, Robert E. L., Jr. "The Administration of the Customs Service of the Republic of Texas." M.A. thesis, University of Texas, 1939.

Crapol, Edward. *John Tyler: The Accidental President*. Chapel Hill: University of North Carolina Press, 2006.

Creighton, James A. *A Narrative History of Brazoria County*. Waco, Tex.: Texian Press, 1975.

Crimm, Ana Carolina Castillo. *De León: A Tejano Family History*. Austin: University of Texas Press, 2003.

Crisp, James. "Anglo-Texan Attitudes toward the Mexican, 1821–1845." Ph.D. diss., Yale University, 1976.

Cummins, Light Townsend. *Emily Austin of Texas, 1795–1851*. Ft. Worth: Texas Christian University Press, 2009.

Curlee, Abigail. "A Study of Texas Slave Plantations, 1822 to 1865." Ph.D. diss., University of Texas, 1932.

Davis, David Brion. *Inhuman Bondage: The Rise and Fall of Slavery in the New World*. New York: Oxford University Press, 2006.

Davis, Ralph. *The Industrial Revolution and British Overseas Trade*. Atlantic Highlands, N. J.: Humanities Press, 1979.

Davis, William C. *The Pirates Laffite: The Treacherous World of the Corsairs of the Gulf.* New York: Harcourt, 2005.

De la Teja, Jesús F. "The Colonization and Independence of Texas: A Tejano Perspective." In *Myths, Misdeeds, and Misunderstandings: The Roots of Conflict in U.S.-Mexican Relations*, edited by Jaime E. Rodríguez O. and Kathryn Vincent. Wilmington, Del.: Scholarly Resources, 1997.

———. *San Antonio de Béxar: A Community on New Spain's Northern Frontier*. Albuquerque: University of New Mexico Press, 1995.

DeLay, Brian. *War of a Thousand Deserts: Indian Raids and the U. S.-Mexican War.* New Haven: Yale University Press, 2008.

Deyle, Stephen. *Carry Me Back: The Domestic Slave Trade in American Life*. New York: Oxford University Press, 2005.

Downs, Fane. "The Administration of Antonio Martinez: Last Spanish Governor of Texas, 1817–1822." M.A. thesis, Texas Tech University, 1963.

Edwards, Michael. *The Growth of the British Cotton Trade, 1780–1815*. New York: Augustus Kelley, 1967.

Eisenhower, John S. D. *So Far from God: The U.S. War with Mexico, 1846–1848*. 1989; reprint, University of Oklahoma Press, 2000.

Elliot, J. H. *Empires of the Atlantic World: Britain and Spain in America, 1492–1830.* New Haven: Yale University Press, 2006.

Ellison, Thomas. *The Cotton Trade of Great Britain*. London, 1886.

Everett, Dianna. *The Texas Cherokees: A People between Two Fires, 1819–1840*. Norman: University of Oklahoma Press, 1990.

Fiege, Mark. *The Republic of Nature: An Environmental History of the United States.* Seattle: University of Washington Press, 2012.

Fogel, Robert, and Stanley Engerman. *Time on the Cross: The Economics of American Negro Slavery.* New York: Little, Brown, 1974.

Foley, Neil. *The White Scourge: Mexicans, Blacks, and Poor Whites in Texas Cotton Culture.* Berkeley: University of California Press, 1997.

Foner, Eric. *Reconstruction: America's Unfinished Revolution, 1863–1877.* New York: Harper, 1988.

Fowler, Will. "Joseph Welch: A British *Santanista* (Mexico, 1832)." *Journal of Latin American Studies* 36 (February 2004): 29–56.

———. *Mexico in the Age of Proposals, 1821–1853.* Westport, Conn.: Greenwood Press, 1998.

———. *Santa Anna of Mexico.* Lincoln: University of Nebraska Press, 2007.

———. *Tornel and Santa Anna: The Writer and the Caudillo, Mexico, 1795–1853.* Westport, Conn.: Greenwood Press, 2000.

Freehling, William. *The Reintegration of American History: Slavery and the Civil War.* New York: Oxford University Press, 1994.

———. *The Road to Disunion.* Vol. 1, *Secessionists at Bay, 1776–1854.* New York: Oxford University Press, 1990.

Genovese, Eugene. *Roll Jordan Roll: The World the Slaves Made.* New York: Random House, 1974.

Gournay, Luke. *Texas Boundaries: Evolution of the State's Counties.* College Station: Texas A&M University Press, 1995.

Green, Stanley. *The Mexican Republic: The First Decade, 1823–1832.* Pittsburgh: University of Pittsburgh Press, 1987.

Hacker, J. David. "A Census-Based Count of the Civil War Dead." *Civil War History* 57 (December 2011): 307–48.

Hale, Charles. *Mexican Liberalism in the Age of Mora, 1821–1853.* New Haven: Yale University Press, 1968.

Haley, James. *Sam Houston.* Norman: University of Oklahoma Press, 2002.

Hämäläinen, Pekka. *The Comanche Empire.* New Haven: Yale University Press, 2008.

———. "Into the Mainstream: The Emergence of a New Texas Indian History." In *Beyond Texas through Time: Breaking Away from Past Interpretations,* edited by Walter Buenger and Arnoldo De León. College Station: Texas A&M University Press, 2011.

———. "The Politics of Grass: European Expansion, Ecological Change, and Indigenous Power in the Southwest Borderlands." *William and Mary Quarterly* 67 (April 2010): 173–208.

Hammond, John Craig. *Slavery, Freedom and Expansion in the Early American West.* Charlottesville: University of Virginia Press, 2007.

Hammond, John Craig, and Matthew Mason, eds. *Contesting Slavery: The Politics of Bondage and Freedom in the New American Nation.* Charlottesville: University of Virginia Press, 2011.

Hardin, Stephen. *Texian Iliad: A Military History of the Texas Revolution.* Austin: University of Texas Press, 1994.

———. *Texian Macabre: The Melancholy Tale of a Hanging in Early Houston.* Abilene, Tex.: State House Press, 2007.

Harrell, Eugene. "Vicente Guerrero and the Birth of Modern Mexico, 1821–1831." Ph.D. diss., Tulane University, 1976.

Harris, Charles. *A Mexican Family Empire: The* Latifundio *of the Sánchez Navarros, 1765–1867.* Austin: University of Texas Press, 1975.

Harris, Helen. "The Public Life of Juan Nepomuceno Almonte." Ph.D. diss., University of Texas, 1935.

Harrison, James. "The Failure of Spain in East Texas: The Occupation and Abandonment of Nacogdoches, 1779–1821." Ph.D. diss., University of Nebraska, 1980.

Haynes, Robert. *The Mississippi Territory and the Southwest Frontier, 1795–1817.* Lexington: University Press of Kentucky, 2010.

Haynes, Sam W. *Soldiers of Misfortune: The Somervell and Mier Expeditions.* Austin: University of Texas Press, 1990.

——— . *Unfinished Revolution: The Early American Republic in a British World.* Charlottesville: University of Virginia Press, 2010.

Henderson, Mary Virginia. "Minor Empresario Contracts for the Colonization of Texas, 1825–1834." *Southwestern Historical Quarterly* 31 (April 1928): 295–324.

Henderson, Timothy. *A Glorious Defeat: Mexico and Its War with the United States.* New York: Hill and Wang, 2007.

——— . *The Mexican Wars for Independence.* New York: Hill and Wang, 2009.

Henson, Margaret S. *Anahuac in 1832: The Cradle of the Texas Revolution.* Anahuac, Tex.: Fort Anahuac Committee of the Chambers County Historical Commission, 1982.

——— . *Juan Davis Bradburn: A Reappraisal of the Mexican Commander of Anahuac.* College Station: Texas A&M University Press, 1982.

——— . "Politics and the Treatment of the Mexican Prisoners after the Battle of San Jacinto." *Southwestern Historical Quarterly* 94 (October 1990): 189–230.

——— . *Samuel May Williams: Early Texas Entrepreneur.* College Station: Texas A&M University Press, 1976.

Hietala, Thomas. *Manifest Design: American Exceptionalism and Empire.* Ithaca: Cornell University Press, 1985.

Hogan, William Ransom. *The Texas Republic: A Social and Economic History.* 1946; reprint, Texas State Historical Association, 2006.

Howe, Daniel Walker. *What Hath God Wrought: The Transformation of America, 1815–1848.* New York: Oxford University Press, 2007.

Howren, Alleine. "Causes and Origins of the Decree of April 6, 1830." *Southwestern Historical Quarterly* 16 (April 1913): 378–422.

Jackson, Jack. *Indian Agent: Peter Ellis Bean in Mexican Texas.* College Station: Texas A&M University Press, 2005.

——— . *Los Mesteños: Spanish Ranching in Texas, 1721–1821.* College Station: Texas A&M University Press, 1986.

Janicek, Ricki. "The Development of Early Mexican Land Policy: Coahuila and Texas, 1810–1825." Ph.D. diss., Tulane University, 1985.

Jenkins, John, and Kenneth Kesselus. *Edward Burleson: Texas Frontier Leader.* Austin: Jenkins, 1990.

Johnson, Walter. *River of Dark Dreams: Slavery and Empire in the Cotton Kingdom.* Cambridge, Mass.: Harvard University Press, 2013.

———. *Soul by Soul: Life Inside the Antebellum Slave Market.* Cambridge, Mass.: Harvard University Press, 1999.

Jones, C. Allan. *Texas Roots: Agriculture and Rural Life before the Civil War.* College Station: Texas A&M University Press, 2005.

Jones, Marie Beth. *Peach Point Plantation: The First 150 Years.* Waco, Tex.: Texian Press, 1982.

Jordan, Jonathan. *Lone Star Navy: Texas, the Fight for the Gulf of Mexico, and the Shaping of the American West.* Washington, D.C.: Potomac Books, 2006.

Kavanagh, Thomas W. *Comanche Political History: An Ethnohistorical Perspective, 1706–1875.* Lincoln: University of Nebraska Press, 1996.

Kearney, James. *Nassau Plantation: The Evolution of a Texas German Slave Plantation.* Denton: University of North Texas Press, 2010.

Kelley, Sean. "Blackbirders and Bozales: African-Born Slaves on the Lower Brazos River of Texas in the Nineteenth Century." *Civil War History* 54 (December 2008): 406–23.

———. "'Mexico in His Head': Slavery and the Texas-Mexico Border, 1810–1860." *Journal of Social History* 37 (March 2004): 709–23.

———. *Los Brazos de Dios: A Plantation Society in the Texas Borderlands, 1821–1865.* Baton Rouge: Louisiana State University Press, 2010.

Knight, Alan. "Mexican Peonage: What Was It and Why Was It?" *Journal of Latin American Studies* 18 (May 1986): 41–74.

Kornblith, Gary. "Rethinking the Coming of the Civil War: A Counterfactual Exercise." *Journal of American History* 90 (June 2003): 76–105.

Lack, Paul. "The Córdova Revolt." In *Tejano Journey, 1770–1850*, edited by Gerald E. Poyo. Austin: University of Texas Press, 1996.

———. "In the Long Shadow of Eugene C. Barker: The Revolution and the Republic." In *Texas through Time*, edited by Walter Buenger and Robert Calvert. College Station: Texas A&M University Press, 1991.

———. "Slavery and the Texas Revolution." *Southwestern Historical Quarterly* 89 (October 1985): 181–202.

———. *The Texas Revolutionary Experience: A Political and Social History, 1835–1836.* College Station: Texas A&M University Press, 1992.

Lathrop, Barnes F. *Migration into East Texas, 1835–1860: A Study from the United States Census.* Austin: Texas State Historical Association, 1949.

Mason, Matthew. *Slavery and Politics in the Early American Republic.* Chapel Hill: University of North Carolina Press, 2006.

May, Robert. *John A. Quitman: Old South Crusader.* Baton Rouge: Louisiana State University Press, 1985.

Meacham, Tina. "The Population of Spanish and Mexican Texas, 1716–1836." Ph.D. diss., University of Texas, 2000.

Merk, Frederick. *Manifest Destiny and Mission in American History.* New York: Knopf, 1963.

———. *Slavery and the Annexation of Texas.* New York: Knopf, 1972.

McDaniel, W. Caleb. *The Problem of Democracy in the Age of Slavery: Garrisonian Abolitionists and Transatlantic Reform.* Baton Rouge: Louisiana State University Press, 2013.

McDonald, David. *José Antonio Navarro: In Search of the American Dream in Nineteenth-Century Texas.* Denton: Texas State Historical Association Press, 2010.

———. "Juan Martín de Veramendi: Tejano Political and Business Leader." In *Tejano*

Leadership in Mexican and Revolutionary Texas, edited by Jesús F. de la Teja. College Station: Texas A&M University Press, 2010.

McElhannon, Joseph Carl. "Imperial Mexico and Texas, 1821–1823." *Southwestern Historical Quarterly* 53 (October 1949): 117–50.

McGrane, Reginald. *The Panic of 1837: Some Financial Problems of the Jacksonian Era.* Chicago: University of Chicago Press, 1924.

McKnight, Joseph. "Stephen F. Austin's Legalistic Concerns." *Southwestern Historical Quarterly* 89 (January 1986): 247–56.

McLemore, Laura Lyons. *Inventing Texas: Early Historians of the Lone Star State.* College Station: Texas A&M University Press, 2004.

McPherson, James. *Battle Cry of Freedom: The Civil War Era.* New York: Oxford University Press, 1988.

Miller, Edmund Thornton. "A Financial History of Texas." *Bulletin of the University of Texas* 37 (July 1916): iv–444.

Miller, Edward. *New Orleans and the Texas Revolution.* College Station: Texas A&M University Press, 2004.

Moore, John Hebron. *The Emergence of the Cotton Kingdom in the Old Southwest: Mississippi, 1770–1860.* Baton Rouge: Louisiana State University Press, 1988.

Morrison, Michael. *Slavery and the American West: The Eclipse of Manifest Destiny and the Coming of the Civil War.* Chapel Hill: University of North Carolina Press, 1997.

Morton, Ohland. *Terán and Texas: A Chapter in Texas-Mexican Relations.* Austin: Texas State Historical Association, 1948.

Nance, Joseph. *Attack and Counterattack: The Texas-Mexican Frontier, 1842.* Austin: University of Texas Press, 1964.

Narrett, David. "A Choice of Destiny: Immigration Policy, Slavery, and the Annexation of Texas." *Southwestern Historical Quarterly* 100 (January 1997): 271–304.

North, Douglass. *The Economic Growth of the United States, 1790–1860.* New York: W. W. Norton, 1961.

Oakes, James. *The Ruling Race: A History of American Slaveholders.* 1982; reprint W. W. Norton, 1998.

Owsley, Frank. *King Cotton Diplomacy: Foreign Relations of the Confederate States of America.* Chicago: University of Chicago Press, 1931.

Parsons, Edmund Morris. "The Fredonian Rebellion." *Texana* 5 (Spring 1967): 11–52.

Pletcher, David. *The Diplomacy of Annexation: Texas, Oregon, and the Mexican War.* Columbia: University of Missouri Press, 1973.

Potter, David. *The Impending Crisis: America before the Civil War, 1848–1861.* New York: Harper, 1976.

Puryear, Pamela Ashworth, and Nath Winfield Jr. *Sandbars and Sternwheelers: Steam Navigation on the Brazos.* College Station: Texas A&M University Press, 1976.

Ramos, Raúl. *Beyond the Alamo: Forging Mexican Ethnicity in San Antonio, 1821–1861.* Chapel Hill: University of North Carolina Press, 2008.

———. "Finding the Balance: Bexar in Mexican/Indian Relations." In *Continental Crossroads: Remapping U.S.-Mexico Borderlands History*, edited by Elliott Young and Samuel Truett. Durham: Duke University Press, 2004.

———. "From Norteño to Tejano: The Roots of Borderlands Ethnicity, Nationalism, and Political Identity in Bexar, 1811–1861." Ph.D. diss., Yale University, 1999.

Reséndez, Andrés. *Changing National Identities at the Frontier: Texas and New Mexico, 1800–1850*. Cambridge: Cambridge University Press, 2005.

———. "National Identity on a Shifting Border: Texas and New Mexico in the Age of Transition, 1821–1848." *Journal of American History* 86 (September 1999): 668–88.

———. "Ramón Músquiz: The Ultimate Insider." In *Tejano Leadership in Mexican and Revolutionary Texas*, edited by Jesús F. de la Teja. College Station: Texas A&M University Press, 2010.

Robles, Vito Alessio. *Coahuila y Texas: Desde la Consumacion de la Independencia Hasta el Tratado de Paz de Guadalupe Hidalgo*. 2 vols. Mexico City, 1945.

Rothman, Adam. *Slave Country: American Expansion and the Origins of the Deep South*. Cambridge, Mass.: Harvard University Press, 2005.

Ruiz y Sandova, Alberto. *El Algodón en México*. Mexico City, 1884.

Santoni, Pedro. *Mexicans at Arms: Puro Federalists and the Politics of War, 1845–1848*. Ft. Worth: Texas Christian University Press, 1996.

Schliz, Thomas Frank. "People of the Cross Timbers: A History of the Tonkawa Indians." Ph.D. diss., Texas Christian University, 1983.

Schmitz, Joseph. *Texan Statecraft, 1836–1845*. San Antonio: Naylor, 1941.

Schoen, Brian. *The Fragile Fabric of Union: Cotton, Federal Politics, and the Global Origins of the Civil War*. Baltimore: The Johns Hopkins University Press, 2009.

Schroeder, John. *Mr. Polk's War: American Opposition and Dissent, 1846–1848*. Madison: University of Wisconsin Press, 1973.

Schwartz, Rosalie. *Across the Rio to Freedom: U.S. Negroes in Mexico*. El Paso: Texas Western Press, 1974.

Siegel, Stanley. *The Poet President of Texas: The Life of Mirabeau B. Lamar, President of the Republic of Texas*. Austin: Pemberton Press, 1977.

———. *A Political History of the Texas Republic, 1836–1845*. Austin: University of Texas Press, 1956.

Silbey, Joel. *Storm over Texas: The Annexation Controversy and the Road to Civil War*. New York: Oxford University Press, 2005.

Silverthorne, Elizabeth. *Plantation Life in Texas*. College Station: Texas A&M University, 1986.

Smith, F. Todd. *From Dominance to Disappearance: The Indians of Texas and the Near Southwest, 1786–1859*. Lincoln: University of Nebraska Press, 2005.

Smith, Justin. *The War with Mexico*. New York: Macmillan, 1919.

Soto, Miguel. "La disputa entre Monclova y Saltillo y la independencia de Texas," In *La Independecia y el Problema de Texas: Dos Eventos en Coahuila*, edited by María Elena Santoscoy, Arturo Villarreal, and Miguel Soto. Saltillo: Municipal Archive of Saltillo, 1997.

Stagg, J. C. A. "The Madison Administration and Mexico: Reinterpreting the Gutiérrez-Magee Raid of 1812–1813." *William and Mary Quarterly* 59 (April 2002): 449–80.

Stern, Madeleine. "Stephen Pearl Andrews, Abolitionist, and the Annexation of Texas." *Southwestern Historical Quarterly* 67 (1964): 491–523.

Stuntz, Jean. *Hers, His, and Theirs: Community and Property Law in Spain and Early Texas*. Lubbock: Texas Tech University Press, 2005.

Taylor, Orville. *Negro Slavery in Arkansas*. 1958; reprint, University of Arkansas Press, 2000.

Taylor, Quintard. *In Search of the Racial Frontier: African Americans in the American West, 1528–1990*. New York: W. W. Norton, 1998.

Tenenbaum, Barbara. *The Politics of Penury: Debts and Taxes in Mexico, 1821–1856.* Albuquerque: University of New Mexico Press, 1986.

Tijerina, Andrés. *Tejanos and Texas under the Mexican Flag, 1821–1836.* College Station: Texas A&M University Press, 1994.

Tjarks, Alicia. "Comparative Demographic Analysis of Texas, 1777–1793." *Southwestern Historical Quarterly* 77 (January 1974): 291–338.

Torget, Andrew J. "Cotton Empire: Slavery and the Texas Borderlands, 1820–1837," Ph.D. diss., University of Virginia, 2009.

———. "Stephen F. Austin's Views on Slavery in Early Texas," In *This Corner of Canaan: Essays on Texas in Honor of Randolph B. Campbell*, edited by Richard McCaslin, Donald Chipman, and Andrew J. Torget. Denton: University of North Texas Press, 2013.

Townes, J. Edward. "Invisible Lines: The Life and Death of a Borderland." Ph.D. diss., Texas Christian University, 2008.

Tyler, Ron. "Fugitive Slaves in Mexico." *Journal of Negro History* 57 (January 1972): 1–12.

Unser, Daniel H., Jr. "American Indians and the Cotton Frontier: Changing Economic Relations with Citizens and Slaves in the Mississippi Territory." *Journal of American History* 72 (September 1985): 297–317.

Van Wagenen, Michael. *Remembering the Forgotten War: The Enduring Legacies of the U.S.-Mexican War.* Amherst: University of Massachusetts Press, 2012.

Van Young, Eric. *The Other Rebellion: Popular Violence, Ideology, and the Mexican Struggle for Independence, 1810–1821.* Stanford: Stanford University Press, 2001.

Vázquez, Josefina Zoraida. "The Colonization and Loss of Texas: A Mexican Perspective." In *Myths, Misdeeds, and Misunderstandings: The Roots of Conflict in U.S.-Mexican Relations*, edited by Jaime E. Rodríguez O. and Kathryn Vincent. Wilmington, Del.: Scholarly Resources, 1997.

———. "The Texas Question in Mexican Politics, 1836–1845." *Southwestern Historical Quarterly* 89 (January 1986): 309–44.

Vincent, Theodore. *The Legacy of Vicente Guerrero, Mexico's First Black Indian President.* Gainesville: University Press of Florida, 2001.

Walther, Eric H. *The Fire-Eaters.* Baton Rouge: Louisiana State University Press, 1992.

Warren, Harris Gaylord. *The Sword Was Their Passport: A History of Filibustering in the Mexican Revolution.* 1943; reprint, Kennikat Press, 1972.

Watkins, James. *King Cotton: A Historical and Statistical Review, 1790–1908.* New York: Watkins and Sons, 1908.

Weber, David J. *Bárbaros: Spaniards and Their Savages in the Age of Enlightenment.* New Haven: Yale University Press, 2005.

———. *The Mexican Frontier, 1821–1846: The American Southwest under Mexico.* Albuquerque: University of New Mexico Press, 1982.

———. *The Spanish Frontier in North America.* New Haven: Yale University Press, 1992.

Weinberg, Albert. *Manifest Destiny: A Study of Nationalist Expansionism in American History.* Baltimore: The Johns Hopkins University Press, 1935.

Wilkins, Frederick. *The Highly Irregular Irregulars: Texas Rangers in the Mexican War.* Austin: Eakin Press, 1990.

Wilson, Maurine T., and Jack Jackson. *Philip Nolan and Texas: Expeditions to the Unknown Land, 1791–1801.* Waco, Tex.: Texian Press, 1987.

Winders, Richard Bruce. *Crisis in the Southwest: The United States, Mexico, and the Struggle over Texas*. Wilmington, Del.: Scholarly Resources, 2002.

———. *Mr. Polk's Army: The American Military Experience in the Mexican War*. College Station: Texas A&M University Press, 1997.

Woodman, Harold. *King Cotton and His Retainers: Financing and Marketing the Cotton Crop of the South, 1800–1925*. 1968; reprint, University of South Carolina Press, 1990.

Wooten, Dudley, ed. *A Comprehensive History of Texas, 1685–1897*. 2 vols. 1898; reprint, Austin: Texas State Historical Association, 1986.

Wright, Robert. "Father Refugio de la Garza: Controverted Religious Leader." In *Tejano Leadership in Mexican and Revolutionary Texas*, edited by Jesús F. de la Teja. College Station: Texas A&M University Press, 2010.

INDEX

Abell, Hammet & Co., 197–98
Aberdeen, Lord, 235, 237–40, 241–42
Abolitionism. *See* Antislavery
Adams, John Quincy, 186, 206, 226
Adams-Onís Treaty, 45
Agrandar, Francisco, 74
Alabama, 4, 23, 35–36, 43, 45, 51, 64–65, 68,
    82, 84–85, 87–88, 90, 92, 95, 129, 154, 155,
    157, 158, 188, 195, 216, 221, 234, 258
Alabamas (Indians), 38
Alamán, Lucas, 151, 153, 155, 156, 175
Alamo. *See* Texas Revolution
Allen, Augustus, 193, 196
Allen, John, 193, 196
Allende, Coahuila, 145
Almonte, Juan Nepomuceno, 158–60, 254
Ambassador (ship), 200–202
Anahuac, Tex., 162
Andrés (enslaved man), 44
Andrews, Stephen Pearl, 238, 240, 243
Annexation, 5, 8, 184–88, 202, 204–6, 208,
    221, 235, 239, 244–54, 255; rejected by
    U.S., 191, 251; support within Republic of
    Texas, 246–49, 252–54, 261; opposition
    within Republic of Texas, 247–48, 253;
    accepted by U.S., 251–52; terms of, 252;
    approved by Republic of Texas, 254
Antislavery: and Great Britain, 4, 7–8, 71,
    107, 111, 128, 170, 182, 188–91, 205, 210,
    212–15, 221, 226, 236–44, 237–45, 260–61;
    and the United States, 4–5, 7–8, 43, 71,
    107–8, 116, 182, 186, 189, 205–8, 209,
    221, 226, 239, 260–61; and Mexico, 8, 10,
    14, 60–61, 72–75, 77–79, 90–92, 95, 138,
    142–50, 152, 153, 169, 172–73, 175, 179, 190,
    195, 211, 215–16, 225, 259, 304 (n. 25); and
    Coahuila, Mexico, 97–98, 100–105, 108–
    13, 116–20, 127–29, 131, 134–35, 142, 163,
    175–76, 259. *See also* Free blacks; Mexican
    national government; U.S. government;
    World Antislavery Convention

Antonia, María (enslaved woman), 145
Apaches (Lipan), 12, 20, 25–27, 32, 38, 40, 203
Aranda, José Mariano, 74–75
Arciniega, José Miguel de, 131
Arizpe, Miguel Ramos, 80
Arkansas, 68, 85, 92, 95, 106
Arkansas Gazette, 63, 91–92, 105–8
Armijo, Manuel, 214
Arredondo, José Joaquín de, 31–34, 37, 39,
    40, 46, 50–51
Article 13. *See* Constitution of 1827
Aury, Louis Michel, 42–43
Austin, James "Brown," 103, 105–6, 108–10,
    112, 152
Austin, Moses, 2–3, 6, 8, 15, 48–52, 57–59
Austin, Stephen F., 59–66, 72, 80, 81, 84–89,
    90–91, 92–96, 97–98, 100, 102, 104–5,
    108, 114–15, 118, 120–22, 125, 128–34,
    141–42, 145, 146, 152–53, 157, 158, 161, 172,
    183–85, 256, 266; focus on cotton, 59,
    64–65, 85–89, 126–27, 142; in Mexico
    City, 66, 69, 72–75, 164–65; arguing for
    slavery, 72–75, 78–89, 90, 95, 102–3, 110,
    115, 117, 127, 128, 155, 156; arguing against
    slavery, 153–55. *See also* Austin's colony
Austin, Tex., 211, 213–14, 219, 232
Austin's colony, 62–66, 72, 76, 78–79,
    81–89, 90–94, 98, 104–5, 108, 118, 121,
    125, 128–30, 135–36, 138–39, 141–42, 147,
    149, 150, 151–57, 158–61, 162–66, 171–73,
    174–75, 295 (n. 63); fears of emancipa-
    tion within, 92, 104–6, 129–30, 146–49,
    171–73; compared to other colonies,
    121–22. *See also* Antislavery; Cotton;
    Migration to Mexico; Slavery; San Felipe
    de Austin; Tejanos
Azcárate, Juan Francisco, 70

Baltimore, Md., 72, 158, 199–200
Baltimore Patriot, 92
Balmaceda, José María, 146

Barry, Diego, 69
Bastrop, Baron de, 49, 94, 100, 105, 108–10, 112, 119, 131
Bastrop, Tex., 234
Battle of Buena Vista, 257–58
Battle of Medina, 32
Bean, Peter Ellis, 97–100, 129–30
Bee, Bernard, 210–11
Beeson, Benjamin, 85
Bell, Thomas, 85
Belgium, 210
Bentham, Jeremy, 111, 128, 299 (n. 40)
Bexar County, Tex., 264
Blaikie, George, 196
Blanco, Victor, 109, 125, 161
Bollaert, William, 232
Borden, John, 192
Boston Commercial Gazette, 107
Bowie, James, 44
Brazil, 245, 263
Brazoria, Tex., 170, 181, 199, 248
Brazoria Planter, 248
Brazos Courier, 228–29
Brazos River, 33, 62, 81, 84, 87–88, 92–94, 121, 124, 137, 156, 158, 160, 162, 170, 171–72, 196–99, 201, 211, 228–29
British and Foreign Antislavery Society, 236
Brougham, Lord Henry, 242
Brown, Henry, 129
Buffalo Bayou, 173, 238
Burleson, Edward, 251
Burnet, David, 214
Burnett, David, 122
Bustamante, Anastasio, 151–52, 153, 162, 175

Caddos, 25–26, 28, 39, 203, 208
Calhoun, John, 244–45, 250–51
California, 13–14, 67, 255, 262
Camino Comanche, 38
Campbell, Randolph, 268
Canary Islands, 69
Capellanía, Coahuila, 145
Caribbean, 245
Carolina, Tex., 232
Carrasco, Gertrudis, 145

Carrillo, Manuel, 101–2, 108, 110, 115, 134
Casiano, José, 71, 161
Centralism. *See* Federalism versus centralism
Cherokees, 203, 208
Chiapas, Mexico, 67
Chihuahua, 30, 67, 224
Chihuahua City, Chihuahua, 30
Chilch (enslaved man), 155
China, 237
Choctaw, Miss., 188
Civilian and Galveston Gazette, 242–43, 247–48, 253
Clarksville Northern Standard, 228, 235
Clay, Henry, 251
Coahuila, 30, 39, 46, 47, 68–69, 71, 80, 97, 98, 100, 101, 102, 103, 105, 108, 109, 111, 113, 114, 115, 119, 127–29, 130, 142, 144–45, 147, 155, 160, 161, 163–64, 175, 226, 257, 259
Coahuila state government. *See* Saltillo Congress
Collinsworth, James, 184
Colorado River, 52, 62, 81, 88, 92–94, 121, 124, 128, 160, 162, 172, 197, 201, 208, 228–29, 241
Columbia, Tex., 185, 196
Comanches, 5, 6, 10, 12, 20, 25–29, 34, 37–42, 47–48, 50, 57–58, 68, 82, 93–94, 125, 203, 208, 216, 233, 258, 265
Confederate States of America, 4–5, 12, 182, 262–64
Connecticut, 106
Constitution of 1824, 79–80, 144, 149–50, 162–65, 174, 256, 295 (n. 55). *See also* Mexican national government
Constitution of 1827, 97–99, 100–103, 104, 105, 108–13, 114–15, 116–20, 142; Article 13 of, 100–103, 104, 105, 108–13, 116–20, 127–28, 131, 134, 142, 259. *See also* Saltillo Congress
Constitution of 1836. *See* Republic of Texas
Córdova, Vicente, 204
Corn, 64, 81–82, 135, 228
Cotton, 1–3, 23–24, 34–37, 59, 61, 82–83, 87–89, 90, 93, 98–99, 104–5, 109, 113, 121,

129, 134–35, 137–38, 147, 154–56, 157–61,
167, 173, 179, 181–82, 187, 193, 196–99,
203, 243, 247, 256; remakes U.S. Gulf
Coast, 2, 4, 7, 23–24, 34–37, 43, 51, 64–66,
68, 72, 258–59; boom of 1810s, 3–4,
34–36, 64, 89; in U.S. politics, 4–5, 126–
27, 142; decimates Spanish settlements,
7, 37–45; U.S. production of, 35–36, 65,
82–83, 87, 126, 157, 212, 221, 241; and
Great Britain, 35–36, 125–27, 137, 157, 189,
200–202, 212–13, 221, 236, 237–38, 241,
245, 263, 282 (n. 8); farming in Texas, 46,
50, 64, 81–89, 116, 121, 122–24, 135–36,
137–40, 157–59, 182, 183, 197–98, 228–31,
264–65; New Orleans as trade center, 72,
87–89, 93, 94, 124–26, 137, 152, 157–58,
162, 165, 167, 181, 183, 194, 197–98, 199,
211–12, 228–30, 247–48, 250, 253; exports
from Texas, 84, 87–89, 94, 95, 122–26,
137, 142, 152, 158–59, 160–61, 162, 181, 183,
187, 196–202, 205, 212, 227–28, 229–31,
247, 250, 264–65; difficulty exporting
from Texas, 88–89, 200–202, 228–29,
231; boom of early 1830s, 141, 157–61, 165,
169, 175, 194, 205, 260; and Republic of
Texas, 166, 181–83, 185–91, 197, 199–202,
205, 209–14, 215–17, 220–21, 224, 227–31,
232, 243, 247–48, 250, 252, 260–61, 264;
bust of late 1830s–early 1840s, 182,
211–12, 214, 215, 220, 223, 229, 231, 243,
247–48, 261; post-1865 price decline,
263–64; boom of 1850s, 264–65. See also
Austin, Stephen F.; Austin's colony;
McKinney-Williams Firm; Republic of
Texas; Tejanos
Cotton gins, 35, 36, 87–88, 121, 127, 137, 157,
161, 197, 202, 233
Coushattas, 38
Creeks, 36
Cuba, 43, 107, 170, 193, 245

Davis, James, 120–21
Decree 56, 129–34, 135–36, 163, 173, 259. See
also Saltillo Congress
Delaware (Indians), 208
Democratic Clarion, 36–37

Democratic Party, 262, 264
DeWitt, Green, 122
Dillard, John, 155
Douglas, Charles, 90
Douglass, Kelsey, 194
Durango, Mexico, 75
Durst, John, 146

Edwards, Amos, 133–34
Edwards, Haden, 69, 114, 122
Edwards, Monroe, 170
Edwardsville Spectator, 63
Egypt, 263
Elizondo, Dionisio, 101, 111, 113, 117–18, 134
Elizondo, Ignacio, 33–34
Elliot, Charles, 237–40, 249, 254
Ellis, Richard, 129
El Voto de Coahuila, 226
England. See Great Britain
Erwin, Andrew, 69
Escuadrón Auxiliar de Béjar, 255–56, 257

Fannin, James, 170
Federalism versus centralism (in Mexico),
76–81, 95, 101, 138–41, 144, 149–52, 156,
161, 162–66, 174–76, 224, 227, 256–57,
260, 261–62
Fisher, S. Rhoads, 154
Flores, Gaspar, 90, 95
Florida, 45, 157
Forsyth, John, 185–86
Forsythe, James, 48–50, 52
France, 24, 27, 49, 125, 128, 154, 185, 188, 202,
209–10, 212, 215, 236–37, 262
Frankfort Argus, 63
Fredonian Rebellion, 114–16
Free blacks, 167, 169, 234, 236, 238, 241
Fulshear, Churchill, 85–86

Galveston, Tex., 42–45, 87, 162, 194,
196–97, 199–200, 202, 220, 231, 234, 237,
238–40, 254; opposition to annexation,
247–48, 253
García, Francisco, 72–73
Garcia, Genobiba (enslaved woman), 145
Garcia, Rafael (enslaved man), 145

Garrison, William Lloyd, 186
Garza, Refugio de, 75–76
Geneva, Tex., 196
Georgia, 35, 82–84, 92, 204, 208
Godoy, Juan Ignacio, 73
Goliad. *See* La Bahía, Tex.
Goliad massacre. *See* Texas Revolution
Gonzales, Tex., 165, 219
Gonzales County, Tex., 234
Gorostiza, Manuel, 226
Gray, Peter, 252–53
Gray, William Fairfax, 167
Grayson, Peter, 184
Great Britain, 4–5, 9, 71, 182, 185–87, 188,
    190, 191–92, 195, 209, 220, 221, 225,
    235, 243, 245, 248–49, 251, 254, 261, 263;
    and cotton industry, 3–4, 7, 8, 35–36, 8,
    125–27, 137, 157, 189, 194, 199, 200–202,
    212–13, 221, 229, 236, 237–38, 241, 245,
    263, 282 (n. 8); and slavery, 4, 7–8, 71,
    107, 111, 128, 170, 182, 188–91, 205, 210,
    212–15, 221, 226, 236–44, 237–45, 260–61;
    Parliament of, 4, 189, 214, 236, 242; rec-
    ognition of Republic of Texas, 191, 202,
    212–14, 221, 235–36. *See also* Antislavery;
    Republic of Texas
Green, Duff, 244–45
Groce, Jared, 84–86, 137–38
Guadalupe (warship), 237
Guadalupe River, 128
Guanajuato, Mexico, 30, 73, 149
Guerrero, Coahuila, 145, 147
Guerrero, Vicente, 142–44, 149–52, 175
Guiana, 237
Guinea, Africa, 147
Gutiérrez de Lara, José Bernardo, 31
Gutiérrez-Magee Expedition, 20, 31–32, 34,
    37, 41, 57, 72

Haiti, 154, 241
Hamilton, James, 210, 213–14
Hannah (enslaved woman), 155
Harrison, James, 188
Harrison, Thomas, 188
Havana, Cuba, 43, 170
Hawkins, Joseph, 62–63

Hays, John "Jack," 219
Henderson, James Pinckney, 187, 188–91,
    209–10
Henry (enslaved man), 155
Hidalgo, Miguel, 30, 31, 35, 70
Holland, 210
Horse trade, 12, 23, 36–42, 46, 50, 52, 57–58,
    68, 93–94, 258
Houston, Sam, 166, 168, 171, 173–74, 183,
    184–85, 187, 191–94, 202–4, 214–15, 217,
    220–21, 222, 226, 227, 230, 232–33, 235,
    237, 244, 249
Houston City, Tex., 193–96, 199, 200, 211,
    220, 229, 235, 238, 239, 252
Houston Democrat, 247
Hunt, Memucan, 187

India, 36, 245, 263
Indians, 5, 6, 10–12, 13, 14, 20, 23, 25–29, 30,
    32, 34, 36–42, 46–48, 50, 57–58, 59, 67,
    68–69, 71–72, 82, 86, 89, 93–94, 102, 105,
    125, 144, 171, 184, 203, 208, 216, 233–34,
    257, 258, 260, 265; raiding Tejano settle-
    ments, 23–24, 26–27, 36–42, 45, 47, 50,
    57–58, 65, 68, 71, 82, 258, 265; trade with,
    26–29, 34–37, 36–42, 46, 57–58, 68, 258;
    and the Republic of Texas, 203, 204,
    208–9, 216, 232–35. *See also individual
    tribal names*
Iturbide, Agustín de, 52–53, 70, 73–74,
    76–77, 150

Jackson, Alexander, 85
Jackson, Andrew, 184, 187, 188, 226
Jalapa, Mexico, 27, 29, 82, 150, 162, 173, 210,
    258
Jalisco, Mexico, 149, 162
Jefferson, Thomas, 28, 36
John (enslaved man), 47
John (enslaved man), 147
John A. Merle & Co., 198
Johnson, Joseph, 188
Jones, Anson, 191, 202, 251
Jones, Randall, 44, 90
Jones, S. L., 200–201

Karankawas, 25–26, 93
Kennedy, William, 240
Kentucky, 15, 59, 63, 92, 106, 133, 198
Kentucky Whig, 91
Kickapoos, 25
Kirkham, James, 1–3, 6, 8, 14–15, 47–52, 265

La Bahía, Tex., 25, 27, 31, 32–34, 40–42,
    45–47, 57–58, 94, 160, 164, 170, 219, 285
    (n. 11)
Laffite, Jean, 43–45, 46
Laffite, Pierre, 43–45
La Luna, 224
Lamar, Mirabeau, 204–12, 214–15, 222, 233,
    234, 248–49, 314 (n. 118)
Lancashire County, England, 126
Land speculation, 49, 84–85, 114, 161, 168,
    180, 195–96, 199, 215
La Quinta (prison), 32, 34, 286 (n. 31)
Laredo, Tex., 288 (n. 64)
Las Casas, Juan Bautista de, 30–31
Latham, Francis, 232
Laura (steamship), 201
Law of April 6, 1830, 138, 152–53, 157, 164
Leftwich, Robert, 69
Leuba, P. B., 69
Lewis, William, 155
Liberator, 186
Liberty, Tex., 196
Lincoln, Abraham, 262
Linnville, Tex., 208
Liverpool, England, 88, 126, 157, 194, 199,
    202, 229
Lombraña, Luis, 145, 147
London, England, 4, 6, 188, 189, 190, 191,
    205, 209, 211, 213, 214, 236, 237, 239, 240,
    242, 244–45
Long, James, 46
Long Expedition, 46
Longín, Coahuila, 145
Loreta, María (enslaved woman), 145
Louisiana, 1, 4, 23, 25, 28, 32–34, 35–36, 37,
    38–39, 43–48, 51–52, 57–59, 63, 65, 68–69,
    82, 85, 87–88, 92, 95, 115, 122, 124–25,
    167–68, 179, 183, 187, 197, 216, 230, 234,
    250, 258, 265. *See also* New Orleans, La.

Louisiana Advertiser, 115
Louisiana State Gazette, 91, 95
Louisville Public Advertiser, 106
Lundy, Benjamin, 205

Madero, José Francisco, 127–28
Madrid, Spain, 25, 29, 45
Magee, Augustus, 31
Manchester, England, 126
Manifest Destiny, 9–10, 266
Marian (enslaved man), 1–3, 6, 14, 47–48, 52,
    265–66
Marsh, Noadiah, 155
Martínez, Antonio, 1, 20, 22, 23, 24, 40–42,
    46–49, 51, 62, 66, 68–69
Martínez, Francisco Pizarro, 155
Martinez de los Rios, Ramon Estévan, 75
Maryland, 72, 106, 158, 199–200
Massachusetts, 106, 206, 238
Matagorda Bay, Tex., 183
Maverick, Andrew, 219
Maverick, William, 219
Maximilian, Ferdinand, 262
McCulloch, Benjamin, 255–56, 257–58
McKinney, Thomas, 158, 167, 197, 199–202
McKinney-Williams Firm, 158, 160–61,
    167–68, 197, 199–202, 224
McLemore, Laura, 266
McNeel, Sterling, 170
Medina River, 31
Menchaca, Antonio, 171
Mexican national government, 66, 68–80,
    138, 144, 149–50, 152–53, 155–57, 161–65,
    174, 190, 210–11, 236, 249, 256, 259;
    debates slavery, 70–71, 72–76, 77–78,
    78–79, 91–92, 95, 144; debates Anglo
    colonization, 72–76, 77; political insta-
    bility within, 73, 76–77, 138–41, 150–52,
    156, 158, 161, 162–65, 224–26, 254, 255,
    261–62; outlaws slavery, 190, 225, 259,
    305 (n. 26); fears of U.S. conspiracy to
    steal Texas, 226–27
Mexican War for Independence, 5, 15, 20,
    22, 29–34, 35–36, 42, 52–53, 59, 61, 67, 70,
    73, 76, 97, 144, 258
Mexico. *See* Annexation; Antislavery;

Constitution of 1824; Constitution of 1827; Cotton; Decree 56; Federalism versus centralism; Mexican national government; Mexican War for Independence; Mexico City; Migration to Mexico; Newspapers; Republic of Texas; Saltillo, Coahuila; Saltillo Congress; Slavery; U.S.-Mexican War

Mexico City, 6, 7, 11, 13, 14, 22–24, 26–30, 32, 41–42, 45, 48, 61, 66–70, 72, 73, 75–81, 87, 90, 93, 94, 95, 97, 98, 100, 102, 103, 124, 125, 129, 138–41, 142, 144, 147, 150, 151–53, 156, 157, 161–65, 172–73, 174–75, 184, 190, 214, 224, 227, 236, 238, 254, 255, 256, 258, 259, 260, 261–62

Michoacán, Mexico, 74, 149

Mier, Mexico, 227

Mier Expedition, 227, 231

Mier y Terán. *See* Terán, Manuel de Mier

Migration to Mexico (of Americans), 2, 5, 8, 12–14, 48–53, 59–62, 68, 78–81, 81–82, 84–87, 89, 90–92, 99–100, 114, 120–22, 124, 129–34, 138–41, 142, 145, 147–48, 152–54, 157–60, 174–75, 187–88, 258–59, 265; Spanish approval of, 3, 24, 50–53, 61; Mexican approval of, 6, 7, 61, 68, 75–76, 258; Anglo motivation for, 9–10, 48–52, 59, 63–65, 71–72, 84, 129, 154–55, 157–58, 174–75, 258–59; Tejano support for, 10, 50, 58–62, 68–69, 71–72, 75–76, 89, 94–95, 99, 130–33, 140–41, 145–46, 163–66, 175, 256–57, 258, 265–66; Mexican opposition to, 98, 101, 138–41, 144, 151–53, 157, 163, 164. *See also* Antislavery; Newspapers

Migration to Republic of Texas: from United States, 169, 182–83, 188, 194–97, 202–3, 208, 213, 215–16, 233, 246, 248, 257, 260–61, 265; pace slowing, 231–33, 243, 261; from Europe, 236, 241, 253

Migration to State of Texas, 255, 264–66

Milam, Benjamin, 69, 121, 122

Miller, Albert, 155

Miller, Washington, 244

Milli (enslaved woman), 155

Mills, David, 199

Mills, Robert, 199, 201

Mina, Francisco, 42

Missions. *See* New Spain

Mississippi, 4, 7, 11, 14, 23, 35–36, 39, 43–46, 51–52, 59, 63, 64–65, 68, 82–83, 87–89, 90, 92, 94, 95, 114, 157, 179, 183, 187, 188, 195, 216, 221, 234, 258

Mississippi River, 88

Mississippi River Valley, 7, 11, 14, 23, 35, 43, 51–52, 59, 64–65, 82–83, 87–89, 94, 157

Missouri, 48–49, 52, 63, 92, 106, 186, 196

Mobile, Ala., 158

Monclova, Coahuila, 109, 130, 163

Monterrey, Nuevo León, 1, 22, 39–41, 47–48, 52, 58, 255–56, 257

Montesquieu, Charles-Louis, 128

Montezuma (warship), 237

Montgomery County, Tex., 252

Músquiz, Ramón, 71, 125, 129, 131, 142, 145, 146, 149–50, 153, 160, 161

Nacogdoches, Tex., 25, 27, 30, 31, 34, 37, 39, 46, 57–58, 81, 84, 104, 110, 114, 122, 128, 146–47, 164, 179, 194, 204, 234

Nashville, Tenn., 36

Natchez, Miss., 35, 45–46, 82, 179

Natchez Republican, 39

Natchitoches, La., 35, 38–39, 48, 57–58

National Intelligencer, 107

National Register, 253

Navarro, José Antonio, 71–72, 125, 131–33, 142, 145–46, 166, 169, 203, 266

Neches River, 46

Netherlands, 210

New Mexico, 13–14, 67, 214

New Orleans, La., 31, 42, 43–45, 57, 62–63, 72, 84, 87, 88–89, 93, 94, 95, 106, 115, 124–26, 127, 129, 133, 137, 147, 152, 155, 157, 158, 162, 165, 167–68, 181, 183, 192, 194–98, 199, 210–12, 228–30, 247–48, 250, 253

New Orleans Halcyon and Literary Repository, 135

New Orleans Picayune, 204

New Spain, 1–3, 6–7, 12, 14, 19, 22–24, 30, 31, 46–53, 67, 76, 258; approves Anglo immigration, 3, 24, 50–53, 61; failure to control Texas, 5, 6, 22–29, 37–42, 42–45, 57–59, 65; rebellions against, 20, 22, 29–34, 35–37, 41–42, 52–53, 57, 59, 61, 67, 70, 72–73, 76, 97, 144, 258; use of missions, 26–27; social stratification within, 29–30

Newspapers: influences migration, 8, 12, 60, 90–92, 95, 99, 116, 120–22, 129, 134, 259; U.S. coverage of Texas under Spain and Mexico, 36–37, 39, 45, 51, 59–60, 63–66, 81, 90–92, 95, 105–8, 113, 115–16, 120–21, 134; U.S. newspapers, 36–37, 39, 63, 91–92, 95, 105–8, 115, 116, 135, 186, 204; Texas newspapers, 194, 197, 199, 201, 206, 212, 215, 223–24, 228–29, 230, 234–35, 242–43, 246, 247–48, 251, 253, 268; Mexican newspapers, 224, 226; U.S. coverage of Texas as Republic, 186, 195, 231, 236

New York City, 87–88, 106, 115, 125, 157, 194–96, 229, 239, 250

New York Daily Advertiser, 107, 115

New York Observer, 116

Niles' Weekly Register, 115

Nolan, Philip, 36

North Carolina, 15

Nueces River, 252, 255

Nuevo León, Mexico, 1, 22, 39–41, 47–48, 52, 58, 69, 71, 255–56, 257

Nuevo Santander, Mexico, 39, 46–47, 73. *See also* Tamaulipas, Mexico

O'Connell, Daniel, 236

Ohio, 131

Oklahoma, 265

Oregon, 67, 251

O'Reilly, Felipe, 69

Ortiz, Tadeo, 69

Padilla, Juan Antonio, 103, 108, 142, 146, 166

Pakenham, Richard, 225, 250–51

Palmerston, Lord Henry, 189–91, 213–14

Panic of 1819, 49, 51, 59, 64, 258

Panic of 1837, 195, 211, 216, 261

Paris, France, 188, 209

Parras, Coahuila, 109, 163

Payton, J. C., 104

Peach Point Plantation, Tex., 197–98, 211

Pecan Point, Tex., 39, 46

Pedraza, Manuel Gómez, 151

Pérez, Ignacio, 46–47

Perry, James, 120, 172, 183, 197–99, 211

Peter (enslaved man), 160

Phelps, A. A., 239

Phelps, James, 90

Philip (enslaved man), 155

Phoebus (enslaved woman), 155

Piedras, José de las, 146–47

Pikesville, Ala., 155

Plum Creek, Tex., 208

Polk, James, 251, 254, 255

Pompeii, Tex., 196

Porras, Salvador, 75

Preston, England, 126

Princeton (warship), 250

Prinnilla (enslaved woman), 155

Puebla, Mexico, 224

Quitman, Eliza, 179

Quitman, John, 179–81, 182–83

R. G. Mills & Co., 199–201

Rabb, William, 85

Railroads. *See* Republic of Texas

Ramos, Raúl, 224

Raphael (enslaved man), 235

Rapides, La., 35

Red Lander, 253

Red River, 37, 39, 46, 230–31

Refugio, Tex., 39, 219

Republican Party, 262

Republic of Texas, 5, 6, 7, 8–9, 10–12, 14, 181–83, 191–94, 209, 260–61; cotton diplomacy of, 7, 8, 14, 185–91, 202, 204, 209–11, 215–16, 220, 227–28, 241, 246–47, 261, 263–64; as precursor to Confederacy, 12, 14, 182, 262–64; and slavery, 14, 166–67, 169–71, 181–83, 186, 189–91, 195–96, 209, 211, 214, 215–17, 219, 220, 233–35, 240, 241, 247, 253–54; and cotton, 166, 181–83, 185–91, 197, 199–202, 205,

209–14, 215–17, 220–21, 224, 227–31, 232, 243, 247–48, 250, 252, 260–61, 264; constitution of, 169–71, 183, 204, 206, 239, 242–43; and diplomatic recognition, 170, 184–91, 202, 210–11, 212–14, 215–16, 235–36, 246–47, 261; financial problems of, 184, 188, 191–92, 202–3, 208–12, 214, 217, 222–24, 227–29, 231, 236–38, 239, 248, 250, 261; population of, 184, 194, 196, 204, 216, 232, 240, 270–71; and Tejanos, 184, 203–4, 216, 220, 222, 227, 257, 260; trade with Europe, 191, 209–10, 235–36, 247; General Land Office of, 192–93; and Indians, 203, 204, 208–9, 216, 232–35; invaded by Mexico, 219–22, 227, 231–32, 249, 253, 257, 264; invades Mexico, 227–28; proposed railroad, 229; smuggling within, 230–31; fears of Great Britain, 236–44, 248–49, 253–54, 261; xenophobia within, 253–54; reasons for failure, 260–61, 264

Republic of Texas Army, 166, 168, 173–74, 179–80, 182–83, 193, 195, 208, 220, 223

Republic of Texas Congress, 192–93, 203, 204, 208, 213–14, 220, 223–24, 228, 233–34, 235, 242, 254

Republic of Texas Navy, 193, 211, 223

Republic of the Río Grande, 224

Rhode Island, 65, 106

Richie, Thomas, 187

Richard (enslaved man), 1–3, 6, 14, 47–48, 52, 265–66

Richmond (enslaved man), 48

Richmond, Tex., 196

Richmond, Va., 106

Richmond Enquirer, 63, 187

Río Grande, 28, 39, 135, 222, 234, 252, 255

Río Grande Valley, Tex., 39

Robert (enslaved man), 147

Robertson, Sterling, 122

Rome, Tex., 196, 232

Rose, Dilue, 172, 179–81, 182–83

Ross, James, 85

Rosset, Juan, 69

Routh, James, 155

Royall, Richard, 183

Runaway scrape. *See* Texas Revolution

Russellville, Ky., 133

Ruíz, Francisco, 41, 71–72, 166, 169, 204

Ruíz, Josefa (enslaved woman), 145

Russia, 67

Sabine Lake, 230

Sabine River, 1, 2, 3, 37, 44–46, 48, 59, 128, 160, 179, 236, 246

Saint-Domingue. *See* Haiti

Saint Landry Parish, La., 47

Saint Louis, Mo., 106

Saint Louis Enquirer, 63

Saligny, Alphonse Dubois de, 209

Saltillo, Coahuila, 69, 80, 97, 100, 102, 103, 105, 108, 115, 119, 129, 142, 145, 147, 155, 160, 163–64, 175, 226, 257

Saltillo Congress, 80–81, 94–96, 97–99, 100–103, 104, 105–6, 108–13, 114–15, 116–20, 121, 127–29, 131, 134–35, 141–42, 146, 155, 156, 162–65, 175, 259; debates slavery, 98–99, 100–103, 105–7, 108–13, 116–20, 126–28, 163, 259. *See also* Constitution of 1827; Decree 56; Saltillo, Coahuila

Saltillo slavery debates. *See* Saltillo Congress

Samuel (enslaved man), 47

San Antonio, Tex., 1, 3, 15, 19, 21, 22, 23, 24–25, 27, 29, 30, 31, 32, 33, 34, 37, 40–42, 45–49, 57–59, 61–62, 68, 75, 89, 94, 100, 101, 103, 105, 108, 110, 114, 125, 128, 130–31, 145, 149, 157, 159, 161, 163–64, 168, 174, 203, 219–20, 222, 227, 233, 234, 264; flood of 1819, 19–24, 45

San Antonio River, 19–20, 25, 219

San Augustine, Tex., 193

Sánchez Navarro family, 130

San Felipe de Austin, Tex., 93, 120, 121, 125, 128, 129, 165, 168

San Francisco Bay, Calif., 67

San Jacinto, Battle of. *See* Texas Revolution

San Jacinto River, 171, 173

San Luis Potosí, Mexico, 149

San Marcos River, 52, 219

San Pedro Creek, 19–20

Santa Anna, Antonio López de, 76, 139, 141,

151, 162, 164–65, 168, 170–74, 179–80, 257–58, 262

Santa Fe, N.M., 13, 67, 214

Santa Fe Expedition, 214

Santa Fe trail, 67

Santos Garcia, María de los (enslaved woman), 145

Saucedo, José Antonio, 86, 100, 102, 103, 105, 114

Saucedo, Manuel, 30–31

Seguín, Erasmo, 57–61, 71, 78–81, 94, 103, 157, 165, 171, 256, 257

Seguín, Juan, 125, 165, 171, 174, 204, 220, 222, 227, 255–58, 264–66

Shawnees, 208

Shepherd, Benjamin, 231–32, 253

Sheridan, Francis, 213, 237

Sibley, John, 28

Slavery, 51–52, 62, 66, 72, 90–92, 95, 97–103, 104–8, 114–16, 120–22, 138–41, 153–57, 192, 259; enslaved people, 1–3, 6, 14, 44, 47, 48, 52, 59, 63, 65, 67, 84, 86, 97–98, 104, 117, 133–35, 145, 147, 155, 158, 160, 184, 220, 232, 235, 262–63, 265–66; fugitive slaves, 1–3, 6, 14, 44–45, 47, 52, 65, 86, 147, 160, 234–35, 238, 265–66; Tejano attitudes toward, 8, 61, 70–72, 75–76, 78–81, 95, 98, 102, 119, 130–34, 141–42, 145–46, 161, 163–64, 175, 259; Mexican attitudes toward, 11, 14, 66, 67, 70–76, 77–81, 108–13, 116–20, 127–29, 142–50, 172–73, 190, 224–26, 259; Anglo-American attitudes toward, 11, 51–52, 66, 70, 72, 75, 78, 90, 95, 102–3, 108–9, 110, 115, 117, 120–22, 127–28, 129–34, 139–41, 153–57, 163–64, 169–70, 179, 195–96, 221, 240, 245, 250–51, 253–54, 259, 260, 262–64; as practiced in Mexico, 14, 71, 79, 190; and Republic of Texas, 14, 166–67, 169–71, 181–83, 186, 189–91, 195–96, 209, 211, 214, 215–17, 219, 220, 233–35, 240, 241, 247, 253–54; smuggling slaves, 23, 43–44, 65, 130–34, 147, 170, 193, 205, 289 (n. 80); slave trade, 25, 43–44, 71, 74, 77–78, 107, 111–13, 118–19, 120, 133, 140, 147, 152, 155–56, 169–70, 189–90, 205, 213–14,

235; as practiced in Texas, 84–87, 92, 128–29, 161, 219, 240; slave population in Texas, 85, 128–29, 216, 232–33, 240, 260, 265–66, 270–71, 295 (n. 63); renting slaves, 85–86; practiced as indentured servitude, 97–100, 129–34, 135–36, 155–57, 163, 173, 259; attempt to abolish in 1829, 138, 142–50, 152, 175, 304 (n. 25); and Texas Revolution, 139–41, 171–76; Anglo-American fears of slave rebellion, 154, 171–72, 233–35. *See also* Antislavery; Constitution of 1827; Decree 56; Free blacks; Mexican national government; Saltillo Congress; U.S. government

Slavery Abolition Act, 189

Smith, Ashbell, 237, 240–42, 244, 245

Smith, Benjamin Fort, 170

Smuggling, 42–44, 59, 192, 230–31. *See also* Slavery

Smyth, George, 135

South Carolina, 1, 15, 35, 84, 92, 186, 188, 210, 226

Spain, 15, 23, 25, 29, 29, 31, 34, 45, 48, 50, 58, 60, 61, 67, 70, 76–77, 80, 144, 151. *See also* New Spain

Sprowl, John, 104

Sugar, 64, 154, 187, 199, 230, 241, 265

Tabasco, Mexico, 224

Tamaulipas, Mexico, 42, 71, 162

Taos, N.M., 13

Tappan, Lewis, 239

Tariff of Abominations, 126–27, 142, 206

Taylor, Zachary, 255–56, 257–58

Tehuacana Creek, 233

Tejanos, 10, 12, 22, 25, 30, 32–34, 41, 47–48, 52, 57–61, 61, 65–66, 68–69, 71–72, 75–76, 78–81, 90, 93–95, 103, 105, 108, 117–18, 124–26, 128–35, 140–42, 145–46, 149, 153, 157, 159–61, 164–66, 169, 171, 174, 184, 203, 204, 220, 222, 227, 255–56, 266; attitudes toward slavery, 8, 61, 70–72, 75–76, 78–81, 95, 98, 102, 119, 130–34, 141–42, 145–46, 161, 163–64, 175, 259; support for American migration, 10, 50, 58–62, 68–69, 71–72, 75–76, 89, 94–95,

99, 130–33, 140–41, 145–46, 163–66, 175, 256–57, 258, 265–66; rebel against New Spain, 30–34; decimated by Indian raids, 37–42, 45, 47, 57, 65, 71, 93–94, 258, 265; interest in cotton trade, 50–52, 58, 60–61, 65, 71–72, 86–87, 89, 124–26, 134–35, 160–61, 165, 256–57, 266; trade with United States, 57, 71–72, 124–26, 160–61, 165–66, 256–57; losing power, 159–60, 257, 266; and Texas Revolution, 165–66, 168, 169, 171–73, 174–75, 222, 255–57, 264; and Republic of Texas, 184, 203–4, 216, 220, 222, 227, 257, 260; and the U.S.-Mexican War, 255–58, 264–66

Telegraph and Texas Register, 194, 197, 199, 201, 206, 212, 215, 223–24, 228, 230, 234–35, 242–43, 246, 248, 251, 253, 268

Tennessee, 36, 63, 69, 92, 169, 195, 232

Terán, Manuel de Mier y, 137–40, 149, 151–52, 155–57

Texas Rangers, 255–56, 257

Texas Revolution, 5, 8, 14, 139–41, 165–68, 170–76, 183, 205, 222, 227, 257, 260, 266; and slavery, 139–41, 171–76; and federalism, 140–41, 162–66, 174–75, 256–57, 260; and Tejanos, 165–66, 168, 169, 171–73, 174–75, 222, 255–57, 264; financed by New Orleans, 167–68; Alamo siege and battle, 168, 171, 179; Goliad massacre, 168, 170, 171; Runaway scrape, 171–73, 179–80; Battle of San Jacinto, 173–74, 179–80, 182–83, 224, 226

Texas Slavery Project, 267–71

Thompson, Alexander, 160

Thompson, Jesse, 104

Thorn, Frost, 122, 133

Tinsley, Isaac, 155

Tivi (enslaved woman), 1–3, 6, 14, 47–48, 52, 265–66

Tobacco, 64, 135, 229

Tom (enslaved man), 160

Tonkawas, 25–26, 38, 93, 203, 208

Tornel, José María, 144

Treaty of Guadalupe-Hidalgo, 264

Trinity River, 33–24, 52, 162, 171, 196, 232

Tyler, John, 244, 249, 250–52

United States. *See* Annexation; Antislavery; Cotton; Mexican national government; Migration to Mexico; Migration to Republic of Texas; Migration to State of Texas; Newspapers; Republic of Texas; Slavery; Tejanos; Texas Revolution; U.S. Anglophobia; U. S. Army; U.S. Civil War; U.S. government; U.S.-Mexican War; Washington, D.C.

U.S. Anglophobia, 244–46, 250, 251–52

U.S. Army, 31, 69, 246, 255–56, 257–58, 261

U.S. Civil War, 4–5, 262–63, 264, 266

U.S. government, 4–5, 28, 34, 36, 43, 45, 49, 52, 64, 68, 71, 101, 107, 126, 142, 167, 169, 170, 171, 182, 184–89, 191, 193, 195, 198, 202, 205, 206, 221, 226–28, 231, 235, 244–54, 255–56; internal politics regarding slavery, 186, 226–27, 244–46, 250–51, 262–63

U.S.-Mexican War, 5, 13, 254, 255–56, 261–64, 266; aftermath in Mexico, 261–62; aftermath in U.S., 262–66

Upshur, Abel, 244, 246, 249, 250

Urrea, José de, 172

Valle, Santiago de, 112–13, 117

Van Buren, Martin, 187, 188, 191

Van Zandt, Isaac, 227–28, 244, 246, 249–51

Vasquez, Rafael, 219–22, 227

Velasco, Tex., 162

Veracruz, Mexico, 27, 29, 82, 162, 173, 210, 258

Veramendi, Juan Martín de, 57, 71, 125

Vermont, 92, 106

Victoria, Guadalupe, 97, 114, 150, 210–11

Victoria, Tex., 172, 208

Viesca, Agustín, 109, 118, 119, 142, 145, 147–50, 160, 163

Viesca, José Maria, 109, 110–13, 118–19, 142, 145–46, 147–49, 156, 160, 163

Virginia, 43, 48, 84, 106, 167, 186, 231

Wacos, 25, 233

War of 1812, 36, 49

Washington, D.C., 6, 43, 45, 63, 106, 184, 185, 191, 195, 205, 221, 228, 245, 246, 251, 254

Washington Gazette, 63
Washington-on-the-Brazos, Tex., 168
Wavell, Arthur, 69, 122
Wharton, William, 185–86, 187
Whig Party, 251
Wichitas, 25–26, 28, 37–38, 40, 203, 233
Wilkinson, James, 69
Williams, Henry, 158, 199
Williams, Samuel May, 158, 167, 197, 199
Woll, Adrian, 227
Woodbury, John, 122

World Antislavery Convention, 239, 240, 244

Ybarvo, José Ygnacio, 146
Yoakum, Henderson, 266
Yucatán, Mexico, 73, 141, 165, 224

Zacatecas, Mexico, 141, 149, 162, 165
Zambrano, Juan Manuel, 41
Zavala, Lorenzo de, 73–74